Fear God, Honor the King

Fear **God,** *Honor* **the King**

Magisterial Power and the Church in the Reformation,
circa 1470–1600

Andrew Allan Chibi

☙PICKWICK *Publications* • Eugene, Oregon

FEAR GOD, HONOR THE KING
Magisterial Power and the Church in the Reformation, circa 1470–1600

Copyright © 2020 Andrew Allan Chibi. All rights reserved. Except for brief quotations in critical publications or reviews, no part of this book may be reproduced in any manner without prior written permission from the publisher. Write: Permissions, Wipf and Stock Publishers, 199 W. 8th Ave., Suite 3, Eugene, OR 97401.

Pickwick Publications
An Imprint of Wipf and Stock Publishers
199 W. 8th Ave., Suite 3
Eugene, OR 97401

www.wipfandstock.com

PAPERBACK ISBN: 978-1-7252-5663-7
HARDCOVER ISBN: 978-1-7252-5664-4
EBOOK ISBN: 978-1-7252-5665-1

Cataloguing-in-Publication data:

Names: Chibi, Andrew Allan, author.

Title: Fear God, honor the king : magisterial power and the church in the Reformation, circa 1470–1600 / Andrew Allan Chibi.

Description: Eugene, OR: Pickwick Publications, 2020. | Includes bibliographical references and index.

Identifiers: ISBN 978-1-7252-5663-7 (paperback). | ISBN 978-1-7252-5664-4 (hardcover). | ISBN 978-1-7252-5665-1 (ebook).

Subjects: LCSH: Reformation. | Reformation—Europe. | Church—History of doctrines—16th century. | Christianity and culture. | 16th Century, C 1500 to C 1599.

Classification: BR145.2 C45 2020 (print). | BR145.2 (ebook).

Manufactured in the U.S.A. 05/12/20

To Ellen with all my love

But you are a chosen generation, a kingly priesthood, a holy nation, a purchased people: that you may declare his virtues who hath called you out of darkness into his marvelous light: Who in times past were not a people: but are now the people of God. Who had not obtained mercy: but now have obtained mercy. Dearly beloved, I beseech you, as strangers and pilgrims, to refrain yourselves from carnal desires which war against the soul, having your conversation good among the Gentiles: that whereas they speak against you as evildoers, they may, by the good works which they shall behold in you, glorify God in the day of visitation. Be ye subject therefore to every human creature for God's sake: whether it be to the king as excelling, or to governors as sent by him for the punishment of evildoers and for the praise of the good. For so is the will of God, that by doing well you may put to silence the ignorance of foolish men: As free and not as making liberty a cloak for malice, but as the servants of God. Honour all men. Love the brotherhood. Fear God. Honour the king. Servants, be subject to your masters with all fear, not only to the good and gentle but also to the contrary. For this is thankworthy: if, for conscience towards God, a man endures sorrows, suffering wrongfully. —1 Pet 2:9–19

Contents

Preface | ix
Acknowledgments | xiii
Abbreviations | xv

Introduction: Historical Survey; How Had the Church Gained Such Vast Temporal Authorities? | 1

1. Luther and "Two Governments" Doctrine | 29
2. Zwingli, Civil Authority, and the Church to 1536 | 56
3. Civil Authority and the Sectarians | 71
4. Secular Authority in the Works of the Second-Generation Reformers | 129
5. Civil Authority and the Church in Tudor England | 191
6. Conclusion: Royal Ecclesiastical Authority in Catholic Europe | 258

Bibliography | 301
Subject Index | 317
Scripture Index | 339

Preface

HISTORIANS, THEOLOGIANS, SCHOLARS OF whichever disciplines and academics in general will be familiar with the process behind the development of a book like this one. For the interested reader, however, the process can seem convoluted but is ultimately understandable. I have written previous books on both the European and English Reformations, sometimes using them in religious history courses. Over the progression of my teaching career, questions were raised that those books did not sufficiently answer, or for which I did not immediately have a useful response. As any professional would, however, I searched for a means of pointing the questioner in the right direction. Together we found the answers they sought. This also gave me good information should anyone ask a similar question in future of course, and, eventually, the collection of books, articles, reports, and websites began to add up and suggest useful revisions of my previous writings and module development.

This book is not merely an updating of those previous books, however. Rather it is an in-depth focus on a theme not sufficiently assessed elsewhere. This book is the result, therefore, of students asking the right questions at the right times, of my searches to give them useful answers quickly, and of the revelation of a topic that has been surprisingly rarely examined on its own terms. I hope that this volume adds something to our historical understanding of the reformers (great and small) mentioned herein, to the work they tried to do, and to the faith they tried to foster and spread. I also hope that it will raise further questions and inspire further research into questions of the historical church and state relationship.

In a previous work, *The Wheat and the Tares*, the main theme was Reformation-era ecclesiology. There I sought to understand and explain what thinkers of the day thought defined the church, what defined who belongs to it, and how to accurately discover what were its authorities, duties, and roles within their wider societies. Having established as comprehensive an understanding as I could there, I decided to take the many models imagined by the different reformers and answer the question of how those churches interacted with the societies in which they assembled.

In late-mediaeval Western Christendom the church was understood as a special hierarchy, headed by a pope who claimed both spiritual supremacy and secular authority over lesser temporal magistrates. The church was institutionally identifiable; it was mandated by God to define scripture, doctrine, and salvation to its members. Its mandate (based on Pauline scriptural writings and Augustinian theology) was to identify, gather, safeguard, and shepherd the faithful (which included kings and commoners alike) toward peace in this life and salvation in the next. At least in theory, therefore, papal supremacy over secular rulers and governors was acknowledged.

Perhaps it is best seen as an ideal, however. In reality it was winked at; special political arrangements were made and cultural norms were discussed. Papal supremacy was often ignored, or circumvented, or otherwise negated. What I sought to do here was to examine and understand how this centuries-old arrangement finally simply broke down so rapidly in the early sixteenth century. Was it nascent nationalism, magisterial greed, cultural innovation, or something more? The Roman Catholic Church claimed to be the only genuine Christian church and the pope its earthly master; but serious doubts and hard questions fostered new ideas and new interpretations of the evidence. This ushered into existence rival sects within the church and later rival churches claiming the same mandates and identifying factors as Rome. Did (could?) the spiritual leaders of these new churches also claim the same secular authorities or were new arrangements necessary? Traditional, doctrinaire Catholics had different ideas compared to their Protestant counterparts about the political nation, but the Protestants were themselves hardly of one mind on the matter of secular authority over the flock and the church. Here I sought an understanding of the major doctrinal controversies separating the various claims. I found significant theoretical conflict just as divisive as rival theologies of salvation or rival interpretations of the sacraments. As my students and I sometimes found, however, this very important aspect of Reformation history, theology, and the study of religion was either inexplicably ignored or relegated to annotated footnotes in many modern textbooks. We wanted a book that tackled this issue and, finally, wanting turned into action.

This book is intended for the interested general reader too because they will recognize (even without having done years of study) many of the questions faced by the reformers. Why, for instance, in the United States are the church and state spheres so vehemently separated in its founding political documents, but so obviously bound together in reality? Why, for instance, in the United Kingdom is the monarch still head of the church, its bishops still sat in the House of Lords, and members of the laity sat in the church's convocation? Why is the church such a factor in Spanish and Irish politics but clearly less so in Canadian and Dutch politics? I have noted in *The Wheat and the Tares* over 40,000 separate modern Christian denominations. Each denomination faces similar issues to those faced by the new churches which sprang up in the late mediaeval—early modern period of European history. Where does the church fit into accepted political structures, for example, or how much authority should the ruling magistrate be ascribed, if any at all, in the local church? In medieval Western Christendom the state, in theory if not in reality, served the church. Now the church appears to serve state purposes (if any purpose at all). *"Fear God, Honor the King"* was conceived as a means of working out how such questions were considered and answered at the most sensitive, divisive time in Christian history, using as much as possible the very sources in which the answers were worked out.

Andrew Allan Chibi

November 2019

Acknowledgments

THIS BOOK HAS GONE through several iterations over a number of years and several people (scholars and laymen alike) have had a hand in the production of it as advisors or consultants, sometimes directing my research down previously unconsidered avenues or pointing out where my meaning was ambiguous. The book grew out of my curiosity over the fact that while trying to save and safeguard the dignity and reputation of the church as well as its right to shepherd the flock, the humanists and reformers of the late medieval and early modern periods moved it either under the auspices of the magistrate and the political sphere or into anti-political isolation. The book grew out of the fact that students (too numerous now to mention individually) asked specific, hard questions, for which there were no immediate satisfactory answers. This book was partially written with them in mind. But it was also written for friends and relatives who also asked interesting questions which led me to wonder how the answers could be addressed to an audience who did not have the benefit of years of research and learning focussing their desires into specific channels. My scholarly debts can never be sufficiently acknowledged or repaid; I formulated this book after discussions over coffee, over the deconstruction of other texts, or over the organization of courses with such luminaries as Mark Greengrass, Kevin Sharpe, Alistair Duke, George Bernard, Terry Hartley, Peter Musgrave, Norman Housley and Ian Campbell among many others. The polyglot linguist James Burtoft helped me to understand certain esoteric German words and phrases that opened up for me previously unconsidered themes, while Paul Shawley, Keith McCormick, and Andy Walker pulled me up short when my discourse become over laden with jargon. I'd like to thank the editors and staff at Wipf & Stock (particularly Matthew Wimmer and Daniel Lanning) and at Pickwick Publications for their belief and support of the project. Obviously, my family gives me the support and strength I've often needed to carry on, particularly my wife Ellen. Friends, family and the staff of libraries too numerous to mention have partially supported me and partially distracted me with their shenanigans when I needed it, so all are equally appreciated. It perhaps should go without saying that while all of these people can take some small measure of satisfaction with the appearance of this book, all gaffs, mistakes, errors of judgement and unsatisfying conclusions (and any royalties garnered) are entirely my own.

Abbreviations

AE	*Luther's Works: American Edition.* 55 vols. Edited by Jaroslav Pelikan and Helmut T. Lehman. St. Louis, MO: Concordia; Philadelphia: Fortress, 1955–86
AHR	*The American Historical Review*
AfR	*Archiv für Reformationsgeschichte*
Baylor	*The Radical Reformation.* Edited by Michael G. Baylor. Cambridge: Cambridge University Press, 1991
Cochrane	*Reformed Confessions of the Sixteenth Century.* Edited by Arthur C. Cochrane. London: SCM, 1966
Companion	*A Companion to the Reformation World.* Edited by R. Po-chia Hsia. Blackwell Companions to European History. Oxford: Blackwell, 2004.
Confessions	*Confessions and Catechisms of the Reformation.* Edited by Mark A. Noll. Grand Rapids: Baker, 1991
CWE	*Collected Works of Erasmus.* 78 vols. Toronto: University of Toronto Press, 1974–2011
CWTM	*The Collected Works of Thomas Müntzer.* Translated and edited by Peter Matheson. Edinburgh: T. & T. Clark, 1988

Decades	Bullinger, Heinrich, *The Decades of Henry Bullinger*. 5 vols. Edited by H. I. Cambridge: Cambridge University Press, 1849
EM	*Ecclesiastical Memorials, Relating Chiefly to Religion, and the Reformation of It and the Emergencies of the Church of England under King Henry VIII., King Edward VI., and Queen Mary I., with Large Appendixes, Containing Original Papers, Records, [etc.]*. 3 vols. in 6. Oxford: Clarendon, 1882
EC	*The Essential Carlstadt*. Translated and edited by E. J. Furcha. Waterloo, ON: Herald, 1995
EE	*The Essential Erasmus*. Translated by John P. Dolan. New York, NY: Mentor, 1964
Elton	*Reformation Europe: 1517–1559*. Edited by G. R. Elton. Oxford: Blackwell, 1999
Formularies	*Formularies of Faith Put Forth by Authority during the Reign of Henry VIII*. Edited by Charles Lloyd. Oxford: Clarendon, 1825
GAMEO	*Global Anabaptist Mennonite Encyclopedia Online*
Grebel	*The Sources of Swiss Anabaptism: The Grebel Letters and Related Documents*. Edited by Leland Harder. Kitchener, ON: Herald, 1985
Handbook	*Handbook of European History 1400–1600: Late Middle Ages, Renaissance and Reformation*. 2 vols. Edited by Thomas A. Brady Jr. et al. Leiden: Brill, 1995–1995
HTR	*Harvard Theological Review*
HJ	*Historical Journal*
Hubmaier	*Balthasar Hubmaier, Theologian of Anabaptism*. Translated and edited by H. Wayne Pipkin and John H. Yoder. Waterloo, ON: Herald, 1989
JBS	*Journal of British Studies*
JEH	*Journal of Ecclesiastical History*
JMH	*Journal of Modern History*
JHI	*Journal of the History of Idea*

Knox	*The Works of John Knox*, 3 vols. Edited by David Laing. Edinburgh: Bainatyne Club, 1864.
NPNF2	*Nicene and Post-Nicene Fathers*. 2nd series. 14 vols. Edited by Peter Schaff and Henry Wace. Edinburgh: T. & T. Clark, 1886–1900
Outline	*Anabaptism in Outline, Selected Primary Resources*. Edited by Walter Klaasen. Waterloo, ON: Herald, 1981
Pocock	*Records of the Reformation*, 2 vols. Edited by Nicholas Pocock. Oxford: Oxford University Press, 1870
Sermons	In *Sermons of Hugh Latimer, Sometime Bishop of Worcester, Martyr, 1555*. Edited by George Elwes Corrie. Cambridge: Cambridge University Press, 1844
Sider	*Karlstadt's Battle with Luther: Documents in a Liberal–Radical Debate*. Edited by Ronald J. Sider. 1978. Reprint, Eugene OR: Wipf & Stock, 2001
SCJ	*Sixteenth Century Journal*
TRHS5	*Transactions of the Royal Historical Society*, 5th series
TRHS6	*Transactions of the Royal Historical Society*, 6th series
Treatises	*Calvin: Theological Treatises*. Edited by J. K. S. Reid. Philadelphia: Westminster, 1954
Tyndale	*The Works of the English Reformers: William Tyndale and John Frith*. 3 vols. Edited by Thomas Russell. London: Palmer, 1831
Works	*Works of Martin Luther*. 6 vols. Edited by Henry E. Jacobs. Albany, NY: Books for the Ages, 1997
Writings	Ulrich Zwingli, *Early Writings*. Edited by Samuel Macauley Jackson. 1912. Reprint, Eugene OR: Wipf & Stock, 1999
Zwingli	*The Latin Works and the Correspondence of Huldreich Zwingli, together with Selections from His German Works*. 2 vols. Edited by Samuel Macauley Jackson. London: Putnam, 1912

Introduction

Historical Survey
How Had the Church Gained Such Vast Temporal Authorities?

THE QUESTION OF HOW is not all that difficult to answer. In essence, the church was handed temporal power by early imperial rulers who had been inconvenienced by the realities of a far-flung empire of diverse political and social characteristics. The church was a convenient means of control and oversight of the masses. Many reformers of the early modern period saw some level of malice behind the Roman Church's brandishing of temporal power, but I take the position that this was little more than a natural progression. Over time, as more and more responsibilities became attached to the church's original mandate to "shepherd, defend, and teach the faithful,"[1] the greater the authority it had by necessity to assume over the faithful. Eventually it got to the point where maintaining and justifying its secular authorities became almost the central focus of its spiritual authority.

As a result of this, tensions built in two critical arenas. First, between what was an international institution's trying to impose hegemony on diverse populations and the rulers of those populations seeking to differentiate themselves as spurred on by nascent nationalism (or at least rising particularism). Second, between the church and its seeming obsession with material gain (e.g., it needed vast sums of money) and the people whose souls were in its care becoming increasingly anxious about their own spiritual welfare (spurred on by rising levels of popular piety and increasing anticlericalism) being ignored. The tensions became uncontainable by the sixteenth century.

— § —

1. For a discussion of the church as an institution, see Chibi, *The Wheat and the Tares*.

The Reformation as a Result of Tension-Producing Causes

Why that series of events that historians call the "Reformation" happened towards the end of the late mediaeval and beginning of the early modern period, and why it happened as it did, can be understood as the result of a series of attempted resolutions to tensions produced by three stressful and long-term conflicts common throughout Christian Europe. The one which fully concerns us here was a centuries' long political and philosophical dispute between an institutionalized church (based in Rome and ruled by a pope) claiming both universal ecclesiastical jurisdiction as well as considerable temporal authority outside of the Italian peninsula with the rapidly developing nation-states of western Europe eager to capture (or in theory recapture) and exploit the political, economic, and social potential of a feudal-like retention of power over ecclesiastical properties, doctrines, and personnel. Churchmen and magistrates faced up to each other over such questions as who held power over the particular clergy, local clerical property and, ultimately, over the membership of the particular (local or regional) church.

Was it the local political authority or the sometimes distant head of the universal church? Put another way, did the king of France rule over French churchmen, control church owned property, and oversee the beliefs of common Frenchmen, or were these in the hands of a distant and almost perpetually non-French pope? On the other side of the issue was the question of how much authority these local powers (whether spiritual or temporal) had over Christians generally.

Of the other sources of tension (with which we need some familiarity but with which we need not deal in depth), one was the result of conflicting intellectual propositions dating back to Plato and Aristotle searching for, but never quite achieving, a means to satisfactorily resolve the contradictions between dogmas thrust upon them by an institutionalized church with control over religious teachings (i.e., revelation) and the conclusions of reason and logic looking into those self-same dogmas and the issues they set out to explain (i.e., rationality). The greatest questions of the period revolved around the issues of predestination and salvation, of course, but explanations of God, Christ, and the church were also very important.

A third source of tension was caused by the conflict between an institutionalized church claiming monopoly over salvation and its associated doctrines (e.g., claiming only its members could be among the elect and only its ceremonies had real influence with God) and the growing attraction for more individualized pursuits of justification-worthy righteousness apart from the institution. While these were expressed in a number of ways, the most significant was the development of an internalized, experiential belief system sometimes called "mysticism" or sometimes "spiritualism." This did not depend upon officially sanctioned external ceremonies, particular dogmas, or even upon membership in any particular church, nor did salvation depend on an accumulation of merits based on material culture (e.g., indulgences, pilgrimages, masses or relics). By the late mediaeval period the tensions caused by such long term conflicts had been exacerbated finally beyond containment by the emotional impact of the Black Death (mid-fourteenth-century) and the exploitation of the printing press (mid-fifteenth-century) to name but two. In other words, the building tensions finally split western Christendom into, as yet, irreconcilable factions. Here, without ignoring the other two tension producing causes we will concern ourselves with the many attempts to resolve the tension around the question of the relationship between the church and the state (or between churchmen and magistrates) exploring such issues as biblical exegesis, spheres of power, morality, discipline and the development of state churches.

On the face of it, "revelation" (i.e., Scripture, the Bible, the Word of God) supports magisterial power. For instance, Matt 22:21 says, "Render unto Caesar the things which are Caesar's, and unto God the things that are God's," while Rom 13:1 says, "Let every soul be subject unto the higher powers. For there is no power but of God: the powers that be are ordained of God." Again, 1 Pet 2:13–14 says, "Submit yourselves to every ordinance of man for the Lord's sake: whether it be to the king, as supreme; Or unto governors, as unto them that are sent by him for the punishment of evildoers, and for the praise of them that do well." Perhaps clearest of all, 1 Pet 2:17 says "Honour all men. Love the brotherhood. Fear God. Honour the king." These are among the most famous and most controversial Bible quotations.

In context, what was addressed here was a simple question of whether the Jews should pay taxes to their Roman overseers. This evolved into a philosophical debate on whether and how much God's chosen people should be involved with government and secular authorities. Indeed, should the chosen people involve themselves in temporal matters at all and, vice versa, should secular powers have influence in the spiritual lives of the chosen people? The answer, nowadays and with our (theoretical) enforced separation of church and state, seems obvious, but in the late mediaeval/early modern western world, where church and state were intertwined, it was not such an easy question and many competing solutions were put forward. Comparing and evaluating these solutions is the basis on this study.

— § —

Throughout most of the Western world nowadays the words "church" and "state" have clear meanings, but the relationship between them can still be vexing. To the modern observer they have clearly defined parameters and define separate entities with specific institutions, hierarchies, and internal logic. Indeed, the constitution of the United States officially separate them in order to avoid any kind of implied social or moral tyranny of one religious group over another. This has become the model of many secularization programs. When these terms are discussed in sociology classes, in popular culture, or on the evening news, we all vaguely know what they mean. And we know mainly because of the answers that evolved throughout the sixteenth century (or the so-called Reformation). But, at the end of the fifteenth century it was almost impossible to disentangle one from the other—churchmen claimed political authorities and temporal leaders tampered with ecclesiastical matters all the time.

The apex of the long struggle on behalf of the temporal power was probably Henry VIII's achievement by the 1530s of recognition for royal supremacy in England from lay and clerical, external or international authorities (but this was not the only one). That king gained for himself (and his successors) not only doctrinal authority over a rapidly evolving state church (e.g., the authority to determine religious truth), but also disciplinary and administrative controls over its many functions and functionaries.[2] This famous quote sums it up nicely: "By the ordinance and sufferance of God, we are king of England, and kings of England in time past have never had any superior but God only."[3] While this is the most famous expression of Henry VIII's thinking on royal sovereignty, it only really summed up political and social reality. Thomas Mayer noted another statement of twenty years earlier which states the king's case even better.

During the English occupation of the French city of Tournai (captured in the 1510s) Henry VIII made several claims of exclusive authority over it, going so far as to isolate the urban clergy of the town from the normative French ecclesiastical patronage networks. In the king's mind was this claim: "we having the supreme power as lord and king in the regalie of Tournai without recognition of any superior owe of right to have the homage fealty

---

2. Elton, "The Reformation in England," in *Elton*, 226–50.
3. Ogle, *Lollard's Tower*, 152–53.

and oath of fidelity as well of the said pretended bishop by reason of his temporalities which he holdeth of us as of other within the precincts of the same territory."[4] What this means, simply, is that well before English parliamentary legislation put it into statute form (in the 1530s) the king recognised no superior authority in any of his territories (inherited or captured) including the universal Church hierarchy. We will look at other similar expressions of royal authority made by other Christian kings in due course.

This crown-centric view was not unopposed.

The opposite case, call it supreme papal authority or superior ecclesiastical power, was the result of a theory formulated as early as the ninth century (but which came more fully to fruition in the thirteenth and fourteenth centuries). This was a doctrine of two estates, or two kingdoms, or two swords which was used as a means of explaining how the spiritual and temporal realms should interact (with the spiritual realm always in a dominant position).[5] The heart of the theory is based on revelation, specifically Luke 22:38, which outlined how Peter found two swords which Jesus allowed him to carry for a time. These two swords came to represent, in papal exegesis, the power wielded by the church—a spiritual power and a temporal power. The first of the swords was carried by the priest (as Peter was allowed to carry one) while the other was *lent out* to the magistrate (to be used only at the discretion of the priest for disciplinary purposes). This formed the basis of the infamous papal bull *Unam Sanctam*, which emphasized both papal leadership of the church and the church's supremacy over the temporal orders. The bull was not without sound justification. The pioneering work of St. Thomas Aquinas, *Summa Theologiae*, was a powerful theoretical pillar for the papal position.

Aquinas considered four types of law to which humanity was subject—eternal law (God's most basic law) and divine law (found in Scripture/revelation) which were both in the purview of the church, while natural laws were the dictates of native human reason and human positive law was that by which society was ordered. By their very nature all four forms are aimed at the well-being of man and, therefore, must be in general agreement. It is easy to see how the theory of two swords could incorporate this division of laws and why, in Aquinas's mind, just as spiritual things are higher than physical things, the spiritual laws must necessarily be superior to the temporal laws (the purview of political authorities).[6] As the spiritual

---

4. PRO, SP 1/13, fol. 127v; BL, Cott. MSS. Vit. B iii, fol. 122v, as quoted in Mayer, "On the Road to 1534," 21.

5. McGrath, *Reformation Thought*, 205.

6. Lane, *Constitutions*, 26.

sword (or kingdom) was the more powerful it was argued that there was no conflict of interest if the pope or some other religious authority was to become involved in temporal affairs which was, basically, nothing more than shepherding the masses. Higher clerical authorities, in England, sat in parliament and voted on temporal issues while, theoretically, temporal authorities were not to interfere in spiritual matters (e.g., no layman sat in convocation). These expressions are at the extreme ends of the issue; the tension between them was as old as the Christian Church itself.

— § —

A Brief Overview of the Church-State Relationship

Fourth-Century Origins

Up to and including the Reformation period, European history witnessed a series of political conflicts (contested authority) between a centralizing body claiming universal spiritual and temporal power with particular, state-focused bodies trying to expand their own rule over geographically or cultural distinctive regions. Any survey of these contests must start in the fourth century, however, when the Christian Church's existence passed through no less than five distinct phases. Beginning as a persecuted minority "sect" of Judaism (subject to vicious suppressions), the Christian Church became a tolerated sect (in which persecution was less severe less often), a favored sect, a mandated state church and, finally, to achieving supreme status as the only legally recognized church in the empire. Each phase also became an important model in the later Reformation era. The fourth century was a "golden era" to which many reformers looked for inspiration and justification; this was the "age" they would so often try to recapture the "spirit" of, thinking of it as that period of Christendom's greatest vitality and dynamism.

— § —

Emperor Constantine ruled a world of severely disparate regional political institutions and conventions no one of which he could fully exploit to establish a central control, relying instead on military might and local loyal representatives. Throughout its brief existence, however, the persecuted Christian sect had developed (by necessity) a clear hierarchy of spiritual and disciplinary authorities over its far-flung membership. Local priests shepherded the local faithful under bishops with regional administrative and disciplinary powers. And even though it had no single leading authority (i.e., Rome, Constantinople, and Antioch were co-equal) it was a model in which the emperor saw potential. Consequently, Constantine turned to the Christian establishment and weeded out rivals. Whether the emperor had any deep seated religious motivations is another question. How did this work?

Well, in North Africa for example, which was considered the breadbasket of Rome, special favor was often shown to the dominant authority there—the Church—so as not to interrupt the food supply. Part political experiment and part political necessity, freedom of assembly and worship was granted to Christians there in AD313 and rival sects were severely restricted). Underpinning imperial unity with a strong common faith had clear and obvious value, which led to Constantine's creation of a state church in the 320s. The "Catholic" (that is to say, empire-wide) church, its institutions, doctrines, and properties were then guaranteed, its clerical officers exempted from public service and normal taxation. Organized religion became part and parcel thereafter of the emperor's total strategy of rule.

Glen Thompson, based on such primary sources as Eusebius's *Life of Constantine*[7], traced a number of imperial favors granted the church as the basis of the imperial "unity" strategy. Properties in Rome were handed over for its use and the church was allowed to receive and inherit legacies (building up its wealth and property holding). In recognition of the growing Christian asceticism it was ruled that citizens who remained celibate or had no children would no longer be punished. In legal disputes Christians could choose to be judged in bishops' courts rather than in temporal courts on particular matters. Sunday became an official day of rest. Indeed, many of the issues that national and regional governments would later take offence at in the mediaeval period clearly stem from this golden century of the Church. For instance, one of Constantine's successors, Constantius, ruled in the 350s that clergy were to be tried only by their peers (setting them apart and above laymen).[8]

The favors shown to the Christians naturally upset other locally entrenched interests and, when these matters were brought to their attention, emperors began to take special, personal interest, even sitting in judgement (as over the grievances of the Donatists) because the bishops told them that it was their duty as a divine agent to preserve orthodoxy (or establish it as when Constantine decided in favor of the Catholics and against the Donatists).

---

7. See *Eusebius: Church History* [*NPNF2*, vol. 1]. This can be found online at http://www.fordham.edu/halsall/basis/vita-constantine.html.

8. Thompson, "Trouble in the Kingdom," 3–4. This can be found online at http://www.wlsessays.net/authors/T/tindex.html.

And, as in North Africa, it was easy enough for the emperor to assume control of the church's occasional gatherings of the local leadership elsewhere too either in person or *via* subordinates. These local synods, of no fixed geographic boundary or commonly recognized authority, had been meeting with regularity to discuss controversial issues but Constantine's establishment of a state church made it possible to assemble a general council of the whole church and, having made it possible he used the established organization and local hierarchies to firmly fix his own authority as well as religious orthodoxy (as in AD325). Consequently, as the political and military stability of the empire deteriorated in the late fourth century, increasingly larger councils, responsive to civil authority, were summoned to replace local synods. The central power looked even more carefully towards the unifying spiritual power as a good fallback position in time of political turmoil.

At Nicaea, for instance, a uniform method for determining the date of the Easter festival was established. Now, to a modern reader this may seem of limited importance, but consider the value an agreed date of celebration, common throughout the empire, would have (if only as a means of downplaying local customs).[9] From the point of view of the emperors' themselves this was sound political strategy and it was just as often beneficial for the church too. In c.AD378, for instance, Emperor Gratian announced the edict *Cunctos populos* which made Catholic Christianity—churches in communion with Rome—the sole recognized religion of the empire. Common spiritual beliefs across the empire, endorsed and enforced by the emperor's authority, turned the church into a firm pillar of imperial power (and *vice- versa*). Theological debates took on political adherents and significance (and *vice-versa*), public order and fiscal policies were weighed against religious freedoms and the hierarchy of clerical officers (increasingly imperial nominations and appointments) took on pseudo-temporal power at all levels. Constantine came to consider himself a special kind of bishop in that, where bishops had jurisdiction within the church he claimed a bishop-like authority over all things. He became *pontifex maximus*—chief priest of the cults—as recognized by the state and which, in the Christian era, came to mean an authority delineated directly from Christ—the king of kings. The emperor became the chief Vicar of Christ even though he did not perform any priestly functions. These claims sometimes necessitated imperial interference in the church's internal business, like the decision against Arius at Nicaea, but provided church matters did not conflict with the emperor's financial interests or public

---

9. Korthals, "The Seven Ecumenical Councils," 3. This can be found online at http://www.wlsessays.net/authors/K/kindex.html.

order needs they often strove to keep their interference to a minimum and let their bishops do their jobs uninterrupted. The only exceptions were cases of heresy and so-called re-baptism as these issues upset public order, unity and challenged orthodoxy. The secular authority retained powers of persecution and death. It was not a perfect solution; there were conflicts between church and state officers[10] and, when Constantine moved the imperial capital to Constantinople (c.330), the Bishop of Rome became the old capital's sole pseudo-political power.

By the end of this most important century an understanding existed between the emperor and the Christian Church. The emperor was God's agent and imperial government had been established not only for the good of the world but for the good of the church too. The bishops remained subordinate regional stabilizing authorities while the emperor summoned councils, declared official legislation and heresy (thus enforcing orthodoxy). The bishops would occasionally sanction the emperor if he overstepped perceived bounds too overtly, but the church rarely, if ever, overstepped any implied bounds into secular affairs except as the voice of morality. In this way the church was able to withstand the political disintegration of the fourth to the tenth centuries and slowly consolidated its own authority. Consolidation, however, came with a price—increasing tension between the institutionalized church authority centered at Rome (and its roughly established doctrinal and jurisdictional authorities over western Christendom) and local political authorities over spiritual issues, disciplinary matters and, increasingly, temporal issues.

The Middle Ages

By the late fifth century Pope Leo I (440–61) was claiming supreme and universal authority in the church based on his interpretation of Matt 16:18–9: "And I tell you that you are Peter, and on this rock I will build my church, and the gates of Hades will not overcome it. I will give you the keys of the kingdom of heaven; whatever you bind on earth will be bound in heaven,

---

10. E.g., *Ambrose: Select Works and Letters* [*NPNF2*, x], 427–29 (letter 21). This can be found online at http://www.fordham.edu/halsall/source/ambrose-let21.html or at *NPNF2*, 4, *Athanasius: Select Works and Letters*, 286.

and whatever you loose on earth will be loosed in heaven."[11] Leo favored a literal interpretation in which Peter was personally the rock upon which the church was built. His name was derived from the Greek *petra* which means "bedrock" or a solid foundation. This interpretation was disputed at the time, in Constantinople and in France, and would be by many reformers in the sixteenth century. Metaphorically it refers to Peter's faith in Christ or in his teachings (which was the general focus of *Matthew* otherwise) as the foundation stone. The second portion, the power of binding and loosing (granting or withholding absolution), was also disputed (examined later). Subsequent general councils of the church whittled away at Imperial supremacy or tried to. At the third council of Constantinople (680–1), for instance, the Bishop of Rome almost slipped "papal infallibility" into the record.[12]

The Dark Ages Period

That famous phrase "*the Dark Ages*" is commonly known, if not precisely understood. It is roughly the period in Western European history between the fall of the Roman Empire and the early twelfth century featuring political fragmentation, the decline in urban life, and the decay of major centers of learning. Consequently there were few renowned intellectuals. Augustine died in AD 430 and no comparable figure arises before Anselm in the eleventh century. The church was able to profit, however; fundamental powers (e.g., Rome's central and supreme authority, Rome's teaching authority, Rome's interpretive power over Scripture) were established. Gregory the Great (590–604) became the virtual civil ruler of the Italian peninsula. The Eastern emperor, far removed, could no longer dependably prevent repeated invasions so Gregory negotiated treaties with the various temporal powers, paid troops, and appointed generals in the service of the church's temporal holdings. Successes in one area, however, raised problems in another.

For instance, while the Bishop of Rome's authority spread (secular power in the Italian peninsula and spiritual authority from Scotland to Africa), the increasing mix of spiritual and secular power led to internal dissent and moral corruption (e.g., bribery in the mid-level clerical hierarchy and Roman bureaucracy). There were successes, like St. Jerome's authoritative version of Scripture (the Vulgate) or the *Decretals of Isidore* (a collection of letters, appeals and decisions from the previous thirty-three popes which limited the authority of bishops but established clerical freedom

---

11 Levi, *Renaissance and Reformation*, 25; Schwerin, "Vicar of Christ," 2–3, which can be found online at http://www.wlsessays.net /authors/S/sindex .html.

12. Korthals, "The Seven Ecumenical Councils," 12; Luke 22:31–32.

from civil authority). Later proved fraudulent, the *Donation of Constantine* gave the bishops of Rome temporal powers and privileges throughout the Italian peninsula. With Leo III's support (c.800), Charlemagne (King of the Franks) was able to forge an empire out of the disparate cultures, states and ecclesiastical realms of central-eastern Europe (a Holy Roman Empire). As Holy Roman Emperor, Charlemagne became protector and temporal head of Christendom and feudal overlord of Rome's temporal holdings, but subject to the Bishop of Rome's spiritual authority (exercised through bishops, archbishops, and overseen by cardinals). Despite a schism in Christianity itself (the *filioque* controversy), faith and salvation had seemingly become subject to the Roman pontiff's sanctions.[13] By the eleventh century, however, tensions between the spiritual and temporal powers could no longer be suppressed.

Leo IX (1049–54) planned a tour of the regions, summoning reforming synods against such evils as simony and clerical incontinence in Italy, France and Germany (the bulk of the Empire). His campaigning, however, clashed with the temporal authorities of the emperor, Henry III. It was understood that God had established civil order in reflection of the spiritual order. For instance, the hierarchy of pope, cardinals, bishops and priests was reflected by a similar hierarchy of emperor, kings, dukes and knights. This civil order was to be a means of disciplining both people and a society marred by the effect of original sin, but a question of how much authority magistrates actually exercised over believers came to a head. Leo used the church's cultural dominance to justify his travels across the continent, his enacting of local reforms, his negotiating arrangements and patronage networks with local magnates, and his trying to enforce a higher standard of clerical and social discipline. Clearly, some of these objectives clashed with the established feudal networks and arrangements. The chains of causality are interesting.

Popular fervor resulting from crusade propaganda, for instance, spread ideals of heightened morality among the laity and clergy alike. This in turned led to the founding of stricter religious orders (e.g., Cistercians, Franciscans and Dominicans) and the standardization of practices made gains only at the expense of local practices (e.g., clerical marriage, local appointment to clerical office). While centralization of power at Rome led to the appointment of more prestigious bishops, abbots and deans, regional political authorities became increasingly nervous as particular conditions were seemingly ignored in the process (e.g., localism—the cultural identification with the region over the state—economic realities, local wealth and class divisions). Just how much real power did the pontiffs have over the rulers of the small, independent

---

13. Schwerin, "Vicar of Christ," 7.

cities, states and all those little kingdoms that had been amalgamated into another empire became a nagging and lasting question. So, the tour not only raised immediate questions but it also led to a long-term crisis which, as V H H Green noted, "was in the long run to exhaust the Empire and to lead to the moral degeneration of the Papacy."[14] The tensions finally exploded with the election of Gregory VII (1073–85) and his so-called "Investiture Contest" (1075–77) with the emperor Henry IV.

Investiture refers to a feudal ceremony during which a vassal (that is, someone who held land from a higher authority) was given tokens symbolic of his relationship with the overlord of the lands. The custom, in relation to the church, was that a new bishop would receive a ring and crosier (a hooked staff) from his king as indication that he was now in possession of the temporalities (i.e., the lands and properties of the diocese). He became a shepherd of bodies and lands just as much as he had become a shepherd of souls. His lordship over the temporalities also gave him the temporary right to appoint officers and spread patronage. A problem arose, however, over the question of whether layman really had the right to empower clergymen in this way. In other words could a lay patron appoint a parish priest and, if so, what did this consequently say about clerical authority?

Pope Gregory VII thought that laymen did not have the power to invest clergy and, in his bull *Dictatus papae* (of March 1075)—wherein he assumed the title "pope and supreme pontiff of the entire west"—he claimed a universal power to deprive and reconcile any other bishop and power above any and all temporal authorities.[15] The aim was to free the church of temporal interference and he went so far as to forbid Emperor Henry IV from making appointments (which he continued to do anyway). Although the power struggle between Gregory and Henry was delayed by the first crusade, the pope emerged from that with a heightened reputation as the defender of international Christendom. When the emperor capitulated, Gregory was able to claim authority to take away and grant property, possessions and even titles to laymen, while they, conversely, had no right of interference in the church.[16] Papal progresses, councils and regional synods in support increased respect and veneration for the pope from the teeming masses and knighthood of Christendom at the same time as individual

---

14. Green, *Renaissance and Reformation*, 16.
15. Green, *Renaissance and Reformation*, 8; Levi, *Renaissance and Reformation*, 6.
16. Holborn, *Reformation*, 19–21.

kings and emperors opposed the popes and made war on each other. In many ways the crusades had established the pope more thoroughly as the moral voice of Christian Europe but also as its diplomatic focal point and across the board clergymen began to arbitrate all disputes between kings thereafter—trade alliances, defensive treaties (any number of issues which nowadays would be the work of diplomats).

The church, as a major land-owning power, exercised all the rights of feudal patronage and expected to (and did) collect feudal privileges. The apex of papal authority came with Innocent III (1198–1216), who transformed reverence and feudal due into political and diplomatic power as the "vicar of Christ." He was able to force England and France into peace as well as install his candidate, Stephan Langton, as Archbishop of Canterbury over King John's choice of John de Grey. Famously, John refused to allow Langton into England. To make his point clear, he also dissolved Christ Church monastery, dispersed the members and secularized its properties. In response Innocent placed England under interdict (removing all ecclesiastical benefits) on 24 March 1208.

Tit-for-tat measures followed leading to John's excommunication in 1209 and deposition in 1212. The pontiff tasked Philip of France with the execution of the order. Tensions rising, the feudal lords and bishops of England forced the king to submit. John acknowledged Langton, re-admitted exiled clergy, made financial compensations and, on 13 May 1213 (of his own accord), surrendered the kingdom into the direct rule of the pope. The assumption was that John would thereafter act as a fief—a feudal client—and pay over an annual tribute). This was a submission too far; the barons rose up to ensure their own privileges and forced the king to endorse *Magna Charta* (against papal wishes).

The Later Middle Ages

Without direct political influence, popes turned to marshal their moral and spiritual supremacy into a substitute. The power of binding and loosing held that popes could wipe away the stains of sin, forgive or condemn anyone. What were regional or local political claims compared to this? By the early thirteenth century the point was driven home when the fourth Lateran Council (1215) enshrined clerical immunity from civil law. A clergyman caught stealing, for example—provided he could prove that he was a clergyman—could no longer be brought to trial in a civilian court but would have his case transferred to a church court (to his obvious advantage). In England, the proof of clerical status was not airtight documentation or testimony from reliable witnesses, but was instead the so-called "neck verse" (*Ps* 51.1).[17] If the accused could read the verse (in Latin) it was presumed that he was a cleric and could claim benefit. This prompted any number of pithy rhymes, like this one: *If a clerk had been taken / for stealing of bacon, for burglary, murder, or rape, / if he could but rehearse (well prompt) his neck-verse, / he never could fail to scape.*[18]

As such rhymes indicate, this claim of immunity to civil prosecution was pushed to the absolute limits and became a real bone of conflict between lay and clerical authorities and a real source of injustice to the victims of clerical abuse. Building on this, Boniface VIII (d.1303) tried but failed to enforce clerical immunity to taxation with the bull *Unam Sanctum*. Here was embodied the principle of supreme papal authority over both spiritual and temporal matters: "[it was] altogether necessary to salvation for every human creature to be subject to the Roman pontiff."[19]

The claim of absolute power is much less serious than having the principle enshrined in documentation. Putting something on paper takes away ambiguity, making claims more difficult to deny or ignore. As a result, in 1303 Boniface was kidnapped by French forces and held prisoner while King Philip (the Fair) procured the election of a compliant French bishop as Pope Clement V (1305). Clement in turn moved the seat of authority away from "corrupt" Rome to "scrupulous" Avignon (a center of trade situated in imperial territory surrounded by France) initiating the so-called seventy-year long "*Babylonian captivity of the papacy.*" It was an audacious act girded by critical examinations of the theological and legal foundation of Roman authority.[20] One such was produced by Marsilio (sometimes Marsiglio) of Padua who theorized that, as the papacy had become the single greatest cause of grief and warfare whether it was now time to place limits on papal authority.

The church's claims to universal dominion over temporal and spiritual matters were addressed by Marsilio in 1324 with *Defensor Pacis*. Marsilio theorized that clerical authority actually depended upon a superior civil power (which itself depended on the willingness of the people to be ruled through the application of agreed laws). The spiritual power therefore had

---

17. "Have mercy upon me, O God, according to thy loving kindness: according unto the multitude of Thy tender mercies blot out my transgressions."

18. See www.websters-online-dictionary.org/ne/Neck-verse.html.

19. Cameron, *European Reformation*, 53; Schwerin, "Vicar of Christ," 12.

20. Lindberg, *The European Reformation*, 45.

no intrinsic jurisdiction in and of itself.[21] The church, he wrote, confused spiritual and temporal authorities and attempted to enforce a kind of hegemony of its own making over temporal society.[22] Power (i.e., control) ultimately was invested in the people as a corporate body. It was this body that delegated rule to those able to meet its material and spiritual needs while retaining a right of censure and powers of dismissal. Marsilio equated citizens with believers and heretics with social outcasts (political theory which predated Constantine). He acknowledged the priesthood as a divine institution but individual priests were in fact subordinate state functionaries—spiritual rather than temporal magistrates. Furthermore, while he held the papacy as legitimate the clerical hierarchy was itself no more significant than any other human institution (and as flawed as any other). As such it should be equally subject to local traditions and customs. Marsilio was making a clear argument for what would later be called "conciliarism."

In the secular sphere the body politic (expressed perhaps in the form of a parliament or senate) agrees laws and conditionally subjects itself to a single ruler for the good of all while, in the spiritual, the general council takes the place of the senate, determines spiritual matters, and agrees to have these decisions enforced through its representative single ruler (perhaps an archbishop). The council, like the representative political body, creates the laws and designates those who will propagate the agreed articles of faith (e.g., bishops).[23] Critics of the church's assumptions and claimed authorities also appealed to the vision of a golden age when the spiritual and temporal authorities had worked hand in hand. They appealed to the idea of reforming the church and removing the abuses that had crept in and, thereby, regain the imagined spiritual and moral perfection the church and Christendom must once have had (say, back in the fourth century). This vision was effective; it could be set alongside the sheer opulence of the Avignon popes in their palaces and with their morally suspect lifestyles all paid for out of the pockets of the faithful. Clerical taxation offended the laity and clergy alike as papal fees, fines, and taxes drew funds away from local needs, giving rise to antipapalism, anticlericalism (which we will examine in due course) and charges of materialism.

To put this into context, the seeming materialism of the church as a whole was in reality no more than a reflection of contemporary socio-economic norms. Expansion and operations required effective administration

---

21. Reardon, *Religious Thought*, 3. Selected readings from *Defensor Pacis* can be found online at http://www.fordham.edu/ halsall/source/marsiglio4.html.

22. Haight, *Christian Community*, 1:362.

23. Haight, *Christian Community*, 1:365.

(bureaucracy) all of which had to be funded, resulting in new accounting and business techniques. The rising importance of towns and the creation and development of centralized markets was changing the economic framework of European society while, at the same time, war, famine and plagues were taking away all the other certainties of life. Money was increasingly replacing these other intangibles, so we cannot be too surprised by a changing mentality in the church. We shall return to this point shortly.

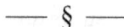

It became increasingly clear to many that the Avignon experience was having a progressively more adverse effect on the papacy's prestige so plans were initiated to move the heart of the church back to Rome in 1377. This led to the so-called "Western Schism."

In the planning stages the Avignon pope died which initiated riots in Rome, demands for the papacy's immediate re-location, and for the election of an Italian pope. Despite the threats of violence, however, the cardinals elected a capable Neapolitan (more French than Italian) administrator as Urban VI. This was meant as a compromise but under pressure from the mobs the cardinals took the drastic step of reversing their decision and declaring his election null and void, slipping away from Avignon and back to Italian territory where they re-assembled, declared Urban uncanonically elected, elevating Clement VII instead. Neither pope resigned, neither accepted the legitimacy of the other, both were excommunicated. Let's pause and consider the repercussions.

This is not the case of a pope and an anti-pope vying for power. Both Urban and Clement were canonically elected. A legitimate conclave had acted unethically (and perhaps illegally) by reversing its own earlier decision, exacerbating a problem of its own creation. For the next few decades the rival popes split the church. It cannot be overstated how spiritually damaging this was to the lives of the masses of Christendom. As Lindberg and others have pointed out, if salvation depended on obedience to the papacy—communion with Rome—would following an excommunicated and possibly illegitimate pope damn one's soul—even if that pope had been lawfully elected and claimed legitimacy? How was anyone to know which was the true Vicar of Christ and which the false? Two popes and two colleges of cardinals led to the absurdity of some parishes having two rival priests baptizing children and marrying couples while claiming the baptisms and marriages performed by the other were illegitimate and rival parishioners as heretics. States were internally and externally divided too; both popes had political supporters among the ruling classes. As the prestige of the church sank, national spiritual movements took root as people were forced to examine why they supported one pope over the other.

The finally settle the matter, the Council of Pisa (March to July 1409) assembled, debated and deposed both popes as both schismatic and heretical, electing Alexander V to heal the divide. Neither pope accepted the new situation. Christendom was left with three canonically elected popes and three warring, mutually hostile factions, a situation not finally ended until the Council of Constance (1414–18) elected one legitimate pope (Martin V). The damage had been done. The Avignon exile/captivity both diminished the spiritual authority of the papacy and contributed to the belief in the pope's real lack of political objectivity. In recognition of the problem the representatives at Constance turned to the "conciliarist" solution in which the authority of the general council was recognized as superior to that of the pope. General councils should be accorded the highest spiritual authority as they were lawful assemblies representing the universal church in a more direct way with power direct from Christ through the Holy Spirit in their midst. It had deposed of the three rivals and elected an agreed upon replacement; surely this gave proof to the claim. Pope Martin agreed to the council's decree (because of course he did), but for obvious reasons subsequent popes viewed conciliarism as a dangerous challenge (rather than aid) to their own authority and few were summoned. With the immediate crisis (multiple popes) averted and widespread heretical movements (e.g., Lollardy and the Hussites—examined below) seen off, the papacy quickly reverted to its worldly, Italy-centric outlook, giving further renewed credence to antipapalism and anticlericalism elsewhere expressed in oral and literary criticisms as well as physical demonstrations with elements of nascent nationalism thrown in. The literate, politically aware classes wanted both the long promised reforms of the church as well as more clearly expressed particular characteristics (e.g., an obviously French church for France).

The church as a mirror of national characteristics brings up a minor but increasingly important aspect of the larger *church v. state* conflict. Local or particular temporal authorities had taken on board all those rising complaints against Rome's universal claims and its spiritual problems and, because of the secular needs of the popes for political allies and funding, had been able to force compromises and win significant powers over their own particular spiritual institutions. If we ignore for the moment the actual practicalities of such claims (on both sides), the greatest climb-down forced upon Rome happened in England.

We noted earlier the height of Roman authority in the reign of John. Since the thirteenth century ecclesiastical benefices (the livings—money—from a church office generated through the attached properties) in England had been made by means of papal provision. Popes collated (i.e., appointed) nominees to vacant positions. By virtue of his supreme spiritual authority, however, a pope might, temporarily, also suspend the (highly contested) rights of the lay patron of any given and soon to be vacant living and provide his own "provisor" nominee (which negated the projected vacancy). In this way English livings had increasingly fallen into the hands of Italian provisors; money was sent out of the country and violence increasingly ensued as lay patrons were cheated of their rights. In response, the *Statute of Provisors* (1350–1) sought to prohibit the practice. Underpinning the stature were arguments of economy (e.g., property rights) and the localities particular spiritual nature (i.e., local candidates for local offices). Legislators argued that the role of the Church *of England*, as founded by the kings and nobles *of England*, was to keep the people *of England* informed of the laws of God as well as the for more practical purposes of establishing hospitals and charity on behalf of locals. Benefices falling into the hands of foreigners undermined these good works and denied the English of all the benefits of religion in a way they could access it.

The statute enacted free election of bishops (in their chapters), enforced the rights of patrons, and endorsed the principle that claimed papal rights would in future revert to the crown. A number of statutes reinforcing or fine-tuning these principles were legislated right up to the reign of Henry VIII (when the Act of Supremacy collated them). The most singular of these fine-tuning statutes was the *Statute of Praemunire*. Although the Roman curia was not mentioned specifically (maintaining the illusion of Roman spiritual supremacy), the statute forbid appeals to any foreign power over patronage disputes. Provisors, Praemunire and others were amended from time to time, often ignored, but never revoked. Henry VIII revived such acts to devastating effect in the 1530s as domestic politics and economic principles forced particularism in the church despite the papacy's on-going march toward centralization. Something similar happened in early fifteenth-century France.

In 1438 Charles VIII summoned a church synod in Bourges to look over some of the major religious issues of the day and come to terms with reform efforts. What emerged was the so-called *Pragmatic Sanction*.[24] As

---

24 This can be found detailed at http://www.fordham.edu/halsall/source/1438

in England, the church in France had been subject to the deprivations of foreigners and the result was plainly negative:

> the churches of the kingdom have been made to suffer from all sorts of insatiable greed . . . given rise to grievous abuses and unbearable burdens; that the most notable and best endowed benefices have fallen into the hands of unknown men, who do not conform at all to the requirement of residence and who do not understand the speech of the people committed to their care, and consequently are neglectful of the needs of their souls . . . thus the worship of Christ is declining, piety is enfeebled, the laws of the Church are violated, and buildings for religious uses are falling in ruin. The [local and French] clergy abandon their theological studies, because there is no hope of advancement. Conflicts without number rage over the possession of benefices, plurality of which is coveted by an execrable ambition. Simony is everywhere glaring; the prelates and other collators are pillaged of their rights and their ministry; the rights of patrons are impaired; and the wealth of the kingdom goes into the hands of foreigners, to the detriment of the clergy.

The solution to these problems was to disallow papal provisions, restrict appeals to Rome, prohibit Annates (i.e., the first year's revenue from a clerical office usually sent to the pope to cover administrative fees), and to enshrine a principle of local elections (which would come to be dominated by royal nominees). The *Sanction* augmented royal authority over the church based on the coronation oath as kings were "bound to defend and protect the holy church, its ministers and its sacred offices, and zealously to guard in their kingdoms the decrees of the holy fathers." Kings had the right, the obligation even, to assemble and oversee local councils and synods, power fine-tuned in 1516 by Francis I with the *Concordat of Bologna*.

A "concordat" is nothing more than an agreement between two parties (in this case Francis and Pope Leo X). Francis ascended the throne with the zeal of a conqueror and almost immediately launched successful invasions of Milan (in support of his "rights" to that duchy and to the Kingdom of Naples). Leo feared that the king would set his armies on papal territory next giving Francis the opportunity to strengthen the crown's grip on the French church. In essence, the *Sanction's* provision of local election was overhauled in favor of royal nominations (and a papal rubber-stamp), which gave the crown a virtual control of over about 100 bishoprics and archbishoprics and about 500 monasteries. In exchange, the papal-states were secure

---

pragmatic.html.

(from French ambitions) and papal spiritual supremacy tacitly recognized.[25] Although Roman Catholic orthodoxy was upheld in both the English and French cases, the underlying argument is that the *universal* Roman church had failed local needs. Temporal rulers had stepped in to successfully remedy the problems. The best example of this was undoubtedly the re-creation of the Inquisition (in Castile in 1478 and in Aragon in 1483). Ferdinand and Isabella molded their successful anti-Turk, anti-Muslim campaigns into greater autonomy over the Iberian church *via* a crown nominated inquisitor-general and a court which served the crown as a useful centralizing tool and means of social control and discipline.[26]

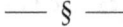

As any student of the Reformation knows, it is nearly impossible to separate the spiritual and political spheres, which explains why the expanding schism between spiritual and temporal authorities produced such shockwaves. Each side wanted to expand its authority and, from either point of view, this was completely reasonable and logical. The problem was pin-pointing precisely where spiritual authority ended and secular authority began and *vice-versa*. This expanding schism, however, raised another in the public trust between how corrupt the institutions of the church were perceived to be and how trustworthy it was imagined they could be.

In crusading times the church had clearly been a unifying influence and a respected authority, but this did not seem so obvious in the latter half of the fifteenth-century. Claiming power is one thing—anyone can claim power—it is the effective use of power that matters and the popes of the period were singularly ineffective. They pursued impressive projects—cathedrals, castles, works of art, limited crusades—but they were seemingly too blinded by their own personal ambitions to take note of the spiritual malaise forming around them. The popes following Martin V were more often than not viewed as petty tyrants and historians reserve especially harsh criticism for Alexander VI and Julius II.

Alexander was the product of family connections and political chicanery and he used his papal authority mainly to break the power of other Italian princes. He rebuilt papal temporal authority and revenue, as well as the power of his Borgia kin (and his own eight illegitimate children, including the

---

25 Spooner, "The Reformation in Difficulties," 211; Knecht, "The Concordat of 1516," 91–112.

26 Roberts, "Ferdinand and Isabella," 48–49; Armstrong, *The European Reformation*, 102. Also see, Kamen, *The Spanish Inquisition*; and Elliot, *Imperial Spain*, 107–8.

infamous Cesare and Lucrecia). With his *The Prince*, Machiavelli permanently refashioned the word Borgia to mean the epitome of cruelty and intrigue.[27] "Borgia" Rome was Avignon recreated. Julius II, also a creature of political maneuvers was, like Alexander, uninterested in providing spiritual leadership, trading the pursuit of vanity projects for military glory instead.

Julius desired political domination of the Italian peninsula and (beyond artists and architects) the driving out of any and all foreign influences. He mounted campaign after campaign in pursuit of military objectives, entering and abandoning political leagues and military agreements with wanton abandon, playing the major European powers off against each other where he could. He became known as the "warrior pope" despite a lack of real lasting success. He could hardly be said to have inspired spiritual respect, but he did inspire others to focus the existing problems. The rebuilding of St Peter's Basilica, for example, ultimately led to the massive indulgence sale that would inspire Luther's righteous anger while an increasingly disgusted Erasmus (a witnessed to Julius's campaigns) was inspired to reimagine an ideal church and question the balance between the spiritual and secular spheres.

Erasmus and the Separation of Church and State Authorities

Neither humanism nor Erasmus needs a detailed introduction; their aims and interests are well documented. For our interests here it is important to note that humanism gave rise to a lay piety movement searching for greater spiritual succor underpinned by published criticism of the church's perceived material orientation and lack of spiritual direction. Humanism also inspired a different kind of intellectual approach to the perceived problems of late mediaeval Christendom (e.g., papal self-aggrandizement and warfare) trying to pin-point where the church and society had gone so badly wrong. They considered the *pax Europa* and searched for Christian renewal as a solution.[28] Not through widespread change but through broad-based moral improvement. Humanism's *ad fontes* approach meant that scriptural correctness was of singular importance; linguistic expertise (in Latin, Greek and Hebrew) and applied critical, literary and historical textual analysis became vital scholarly pursuits. Bible stories were reconsidered as records of human activity and development, sacred and secular history with moral overtones.

Erasmus (although not the only scholar to do so) recognized the weaknesses of the institutionalized church and the obstacles that lay in the

27. An online text can be found at http://www.constitution.org/mac/prince.txt.
28. McGrath, *The Intellectual Origins*, 34.

path of Christian renewal and peace. Like his fellow humanists he was not interested in challenging the church's power, or the position of the pope, or its theology, but he was interested in extracting from its most important historical documents moral and doctrinal insights for practical applications. They were in the vanguard of an intellectual movement which discounted traditional *Sentences*, glosses, and commentaries on the Bible in favor of the actual source material. They were searching for a living, breathing Christ and the once vital and dynamic church to revive them. The lessons and wisdom gleaned from his words and works could then be applied to a recapturing of the vitality and energy of the early church. Humanists, particularly northern European or Christian humanists, looked increasingly at the New Testament and the writings of the ancient Church Fathers (Christianity in its purest form) in the attempt to exact practical solutions. As McGrath pointed out, the humanist program was not *sola scriptura*; the Bible was but one source of doctrine and morality among many.[29] *Sola scriptura* grew out of it as the reformers (influenced by the humanists) became focused on correct doctrine and the earliest less worldly, less materialistic church practices. Humanists pursued their ideals by exposing and condemning the abuses and weaknesses in the church (as an institution and among its custodians), comparing the contemporary with the ancient to encourage a more practical, spiritual Christianity and inspire renewal and peace. The reformers would take this one step further to compel the ideal.

Staying with Erasmus (a pacifist), his frustrations were especially aroused by internecine Christian warfare, egged on by the Vicar of Christ and churchmen. Some clergy even took on a pro-active role, exchanging righteousness for temporary and meaningless material gain. Erasmus saw Christians as part of a single corporate entity. They were, together, and despite ranks of dignity or function, the physical manifestation of the body of Christ. They should be dedicated to spiritual pursuits and a Christ-like existence. In his view all souls are of equal value within the church because of their common head, Christ. It was unthinkable, therefore, that this body should wage war against itself—peace should be the goal of each and every Christian in imitation of Christ "the prince of peace." The church—the "house" of Christ—is a spiritual entity meant to shepherd Christians—the "people" or "flock" of Christ—and should be entirely unconcerned with materialism and physical matters—ideally. Nowhere does Erasmus doubt the legitimacy of the office

---

29. McGrath, *The Intellectual Origins*, 42.

of the pope, or that the church as an institution has need of physical properties, but he wanted its overall focus turned back in the direction for which it had been originally established—those original Pauline and Augustinian mandates to gather, instruct and shepherd the flock. Much of his writing, therefore, and much of his specific ecclesiology, is geared toward extoling the church's spiritual mandate and detailing the implications of it for the lives of individual Christians. To do this effectively meant, without advocating its destruction, exposing and condemning the abuses and weaknesses within the Church (both the institution and in its custodians) in order to effect or inspire basic reform. One of the earliest illustrations of Erasmus's viewpoint can be found in his *Handbook of the Christian Soldier* or *Enchiridion militis christiani* (of 1503).[30]

Handbook was written as an improving text for an anonymous friend and is the type of manual with which we are all quite familiar; nowadays it might have some self-deprecating and amusing title like *Christianity for Dummies*. Erasmus was writing for an interested audience (more than just professional theologians) so he emphasized the individual and the development of a personal, inward spirituality dependent on nothing but a genuine pursuit of faith. Erasmus's friend was a soldier so the lessons were couched in military language. Christian life became a war on evil, so what did it mean to be a good Christian soldier? Can one focus on the war without becoming isolated from life outside the war?[31]

We have seen this kind of dual spheres of influence model many times already. The divine governs the soul and the physical, animal world governs the body.[32] The church, which should be part and parcel of the divine is, however, so mired in the latter (the sphere of the secular government) that would-be Christians need to take a hand in turning this situation around before all trust in the church is lost.

What does this mean?

It means that due to the political and temporal responsibilities which (with all the best intentions) have been piled upon the church over the centuries it has been left with a less than spiritually satisfying, but necessarily heavy material emphasis in much of its dealings. The Mass, pilgrimages, veneration of saints, images, indulgences, all have monetary aspects somewhere in their make-up, and these have largely replaced and overwhelmed the actual central spiritual messages. Similarly, rigid dogma and doctrine has replaced the concepts they were originally meant to explain. To address

---

30. Here I will be using Erasmus, "Handbook of the Christian soldier," in *EE*, 24–93.
31. Augustijn, *Erasmus*, 43–55.
32. Augustijn, *Erasmus*, 42.

this perceived disorder Erasmus wanted to switch the emphasis for Christians back to the words, teachings, actions and example of the Christ himself—*ad fontes* in the most literal sense.

Reardon read into this a focus on charity; not the mere mechanical donation of money and materials but actual involvement—the edification of one's neighbor, counting all as equal under Christ, rejoicing in a friend's triumphs and commiserating in his failures (as if these were personal)—genuine charitable activities.[33] Erasmus wrote that all the physical, material aspects—church visits, prostrations before statues, lighting candles, mechanical repetition of prayers, prettifying buildings—were simply unnecessary.[34] What was necessary was the study of Scripture, mediation on the divine, and a sensible reading of the pagan philosophers.[35] He saw Christianity in the mind, heart and soul, unconcerned with the physical. At a stroke he repudiated a great deal of the external structures of organized religion: there was no real place for excessive ceremonial, rules, regulations, usages, church buildings. Even the special place usually accorded clerics and monks was played down in favor of an internal dialogue and personal relationship with Christ. What Erasmus was recommending was a turning away from the visible aspects of life, from the imperfect, the indifferent, towards those invisible things of the spiritual. It is an anti-materialistic message that almost all the reformers will, in one way or another, repeat.[36]

Underlying charity was a notion that within the spiritual sphere there were no degrees or ranks of individuals. Certainly the body of Christ encompasses members from various ranks of social or political dignity and of all sorts of functions in the secular world, but all souls in the spiritual sphere are of equal value because of their common head in Christ. There is in reality no difference between clergymen and laity within the spiritual sphere save for function; baptism being the great equalizer.[37] By emphasizing charity, brotherly love, commonality, and faith, Erasmus sought to lessen the ties of citizenship and nationality which could sometimes assert much more violent influence, hampering charitable efforts. Turning to the physical sphere he acknowledged different ranks of dignity without really focusing his critical eye on political systems or temporal power structures *per se*. He basically accepted these things (outside the spiritual sphere) largely as they were presented. Nor did Erasmus fuss much with the conflicting theories of relative

---

33. Reardon, *Religious Thought*, 36.
34. Erasmus, "Handbook," 68.
35. Reardon, *Religious Thought*, 36.
36. Erasmus, "Handbook," 61–62, 63, 67, 68–69.
37. Pabel, "The Peaceful People of Christ," 62–63.

powers and spheres of influence as some others had (e.g., Marsilio), and nor did he write a dedicated treatise on the relationship between the church and the temporal authority, seeing as they were concerned with separate matters. There are, however, hints of an ideal Christian Commonwealth in his writings wherein each is accorded the respect their function deserves provided they perform their function virtuously.

For example, in his every expanding collection of *Adages* it seems clear that Erasmus was uninterested in extoling one sphere at the expense of the other, searching instead for balance. If such a balance could be found then "each part of the body politic would retain its rightful authority, the people would be given their due; the councilors and magistrates would be paid the proper respect to their learning, to law and to justice; the bishops and priests would receive the honour due to them" and presumably there would be no internecine warfare.[38] The basic theme of harmonious interaction was taken up later in *Panegyric for Archduke Philip of Austria* (1504), an anti-war diatribe in which he visualized Christendom as one country, family, or body all "redeemed at the same price."[39] As for specifics, Erasmus cast doubt on popular assumptions about the Petrine doctrine of the two swords (examined earlier) in (but not exclusive to) *Adages*,[40] *Complaint of Peace* (1517), *Paraphrase on Mark* and *Paraphrase on Luke* (both of 1523).

In *Complaint of Peace* (*Querela pacis*) Erasmus divested the church of its sword, making it impossible for any engagement in war (where the church does not belong) other than as advocates of peace.[41] "The world had its own laws and its own established practices before the gospel appeared; it punished with death, it waged war . . ."—but Christ's purpose was to exemplify another way, that of peaceful resolution. Bishops and priests teach the gospel; magistrates and rulers expound the laws, maintain justice, defend the public peace and relieve the oppressed.[42] Instead of a sword, therefore, the church brandishes Scripture, "the sword of the gospel" to "cut the throat of wickedness and lop off human greed."[43] Still speaking of balance and dignity Erasmus was concern to prevent temporal authorities interfering in

---

38. Dickens and Jones, *Erasmus*, 66. The quote is from Phillips, ed., *The "Adages" of Erasmus*, 183 (1508 edition). Also see Schoeck, *Erasmus of Europe*, 76.

39. Pabel, "The Peaceful People of Christ," 67–68, quoting "Panegyric for Archduke Philip of Austria" (1504), in Levi, ed., *CWE*, 27:54–56.

40. "Adages III iv 1 to IV ii 100," in Grant, ed., *CWE*, 35:424.

41. Dickens and Jones, *Erasmus*, 71.

42. Erasmus, *The Complaint of Peace*, 69, 72, 101–2.

43. Erasmus, "Paraphrase on Luke 11–24," in *CWE*, 48:197; Erasmus, "Paraphrase on Mark," in *CWE*, 49:4.

church affairs as well.[44] Where Luther would later suggest that princes simply take over their regional churches and reform them, Erasmus suggested instead that rulers, as the heart of the body politic, had certain priest-like responsibilities. In the *Education of a Christian Prince* (1516), for example, the prince was a father-figure and shepherd of the flock. Perhaps the best illustration of Erasmus's idealism can be found in *Julius barred from Heaven* (*Julius exclusus e coelis*, 1518), where mockery underscored the seriousness of the message.[45]

Noted earlier, Julius is remembered in history as a man of letters, a patron of the arts and architecture, but also as an untrustworthy war-monger. In his dialogue, Erasmus sees Julius arguing with St Peter at the gates of heaven. Julius (who died in 1513) defends his war-like pontificate[46], his failure to call general councils[47], and his tolerance of the many weaknesses of the church. Erasmus witnessed a decline in public trust of the church suggesting, through the saint, that pursuit of the spiritual would better serve both it and Christendom. Where the saint laments the decrease of faith and doctrine, Julius responds that he had made the church splendid through "palaces, trains of mules and horses, troops of servants, armies and officers."[48] Where Erasmus suggested change from within, as we shall see later, many reformers would develop arguments in recommendation of temporal authorities assuming at least a supervisory role over their local spiritual establishments as a better reflection of both local conditions and biblical evidence. Historians tend to refer to such thinkers as "magisterial reformers", and count Luther, Zwingli and Calvin first among them. More radical reformers, however, will recommend a complete termination of a distinctly separate spiritual authority and others still will simply disregard both church and state.

Erasmus advocated a non-materialistic approach to God. The church, as an institution and with such leaders as Julius, came under increasing criticism because all of its solutions to the problems of Christendom seemingly had little to do with the spirit and more to do with acquisitiveness, money and military adventurism. By de-emphasizing the externals, the materials of religious faith (the visible, the buildings, the rites and ceremonies, the mechanical aspects), and concentrating on the internal matters (the invisible,

---

44. Dodds, *Exploiting Erasmus*, 280 (no. 11). Also see, Bickenhotz, *Encounters*, 75.

45. Written in 1513. Here I am using the translation of the work found in Froude, *Life and Letters*, 156–74. Also see the edition in Erasmus, *The Praise of Folly and Other Writings*, 142–73. This can be found online at http://triablogue.blogspot.com/2007/01/Julius-excluded-from-heaven.html.

46. Froude, *Life and Letters*, 152–53.

47. Froude, *Life and Letters*, 163.

48. Froude, *Life and Letters*, 167, 170, and 172.

genuine faith, genuine charity), Erasmus offered a genuinely new approach to familiar problems. Standing in the way of renewed Christianity and *pax Europa*, however, were the clergy themselves, dedicated to the pursuit of money rather than spirituality. They became the special target of his most famous work, *Praise of Folly* (or *Encomium Moriae*, 1509).[49]

No member of the clerical estate is spared mockery and criticism. Monks and friars are portrayed as stupid, prideful and falsely pious, more concerned to differentiate between their orders—through knots, color, habits and a bewildering variety of rules and regulations—than they are to emulate Christ through faith and charity.[50] Priests have forgotten their duty to preach for the edification of the laity, while bishops (cardinals and popes) forego spiritual credentials in exchange for secular achievement. The "blameless life", the "perfect knowledge of the Old and New Testaments" and the "sincere administration of the Sacraments" have all been pushed aside for "worldly business." The mandate of the early church—to gather, keep and instruct the flock—has given way to jealously guarded titles and excessive bureaucracy.[51]

We may take Erasmus's writings as a point of departure or as a sampling of ideas in the air in the early sixteenth century. Many of the same themes will feature repeatedly in the works of the reformers, some with a light touch, nuanced and thoughtful, some with a hammer stroke, loud and blunt. They were all looking for the same thing as Erasmus; that is, how to recreate that ideal world where magistrates oversaw justice, protected the weak from the strong and safeguarded both lives and possessions, while the churchmen guided the flock toward salvation. If Erasmus gave any particular thought to the power structures and parliaments of the secular world, however, it does not show in his works. We might see instances of conciliarism or democratic theory approaching that of Marsilio but he was really more interested in disabusing his readers of a great many debilitating mediaeval ideas about the church and church/state relations. He sought a balance between them, and a mutual respect for the work each was responsible to perform within a unified, Christocentric society, seeing even papal supremacy as a point lending itself

---

49. *Praise of Folly* can be read in several modern editions. Here I have used Erasmus, *Praise of Folly and Letter to Martin Dorp 1515*, 55–208 but *EE* (94–173) is also useful. There is a good online edition at http://smith2.sewanee.edu/erasmus/pof.html.

50. Wilson, ed., *Praise of Folly*, 65.

51. Wilson, ed., *Praise of Folly*, 66, 73, 74, 75, 76. Also useful is Augustijn, *Erasmus*, 63–68 (a useful study of Erasmus's criticisms of churchmen).

to polite debate rather than dogmatic dispute. Ultimately his was a question of functionality. Temporal authorities had a function and spiritual authorities had a function and, provided each carried out its task properly tensions between civil and clerical offices should cease as should warfare itself. The institutions of the church mattered to Erasmus because he accepted much of the papal justifications underlying their own authority as debatable, but firmly traditional and entrenched. Luther did not agree.

1

Luther and "Two Governments" Doctrine

Erasmus did not explicitly deny the mediaeval doctrine of the two swords. He agreed that the spiritual (divine) and material (physical) spheres had unique and distinctive elements—the latter perhaps diabolical in origin—and wrote that the officers of one should not interfere in the workings of the other. Traditionally, the church claimed control over both swords, loaning out the temporal sword to lay magistrates under temporary and supervised conditions. Martin Luther also recognized two spheres, or sometimes kingdoms or governments, but was more than willing to take an additional step. He wanted to find a means of separating the two spheres without losing sight of God's (not the church's) ultimate domain. Granted, this does not appear all that different from the traditional.

Luther reformulated the basic mediaeval doctrine in a way consistent with his emerging scriptural exegesis, making a comparison between his understanding (the two kingdoms doctrine) and the built up misconceptions of the Roman position (the two swords), and he used this to attack the pope's willingness to use the doctrine as a means of placing the temporal sphere firmly under the control of the spiritual. Instead, for Luther, the two kingdoms interlaced—Ebeling termed this an "inseparable interrelationship"—in which each kingdom was fully functioning but also in some ways limited by the other kingdom. The limits of each kingdom depended upon a proper understanding of a much clearer distinction between the things of God and the things of the world.[1] The built up and reinforced Catholic misunderstanding of biblical meaning (in Luther's opinion) thus became the first wall to be demolished in his *To the Christian nobility*[2] one of Luther's three great treatises of 1520.

---

1. Ebeling, *Luther*, 178.
2. I have used the Steinäuser translation in *Three Treatises*, 1–112.

The traditional socio-political structure of Christendom was built upon a division of people into one of two classes, spheres or regiments—laity or clergy—reflecting the traditional state/church separation. The historical fallacy that the clergy formed a separate caste above and purer than the temporal had come to exercise Luther greatly, however, and he subjected it to a radical revision. Erasmus sought, through persuasion, to put all Christians into one *body politic*—a Christocentric commonwealth—and he assigned everyone a proper function within it. For Erasmus, receiving the sacraments (pruned of material embellishments) placed every individual on the same level spiritually, hearing the gospel would help order their lives ethically. In this way he anticipated *priesthood of all believers'* doctrine while still differentiating Christians on the basis of their secular occupation (i.e., function). The finer political details did not interest him except insofar as they could be related to a Platonic body metaphor. As his theology was largely Catholic and traditional Erasmus also accepted that the commonwealth was possible based on human volition in cooperation with divine grace.

It may be said that Luther appropriated Erasmian idealism and turned it on its head. He spoke of Christians differentiated by duties and functions, but where the traditional system was based on protected rights and privileges his was a system based on service (the duties and obligations incumbent upon Christians toward each other). Even so, it was still idealism. In reality, a commonwealth could never work "for the wicked always outnumber the good."[3] No one can naturally and of their own volition attach themselves to the body of Christ, Luther's justification theology forbad such a notion. Salvation is based on God's own will, the divine imputation of righteousness, the teaching of the Holy Spirit in the heart, and *eventual* redemption. As non-true believers and true believers live together in the kingdoms of the world they must be subject to its rulers and its laws for their own good and protection. Luther's two kingdoms replaced Erasmus's one Christian commonwealth of distinctive clerical and lay functionality. As time went on, however, and new challenges emerged—like radical sectarianism and the *Peasants' Revolt*—Luther came to emphasize temporal authority more and more forcefully. Christians, for Luther, were members of both kingdoms because no one knew who the true believers were, and he gave each person both secular and religious tasks to perform.

— § —

---

3. Luther, "Temporal Authority," in *AE*, 45:91.

Luther's Writings on Civil Authority and the Church up to the Peasants' Revolt

Much like Erasmus, Luther was not particularly interested in dismantling the clerical hierarchy or founding a new sect within the church, but there were a number of influences on him in the late 1510s and early 1520s which led him away from traditional ecclesiology. He came to look positively toward the imperial and princely authorities to take back non-spiritual powers from the church and redistribute its vast wealth. The assumption was that both the realm (materially) and the church (spiritually) would benefit. He wanted a German general council and, when this failed to materialize, tasked the magistrates with the religious reform of their states. The *Ninety-five thesis* contains fine illustrations of Luther's basic positions.

Beyond the indulgences controversy he saw the church failing his people. The mass of Germans were not happy (thesis ninety), nor taught the gospel (thesis seventy-four)—bishops actually silenced it. Unorthodox ideas spread (theses seventy, seventy-two and eighty) while the sheep were not gathered and protected by the shepherds. The hospital could not care for either the curably or incurably sick.[4] Germans were made poorer (as money flowed to Rome) without any perceivable spiritual benefit, and no one was acknowledging the many abuses that needed immediate redress. That people belong to two incompatible kingdoms (thesis fifty-eight) was where Luther differentiated the needs of the inner spiritual man from those of the outer physical man—a duality which impacted on both the church and secular society. As only God knew who were the righteous, however, Luther postulated an inner, invisible, true church of believers (the elect) within the collective visible church of all professed believers (Christians), all of whom live undifferentiated in both the church and society. What was meant as a private letter full of rage, scattershot complaint, and spur of the moment suggestion quickly spread far and wide and out of Luther's control. He and Wittenberg became the nexus of anti-papal protest and resistance and, in rapid succession the "Luther problem" was raised at a plenary meeting of the Augustinians in Heidelberg; a letter to the pope (attached to which was a small treatise entitled *Explanation of the Ninety-five Theses*); a letter to Spalatin (with an explanation for the duke of Saxony)[5];

---

4. Luther, "To Cardinal Albrecht," in *AE*, 48:47. For the hospital imagery see Karkkainen, *An introduction to ecclesiology*, 47. Also see, Luther, "Sermon on the gospel," in Lenker, ed., *The Sermons of Martin Luther*, 5:19–20.

5. E.g., Luther, "To John von Staupitz," in *AE*, 48:64–70 and Luther, "To George Spalatin" in *AE*, 48:75.

a summons to Augsburg in October 1518; to the Diet of Worms, and to Luther's formal excommunication in 1521.

Consider the Augsburg meetings where Luther was interrogated by Cardinal Thomas Cajetan. Cajetan, something of a scholar, a lawyer, a humanist and theologian, was not unsympathetic to the calls for reform in the church (there was a reform party growing in Rome), but he realized that, even if Luther did not yet know it himself, the reform he was calling for would eventually lead to the foundation of an entirely new church. Although *Ninety-five theses* was meant to spur on a much needed discussion of the many faults in the church's sacramental system it also threw shade on basic questions over authority. Cajetan saw in Luther's increased reliance on Scripture (*sola scriptura*) an eventual secularization of the church and the particularization of religious expression.[6] Luther's doubts on the indulgences issue and sacrament of penance begot doubts about the church's penitential and sacramental systems, its rules, regulations and ceremonies and, finally, the power of the papacy.[7] Soon everything was being tested against the keystone of Scripture and much of it was found severely wanting. Cajetan's concerns were soon realized.

Augustine von Alveld, a Franciscan in Leipzig who followed the growing controversy, hastily wrote and published a little Latin defense of the divine nature of the papacy entitled *On the Apostolic See, whether it is of divine legitimacy or not*. Luther found the treatise amateurish in its assertions of evidence out of Scripture intermingled with reason, scholastic tradition, piety, logic, innate human wisdom, and "science." Apart from *ad hominem* attacks, Alveld applied natural reason as the basis of universal monarchy theory. In essence, as every community must have a head, the corps of Christendom (a community universal in nature) as both physical and spiritual must have both a bodily (the pope) and spiritual (Christ) head. Luther would have ignored it had Alveld not subsequently re-published in German.[8]

In his response (26 May), *The papacy at Rome, an answer to the celebrated Romanist at Leipzig*[9], Luther dismantled the idea of a necessary universal structure with a universal earthly head, arguing instead that the church is a spiritual community of believers (rather than a physical assembly) and, as such, should have no absolute external structures or

---

6. For a discussion see, Wriedt, "Founding a New Church," 53–54; or Wriedt, "Luther on Call and Ordination," 256.
7. E.g., Luther, "To John Lang," in *AE*, 48:149.
8. Luther, "To George Spalatin," in *AE*, 48:164.
9. This can be found in *AE*, 39:55–104.

ordinances binding it to particulars. External unity was an indifferent matter; those who would try to force adherence to minutiae (e.g., regulations or statutory orders) were in reality no better than Jews relying on codes and legalism.[10] The true church is not specific to any human visualization as human reason is clearly inferior to divine will, word and law. Indeed, Luther lamented both Rome's obsession with money and the Germans' acceptance that ecclesiastical appointments were dependent upon papal confirmation (for a fee) for legitimacy.

Luther's response is an interesting expansion on the church visible/invisible dichotomy. The invisible true church does not, indeed cannot, depend upon physical proximity as it is a spiritual unity separate from all temporal communities so Alveld's external community argument had no validity. The true, invisible church cannot be bound to Rome. The visible church of professed believers, however, is temporal, earthly, a blend of believers and non-believers. True believers obviously still live in the physical world. Luther found it valuable as well; people still need to hear the gospel preached, taught, and they still need the sacraments administered. Professed believers need shepherding. The Holy Spirit sanctifies through the church as an instrument—Luther's theology of salvation is actualized within the church. This visible congregation or "external Christendom" is ruled by canon law, man's law, decretals, prelates and a pope, and can certainly include true believers but includes the false as well. The physical body can possess material objects (which are subject to many arguments, debates and violence). It follows that the visible, external church could have a visible, material head (or many in fact) but the true, invisible, spiritual church could have only one head in Christ. What then are popes, bishops and priests for? Luther's answer is that these officers are messengers of Christ conveying the same message of salvation to the masses. The messengers can be arranged at the whim of the community because such external designs have no impact on the essential message itself. Luther's doctrines of salvation and predestination leads to a clear delineation between true and professed believers and reduces the church to any place where baptism and the Eucharist are correctly performed and where the gospel is purely preached, there is the church.

On the basis of Scripture, Alveld's argument was simple. The Old Testament provided the foundations and the New Testament fulfilled them. Thus, as the Old Testament featured high-priests as leaders and bodily (earthly) heads (like Aaron) so the New Testament, as fulfilment, must have some like authority figure understood (St Peter and his successors). Rome is the New Jerusalem based on the pre-eminent authority of Peter; the priestly power

---

10. Luther, "The Papacy at Rome," in *Works*, i, 257, 270.

of binding and loosing creates a special priesthood as a means of creation (the sacrament of ordination). Luther agreed that while the Old Testament does configure a bodily, worldly, law-ridden and external church (authorities as guides to right living), the New Testament instead features a spiritual, internal, law-free church (the Christ having fulfilled the previous needs and conditions). The church of the former (Jewish in nature and function) prefigured and then gave way to the church of the latter (Christian in nature and function). The pope can be considered as a type of Old Testament high priest figure, but he could never be considered spiritual and able to give spiritual succor. Luther concluded that the Church of Rome as it is configured has no specific gospel support.[11]

Luther's early writings established an ecclesiology of two "churches", one of which is visible and external and to which all local political rules and regulations apply and wherein rites and ceremonies were subject to local practice. This visible institution is not universally consistent, and counted among its members are saints and sinners, believers and non-believers, the genuine and the merely professed. Popes, bishops and priests are, or should be, messengers of the gospel; titles, positions in the hierarchy and office-holding have no meaning except in regard to the visible structures. The other church (the genuine Christian Church) is invisible and internal, composed only of true believers to which only divine law and the gospel apply. Luther's famous works of 1520 more or less develop this standpoint.

For instance, in *To the Christian nobility* Luther developed *priesthood of all believers'* doctrine out of his considerations. Drawing on Erasmus's shared and undifferentiated reception of the sacrament, Luther made no distinction between members of the visible church save in terms of function or office, nullifying the idea that priests had both temporal and religious duties. "All Christians are truly of the "spiritual estate," and there is among them no difference at all but that of office ... we are all one body, yet every member has its own work, where by it serves every other, all because we have one baptism, one Gospel, one faith, and are all alike Christians."[12] Luther rejected the traditional division of two separate classes of people, envisioning a division of function within one all-encompassing spiritual class. The Roman sect had built up three walls around its usurpation of temporal authority in order to deny princes, lords and magistrates their rightful powers, to justify their own exercise of temporal powers, and to block much needed reform. Heresy charges soon followed as did threats

---

11. Luther, "The papacy at Rome," 267, 268, 270, 280, 286.
12. Luther, *To the Christian Nobility*, 127; McGrath, *Reformation Thought*, 205.

on his life as well as offers of military protection (most notably from Ulrich von Hutten and Franz von Sickingen).

Both Luther and Erasmus denied any essential difference between Christians, except through office or function, and both made all Christians priests by virtue of the sacraments. If the gospel was presented to the masses in a straightforward manner, mutual respect would grow and necessary changes would be enacted. Erasmus left it at that but Luther took another step. Given the *priesthood of all believers* and common membership in the spiritual estate he turned his attention to those "priests" who exercised civil authority—that is, civil magistrates. If only temporal authorities, like the imperial knights, were willing to protect him and safeguard his ideas, Luther began to consider whether there was not more to the duty of secular princes with regard to the church and the restoration of right order? If the traditional clergy was not a protected, superior caste of perfect men, could magistrates not somehow assume control in their place? Magistrates were already tasked to "bear the sword and rod with which to punish the evil and to protect the good . . . for the bodily and spiritual welfare of the community."[13] While it was not their function to preach or perform the offices and sacraments, surely it was not beyond the German nobility the right to summon a general council for Germany and begin the reformation process (unilaterally if necessary). Magistrates, for Luther, would be ordering the conditions by which the clergy could perform their own functions properly and he developed a doctrine of two kingdoms in order to explain why they (magistrates) had the right to proceed.[14]

Given his justification doctrine Luther recognised that not all professed believers were *true* believers, otherwise in that ideal world there would be no need for worldly government, legal concepts of justice, equity, coercion or soldiers of war. But because faith is invisible, and because *true* believers are invisible and unknown to each other (not to mention few in number), worldly government is necessary to protect good order, civil society and the visible church. Those scholars who have studied Luther understand that *sola fide* (justification by faith alone) and the consequent denial of any salvific value for good works had created a potential for *antinomianism* (or extreme lawlessness). Kings, magistrates and other civil authorities, by necessity, wield the sword of order and law against the prospect. These authorities concern themselves with the affairs of the world and perform God's work. Thus, it is the common duty of all Christians to fully cooperate with civil authorities.

13. Marius, *Martin Luther*, 237.
14. McGrath, *Reformation Thought*, 206–7.

§

As early as his lectures on the Pauline epistle (1515–1516) Luther recognised that civil authority was divine in origin. Christians must subject themselves to the higher powers—even if they are wicked or unbelieving men occupying the offices because the office is necessary and God's own creation.[15] Christians do not violate the order of the institution of the church because it serves to guide and soothe the inner spiritual nature of man (ruled through the Word and the Holy Spirit) toward redemption while the temporal authority serves to guide and soothe the outer, worldly nature of man. It is hierarchical, rules-laden, sometimes violent, but all-inclusive. And, just as Jesus was both man and God, man too is of two natures. The inner spiritual nature cannot, however, exist without the outer, earthy nature. Christians cannot live without the power of the state—they are constantly confronted by sin, moral choices, ethical dilemmas, evil, and the needs of the neighbour.[16] The ordering power of the magistrate is essential simply because the vast majority are not *true* believers and governed only by the Word and faith. Since it is impossible to distinguish one from the other, all of them must be so governed for the good of all. "The spiritual authority of the church is thus persuasive, not coercive, and concerns the individual's soul, rather than his body or goods. The temporal authority of the state is coercive, rather than persuasive, and concerns the individual's body and goods, rather than his soul."[17]

Luther described the Christian prince as a hard-working shepherd and model of both personal and public morality, but could point to few real life examples. Although his ideal was Erasmian—a Christian commonwealth based on *sola scriptura* ethical standards and the teachings of the Holy Spirit—Luther was less idealistic and more practical. To his way of thinking the papacy had confused the two separate ethics or spheres of authority over the centuries, evinced by extensive and self-contradictory canon laws. The two kingdoms are not opposed but are rather two aspects of the same thing—the means by which God rules a world fallen into sin. God governs the world through princes and magistrates and the church is part of the world.

In his treatise he invited temporal authorities to grasp the reins, direct local reformation efforts and, afterwards, humbly stand down and direct their efforts purely toward physical concerns and the protection of good social order. Luther encouraged cooperation between the governments of the two kingdoms, asking each to respect not unreasonable limitations

---

15. Lohse, *Martin Luther*, 53.
16. Luther, *Commentary on Romans*, 179–92; Lausten, "Lutherus," 56.
17. McGrath, *Reformation Thought*, 208.

as the other kingdom's concern. For instance, the clergy would no longer meddle in earthly politics concentrating instead on teaching and preaching. Magistrates, likewise, would no longer meddle in religious doctrine concentrating instead on good social order and the protection of the church. It was a hard sell; neither religious nor secular leaders were likely to restrain themselves as Luther suggested and the rise of sectarianism in the early 1520s became another source of tension. Catholic leaders misunderstood (on purpose perhaps) the inseparable interrelationship of the two kingdoms, while sectarians began to call into question the need for secular authority. Some hived off into non-cooperating sects while others formed militant groups preparing to purge Christendom by the sword.[18] On 7 November 1522 Duke George of Ducal Saxony issued an edict prohibiting the sale and possession of Luther's translation of the New Testament. Luther considered this a hostile step over the boundary of temporal power and set pen to paper to explain the boundaries again.[19]

We have noted already that duality features strongly in Luther's theology: Christ is man and God; the church is visible and invisible; man is spiritual and natural, saint and sinner; a Christian is both servant to and master of others and a member of two kingdoms. In 1523, his treatise *Temporal authority*, written in German for the literate masses, delved a little more deeply into this doctrine and laid the groundwork for a complete break from mediaeval principles.

Luther made a sharper distinction between the two kingdoms (e.g., duties and responsibilities) and between true and professed believers. True believers, the justified, live in the kingdom of God and do not need the kingdom of the world *as such* because they know that God provides for all their needs as they, in turn, look out for the needs of others as taught by the gospel and guided by the Holy Spirit. For themselves, ideally, they have no need for worldly authorities except insofar as the needs of the neighbour come into play. Looking out for the needs of the neighbour (unlikely to be a *true* believer) places them both within the bounds of the civil authority. In theory, secular rules and laws no longer apply to the justified because they need no coercion to do the right thing and they accept bad things happening to them with good grace. That said, however, the *true* believer must be prepared to cooperate with secular authority nonetheless—working for

---

18. Ebeling, *Luther*, 181.
19. Höpfl, ed., *Luther and Calvin on Secular Authority*.

the good of all, doing what is best for the neighbour (which may include law enforcement): "Therefore, if you see that there is a lack of hangmen, constables, judges, lords or princes, and you find that you are qualified, you should offer your services and seek the position, that the essential governmental authority may not be despised and become enfeebled or perish. The world cannot and dare not dispense with it."[20]

This is not a philosophy new to Luther of course, it could be traced back passed Augustine to St Paul and even further. Secular government maintains order. Given his opinion of most princes, however, it is perhaps not surprising that Luther accepted that the prince need not himself be a true believer or even a Christian—it is the office that counts. The only necessary qualification was reason (which, of course, is folly to the true believer) and that the office is honoured and obeyed. Ideally, those who possess civil authority would also be genuine believers, but his was not the ideal world. And since neither he nor princes were perfect, Luther felt free to criticise them and disobey imperial edicts he saw as evidence of the church's meddling in civic affairs. He was no hypocrite; he accepted due punishment for his defiance of the magistrates. Sadly, Luther had not explained himself as clearly as he might have done and radical sectarians followed what they thought was Luther's message. They pointed out that the earliest Christian sects were actually opposed to the governments of their day too. This, Scripture, and Luther's own words justified non-cooperation. It was *verkehrt herum*—a topsy-turvy situation.[21]

Before the *Peasants' Revolt* changed everything Luther's recommendations on the extent of secular authority can be summed up in a few key phrases: the keeping and assurance of peace and order; the safeguarding of creation against evil and destruction; the creation of conditions conducive to social tranquillity; and, the proclamation of the gospel.[22] The spiritual authority has usurped some of these duties consequently upsetting God's plan. It must stay focussed on rule by the Word, love of neighbour, and the sacraments by way of persuasion not coercion. As noted, the life of the *genuinely* Christian prince was tempestuous. He must be a model in both kingdoms. He must serve God with inherent sincerity and serve his subjects as a good Christian would, that is, without thought to his own base needs and desires. The ideal Christian prince must be held to an impossible standard. He must assess his advisers with an eye trained on their own Christian virtues and he must deal swiftly with evil-doers. Princes

20. Luther, "Temporal Authority," 95.
21. Luther, "Temporal Authority," 109.
22. Lausten, "Lutherus," 54.

were warned to keep justice ever before their eyes as, while true Christians will not rebel God could make a hammer of all the non-true believers. This was certainly a potent threat. Tension always existed just below the surface in the life of the mediaeval peasant and Luther appeared to be justifying mob action against unjust princes.

— § —

In the mid-1520s both Luther and his doctrine of the two kingdoms were tested. Access to God's Word and appropriate preaching was severely limited while secular leaders misused his treatises to take on a leadership roles in the reformation of the church and the determination of orthodoxy. His democratic principle of the *priesthood of all believers* in theory allowed congregations to choose their own pastors but, as this conflicted with established patronage networks, princes and nobles forcefully insisted on their own candidates, quoting Luther as a means of defying both the papacy and local desire. As a means of easing tensions Luther suggested that as "pseudo-bishops" it was the "duty" of princes to *at least* select pastors who could preach and ensure the spread of the Word in their territories. While involved in the process, princes would then step back and let the pastors' work curb harmful traditional practices. Unjust princes, he warned, might find themselves subject to mob action or foreign invaders (as tools of divine vengeance) if they did not moderate their own behaviour. At what point, however, does mob action change from a defiance of God's sovereignty into an expression of divine intervention? The defining principles seem indistinguishable, but such were the questions raised by the *Peasants' Revolt*.

The Influence of the Peasants' Revolt on Luther's Doctrine

The so-called *Peasants' Revolt* was the latest in a series of not unrelated upheavals to take place across mediaeval European. The rural and urban under-privileged were roused to violence by strong political figures and/or charismatic churchmen through a mix of not unreasonable literal interpretations of the Bible in the context of political, social or economic failures. Uprisings could be sparked by something as innocuous as a perceived insult, by anticlerical jealousy against a local monastery, or by the continuous annoyances of the bastard feudalism under which the peasants were bound and laboured. This was not unusual. What was atypical in this case was a sophisticated level of organization.

A few peasant uprisings here and there across the southern portions of the empire in the early 1520s, in an otherwise inflationary period and when intense religious issues were coming to the fore, would not necessarily have given Luther particular cause for concern. He may have thought unjust rulers were getting their just rewards as property damage was done mostly to Catholic institutions and the castles of Catholic rulers. To him this was no great loss and not really unexpected. From 1524, however, the many waves of peasant unrest, vague claims to scriptural justification, and golden-age imagery of long-gone rights guaranteed by ancient charters began to be organized much more effectively by a so-called "Christian union or brotherhood" emerging in one territory after another. The union came to Luther's attention and some of its claims were offensive to him.[23]

Peasants, under the union banner, press-ganged the (almost always Catholic) rulers into acceptance of the gospel. Luther found this objectionable because they were misusing the name Christian for secular gain, mixing up civil and spiritual issues, and pressing the gospel into secular service. Moreover, by revolting, by taking action into their own hands they were trying to gain justice for themselves by their own efforts. Nowadays we might not object, but in Luther's eyes they were acting as their own judges—an offence to natural law. Finally, by demanding divine rights they were sinning against God and the second commandment (in that they were acting upon the claims of such false prophets as Thomas Müntzer).[24] Luther also found himself named in some manifestos as an acceptable intermediary, implying influence and complicity.

But it is easy to see where this came from. Much of what Luther had written about necessary reformation would have filtered down to the illiterate masses through only slightly more literate associates and friends and would have been very welcome to their ears. Unjust princes were withholding the gospel; when, for example, were these princes going to take the properties and wealth off the Roman Church and pass this largess around in a fairer re-distribution? The peasants heard that unjust princes could be rebelled against as the mob was God's means of vengeance so, by rebelling were they not acting in accordance to God's will? Were the princes (of which so few were genuinely Christian) not unjust in their array of backbreaking demands? While this is not what Luther meant, a clever, partially literate man could make the case or radical prophets could present it that way. Luther tried to hurry out a new treatise to ease tensions and explain

---

23. Bornkamm, *Luther in Mid-Career*, 359.
24. Lohse, *Martin Luther*, 55. Also see, Luther, "Admonition to Peace," in *AE*, 46:27.

his case more clearly. The *Admonition to Peace* (1525), however, really only stated the case more forcefully.

Luther accused both sides (albeit much more the rulers). While the peasants had acted in haste and irrationally, they were not entirely in the wrong. The princes and nobles, however, sinned by their great misuse and abuse of their rights as civil authorities. Luther called out their unethical, selfish behaviours. True, both sides had fallen prey to false prophets and radical sectarians, like Müntzer and Karlstadt[25], the magnates and prince-bishops were advised to see the mob as the scourge of God against their display and pride. They should seek reconciliation before it was too late, moderate their future behaviour, and make fewer demands on the peasantry. It was not the temporal authority's role to force belief and theology, but to ensure peace, order and ensure that proper religion can grow and prosper. The princes should take steps to self-reform, become "different men."[26] Luther pleaded with the magistrates to "give way a little to the will and wrath of God . . . stop your raging and obstinate tyranny and not deal unreasonable with the peasants . . . try kindness first . . ."[27] Marius points out that Luther's tone was mild toward the princes but the second part of the treatise, aimed at the peasants, was quite the opposite.[28]

For Luther, the revolt brought a particularly nagging question into sharp relief. It seemed that civil authorities could be tyrants and the church and the masses would just have to live with it until such time as God dealt with the issue through the dispatch of some raging force of divine wrath. As God provided for all the needs of true believers the appearance of a tyrant ruling over them must, by virtue of God's goodness, have a good reason or else it could be taken as clear evidence of the wickedness of the population itself. A tyrant may open himself up to criticism, certainly, but on the mortal plain that is about as far as a good Christian can take the issue. If no other lesson is learned from early antiquity this one is clear: genuine Christians must sometimes die for their faith. The peasants did not appear to be accepting of this, however. The prince, nobles, magistrates and rulers could use the sword—violent coercion—to enforce order but Christians were to live according to the private ethic and obey for the good of all. As priests, all *true* believers *are* equal in the eyes of God (spiritually speaking), all exercise equal (transferable) authority in the church while the magistrates exercise authority otherwise. As McGrath noted it was virtually impossible for the

---

25. Bornkamm, *Luther in Mid–Career*, 366.
26. Luther, "Admonition," 20.
27. Luther, "Admonition," 21–22.
28. Marius, *Luther*, 425.

magistrate not to exercise authority over the church and, indeed, this is what came to pass (hence the term *magisterial* reformation). God may rule the church directly through the gospel but He rules the world (including the church) through "law, wisdom, natural law and coercion"—all of which the peasant rebels were defying.

"The fact that rulers are wicked and intolerable," Luther wrote near the start of the second part of the treatise, "does not excuse disorder and rebellion, for the punishing of wickedness is not the responsibility of everyone, but of the worldly rulers who bear the sword."[29] It was an unnatural situation; the peasants set themselves up in the place of temporal authorities—judging their own causes, seeking their own vengeance—when by so doing they merely confounded God's order and sought to usurp his sovereignty. "You confess that you are causing disturbances and revolting. And then you try to excuse this behaviour with the gospel. You have heard above that the gospel teaches Christians to endure and suffer wrong and to pray to God in every need. You, however, are not willing to suffer, but like heathens you want to force the rulers to conform to your impatient will."[30] Moreover, they had read too much into *priesthood of all believers*.

For instance, Luther agreed that they should be allowed to choose their own pastors so that they can hear the gospel freely preached, provided they were willing to pay out of their own funds. Confiscating the prince's wealth and properties to fund pastors and teaching was an illegitimate approach amounting to theft. The ruler may make these properties available to them but if he did not it was up to the congregation to support the pastor. Withholding the tithe was not an option either as this too amounted to theft and nothing more than a scheme to set themselves up as lords of the land in denial of natural law and God's sovereignty. If the ruler did not tolerate the locally selected pastor, the pastor should flee elsewhere and supporters could flee with him. While all men were equal in the spiritual sphere, no such equality existed in the temporal and nor could equality be forced.

While the treatise was in the printing stage Luther visited parts of Thuringia to both access the situation and disseminate his latest writing. His was not a welcomed message. Luther encountered stiff resistance and threats to his own life. As he toured and preached (and was heckled and criticized) reports of peasant violence grew increasingly frequent and widespread but most shocking for Luther, perhaps, was that his own words were coming back to haunt him. Peasants were demanding the social equality that the *priesthood*

---

29. Luther, "Admonition," 25.
30. Luther, "Admonition," 35.

of all believers implied and, while they claimed a willingness to be corrected in their manifestos, Luther's teaching was resisted.

In response Luther turned to the princes and nobles as a means of putting an end to the peasants' false interpretations "presented under the name of the gospel."[31] They were attempting to, and often succeeding in, overturning order and thereby they were challenging God's sovereignty. Duty and function were all important to his understanding of the relationship between the church and the civil powers and, since the peasant rebels had abandoned their God-given duties it was up to the princes and lords to do theirs and set matters right again. Count Albrecht of Mansfeld became Luther's standard. The count had already acted and Luther wanted more. "There never can be any doubt that the count's office was decreed and ordained by God. Therefore, as long as life is in him, His Grace ought to use his sword for punishing of the wicked."[32] Duty was also the central point of *Against the Robbing and Murdering Hordes of Peasants*, originally a supplement attached to a re-printed *Admonition*, now expanded and printed separately as a princely instruction manual to their role as responsible Christian leaders. In essence he wrote that the peasants had abandoned the gospel and their duties, thus betraying their own spiritual selves. They had become heathens, seditious, rebels to the social order and "outlaws before God and the emperor." As such they had forfeited all temporal and spiritual consideration. "Whoever is the first to put him to death does right and well . . . therefore let everyone who can, smite; slay, and stab, secretly or openly, remembering that nothing can be more poisonous, hurtful, or devilish than a rebel."[33]

The *Peasants' Revolt* clarified for Luther the rights and duties of civil authorities as protectors and scourges but *Against the murderous Hordes* was badly timed. It was published at a time when the revolt was in collapse and appears to have been written after the fact. What had been written at the height of the chaos to shake up the consciences of the princes to do their God-given duty and restore order now appeared, along with Luther's preaching of obedience and duty, as a recommendation of senseless slaughter and revenge. Luther's stock rose with the magistrates (even with Henry VIII for a time) but bottomed out with the masses. Princes seemingly had the power of life and death over their subjects. Even when Luther railed against their

---

31. Luther, "Hordes of Peasants," in *AE*, 46:49.
32. Luther, "To John Rühel," in *AE*, 49:108–9.
33. Luther, "Hordes of Peasants," 50.

lack of morality, or their social injustice, or their bad behaviour, ultimately he did not challenge their right to rule. Indeed, he continuously counselled obedience and submission to political authorities in expectation that God would punish the evil. Even after the rebellion finally collapsed at the battle of Frankenhausen (15 May 1525), some princes enthusiastically carried out further reprisals, killing, torturing and harassing even peasants who had only been coerced into joining the revolt, using Luther's writings as justification. Princes friendly to Luther's reform used *Against the murderous Hordes* to justify their bloody deeds while those unfriendly blamed him for encouraging the revolt in the first place with his ill-considered, pseudo-democratic theology and his counselling of arbitration in *Admonition*.

If we take away the extenuating circumstances, the chaos of the times, and the bad timing of the publishing process, Luther's doctrine of the two kingdoms rested on questions of duty and conscience. In subsequent letters, sermons, and even in a new treatise entitled *An open letter on the harsh book against the peasants* (of July 1525)[34]—in which Luther defended *Admonition* and *Against the murderous Hordes*—he tried to explain himself again.

The emphasis of *Open Letter* was duty—of the peasants to obey and of the princes to enforce order to ensure the safety of both professed and true believers but neither side was entirely in the right. The peasant rebels had taken sword in hand without authority from God, transgressing both divine and natural laws. Those sympathetic to the rebels had shown themselves in opposition to God's dominion and, harsh as it may sound to modern sensibilities, those coerced into action were not innocent as they could have resisted giving in to the pressure of their peers. True, the princes had often reacted too violently but they had acted in God's name to safeguard the two kingdoms.[35]

> The Scriptures, therefore, have good, clear eyes [Matt.6:22–23] and see the temporal sword aright. They see that out of great mercy, it must be unmerciful, and from utter kindliness, it must exercise wrath and severity . . . it is God's servant for vengeance, wrath, and punishment upon the wicked, but for the protection, praise, and honour of the righteous [I Pet.2:14; Rom.13:4]. It looks upon the righteous with mercy, and so that they may not suffer, it guards, bites, stabs, cuts, hews, and slays, as God has commanded; and it knows that it serves God in doing even this. The merciless punishment of the wicked is not being carried out just to punish the wicked and make them atone for the

---

34. Luther, "Against the Peasants," in *AE*, 46:58–85.
35. Luther, "Against the Peasants," in *AE*, 46:65.

evil desires that are in their blood, but to protect the righteous and to maintain peace and safety. And beyond all doubt, these are precious works of mercy, love, and kindness, since there is nothing on earth that is worse than disturbance, insecurity, oppression, violence and injustice . . . the wrath and severity of the sword is just as necessary to a people as eating and drinking, even as life itself.[36]

Magistrates take up the sword to punish and to preserve. In this way Luther became the reformer of choice for the temporal leaders. He was drafted into politics as princes adopted the evangelical cause for personal reasons of conscience, religious conviction, or for less savoury reasons. As such, Luther was forced to consider the wider implications of his doctrine of the two kingdoms or allow it to become hopelessly confused and ill-used. Here we will consider two areas of concern—war and marriage.

Warfare

The ramifications of Luther's doctrine of the two kingdoms went beyond questions of organization of the visible church and socio-political conditions as it impacted widely in a world steeped in piety, moribund religious traditions, and an almost impossible-to-un-weave interlacing of church and state authorities. In the aftermath of the *Peasants' Revolt* and with the rise of radical sectarianism other religious questions were being raised beyond the meaning of the sacraments. The conduct of war was one of these questions. Here was an issue itself steeped in pseudo-religious and secular philosophies close to the heart of early modern society. Luther became the correspondent of choice for every person with a question; a virtual republic of letters grew up around him. One letter, from a professional soldier who worried that his Christianity and his profession (as a professional killer for hire) were incompatible, inspired Luther to write *Whether soldiers, too, can be saved* (published in 1527).[37] In this case, timing worked on Luther's behalf. The Emperor and the King of France were trying to reconcile differences and join forces, first against Turkish invaders and, second, with other Catholic rulers against so-called heretics. Proposed alliances included

---

36. Luther, "Against the Peasants," 73.

37. Luther, "Whether Soldiers," in *AE*, 46:87–137. Also see Bornkamm, *Luther in Mid-Career*, 581.

Duke George and inspired the formation of a league of evangelical powers centred on Electoral Saxony and Hess.

On the titular theme Luther considered duty, conscience, warfare, and even types of war. In many ways the soldier's was not a unique profession. It was an office with duties and obligations from God in the civil kingdom and these were to be performed conscientiously. As elsewhere Luther drew a distinction between the office and the holder (not all soldiers would be true Christians) and not all holders will be honourable. The military is an adjunct of secular government aiding the prince as a means of providing order, preserving peace, and punishing the wicked. As such he can accept pay (he must be satisfied with his wages and act with moderation and avoid greed) and, like any craftsman, he can sell his services to any buyer. If, however, the prince is in pursuit of an unjust cause he need not fight. He has to be sure that the prince's cause is just and he must act accordingly.[38]

War is presented as God's means of punishing the wicked through the prince, developing new themes on the issue of civil authority. The peasants' uprising came about through a too strict application of the laws, leading to injustice. Princes must temper the application of law with equity and fairness as the surest way to secure good order and due obedience.[39] The prince must stand watch that equity (or at least the claims of inequity) was not also abused (as the peasants tried).[40] Of course, in the ideal world of true Christians this would not be a concern, but "as far as the body and property are concerned, they are subject to worldly rulers and owe them obedience. If worldly rulers call upon them to fight, then they ought to and must fight and be obedient subjects. Christians therefore do not fight as individuals or for their own benefit but as obedient servants of the authorities under whom they live."[41] In a very clear way Luther was pursuing a theme of socio-political organization. Society is hierarchical as is the exercise of authority: "What would become of the world if everyone who was in the right punished everyone who did wrong? The servant would strike his master, the maid her mistress, the children the parents, the pupils the teacher . . . What need would there be, then, for judges and temporal rulers appointed by God?"[42] This segues neatly into a discussion of power relationships revolving around two types or labels—"general persons" and "individual persons."

---

38. Luther, "Whether Soldiers," 94, 127–32.
39. Luther, "Whether Soldiers," 103.
40. Bornkamm, *Luther in Mid-Career*, 583.
41. Luther, "Whether Soldiers," 99.
42. Luther, "Whether Soldiers," 114.

In Luther's vision of political reality every post-holder—whether judge or emperor—is a general to his inferiors, but an individual to his superiors. The general person, a prince for instance, has authority over every individual under his command. In a way he comes to symbolize all of them—he is the sum total of them—or he is them *in general*. The prince is, however, merely an individual to his superior—the Emperor. The emperor is the general person of all the empire with all the individual princes beneath him but, for all that, he is still an individual to God—the sum total of everything. Ultimately, all authority and power comes from above, finally from God alone who exercises that singular power through the many individual persons on Earth. Authority is expressed down the scale and responsibility is expressed up—peasants have duties to their lords, who have duties to their nobles, to princes, to the emperor, finally to God. While not all princes will be true Christians they should still act within reason and the natural laws.[43]

Armies and soldiers are the means by which Christian princes punish the wicked among them and protect their own from the ravages of other non-Christian princes. Can warfare be misdirected? For Luther the answer is yes; warfare has often been confused by the papacy as a spiritual mission, subsequently used as a means of political control, and as a means of augmenting its own political authority (e.g., crusades). What should perhaps be the ultimate expression of the emperor's duty to order society and punish the wicked has become hopelessly confused thereby with spiritual power and expectations, and Luther's treatises on the war against the Turk thus represents for us one of the key themes in the separating of the church from civil matters.

Untangling of the two was no easy matter; Luther had considered the matter as early as thesis five and subsequently in his clarification treatise *Explanation of the ninety-five theses*.[44] Luther thought that papal calls to crusade were little more than deflection; a smokescreen to their own paltry acts. The Turks represent a necessary divine scourge for Luther, however, against all the sins of popes and Christians, and he equated resisting the Turk to resisting God's will. This gave his enemies a stick with which to beat him and every subsequent defeat of European armies by Turkish invasion forces was partially laid at Luther's door. To Luther, not unlike the peasants in the mid-1520s, the papacy had been trying to act as its own judge and avoid facing the penalties of its own iniquity, trying to turn all attention against the instrument of the scourging rather than admitting to the cause of the scourging. Purposeful misunderstanding of his point forced Luther to abandon the

---

43. Luther, "Whether Soldiers," 122, 126.
44. Luther, "Explanation of the Ninety-Five Theses," in *AE*, 31:79–252 (91–92).

metaphor for over a decade, only taking up the point again in April 1529 when he wrote a pastoral study entitled *On war against the Turks*, focused mainly on the confusion of causes or *false motivations*.[45]

The papal authorities called the war against the Turks a "crusade"—a holy war—and a fight for the sake of the Christian faith and church, but this was precisely opposite to the way Luther argued war against the Turk should be portrayed. It was emphatically not the church's business to promote wars or to wage wars as this fused the spiritual and political, although popes traditionally treated warfare as if it were a good, meritorious work—salvific even—which offended Luther's theology.[46] Such claims were misleading; the goal was to disentangle the spiritual from the political and to disabuse people of the notion of salvific good works altogether. Luther wanted men to fight with a clear conscience, however, using the characters of Sir Christian and Emperor Charles to illustrate his general principles.

Sir Christian takes up a weapon in support of the emperor only by virtue of his godly duty to obey his political master. To be sure that he can do so with a clear conscience he must pray and repent his sins prior to any fighting. That way he knows that if the emperor is fighting for the wrong reasons God will not be angry with him for participating. Because of the way that the papacy and other Catholic princes have suppressed the gospel and mixed up the two kingdoms, the Turk is the scourge or rod of God's anger, winning battle after battle and more and more territory in Christendom and will continue to do so until motivations are set right and consciences cleared. For Sir Christian the Turk is the devil to be opposed by prayer; for Emperor Charles the Turk is an evil, wicked threat to order, property and discipline within his realms. The Christian takes up arms against the works of the devil in spiritual ways while swords and shields are the weapons of Emperor Charles, used to fight physical, worldly battles in the protection of good order, property and for the punishment of evil.[47] It is a war with two fronts—appeals to God and the threat of physical violence. Sir Christian is active on both fronts, but must not co-mingle them. The physical fighting is one front, the temporal issue, and the individual Christians must avoid thinking of it in any terms other than having been called to do their godly duty as *subjects of the emperor*. Thinking about war and combat beyond its purely temporal terms—the defence of Europe, the realm of the emperor—perverts the doctrine of the two kingdoms, confuses the issues and ultimately offends God's sovereignty.[48]

---

45. Luther, "War against the Turk," in *AE*, 46:155–205.
46. Luther, "War against the Turk," in *AE*, 46:167–68, 180.
47. Luther, "War against the Turk," in *AE*, 46:165, 167, 170, 185.
48. Luther, "War against the Turk," 184.

Thinking about it in purely civil terms allows the states to work united under their temporal ruler—Charles—rather than as spiritually separate and perhaps even mutually hostile individual states.

Later in the same year Luther published a follow-up treatise called *Army sermon against the Turks*, now ascribing prophetic properties and biblical symbolism to the Turkish invasion. He was ascribing *end of the world* or millenarian thinking and emphasized the Turks as God's final scourge. In 1524/5 the peasants had been the devil's means to batter down society, an internal foe to disrupt Christendom for demonic ends. Now, closer to the second coming and the end times, the devil has upped the ante trying to bring about internal unrest, anarchy and collapse through the means of a fearsome external—indeed almost "godless"—foe. The war, although fought by Christians doing their godly duty was still a temporal, worldly matter, and they run the risk of offending God should they forget this and again mix up spiritual and political motivations. Christian men obey their political superiors and in so doing fulfil godly obligations. They should be satisfied in their consciences that this is the right thing to do. At once, Luther put an end to the mediaeval concept of "crusade" as a fusion of spiritual and civil causes and placed the struggle with the Turk firmly into the more modern sphere of geo-political conflict—land, property, wealth, politics, economics—as well as staying true to his millenarian beliefs.[49]

Marriage

Marriage has had a long history of confused spiritual and civil regulations and motivations by the late mediaeval period. It was held as a sacrament (at least from 1439 and the council of Florence), already stressed by a large body of sometimes contradictory canon laws—admittedly Scripture based—and an equally large body of civil laws. These laws became attached, subordinated sometimes one to the other form, but as they were meant to direct religious and civil authorities in the matter the hopeless confusion that sometimes resulted often just led to more regulations (for which the church could charge costs) further confusing the issue. When Luther began to question (and finally deny) marriage as a sacrament he came to regard it, like war, as an exclusively civil matter in which Christians participate due to divine ordinances and the fact that the world needs ordering: "No one can deny that marriage is an external, worldly matter, like clothing and food, house and property, subject to

---

49. Bornkamm, *Luther in Mid-Career*, 590–95.

temporal authority, as the many imperial laws enacted on the subject prove."[50] This was his judgement in a work of 1530, by which point he had already formulated the two kingdoms doctrine.

In the early stages of the spreading reformation, say the 1520s, Luther's evangelical followers were trying to jettison much of the confused, self-serving Roman tradition. Sadly, they had no firm regulations of their own prepared and ready to be implemented, and this resulted in a great many nervous consciences. Pastors worried that they could not serve their flocks correctly. In a kind of circular way, however, just as the civil authorities confirmed the canon law, the church tended to confirm local civil customs and traditions, and this became another source of tension. Because of the unique nature of the sacrament of marriage in traditional eyes, the priest acted as a witness (on behalf of the church) to the event, even though civil law did not necessarily require a witness. Over the late mediaeval period national customs were also increasingly incorporated into the already expansive mass of conflicting laws resulting in conflicting views and many "types" of marriage. It seemed that within obvious and necessary limits anyone could marry just about anyone if the price was right. Divorce, on the other hand, was tricky. The church considered marriage indissoluble (unless one had the money) and this thinking spilled over into civil society. When Luther came to consider the issues in the early 1520s (many letters) his initial considerations where published in *The Estate of Marriage* (1522).[51] Therein, the doctrine of the two kingdoms was perfectly clear, perhaps because in had been on his mind long before.

In a dedicated sermon of 1519, for instance, and in his seminal work of 1520, *Babylonian captivity*, Luther had given much thought to marriage (in relation to monastic vows and clerical celibacy)[52], and in 1522 he undertook a preaching tour, one goal of which was to strip marriage of its too ponderous church-baggage and unnecessary human innovations. Scripture was clear; Lev 18 (famous as Henry VIII's justification for the annulment of his marriage to Catherine of Aragon[53]) identified the forbidden degrees, anything else was human additions meant to confuse or bring profit.[54] So, even before the doctrine of the two kingdoms, Luther was trying to correct false motivations and practices which tended towards insult to God's sovereignty. Marriage, for

---

50. Luther, "On Marriage Matters," in *AE*, 46:259–320.

51. Luther, "The Estate of Marriage," in *AE*, 45:11–49.

52. Luther, "Babylonian Captivity," in *AE*, 36:92–96.

53. Chibi, "The Interpretation and Use of Moral and Natural Law," 265–86; Chibi, "John Stokesley and the Divorce Question," 387–97.

54. Luther, "Consanguinity and Affinity," in *AE*, 45:8. Luther also discusses the issues in "The Estate of Marriage," 24.

Luther, "is an outward, bodily thing, like any other worldly undertaking. Just as I may eat, drink, sleep, walk, trade with, buy from, speak to, and deal with a heathen, Jew, Turk or heretic, so I may also marry and continue in wedlock with him."[55] Just as the soldier in warfare, marriage has spiritual overtones, but to allow civil authorities to better keep society in order he wanted all the false (i.e., Roman Catholic) "spiritual" innovations removed and allow those who could to marry with clear consciences.

Divorce had been similarly regulated and confused by admixing spiritual and temporal conditions. Luther found only three legitimate grounds. Where the husband or wife were "not equipped" for it due to "bodily or natural deficiencies", like impotence. As such persons could not fulfil the divine ordinance to multiply their spouses should be freed. Adultery freed the innocent party to remarry, as did the case of one spouse denying the other conjugal use of their body (which they had pledged to the spouse after all). Luther's reasoning is consistent with two kingdoms doctrine. The righteous tolerate the conduct of their spouses (as a means of frustrating the work of the devil); the worldly try to place limitations on misbehaviour.[56] As the vast majority are of the latter condition they must apply themselves conscientiously to the civil regulations as best they can. So, both church and state have a role to play in marriage—the former brings to light immoral behaviour while the latter punishes misbehaviour—these roles need to be assessed and understood correctly and separately (else God be challenged and good order perverted).

Luther, in his winter sermons of 1522, called upon civil authorities to do their duty, to weed out papal interference, ensure that children follow the wishes of their parents in the case of arranged marriages (or even coerced marriages). Ideally, the parents were looking out for the best interests of their children and, without doubt, papal regulations had led only to a jumble of ordinances from which it is nearly impossible to extract good order—"obedience is a mere farce"—so Christendom itself stands confused.[57] In 1523 Luther restated his principles in an address to the Teutonic knights, returning to the subject as needed in 1524 with *That Parents should neither compel nor hinder the marriage of their children and that children should not become engaged without their parents' consent*[58] and again in 1530 with *On marriage matters*.

---

55. Luther, "Estate of Marriage," 25.
56. Luther, "The Estate of Marriage," 31.
57. Luther, "Sermons," *Works*, 1/4:368–70.
58. Luther, "An Exhortation to the Knights," in *AE*, 45:131–58; Luther, "Parents," in *AE*, 45:379–93.

The message was simple—marriage is a civil, worldly matter.[59] By interfering, the pope, pastors, clerics of all type wrongly set themselves up as temporal judges and muddy the waters. "I am still toiling to see that the two authorities or realms, the temporal and the spiritual, are kept distinct and separate from each other and that each is specifically instructed and restricted to its own task." Luther advised the clergy to refuse to deal with marriage issues altogether, "except where their pastoral advice is needed in matters of conscience."[60] Pastors, working in the spiritual kingdom, care for the consciences of their flocks. Princes, working in the civil kingdom, promote laws tending to the settling of order and peace and enforce them. In the ideal world of true Christian believers there would be no real need for these two separate spheres but, faced with the hard realities, Luther's advice to political and religious correspondents from this point remained consistent.

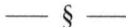

Luther and Imperial Politics to the Augsburg Confession

Readers of early modern European history are well aware of the divisions, both religious and political, tearing at the seams of the Holy Roman Empire in the sixteenth century. Archly Catholic, sometimes even reactionary, territorial rulers blamed Luther for all of their problems (especially since the *Peasants' Revolt*) while evangelical leaders looked out for any sign of impending papal-sponsored crusades against Luther or themselves—seeing Catholic conspiracies everywhere. While in Spain Charles had limited engagement with internal German problems, and the success of the Turks in south-eastern Europe kept his brother and regent—Ferdinand of Austria—focused on defense. The absence of the top political authorities left the lesser authorities—electors, dukes, landgraves and counts—largely free to act as they would and, naturally perhaps, they divided along religious lines. The development of political alliances determined by religious motivation was offensive to Luther's ideals and he made no secret of his hostility (comparing them to earlier peasant associations). He was not opposed to purely political defence initiatives but rather to the division of the empire into religion-driven camps. Civil war, based on religion, hung over the empire for about twenty years from the end of the *revolt* exacerbated by such external pressures as the *League of Cognac* or Francis I's alliance *of sorts*

---

59. Luther, "On Marriage Matters," 265.
60. Luther, "On Marriage Matters," 266, 317–18.

with Sultan Suleiman II.[61] Luther was not opposed to the drawing up of articles of faith, confessions, or religious statements of evangelical principles (as suited to the work of pastors and theologians), and he could not himself resist (sometimes) interfering[62], but he was determined not to emerge as any kind of political leader or pseudo-pope. He always advised legal and diplomatic solutions first and foremost.

This would explain why Luther did not comment much on the events of the Diet of Speyer of 1526—a political assembly summoned for the purpose of dealing with the church and faith issues. Moreover, he rarely favoured military action in support of religious positions. In March 1528, for example, the Elector John sought his opinion on the plan of his ally, Philip of Hess, to launch a surprise attack against Duke George—the proposed *Weimar alliance* (9 March 1528). The alliance acted on evidence of Catholic war preparations (subsequently shown to have been forgeries), but Luther opposed the enterprise. He was morally opposed to the idea of surprise military actions and was worried that his work as a pastor and theologian would consequently be forever compromised by association. He suggested the elector seek out the appropriate legal and diplomatic resolutions to this essentially political issue and leave religion out of it. Had it been real, the duke's surprise attack against evangelical territories would have been a violation of the peace worked out at Speyer as well as the Regency council's mandate as would any surprise attack against the duke.

The mandate required all parties to keep the peace and seek legal solutions and Luther supported this advice as the Regency council spoke for the emperor, "our regular governmental authority, which has been established by God, and which we are duty bound to obey." The mandate clearly considered the peace and good order of the empire rather than either religious faction which, in Luther's mind, was right and proper. Should the elector support the landgrave in a surprise attack, Electoral Saxony could rightfully be classified as rebellious—"the case of our party would get so far that [we] would have no good conscience before God, no legal ground before the Empire, and no honour before the world."[63] Luther's advice was accepted.[64] In a subsequent meeting at Weimar the following month both he and Philip Melanchthon were invited to the discussions. Again, Luther opposed this first strike scheme. "One can be sure that God calls for a defence against war and insurrection

---

61. Bornkamm, *Luther in Mid-Career*, 610.

62. Bornkamm, *Luther in Mid-Career*, 613; Luther et al., "To Elector John," in *AE*, 49:129–30.

63. Luther and Melanchthon, "To Elector John," in *AE*, 49:193.

64. Luther and Melanchthon, "To Duke John Frederick," in *AE*, 49:195–96; Luther, "To John Hess," in *AE*, 49:19.

and for the protection of one's subjects. But to start a war and to attack others, of this one cannot be at all certain that it pleases God. Much more certain is it that this sort of thing does not please him."[65] Three years later, at the second diet of Speyer (1529), Luther repeated his warning to his elector to avoid the alliance-building works of Hess as this might easily move, too swiftly to stop, from an alliance of defence into one of attack. Increasingly difficult, Luther could not prevent alliance building so he concentrated on theologian-to-theologian discussions and the writing of confessions. The most famous of which is the *Augsburg Confession*.

Charles V had summoned a Diet at Augsburg to discuss both the Turkish threat and religious divisions, although magistrates and theologians met separately. The second issue clearly needed to be resolved so that the states of the empire could unite (freely) to deal with the first (that admixture of motivations Luther opposed). The diet was to convene on 8 April 1530. Given the second reason, and the fact that he was advised to have "controversial points" drawn up and explained through Scripture, Elector John commissioned Luther, Melanchthon and others to write a document which would justify the evangelical stance of Electoral Saxony. Melanchthon presented the committee's preliminary results to the evangelicals at Torgau on 27 March—church/state relations and civil authority did not feature. The theologians decided to pursue only those articles in controversy and Melanchthon continuously modified the materials while keeping Luther abreast of changes. The two kingdoms doctrine is implicit in his adjustments and preface materials.[66] For the sake of clarity, however, Luther's *Confession* of 1528 (written against radical sectarian views on the sacrament), which formed the basis of the *Articles of Schwabach*, were rejected at the conference of the same city by Strasbourg and Ulm and the southern German cities. Evangelical and Catholic differences (limited on the issue of civil authority) were becoming overshadowed by Swiss objections wherein another view on the question of magisterial power was emerging.[67]

We can acknowledge that the *Augsburg Confession* did not give any more definition to Luther's understanding of church/state relations and civil authority. That had not been the purpose either. Melanchthon had revamped past Lutheran statements (forming article sixteen) to place clear blue water between the evangelicals and the radicals. The civil sphere was acknowledged as godly; it is lawful and moral and ethical for Christians to

---

65. Bornkamm, *Luther in Mid-Career*, 620.

66. Bente, *Historical Introductions*, 28–31.

67. For the text of the articles, see "The Schwabach Articles," in Kolb and Nestingen, eds., *Sources and Contexts*, 83–87.

"to bear civil office, to sit as judges, to judge matters by the Imperial and other existing laws, to award just punishments, to engage in just wars, to serve as soldiers, to make legal contracts, to hold property, to make oath when required by the magistrates, to marry a wife, to be given in marriage."[68] Anabaptism was condemned for its failures to hold these truths. Melanchthon concluded the statement with the warning that while Christians were bound to obey their magistrates they must be careful to obey God first. Melanchthon strengthened the statement in his subsequent, explanatory *Apology*, to more forcefully drive home the message of Luther's criticisms of the way Catholics had dangerously melded to two kingdoms over time or misunderstood the gospel message as it pertained to civil authority.

To Luther and the subsequent "Lutheran" view, the church was a godly institution defined (and limited) by its godly mandates (as found in Pauline and Augustinian statements) rather than by its Earthly format. The same can be said for the civil authority, with an added recognition that Earthly format was determined by the history and customs of the particular location. In considering the relationship between the two kingdoms, as of 1530, we have for the Lutherans two fully functional, divine establishments, each limited, however, by the extent of the other. The civil, princely or magisterial authority (whichever was locally established) had to be acknowledged and accommodated, particularly if an effective reformation of the church was to be undertaken (that is, in an orderly fashion). Luther lived in an empire which featured a hierarchy of political authorities each subject, ideally, to the one above it and, ultimately, through the emperor each responsible to God. Because of its local implications princely authority became for Luther the normative foundation upon which society was built and necessary order maintained and his doctrine reflected these conditions. Turning to the Swiss and the other major reformer of the first generation, we find that Zwingli grew up more familiar with aristocratic rule—councils and collective magisterial authorities of a more pluralistic nature. How this impacted his understanding of the relationship between the church and the civil authority, and how this differed to Luther's two kingdoms, is the focus of the next chapter.

---

68. *Augsburg Confession* (and supporting documents) can be found online at http://www.reformed.org/documents/ index.html/.

2

Zwingli, Civil Authority, and the Church to 1536

LUTHER'S DOCTRINE OF THE two kingdoms consistently expressed the idea that God ruled the world through two complimentary but distinctive agencies. In the physical kingdom this was through secular government (using laws, sword and compulsion) and in the heavenly kingdom this was through the gospel (preaching, teaching and moral advocacy). In this way he distinguished the material from the spiritual and the mass of humanity (including professed believers) from true believers. The role of magistrates, secular government and rulers in Luther's doctrine was to govern external lives—property, life, social and economic relationships, defence of the state, and the punishment of crime. It was decidedly not the function of civil government to legislate or enforce religious beliefs, although obviously it had the means to ensure that the gospel was taught and preached in a clear and correct manner—it ensured the necessary external conditions.

To a great extent Luther's target had been Catholic rulers who suppressed religious reform; only later did he begin encouraging civil disobedience towards governments which attempted to bind consciences. He argued against the, albeit similar sounding, Catholic theory of the two swords which recognized only one kingdom in which the higher power, the church, controlled the spiritual sword and the lower power, the state, controlled a temporal sword in the service of and at the sufferance of the church. Luther recognized two kingdoms but separated them into near-exclusive functions. His doctrine relied upon and reflected the political reality of a religious leader protected and encouraged by his prince. Some of the Reformed theologians of Switzerland and southern Germany would develop church and state theories with elements similar to Luther's, although their own political realities influenced different outcomes to his. Oecolampadius and Calvin, for example, would treat the church and state as separate but complimentary entities whereas Zwingli, and to a greater extent Bullinger, would ascribe to them a much closer, intertwined relationship due to their own more covenant, commune-focused doctrine and the pre-eminence of the city council as the political authority in Zürich. The reason for this minor schism of opinion among the Swiss was the impact of radical sectarianism, much greater in Zürich than in either Basel or Geneva.

Zwingli did not separate the two communities, finding it important that both preacher and magistrate cooperate for the betterment of the life of the whole. Given the stress he laid on communal organization and a covenant-based salvation doctrine (divine providence) there is a subsequently complex relationship in his thought between civil authority and the church.[1] As in Luther's philosophy, however, the community for Zwingli was ultimately under the sovereign rule of God. For this reason historians and theologians speak of Zwingli as a "theocrat."

Ideological differences which emerged between Luther and Zwingli were the result of far different political situations and doctrine. Luther, the monk, thought in much more personal terms than did Zwingli, the parish priest, who for his part took a wider communal point of view. At the heart of all of Luther's doctrine stood the individual (the true believer or non-believer) whereas at the heart of Zwingli's stood the entire community (true believer and non-believers mixed). So, where Luther examined the conditions under which the true believer would have to act in the temporal sphere—as in his relationship with a non-believing neighbour—Zwingli expected everyone to actively participate and serve the community as a whole. Luther expected, as a preacher/teacher and religious leader, to be left out of the political sphere and to be left without interference from political figures in the spiritual sphere (he would often be disappointed). Zwingli expected to participate in the political life of the community as a religious leader and he expected the magistrates to fulfil religious obligations as a matter of course (as key figures and leaders in the community). Zwingli, more directly and obviously than Luther, fostered a working relationship with magistrates as the means of bringing his reforms to life.

The introduction of religious reform in the Swiss and southern German cities was often through temporal councils authorizing limited, initial change (e.g., the removal of abused images, the introduction of a vernacular liturgy, or gospel-based preaching and instruction). Zwingli expected the magistrates (the burgomaster and the Small and Great councils) to be involved in changes to doctrine and worship, to enforce the gospel and in the re-ordering of the community in light of the Word of God properly

1. Chibi, *The Wheat and the Tares*, 83–85.

understood. The "proper understanding" of the gospel was his purpose as a preacher and a prophet. Luther turned to the Christian princes, even if he could not accurately identify a true one, to act where the bishops of the Catholic tradition would not. This was an act of necessity; there was no one else who could take the initiative. Zwingli also turned to the political authorities; but this was not out of historical necessity but as a result of his so-called "theocratic view of society."[2]

In his view both priest and politician were servants of the sovereign rule of God. Indeed, all things for him ultimately served the glory of God, subject to his divine will. For Zwingli the community was both church and state, both preacher and politician, serving both—one by preaching and the other by ruling—both acting in accordance with the gospel. The council was to formulate laws by which to rule in accordance with the Word. If there was some doubt or disputed doctrine the council summoned disputants to debate the fine points of theology in its presence and then acted upon the results of the disputation under the auspices of the gospel. The council, for Zwingli, became the Reformation's bulwark against the rulings of the far distant Bishop of Constance (who still claimed authority) as well as the immediate forum in which the claims of the radical sectarians were to be argued out, examined, and ultimately rejected. Zwingli's doctrine was worked out in public disputations and supporting treatises in a way Luther's never could have been.

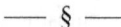

The occasion of the first Zürich disputation (29 January 1523) was the cumulative effect of Zwingli's preaching challenges against traditional church claims, practices, regulations and rules (e.g., on food restrictions, images, both kinds in the sacrament), based on what he found to be the clear message of Scripture. Indeed, his preaching against military alliances (he had been an army chaplain) and mercenary service was so powerful that the magistrates of Zürich took it all on-board and forbad its citizens of selling their mercenary services (on 11 January 1522).[3] Zwingli (the humanist) founded his philosophy on the moral standard of the *imitatio Christi* and an *ad fontes* approach to biblical exegesis, only now combined with gospel-based preaching. He also took the occasion of Luther's persecution by church officials as a base for a number of writings against Rome's abuses of power and position (e.g., exemptions from taxation for instance) which

---

2. Stephens, *Huldrych Zwingli*, 286.
3. Potter, *Huldrych Zwingli*, 7. Also see, Zwingli, "A Solemn Warning," 130–49.

had widespread repercussions. So effective were his sermons and treatises that the traditional authorities in the cathedral and in the monasteries laid a heresy charge against him.

The charge attracted the attention of the bishop (Hugo von Hohenlandenberg) as well as the political authorities of the other Swiss cantons, giving Zwingli's doctrine a national stage. As with Luther, timing was on his side as Rome had just reneged on their financial obligations (i.e., the agreed payment to hired Swiss mercenaries).[4] The bishop and the other cantons sent delegates to Zürich to investigate (7–9 April 1522) the issues and advise the magistrates on possible action.[5] Zwingli was nowhere singled out by name (perhaps the bishop did not want to create another Luther), but he forced the issue by addressing the complaints raised by the delegates in a meeting of the Zürich clergy and again later in the Senate chamber (bringing in the political authority).

In so doing he initiated a period of tense polemic dispute with Catholic authorities on a wide variety of issues—theological, social, regulatory—mounting to a contest between traditional practices and Zwingli's gospel-based testing of those practices. The tension eventually forced the magistrates to step in providing a platform to both parties in the form of an official disputation. Zwingli prepared a short statement of faith, his Sixty-seven articles, which provided the basic points of debate. The Articles (and debate) addressed all of the recent controversies, Zwingli's stance on social morality, and the provision of ethical guidelines. The bishop's delegates (his vicar-general John Faber or Fabri and Martin Blansch, a preacher from Tübingen) in the event were unwilling to challenge those articles directly with scriptural arguments or even to recognize the authority of the magistrates to deal with matters of doctrinal reform. Of the disputation itself there are several accounts of varying credibility, but the end result was the approval of Zwingli's teaching and an order to all the other priests of Zürich to follow his lead.[6] Most interesting is the illustration of Zwingli's ecclesiology (doctrine of the church) and his stance on temporal authority in relation to the church which the Articles provide.

Traditional ecclesiology, which I have examined elsewhere, saw the church universal sufficiently expressed by Rome—the visible, institutional, hierarchical body which embodied all Christians, which had the authority to interpret Scripture, and apart from which there was no means of salvation.[7]

4. Birnbaum, "The Zwinglian Reformation," 33.
5. Zwingli, "To Erasmus Fabricius," in *Writings*, 113–29.
6. Hegenwald, "Acts," 40–117.
7. See Chibi, *The Wheat and the Tares*.

There was no distinction between the visible and invisible congregation, the spiritual or material, and there was no need for it. Faber refused to discuss old practices, customs and traditions outside of a general council because, in his mind, any decision made in Zürich might not find favor with other Christians "in Spain, in Italy, in France and in the north"—those not privy to the decision making process through their own representatives.[8] He recommended that the issues should be written out and brought to the universities at Paris, Cologne or Louvain for comparison and judgement (a traditional process). He appears to misunderstand Zwingli's call for the faithful, or members of the congregation, to judge the dispute based on Scripture alone and/or the legitimacy of such an act.

As early as his eighth article (following immediately upon Christological statements) Zwingli was careful to distinguish the faithful as "members and children of God" based on his salvation doctrine and providential principles. This body of believers is the church, the "communion of saints, the bride of Christ" or what he identified as the Catholic or Universal Church. Christ is the head, the residing intelligence without which the body falls into dangerous internal conflict. The result would be pointless and burdensome laws, traditions, regulations, and practices.[9] So that the communion of saints in Zürich is perfectly capable of deciding whether doctrine or practices are legitimate because they are led by Christ and inspired by the Holy Spirit. For this reason their decisions would not contradict those made by the communion of saints in Spain or the north (although there might be certain external variations more suited to their own geographic, economic or political circumstances). For Zwingli the church is communal and bishops are watchmen or overseers of the flock whose duty is to instruct the congregation. This clashed with Faber's hierarchical principle wherein bishops embody the church as the inheritors of the apostles on behalf of the congregation. This difference hampered any discussion on clerical marriage, food regulations, intercession of the saints and Mary—that is, on human traditions and customs which currently took precedent over the gospel.

Later, while expanding and explaining his articles Zwingli took great pains to distinguish the gospel meaning of words like "church" or "ecclesia"—referring to the community of the faithful (as per John 6:40) or "all Christians united in one faith by the Spirit of God"[10]—from the German word *kirck* which refers only to the physical structure or place where the community gathers (dividing the spiritual from the material). The gospel

8. Hegenwald, "Acts," 51, 66; Zwingli's objections can be found at 85.
9. Noll, *Turning Points*, 40.
10. Zwingli, "Exposition," 44.

understanding refers to a community which cannot gather together in one physical, visible location, although they are gathered together, invisibly, in the Holy Spirit. So, while contrary to its claims, Rome does not represent (i.e., embody) the universal church (in the first spiritual, universal sense), it would certainly be a local expression of the community (in the later, material sense), as too would any parish or ecclesiastical division. The true invisible community is contained within that wider, variable, visible expression for which there is scriptural support (e.g., 1 Cor 1:2). The church (the bride of Christ) in the form of a community is the faithful invisibly united in spirit (whether universally or locally focused). In this way papal claims that the universal church is expressed in the pope and the hierarchy of bishops, who have interpretative authority over Scripture and who make decretals and canons, can be dismissed as little more than human innovation and wishful thinking.

For Zwingli, the first mark of the true congregation (articles thirteen to sixteen) is primacy of the gospel. The gospel, the promise of God and faith in that promise, constitutes the church, the community of the faithful, as opposed to papal claims which have the roles reversed—the church claiming power to constitute the gospel. The pope, whatever other good things he may represent, cannot be the head of the universal body. This is the clear meaning of article seventeen (although the pope can certainly be the leader of a local congregation). Zwingli's exposition on his eighteenth article discussed the familiar image of the pope as an expression of the old style, Old Testament sacrificing high priest juxtaposed with the "eternal high priest" of the New Testament and his one-time for all time self-sacrifice which signaled the end of that old order. Those who would claim that high priest role—popes—are to be rejected as in denial of God's sovereign authority.

Zwingli's exegesis of Matt 23:9 supports this interpretation from which he went on to examine the usual scriptural justifications made underlying papal supremacy—Peter as the rock upon which the church was built, the power of the keys, etc. The role of the clergy was subsequently examined in a large block (articles twenty-three to thirty-two), augmented later with dedicated treatises. Zwingli condemned material orientation, traditions, vows of purity and sumptuary regulations distinguishing the clergy from the laity much as Luther had. Other marks of the true church include excommunication and the priesthood of all believers. Zwingli placed the power of the keys into the hands of the visible congregation, dealing with issues of public scandal rather than with issues of private dispute between members (articles sixty-one to sixty-three). He took to task, in these later articles, anyone who saw the ministry, the priesthood, as anything more than one office among others, an office which grants nothing like the "indelible character" claimed by Rome. Just like a mayor who fails to carry out his functions properly, the priest can be dismissed becoming, once again, nothing more or less than a private citizen. As for the correct functions of a priest: "those who teach in the church, who proclaim the word of God, who translate Greek and Hebrew, who preach, heal, visit the sick, give help and alms to the poor and feed them; for all these tasks belong to the word of God."[11] For this service they are to be supported by the community. Turning to the position of the magistrates, ten of the Sixty-seven articles deal with temporal authority either directly or indirectly—articles fourteen and thirty-five through forty-three (all of which were subsequently expanded upon in Zwingli's *Exposition*). Article fourteen is indirect as an expression of Zwingli's general expectation: "Hence all Christians should do their utmost so that everywhere only the gospel of Christ be preached"—a simple mission statement. The later block of nine articles gives us a more direct understanding of the magistrate's role.

Zwingli was making a point of contrast between the assumed traditional powers of priests and bishops and the natural rule of magistrates (hereditary or elected). Predicated upon, and legitimized by adherence to the gospel, the work of magistrates encompasses all judicial powers and can expect obedience from all Christians. The only condition he placed upon this authority was the provision that "they do not command anything which is opposed to God." Natural justice and divine law (as made known in the gospel) should always be their guide. The civil power protects the weak and oppressed (for their own good), imposes sentences and punishments (including death) for public offences, and provides aid in exchange for "physical support." Zwingli made it clear from the start that this authority, divine though it is, is also subject to the judgement of the gospel and that magistrates could be deposed if they did not act "according to the precepts of Christ"—that is, if they became unfaithful to the word of God. "In short, the dominion of the one who rules with God alone is the best and most stable; but the dominion of one who rules by his own whim, is the worst and most insecure."[12] He never wavered from this position. In answer to the main question, however, he placed social control and discipline into the hands of the magistrate. *Articles* had been aimed at the traditional clergy, that is teachers and preachers of the Word rather than political leaders, and it was from the traditional clergy he met the most resistance.

We saw Faber refuse to acknowledge that public disputations overseen by magistrates could have authority to deal with questions of doctrine. Zwingli

---

11. Zwingli, "Exposition," 355, 357.

12. *The Sixty-Seven Articles* can also be found in Jackson, ed., *Selected Works*, 111–17.

found that as the public—the community—had assented to the authority of Scripture, their government was thereupon provided a mandate to authorize the preaching of the gospel. He would later marshal the relevant Bible sources to prove the assertion. The decision of the magistrates was to give Zwingli permission to carry on as he was, preaching unhindered by the Catholic powers, and any clerics not preaching in like manner were to be removed by the council for the good of the whole church of Zürich. Zwingli followed up the magistrates' decision with two supporting treatises—*Divine and Human Righteousness* and *An exposition of the articles* (both of 1523).

In 1523 radical sectarians in the environs of Zürich were starting to question the viability of government within the context of the genuine Christian life. Zwingli took up the issue in the first treatise (*Righteousness*), the text of an earlier sermon addressed to a friend in Bern. Zwingli's purpose was to prove that the work of the magistrate was divine and based on sound scriptural interpretations, as well as to show that clerical authority had no business in material affairs. His starting point was the well-established Lutheran trope that divine and human righteousness are not the same thing (i.e., no man can attain righteousness in the face of God, although expected to strive for it). People are expected to forgive trespasses, to not murder, to not engage in frivolous lawsuits and quarrels, to not commit adultery, swear oaths, and strive to do good turns to both friends and enemies alike, to not steal or slander and to love our neighbours.[13] In the face of such expectations man exposes his own impotence and turns finally and fully to God alone as the source of his strength and his salvation. Just as Luther did, Zwingli recognized that these were impossible standards for Christians to maintain and that, moreover, they must also treat with non-believers on a regular basis. Of course, if everyone were a true believer and fully submitted to God's will and law nothing further would be needed and radical sectarians would be correct in their interpretation of the "sermon on the mount"—that is oaths, tithes and interest payments are non-Christian. But this was not the reality Zwingli knew.

It is for the sake of peace that human laws and governments were created and are necessary. Their remit is human righteousness—the enforcement of good behaviour. In essence we need temporal authorities to regulate the wicked for the sake of those striving to submit themselves to the will of God. Man cannot of his own volition achieve divine righteousness (he can only aspire to it) but he can achieve human righteousness (he can be good in the estimation of his fellow men). Although human righteousness means nothing in terms of salvation—good works and acts of charity

---

13. Zwingli, "Divine and Human Righteousness," 10.

are non-salvific—it does at least provide those trying to strive for divine righteousness the peace to do so. Thus, while Christians try (and fail) to conform to God's law and demands for interior perfection (under the guidance of preachers), to love God and neighbours, they can try (and succeed) to conform to human laws, perfect their exterior selves, and learn how to behave properly within society (under the eye of civil leaders).

The priests, pastors and bishops should endeavour to hammer home the message of striving for divine righteousness, teaching the gospel, leading or shepherding their flocks toward salvation. Through hearing the gospel, the individual is transformed, changed, improved, although perfection is never attained in life—human nature cannot be altered by man's own effort. This is where clerical authority ends; teaching and shepherding is the limit of their responsibility. They are to explain what man is striving for, provide models of behaviour, advise the weak and aid the poor. Some men will not strive toward salvation and some are not believers at all (genuine or merely professing), so God provided the test of human righteousness and its related ordinances so that we can live peacefully, human nature can be restricted, and He gave us rulers to protect Christians against the wicked and the evil (against those who refuse even to behave to a certain agreed standard). The authority of rulers, therefore, includes compulsion (i.e., the sword) and they can expect cooperation and assistance from everyone. Luther, however, saw a degree of tension between these forms of righteousness, even contradiction (not unreasonable given his doctrines of predestination and imputed salvation). Zwingli's wider communal view eliminated the contradiction. Divine and human righteousness cooperate toward the improvement of the whole man and the benefit of the entire community. A well-ordered external life—human righteousness—reflected or symbolized that internal striving for divine righteousness.[14]

In the second treatise referred to earlier, *Exposition*, Zwingli amassed biblical evidence against the papal claim that priests and bishops have a leading secular role. For Zwingli they are servants of the gospel, the moral guardians of the flock, without power of compulsion (i.e., temporal power). Christ sent out his disciples to preach and teach, "without bag, purse or staff, so that they might not amass a pile, nor bag anything, nor beat anyone, nor rule harshly" rather than to oppose temporal powers.[15] This was followed up with an examination of the scriptural foundations of temporal authority (e.g., Matt 22:21) and the obligations of paying taxes and customs duties and giving obedience.

---

14. Zwingli, "Divine and Human Righteousness," 28.
15. Zwingli, *Exposition*, 246 (using Luke 9:1–11 and 10:1–16).

The magistrate is the "painful medicine", "iron" or "fire" used to correct social disturbances. In essence, because "not everyone is giving to God his due" it is necessary that everyone be compelled to at least give the magistrate his due for "if everyone were to give God what is his due there should be no need of a prince or ruler; indeed, we should never have lost Paradise."[16] The traditional Catholic establishment had turned the world upside down. For example, no one is exempt from paying taxes (e.g., Matt 17:24-7). Zwingli found a certain duality and symbolism in the roles of priests and princes. Each had an office with particular duties and at the same time each was an individual Christian among Christians with all the same duties and obligations to one another.

In his exposition of his thirty-sixth article regarding the administration of justice, Zwingli placed this firmly under worldly authorities based on Christ's own refusal to judge (Luke 12:13ff). Like Luther he used the example of the papacy's involvement in crusades (e.g., compulsion, the use of arms) as an example of wrong-headed thinking and for the same reason—clerical interference had led to countless unnecessary and avoidable deaths. Zwingli wrote that the worldly authorities are well capable of defending their lands and, provided they are employing Christian principles, there should be no problem. Using Rom 13:1ff and 1 Pet 2:13-17 to show how the clergy are bound to obey the temporal powers, Zwingli continued to hammer at the evil of the papal position (remember that the mercenaries had not been paid) which has led the Swiss to repeated disasters in the past. Those Christian principles (article thirty-eight) include the support for gospel preaching and learning from the mistakes of history.

Zwingli equated the law of nature with the law of God and used these interchangeably, but it would seem that the position of the prince—ordained by the law of God—actually contradicted the law of nature. The good Christian, according to nature, treats his neighbours as he would himself wish to be treated by others (Matt 7:12). But, clearly, in order to rule effectively a king must be obeyed and be treated differently from, say, a cobbler. Here we have another example of duality. If everyone was a believer, a good Christian, then there would be no need of political authorities and no contradictions if everyone could live up to the dictates of divine righteousness. Because man is fallen from this ideal, the prince must act according to his office in public—rule, judge others, make laws that enforce human righteousness—and adhere to these as an ordinary Christian otherwise. The princely office is established, therefore, mainly against the wicked (i.e., those

---

16. Zwingli, *Exposition*, 248.

who cannot conform even to human righteousness) as the protector of the oppressed. How is this to be done?

Princely rule must conform itself to divine laws (e.g., the Ten Commandments) and the prince be as any other ordinary Christian. If the ruler should witness or hear of a transgression to divine or natural law it is his duty to act (to love his neighbour). Since the temporal authority is the only office established with the power of compulsion and punishment, it follows (in article forty) that the ruler can impose the death penalty (in his office as prince rather than as a citizen or ordinary Christian) and then only in the case of public offences. Like all other men he cannot see what is in the heart of the wicked and can only judge by their actions (external evidence). As a citizen and as a Christian the magistrate must obey the divine law, "thou shalt not murder" but, as ruler he sometimes must kill (with the norms of human righteousness as his guide). The ruler can expect recompense for his work (in moderation); he can expect taxation, aid (e.g., military support or bureaucratic service), but he should also avoid excess. God will deal harshly with those who abuse the system for unlawful or unreasonable personal gain (e.g., tyrants and despots). How can the ordinary citizen, the ordinary Christian deal with a tyrant?

Article forty-two tells us that the despot may be deposed by whatever method was used to elect him (although Zwingli is vague in the case of the hereditary monarch). When a temporal ruler crosses the line (in terms of human righteousness and in keeping divine/natural law before his eyes) he must be deposed according to divine law, not through violent revolt, but with "common piety" in mind.[17] In other words God will sort out the tyrants on behalf of his people. Once it was established that the council, the temporal authority, has a clear role to play it became a regular feature in Zürich's Reformation thereafter, placing a great deal of responsibility on the political office.

Due to Zwingli's efforts, the Zürich magistrates (the Council of Two Hundred) had accepted and enforced the authority of the Scriptures (i.e., the Word) in determining what was to be preached and how it was to be taught. It is certainly a lesser issue that the council determined thereafter when and how changes based on these preliminary principles were to proceed. So, for instance, while the theologians debated a true understanding of baptism, infant baptism and the physical elements in the sacrament, the council

---

17. Zwingli, *Exposition*, 268–69, 273, 279, 280.

enforced compliance (e.g., compulsory baptism came into effect in the city in 1525). By the time of the second disputation the council's authority to act was clear and established. Zwingli thought it was correct to leave all external matters in their hands—images, aspects of the Mass—and only the most ardent opponent, papist or radical, was prepared to argue the point.

Having discussed divine and human righteousness, and having determined that earthly, external matters are firmly in the realm of the temporal authority, it followed by the time of the second disputation that all external matters, religious and secular, could best be left to the magistrates. In his emerging dispute with radical sectarianism, however, it became more and more a heated discussion, but Zwingli never wavered. The magistrates, in effect, took the place of the entire church (i.e., the entirety of the community) by virtue of delegated representation (supported with reference to Acts 15). The council acts in line with divine law and the gospel so that its decisions have already, in a manner of speaking, been approved and discussed by the entire community. What Zwingli meant by this is that the gospel is preached and a correct understanding widely taught so that the congregation understands finally, for example, that images have no salvific value, leaving it to the council to determine when was the optimal time to remove them from the public space. This delegation of authority was also useful in that not all decisions are of interest to all the community (and some issues inspire the wrong kind of interest in some people) and, particularly in 1525, it was clear that some of the community pulled in a direction opposite to the correct understanding of the gospel on certain issues (e.g., papists or sectarians). In many ways the doctrine of the Eucharist became a test case of Zwingli's point on temporal authority. A good illustration of this is Zwingli's treatise of August 1525, *Subsidiary essay on the Eucharist*.[18]

Under Zwingli's direction the council turned to the issue of the external elements of the Mass and eventually abolished the Catholic ceremony. That decision was not taken lightly, however, as Zwingli and the councilmen held talks and meetings on a number of occasions. Zwingli also took pains to answer the objections of Catholics that the matter had been brought to the council in the first place. His reasoning, now familiar, was based on the achieved cooperation between church and state:

> I who am set over the preaching of the word at Zurich have previously given free warning to the Two Hundred that I suffer the things that belong to the jurisdiction of the whole Church to be put in their hands for decision only on condition that their

---

18. Zwingli, "Subsidiary Essay on the Eucharist," 187–231. For commentary, see Stephens, *Theology of Zwingli*, 290.

deliberations and decisions be under the guidance of the word, also that they themselves do not occupy the place of the Church except insofar that the Church itself has by silent consent thus far kindly accepted their enactments or decisions.[19]

Given his dual key elements of gospel agreement and the needs of peace, "whatever, therefore, comes up in regard to changes in rites and ceremonies is referred to the Council of Two Hundred" on the principle that the larger the assembly the more opportunity for violence and descent into "senseless feelings" there was. The magistrates act, therefore, in the name of the whole community.

Preachers prepare the groundwork by preaching the gospel, explaining its meaning and ramifications for the church and, once this is done, issues like images and the Mass, properly understood and accessed, can be turned over to the magistrates to act on the collective will of the church and society combined. It was noted earlier that Acts 15 was Zwingli's proof text here. Later in the same treatise he equated magistrates with the *presbyteroi* or elders mentioned in that chapter (and he would do so again in 1528 in an important letter to Ambrosius Blarer).[20] While clearly the council and the church are not the same institution, the council represents the church in its capacity as the representative body of the entire populace, which itself equals the church. Each member has basic obligations as a Christian and as a citizen and the magistrates act upon these obligations. But, as rulers, they also have the power and duty of compulsion (i.e. discipline or social control). It is not a question of absolutes though. The council, for Zwingli, was the best available route for the furthering of the gospel and of reform. Purely theological issues were debated, conclusions agreed, and then turned over to the magistrates for implementation and enforcement. These issues were subsequently explored in *Commentary on True and False Religion*.

Some of this bears repetition. For Zwingli, "the church is a congregation, an assemblage, the whole people, the whole multitude gathered together."[21] He was trying to distinguish the church from its past associations and meanings—the church, for example, as only the pope and the bishops—in the same way that the king is not the entirety of the people although he may represent them in clear cut and obvious ways. The pope and the bishops as they were in the 1520s cannot represent the church in Zwingli's view because they were not led by the gospel. The council, magistracy, prince or king, however, can represent the people in terms of his

---

19. Zwingli, "Eucharist," 206.
20. Potter, "Church and State, 1528," 114–15.
21. Zwingli, "Commentary on True and False Religion," 176.

office. The council was not the church but, led by the gospel it could speak on behalf of the church and enforce decisions made by the church. Zwingli also now had an ear toward the claims of his more radical supporters and their growing opposition to the participation of Christians in government (discussed below). He examined the issue to show that, on the contrary, participation in government was a clear Christian duty.

This would be a continuous sore-point, however, between himself and some of his former disciples and students. Once it was clear beyond any further need of justification (in his own mind) Zwingli turned his attention to a review of the scriptural evidence against his anti-government opponents in the radical camp. To them, Christians were not to get involved in government. The problem faced by Zwingli was that they were conditionally correct. If everyone was a Christian and everyone knew who the genuine Christians were there would be no need of government and no question of involvement. But, conditions being what they were, for Zwingli, the sum of Scripture relative to the issue suggested that only a Christian could be an effective magistrate. The reason is familiar enough—the connections and parallels between the church and state and the realistic demands of divine and human righteousness. Zwingli considered, within the demands of human righteousness, just what the state requires of its citizens: "serve the commonweal, not your own [needs]; that dangers be shared in common, and fortunes also, if necessity arises; that no one exercise a selfish prudence; that no one exult himself; that no one stir up strife."[22] The church, worded slightly differently, expects much the same behaviour of the congregation. The difference being that the state is content with outward conformity while the church demands sincerity in the inner man—genuine love of neighbour rather than compelled good behaviour.

"There can be no Church without government" is one of the concluding statements of Zwingli's last major treatise, *An Exposition of the Faith*.[23] Forces out of his control forced his hand and Zwingli accepted the need to try and find common ground with Luther on the spiritual front and, politically, on behalf of Zürich he sought closer alliances with Hess, Venice, and even France. On the advice of Lambert Maigret, a French envoy, therefore Zwingli wrote a confession of faith addressed to Francis I, but the second war of Kappel and Zwingli's death on the battlefield delayed publication to February 1536. It was seen into print by Bullinger in conjunction with the publication of the *First Helvetic Confession*. Although he had little more to

---

22. Zwingli, "Commentary on True and False Religion," 294.
23. Zwingli, *Exposition*, 268.

say on civil governments and magistrates, he tried to hammer the points made earlier to the king.

Government is necessary within the very nature of the visible church. It houses both genuine believers and false, "insolent and hostile" non-genuinely-Christian men who are the special responsibility of human authorities—princes, magistrates—without whom the church would be "maimed and impotent."[24] With specific regard to government Zwingli explored many types and their corrupted counterparts—monarchy and tyranny, aristocracy and oligarchy, democracy and sedition. If the rulers are directed by pious considerations, justice and equity, rule will not break down into the corrupted forms and the church will thrive because its members are protected against the wicked among them. And, although tyrants, oligarchs, and the seditious are still to be obeyed by Christians, it is to be expected that God will soon deliver his people from them. The Bible gives many examples illustrating the downfall or recovery of evil rulers—Saul, David, Ahab, and Herod—the error of their ways was always pointed out to them by a churchman, a prophet—Samuel, Nathan, Elijah and John—showing both good governors and prophets are necessary for the survival of the church. Yes, prophets are more important in that they teach and preach the gospel, but there can still be no church without magistrates or governors to protect it. So, although Francis I may not agree with Zwingli's opposition to Swiss mercenaries selling their services to his causes he can clearly see that Zwingli supports his rights as a king and as the guardian of the church in France otherwise. The appeal was three-fold: defend the church against papal bishops who oppose the spread of the gospel; defend it against the wicked who trouble the lives of the faithful; and, defend it against radicals who seek to destroy the integrity of the church from within and without.

---

24. Zwingli, *Exposition*, 266.

3

Civil Authority and the Sectarians

THE TWO MAJOR REFORMERS of the dynamic years of the Reformation period, Luther and Zwingli, agreed and asserted, based on some very convincing scriptural, philosophical and natural law evidence, that civil government had been established by God for good and sure reasons and it was supplied by God with the authority and the tools (i.e., the sword) to perform its role effectively. The extent of this role into specifically church matters, however, separated their views, but not radically so. For Luther, the extent of civil authority was a more crucial issue perhaps than it was for Zwingli.

Luther wrote that secular rulers could not rule over the soul, over salvation itself, as these were God's own matters. Moreover, government does not coerce faith although it does protect the people against false teachings (as determined by the priests and bishops according to the word of God). We shall later find Calvin (in Geneva) and Knox (in Scotland) establishing similar positions. For both Luther and Zwingli, however, secular authorities were clearly necessary for society (and for the church) to properly function. While it was not charged with determining matters of faith, the pace of reform was in its collective hands. And yet, taken to its logical conclusions, the *priesthood of all believers* would seem to suggest that all civil leaders are also priests with the authority and duties of priests.

Luther circumvented this logical knot first with the separation of the two kingdoms (earthly and spiritual) and, second, with an emphasis on the differences between the holder and the office. Turning to Zwingli, it is clear that he largely agreed with Luther on many issues but, because he developed a communal point of view, his doctrine led him to do away with the notion of two separate kingdoms. The magistrates have certain authorities even within the church (as magistrates), acting upon the necessary advice of priests, teachers and preachers (who themselves participate to a certain extent in the civil sphere as citizens). After it is known that the church/community as a whole has accepted a change, then action by the magistrates to bring the change into reality became necessary and expected. These actions could be setting the agenda for the removal of images or agreeing official changes to the Mass and enforcing these changes. Both first generation leaders of the magisterial position sought to balance the wider implications of the *priesthood of all believers* with their own doctrines of salvation and with the needs of Christian society and their own unique political situations. The "radical" sectarians who followed them—mystics, spiritualists and Anabaptists among them—recognized no need for that compromise.

The Swiss Brethren in Switzerland and Hoffman and Hubmaier in Southern Germany, for instance, came to associate temporal influence with corruption and temptation for the church. Such doctrine as believers' baptism and the profession of faith as the sign of genuine belief became their means to distinguish members of the true church as well as spiritual from secular matters. Thomas Münzter in Austrian territory and Karlstadt in Saxony took more radical spiritualist views which sought, eventually, to separate the believer from all external authorities. For all the radicals, however, the half-measures and delay tactics of the magisterial reformers were to be rejected and, due to the *Peasants' Revolt* and the polemic opposition of such figures as Luther and Bullinger, all sectarians (radicals and moderates alike) became tarred with the brush of radicalism.

Generally speaking, Alistair McGrath noted that the radical opponents of the mainstream magisterial reformers adopted a model of the church which corresponded, sociologically, to sects, and hence the term sectarian is used by historians to describe them somewhat indiscriminately. What this means is that each group in their own way advanced a particular and exclusive view of a distinct society within but separate from mainstream culture, and then they equated this with the church or congregation of the genuine people of God.[1] Membership of this congregation then became evidence of salvation. Although they subscribed different views of the relationship between the church (as they understood it) and the various civil authorities, they all tended to look back to an ideal golden age—that period before Christianity was the state religion of the Roman Empire when it was persecuted but self-assured of its righteousness. This is certainly a heroic image, one which, under persecution before, during and after the *Peasants' Revolt*, must have been quite attractive to oppressed individuals. From Karlstadt to Grebel, Müntzer to the *Schleithiem Articles* there are many repeating elements within sectarian thought regarding civil authority—policies of non-resistance and non-cooperation, against the swearing of oaths, involvement in secular affairs—but unity (save for those

---

1. McGrath, *Reformation Thought*, 202.

golden age associations with the primitive church) was beyond them. The word "archetype" gets thrown around a lot and sometimes unfairly, but we can use it here to divide the many radical visions into two relatively homogeneous groups based on what we know already of their theological and doctrinal positions. So, with men like Karlstadt or Müntzer as examples we can discuss a "spiritualist" position whereas, with men like Grebel or Hubmaier, we can discuss a "Biblicist" position. These paradigms (however imperfect) help us better understand differing sectarian perspectives on questions of civil authority and the church.

—— § ——

Karlstadt and the Doctrine of One Kingdom, c.1521–25

In a previous study Karlstadt's prototypical Puritan doctrinal stance was established.[2] Moreover, as both a theologian and a jurist, his study of the law influenced his understanding of, and approaches to, theology, the Bible, and society itself. Still, up to the aftermath of the Wittenberg disturbances his thinking on civil authority and the church largely reflected Luther's. The prince essentially cleared the path to reform, stepped back, and did all he could to protect it (protecting it from the wicked, etc.) We noted that Luther considered the external format of the church as *adiaphora*, non-salvific external material, or as just another expression of human righteousness. So long as the political authority performed its Christian duty to protect the faithful from the sinful, Luther was satisfied. Pastors got on with the more important serious work of stirring the faithful toward a divine righteousness they would never reach in their lifetime. Prior to 1522 Karlstadt echoed Luther's thinking.

It was not exactly the same, however, as Karlstadt incorporated a more extensive element of a pre-existing mysticism into his writings (based on his attraction to the *German Theology*), along with a *sola scriptura* that included a legalistic element. This was a different appreciation of some books of the Bible with a heavier emphasis on Old Testament legalism (which Luther opposed) and considerations of how these still applied to Christians.

In his writings before the schism developed between them, Karlstadt enthusiastically embraced much of the Augustinian/Lutheran view, and their differences produced only good natured points of debate. Karlstadt endorsed Luther's thinking on the difference between human and divine

2. Chibi, *The Wheat and the Tares*, 46–57.

righteousness, the harsh expectations of the latter, and humanity's inability to meet those expectations. He would, however, come to expect humans to strive to meet them through ultimate submission to the will of God and abandonment of egocentricity. He also subscribed Luther's *priesthood of all believers* and *theology of the cross* (i.e., the search for God in the least likely places). Indeed, he embraced some of this with more enthusiasm than did Luther himself. As events in Wittenberg proceeded, Karlstadt's view of the extent of civil authority (the local leadership of the immediate community) became clearer too. Not merely compulsion, however. For him, the magistrates had an extensive role to play in the ordering of the community in both religious and sociological terms. In other words the magistrates both determined *and* safe-guarded doctrine, examined *and* enacted the needs of the community, determined its character *and* set the conditions by which the church and the Christian congregation could grow in perpetuity. The greater extent of lay authority in religious matters sprang out of the combination of this and other writings.

Karlstadt held all "priests" as essentially elected to specific offices and functions (lay or clerical) whichever suited their talents best—shoemaker or councillor. Consequently, *priesthood of all believers* also meant that each and every priest was permitted to participate in and/or judge religious debates and theological disputes.[3] The difficulty was getting them access to the gospels so they could be properly shepherded. Karlstadt saw much more potential in the capabilities of the common man than Luther but, as a result of the *Peasants' Revolt*, he became inextricably (and unfairly) connected to a radicalism which tainted his works. His enthusiasm, clear in his writings, emerged more fully in practice in the mid-1520s when it is also clear that he had turned his back on the self-righteousness of authority figures in the Roman Church, in the university, and in the political sphere. Karlstadt had already by then granted that laymen could perform church functions—hearing confessions, granting absolution—just as well, if not better (more purely) than titled clergy. This was the gist of his treatise against Eck, *Verba Dei* (1520), wherein he suggested that the reading of theology in schools could actually be detrimental to a proper understanding of Scripture.

Following Luther's lead Karlstadt agreed that many of the ceremonies of the church were merely the functions of office rather than the special powers/privileges of ordained men, but a serious disagreement came about in

---

3. Sider, ed., *Karlstadt*, 137.

the aftermath of the local disturbances when, in Luther's absence, Karlstadt led their colleagues in putting Luther's doctrines into practice in the town. Whereas, for perhaps obvious reasons, Luther looked to the elector for political backing to his reform efforts, Karlstadt instead looked locally to the city council (an expression of his own communal interests). His more radically Lutheran and mystical positions began to emerge following disputes when Luther returned to Wittenberg and delivered his *Invocavit* sermons. Therein he called on delaying the destruction of images and slowing down key doctrinal changes for the sake of domestic peace. At that stage both men were in pursuit of the same end but, when Luther disappointed him Karlstadt began to pursue his goals without reference to authority—whether religious or civil—external to the immediate community. This was the first step in Karlstadt's modification of Luther's doctrine of the two kingdoms.

Recall that Luther theorized the existence of two kingdoms (one divine the other mundane). These were separate (in terms of function) but still under the ultimate sovereignty of God. He used priests or politicians to his own ends. Karlstadt moved closer to the Zwinglian position of common Christian duties differentiated only by the lay authority's duty to use compulsion and direct dealing with the wicked as led by the prophets. Karlstadt developed a "one kingdom" theology which ultimately rejected the clerical hierarchy *per se*, and featured an advocacy of "lay Christianity"—focussing much lower down the traditional social scale. As with Zwingli, Karlstadt's evangelical pastors held no disciplinary authority. This gave magistrates the power to impose God's law (spread the gospel, advance Scripture) in reflection of a more Old Testament model. There are many worthy examples showing magistrates with ultimate and direct authority over the church (e.g., Moses's authority over Aaron or David's authority over the priesthood itself) so it seems clear that he was taking the priesthood of all believers only to certain logical conclusions.[4] The question for many historians, however, is whether, like some of his colleagues, Karlstadt had become attached to the ideas of one or other of the Zwickau Prophets—in this case with the ideas of Nicolas Stork—and thereby corrupting what should have been a pure evangelical position.

Stork advocated a so-called "Free Republic of Christ" ideal which relied on no particular external authority. It was an idea later taken up by Müntzer

---

4. Nelson-Burnett, "Kilchen ist uff dem Radthus," 62–3. Also see, Sider, ed., *Karlstadt*, 277–83, 288–91; and Pater, *Karlstadt*, 78–91.

which, in Luther's mind established an indelible link with Karlstadt and the prophets (despite contrary evidence).[5]

The reformers had made the Bible—the Word in literary form—the cornerstone of the Reformation. Stork and the prophets, Müntzer, and eventually Karlstadt, took one further step back to interior revelation—the Word as spoken by God directly to the internal conscience of the chosen or, in Stork's view, direct revelation from the Archangel Gabriel (as in Mohammad's case). For the prophets, the gospel, internalised in this way, meant the abandonment or overthrowing of all current external powers—church and state and written revelation—in exchange for the guidance of direct interior illumination. This would be under the watchful eye of the prophets, of course, the mediums of this new spiritual enlightenment. For an interested mystic like Karlstadt the ideas of the prophets may have been quite intriguing (perhaps even thrilling), but there is no evidence to say that he was influenced by the prophets to any large extent. Yes, later, he did go to lengths to extradite himself from the church's financial controls, but he was already dubious of church authority prior to the arrival of the prophets in Wittenberg and he never joined Müntzer in revolt.[6]

Historians know (from Preus's valuable study of the events of the Wittenberg disturbances) that Karlstadt was certainly willing and able to work with the local political authorities toward much needed religious reform. On 10 October 1521 he participated on the elector's commission (with university and church leaders like Jonas, Amsdorf and Melanchthon) to investigate the actions of the local Augustinians who had abandoned both private Masses and monastic vows. The investigations put Karlstadt in a good position to see the convergence of forces—whether conservative v. evangelical or spiritual v. lay leadership—as well as to assess conflicting political, academic and religious claims and counter-claims. He noted the atmosphere of tension created by something as simple as advocating for the gospel. It is certainly possible that within the competing authorities and resulting violence he began to draw historical connections between the persecuted minorities of the primitive Christian church and the treatment of the "people of God" in his own time.

In his exegesis of Matt 11:12 and Luke 20:9-18 (the parable of the vineyard), for example, Karlstadt drew comparisons between the people of God or kingdom of God and the persecuted primitives but he was witnessing in Wittenberg more than persecution at the hands of religious authorities. Lay political authorities were also setting up in opposition

---

5. Sider, ed., *Karlstadt*, 147.
6. Wylie, *Protestantism*, 1:508–9.

to the "prophetic minority."[7] To combat these reactionary forces he went through the applications of *sola scriptura*, the lessons of sacred history, Lutheran salvation theology and the *theology of the cross* and prepared a thesis selection, later presiding over a consequent public disputation on the Mass. During the disputation he remained the voice of moderation and cautious optimism even in the face of Melanchthon's frustrations, insisting that any changes must be brought about through the consent of the Wittenberg magistrates. In his view this was necessary to prevent violence and limit occasion for slanderous charges. Differences over doctrines of the Mass and the sacrament aside, Karlstadt searched for the widest common consensus on all the issues, forcing both sides into deeper consideration of their own opinions. Later he drafted the commission report of 20 October, dispatched to Frederick, which urged the elector to do his Christian duty and clear the way to certain moderate religious reforms in Electoral Saxony.[8] Although, at this stage, Karlstadt was no more than applying sound Lutheran principles in the call for reform, the effort ran into the wall of the elector's demands for unanimous consensus. This may have given Karlstadt pause—was a total consensus possible?

On 20 October he drafted papers from the commission calling on the elector to initiate major reforms and, in so doing he had done no more than Luther would have done—calling upon the prince to clear the way for the gospel to have its place, and Luther approved. Tension escalated at the elector's call from unanimous support—impossible at the time. The city council consequently found itself at the centre of a problem. A majority (including the citizens at large) followed Karlstadt in demanding specific reforms but were opposed by a vocal minority of traditionalists. In the event the elector resisted acting upon the recommendations of the commission to direct a reformation program himself and, with the traditionalist authorities—like the canons of the Collegiate Church—doing nothing otherwise (there would be no unanimous vote) this drove the pro-reform community to frustration and sometimes violent extremes.[9]

The magistrates emerged as the centre of the reform movement as representatives of the wider community. As such, the quartermasters, representatives of the guild leadership and members of the council of forty, pressed six demands. The preaching of the pastors and the tracts of the reformers had here, as elsewhere, laid the groundwork for widespread calls for reforms to be instituted and legitimized by law. Zwingli had used the same situation

---

7. Preus, *Carlstadt's Ordinaciones*, 16.
8. Preus, *Carlstadt's Ordinaciones*, 19.
9. Sider, ed., *Karlstadt*, 156.

in Zürich to the benefit of the reform-minded community, and Karlstadt made the same approach, by-passing "superior" spiritual authorities as obstructions. The demands of this cross section of the community are familiar enough—gospel preaching, changes to the Mass, etc. The revamped commission, now shorn of former conservative voices, positioned itself solidly behind the six articles delivering that unanimous statement which reflected Karlstadt's developing interpretation of key Lutheran points. They advised that the elector should proceed to allow reforms without regard to the scandal these may cause as it is not the reformers causing trouble but the Roman Catholic authorities who refuse to free the gospel. In the primitive church, a small minority of poor people and common folk received the original revelation against the persecution of the high and mighty. For Karlstadt, sacred history was just repeating itself in the present.

But only so far; by December Karlstadt performed an innovative evangelical Mass in defiance of the elector's call for a return to traditional usages and customs. With the arrival of the Zwickau Prophets, and with the issue of an imperial mandate in January, an already tense local situation intensified. Even as the prophets upset the laity with claims of direct revelation Karlstadt remained convinced that Scripture was the sure authority to direct what changes were needed, and he argued that it was hardly beyond the capacity of the laity (all equally priests) to discern what were the correct procedures based on the gospel rather than the visions of so-called prophets. In direct terms the city council, as representative of the entirety of the community, acts upon the will of the community and is thus able to institute gospel-led changes against the stalling pretensions of traditionalist churchmen obstructing the effort. Karlstadt, Melanchthon, Jonas and Amsdorf negotiated with the magistrates over the terms of the *Ordinance* (of 24 January 1522) to meet two important objectives.

The first was to ensure and perpetuate gospel-based reform. The order gave reform "statutory reality" which, in Preus's words, "constituted" a small revolution.[10] The second was to direct community life into a much more clearly Christian model which it presumably once had but lost through clerical tyranny.[11] The order envisioned a Christian community—God's kingdom on earth—a church, a people of God, and set out to remove those practices which hindered bringing of the vision to life.

The city council, in Wittenberg became "the means for legitimizing and institutionalizing reform" as, although politically responsible to the elector, it had significant and autonomous local powers with regard to religious issues.

10. Preus, *Carlstadt's Ordinaciones*, 25, 34.
11. Goertz, "Reformation of the Commoners," 7.

The resulting seventeen articles are of a familiar type, little beyond Luther's appeal to the Christian nobility two years earlier. Karlstadt's lawyer's mind, however, zeroed in and expanded (in fourteen of the seventeen articles) on the existing poor chest regulations as key to his communal vision. With his active (perhaps even dominating) presence, a lay political authority gave clear definition to the church (using the six articles as a base statement of community desires), abolished begging, assumed authority over previous clerical functions and, ultimately, cleared the path to an exclusive focus on the word of God (total *sola scriptura*), but it was not enough.

Karlstadt would not be satisfied until laymen were equated as priests and considered able to take the initiative in their own reform movement. They must also be pro-active, joyous and altruistic in their faith. In his *Homily on Malachi* (1522), for example, he argued that Christians must take responsibility for their own religious lives and not merely be subject to the judgement of authorities—religious or political. Later, he would advocate communal autonomy from all "external authorities"—that is, authorities external to the congregation. In Karlstadt's vision "housefathers"—the heads of households—should themselves diligently learn the gospel so that they can instruct their children to become the next generation of messengers of God.[12] How this was to be accomplished (*via* the rededication of religious incomes and endowments, redirection of the income of fraternities and guilds, and with the secularization of church properties) was outlined in *On the removal of Images* (27 January 1522) published a few days after the official release of the magisterial *Ordinance* which outlined the official process. Karlstadt published so as to bolster the magistrates who, in his mind, were not acting fast or diligently enough, directing official attentions toward the care of unfortunates like widows, beggars, and orphans.[13] This was a key area.

Both he and Luther criticized the church for its failures in dealing with and caring for the poor, and portrayed abject poverty as a communal failure of human righteousness. Karlstadt was, at this date, in the formulation process of a salvation theology which assigned great significance to the external deeds of Christians (as evidence of interior regeneration) and was looking to encourage root and stem, Christian, gospel-led, solutions. Sadly, this clashed with the traditional church view of poverty as the foundation for its doctrines of grace and salvation *via* good works, in which the poor were seen as either loathsome creatures or noble, holy innocents. Karlstadt rejected the paradigm; in 1523 he renounced his academic degrees,

---

12. Preus, *Carlstadt's Ordinaciones*, 49–50.
13. Karlstadt, "Images," in *EC*, 101–2.

responsibilities, dress, and privileges to emerge as only "Brother Andrew"—identifying himself with the mass of humanity.[14]

It was a clash of approaches to the same problem. By redirecting church incomes the council was providing the means by which the supply of future preachers, teachers and even political leaders was perpetuated; nowadays we would call it a "level playing field" or "equality of opportunity." Freed from begging and the disadvantages of abject poverty, the peasantry could begin the process of self-improvement at the hands of the entire community. Karlstadt knew that whatever was done there would always be poor people, just as there would always be rich people—God's creation. He equated the existence of beggars with the absence of genuine Christian charity rather than an economic equation. He had managed to get the magistrates focussed on the begging issue as a perfect example of their role in nurturing the spiritual and moral progress of the whole community. Responsible magistrates could/should engineer poor relief in such a way as to eliminate begging (although not necessarily to eliminate poverty).[15]

To Luther's functionality aspect (i.e., that cobblers, cooks, and preachers are all equally priests too) Karlstadt added magisterial responsibility for socio-economic engineering (in which we can see an early form of socialism). In *Images*, written in German and aimed at a literate rather than simply academic audience, Karlstadt wrote: "they shall help everyone according to his requirements whether one desires to be a printer, goldsmith, baker, tailor, shoemaker, learn a secular craft, or engage in business."[16] The extended list includes preachers, teachers and even future political leaders but it all depends on a Christian magistracy and population. Karlstadt nowhere intended to eliminate the poor; the idea was only to eliminate the moral stain of begging and to foster joyous, altruistic care one for another.

This is a key difference in doctrine between the two reformers. Luther more forcefully and fatally isolated secular and spiritual tasks. Nor did Luther accept that compulsion, a secular power, could change hearts or minds or really mould a truer Christian existence. The two reformers agreed that hearts and minds would be changed by the hearing of the gospel, a precursor to action, but for Luther the spiritual kingdom was key, and the political followed its lead, protecting it from the wicked, the sinners, and the non-believers. Karlstadt no longer made the separation. But it was not only begging and abject poverty that exercised his mind; it was the *duty* of the magistrates to

---

14. Lindberg, "Poor Relief," 318.
15. Leroux, "Images and Begging," 87.
16. Leroux, "Images and Begging," 79; Karlstadt, "Images," in *EC*, 122.

release monks and nuns from their vows and to help them resettle into the community (based on the biblical seven-year slave cycle.).[17]

According to Lindberg, Karlstadt's assigning importance to Old Testament texts, which Luther did not do, also signalled a more important schism than contemporary appearances would seem to suggest. Karlstadt used Old Testament sources to underline his theological position that a Christian commonwealth (or Christian city) was a theological and sociological possibility and a distinctive entity in its own right. We noted that income from certain clerical offices and other means would be re-dedicated by the local political authority. The educational duties of the fraternities and guilds would be taken up by the poor chest, which would then be augmented by the council and the natural wastage of existing clerical title holders. Yes, we will always have the poor in society, but God created the poor as a means by which the wealthy could fulfil their Christian duties (a conclusion of Karlstadt's salvation theology).[18] He was not, however, particularly optimistic; Images served as a kind of warning to the magistrates that the retention of images, statues, and idols hindered spiritual growth and risked divine displeasure. Old Testament sources seemed to favour his position[19], as well as providing authorisations (e.g., Ezekiel 14:19) against the moaning of traditionalists and "false prophets." The subsequent *Ordinance* closely followed the weave of Karlstadt's teachings.[20]

It is important to recognize, however, that Karlstadt was not placing sole and direct responsibility for all spiritual issues on the shoulders of the magistrates alone. Duty fell universally and communally; "Each city must look after its own citizens", the combined effort of town-folk and farm-folk.[21] The city, town or local council encapsulates the local community—as it was to do politically—and has the power of compulsion as God's agent in temporal matters and spiritual matters alike. The success of *Ordinance* spurred Karlstadt and his colleagues on to a more dedicated, detail oriented preaching campaign. This drew the ire of the elector and forced the magistrates to step back. Historians know that over-zealous laymen in Wittenberg, anxious to have the council's order fulfilled, acted prematurely and violently, unfairly blackening Karlstadt's reputation.

17. Karlstadt, "Images," in *EC*, 121–22.
18. Lindberg, *Beyond Charity*, 122; Arffman, "The Lutheran Reformation," 213.
19. Lindberg, *Beyond Charity*, 118. Hezekiah had been praised by the Holy Spirit for the destruction of images (in 2 Kgs 18:3–4), and Josiah illustrates the rule of civil authorities over priests (in 2 Kgs 23:4).
20. Lindberg, "Poor Relief," 323–24.
21. Karlstadt, "Images," in *EC*, 122.

Karlstadt, perhaps, missed the true significance of these acts, which he dismissed as righteous fervour and over-zealousness. The gospel was finally inspiring the community; a minority took things too far in their enthusiasm. Obviously, there would be a settling in period; this was a highly motivated local community exercising its rights to determine its own religious identity through its own political leaders. For others Karlstadt had become an instigator of violence[22] and civil disobedience while, ironically, the magistrates (acting on his advice) were praised for their actions. Just as support for him dried up—from his church, university, and political colleagues Luther returned to direct the local reform movement.

It is difficult to see where Karlstadt had been wrong. He had been up to this point the very model of caution. He had advised Melanchthon to modify his violent tone; he had pressed for change within the system; he had remained consistent with Luther's doctrine; and, the magistrates who acted on his advice had been praised for their work. We can only assume that the elector was nervous of imperial reaction as reactionary Catholic institutions feared popular uprising (which did later happen).

Karlstadt had taken Luther's own doctrine closer to its logical conclusion having recognized that change was necessary and welcomed. Perhaps his misstep had been to jettison Luther's self-imposed limitations, imposing instead his own emerging mysticism with emphasis on internal regeneration. After Luther's return restrictions were placed on Karlstadt's preaching opportunities and this inspired him to move away from all external sources of authority as corruptible. On 3 February 1523 he renounced Wittenberg and moved the experiment to Orlamünde.

The split with Luther eventually moved beyond questions of civil authority and ecclesiology. They agreed to restrict clergymen from purely temporal matters but Karlstadt moved beyond Luther's doctrine that temporal authorities had no place in purely spiritual matters. And, by "authority" Karlstadt favoured the local authority (as selected at the local level[23]) whereas Luther favoured the princely, even the imperial, influence (which Karlstadt viewed as self-electing). Karlstadt's reasoning was convincing—the Old Testament is chalk full of princes and kings ordering the church and doctrine to God's plan and, in the New Testament Christ's many statements on obedience to the civil powers are as clear as St Paul's own. Luther

---

22. Preus, *Carlstadt's Ordinaciones*, 42; Hillerbrand, "Andreas Bodenstein," 386.
23. Goertz, "Karlstadt," 12; Preus, *Carlstadt's Ordinaciones*, 17 (no. 21).

bowed under electoral pressure and the local magistrates scaled back and delayed the reform effort in Wittenberg. In Orlamünde, Karlstadt found a receptive community and focussed more and more attention on the civil power, communal reformation, and the needs of the lowest social echelons (at an unfortunate moment in time) but was never able to re-capture the energy of those Wittenberg years. His internally focused salvation doctrine also coloured his views on the claims of the established church authority to determine the spiritual, economic and political nature of the town and also its religious claims (which seemed geared only to perpetuate a permanent schism between an inferior laity and a superior, purer clergy). Karlstadt began to reverse the roles using *priesthood of all believers* to eliminate the need for a specific clerical hierarchy. Every member of the community could (or would eventually be able to) read and discuss the Scriptures with every other member so there was nothing in the way of their political leaders representing their desires in purely spiritual matters.

This then was the doctrine of the one kingdom—not the clerical hierarchy and the political hierarchy separately under God, but the church (as defined wherever the faithful gathered) or congregation empowered to self-determination (that is, to judge doctrine, approve, appoint, remove teachers and pastors) by raising questions and learning the gospel faithfully. Out of the congregation the faithful choose their own political leaders, who are just as equally involved in the discussion forums but also oversee all those issues Luther otherwise ascribed to the temporal and spiritual kingdoms separately.[24] Karlstadt may have expressed some sympathies for the peasant armies and their aims, but he distanced himself from violence and particularly from Thomas Müntzer despite some shared theology. Catholic authorities who refused to advance the Reformation and the gospel were not representative of the congregations who wanted it; Karlstadt advocated the separation of believers from non-believers as did Müntzer.

Thomas Müntzer:
Secular Princes and the Sword of God

Müntzer presents a small problem in that his very few published works do not present a fully formed theory on the question of secular authority and the church. Essentially, his is an extended (and some might say radical) version of Luther's *priesthood of all believers*, which Müntzer found much too

---

24. Goertz, "Karlstadt," 12–13.

conservative. He explored the extremes; he mixed in his own understanding of Luther's *theology of the cross* and removed many elements of the *doctrine of two kingdoms* as unnecessary divisions within the ranks of the elect.[25]

Historians need to be cautious when dealing with Müntzer. His position as a leader in the *Peasants' Revolt* has coloured everything he wrote as class war propaganda and proto-communism. We can acknowledge there were elements of this in some of his letters, but retrofitting everything into a Marxist model is less than helpful. He was a "Martinian" early in his career, and he was prepared to gather Christians (true believers or the elect) under the rule of their local secular princes, to work with them, and to recognize their place in the political and religious spheres (provided they were also among the elect—unlikely as this was). Like Luther, Müntzer looked to the magistrates, mayors and princes, to protect the people of God and the gospel and the Reformation; like Zwingli, he accepted that secular rulers had a clear godly role to play (as among the elect) and a divine mandate (e.g., Rom 13) for their rule over the church (i.e., the community of the elect), using the sword to protect it when called upon to do so. Like the magisterial reformers Müntzer also found allies for his spiritual position among the secular rulers—local magistrates and electoral officers alike. Mighty Catholic authorities, like Duke George, Count Ernst or the Archbishop of Mainz, however, opposed him and his preaching, rounded up his followers, and influenced lesser rulers against him. This led to bitter counter-blasts against princely power, "big-wigs", and an increasingly Karlstadt-like leaning toward the common man as the source of hope for a new kind of church.

By 1524 Müntzer had abandoned Luther's caution against the rising up against even tyrannical authorities and over turned the traditional interpretation of the text of Rom 13. As Rupp noted, however, it was not necessarily a social revolution Müntzer finally came to support but simply moderate equalization. Even in his last confessions he recognized that hierarchies existed, that tyrants have power over the material world calling merely for a little less obvious exploitation and ostentatious show: "says he declares that when they ride out [in public] princes should ride with eight horses, a count with four, and a nobleman with two, but no more than that."[26]

Like less radical reformers he had been more than willing to acknowledge secular authority. He insisted, however, that they use the sword to defend the elect, to recognize that they were all equal in the covenant (if not socially or economically outside of it) and in these ends times use

---

25. Chibi, *The Wheat and the Tares*, 124.

26. "Interrogation and 'Recantation' of Müntzer," in *CWTM*, 434; Rupp, *Patterns*, 301.

their power to wipe out the godless. By 1525, with the many betrayals behind him (it seemed that it was only ever princes and nobles who opposed the spread of the gospel), revolt against non-elect secular princes and landlords dovetailed with Müntzer's verbose and bitter preaching against these same figures, and against Luther. He wanted the sword removed from those who refused their divine duty and used against them. As Goertz noted this was not a criticism against secular authority merely for being secular—good or bad, benevolent or tyrannical—but a criticism against those unwilling to protect the godly and destroy the enemies of the gospel.[27] Hubmaier and Hoffman will echo this view.

There were many parallels in the thought of Müntzer, Luther and Karlstadt: their adherence to Augustinian theology; their love of that unique German mystical tradition; and, Platonic philosophy. Never in Luther's immediate circle, however, Müntzer was an acquaintance and both Karlstadt and Luther helped secure him beneficial positions in the regional church—in Orlamünde in 1519 and as a preacher in Zwickau at St Mary's Church in April 1520. Bradstock suspected that it was in the latter where he fell under the influence of Storch's intense brand of experiential, apocalyptic mysticism in which visions are the means of ascertaining gospel truth. Despite this foreshadowing Müntzer's expressed opinions were nothing that could not be found in Luther treatises and, like him Müntzer turned to the magistrates to protect the Reformation process against the objections of the local Catholic obscurantists. In Zwickau this was the local Franciscans. Indeed, it was with the support of the council that he wrote to Luther (on 13 July 1520) seeking advice, and defending the reform effort he fronted.

Müntzer objected to having been summoned to appear before the Franciscan provincial in Breslau. At the same time the council appealed to Duke John for his protection and support in their effort to spread the gospel. Müntzer had been trying to instil an evangelical, Lutheran model of reform, advocating the rights of the local community to select their own preachers. He expected pro-active Christians (especially from those in authority positions), and he had already taken the laity to task for not doing enough: "I said that the laity, too, were likewise guilty who had failed hitherto to pray and sigh for shepherds of souls, hence the Lord had justly set blind watchers over the blind sheep [Isaiah 56:10]"[28] Later in the same letter he mentioned

---

27. Goertz, "Radical Religiosity," 81.
28. *CWTM*, 18–19 (letter no. 13).

that "the whole council supports me and almost the whole town"—clearly he thought his efforts were paying off. He noted that the magistrates were well involved in the effort having read and taken in the message of his sermons. Although some feared his violent tone, Müntzer name was on the rise. He appealed to the mayor and the city council of nearby Neustadt, advising them that it was within their authority to take the lead in a local marriage controversy and thereby resolve it.

His letter, of 27 January 1521, contains all the anticlerical vitriol one might expect from so-called "Martinian" preachers.[29] Müntzer was actively opposed to clerical interference in what he saw as representative social and communal issues. At least, that of the existing institutionalized church, which he saw as a corrupted echo of the pure, primitive church.[30] This was a familiar theme found in all his writings. Müntzer was expelled from his position in Zwickau shortly afterwards, the first "betrayal" which eventually led him to advocate revolt and violence against anti-gospel political leaders (or tyrants). He was expelled in April, making his way to Prague in June. Most accounts hold that he was welcomed in Prague, feted even by other followers of Luther and all evangelicals. Living accommodations were provided and he was invited to preach.

There he wrote one of his most infamous works, the so-called *Prague Manifesto*, an unpublished attack on the existing church and its hierarchy of priests, outlining a "theocratic" political ideal (in the sense that God's rule was to be elevated above all earthly, "creaturely" authorities). Although rather vague on the nitty-gritty of day-to-day politics and the influence of secular authorities on the church specifically, there is much that can be inferred. For instance, four versions of the *Manifesto* exist—a long and a short German format (for the exile community), a Latin format (for scholars) and an unfinished Czech format (an appeal to the native population in the spirit of John Hus). According to Matheson, the purpose of the work was to inspire the laity and their leaders to put forth another Hus-like effort to recapture the spirit of, and emulate, the early Christians in the "apostolic renovation" of the church, rejecting Roman Catholicism, stale Biblicism, and accepting Müntzer's own mystical understanding of personal salvation. Vague also are his socio-political assumptions and no concrete plan was offered up on how this recapturing was to take place. In Müntzer's mind the *Manifesto* was a clarion call; he was rallying believers to action.[31] In the short German version of the work he wrote: "I summon every single person to help in the defence

---

29. *CWTM*, 27–28 (letter no. 19).
30. Gritsch, *Müntzer*, 26.
31. *CWTM*, 355.

of God's word . . ."[32]—an application of the *priesthood of all believers* doctrine writ large. For Müntzer, as for Karlstadt, this was not mere metaphor; Müntzer expected people to live it. In the large German, and in the Czech version, anti-clerical vitriol was given full expression. The message was subdued in the Latin version; the educated elite and nobility were expected to take charge of the effort. Sadly, no one showed up.

According to *Manifesto,* the church has failed both to explain to the world, and protect from its enemies, the genuine Christian faith. Substituted into its place by the greedy clergy and book theologians was a false church based on the dead letter of Scripture and human improvisation. Müntzer thought, perhaps due to relevant history, that the Bohemians would take up the call to arms against this falsified church (and its resultant impure faith) and teach the rest of the world what true faith was (at least according to Müntzer's own spiritual interpretation). The appeal to action was surprisingly vague and uninformed, however; temporal leaders were to take seriously their role in the community. Secular lords were to halt the social and spiritual rot that had set in to Christendom, expose the corruption of the greedy, Roman clergy and, presumably, cut it out and overthrow the current ruling elites ensconced within the church and bring to an end to their assumed economic, social and political domination. There is a hint of Luther's two kingdoms doctrine and an appeal to the temporal to restore and re-establish the spiritual.

Baylor termed Müntzer's political scheme as "congregationalism", explaining it as a "democratic localism" in which "the laity finally do exercise their right to select their own clergy" and thus determine the nature of the local church (suited to local conditions but reflective of primitive Christendom). Unfortunately there is no explicit appeal to temporal authority and it is unclear why Müntzer failed to make one. Perhaps he thought it should not have been necessary.[33] No self-cleansing crusade came about; instead the Prague authorities arrested Müntzer and forced him into exile, another betrayal.

Müntzer spent 1522 unsettled, explaining to Melanchthon (in a letter of 29 March 1522) the dangers of trusting in secular authority and flattering princes—"you will live to see your undoing." The reference to 2 Tim 2:14 was meant to instil in his correspondent a striving for meaningful reform rather than a mere contesting of words.[34] Gritsch explained that Müntzer could find little or no support for his theocratic views among the territorial

32. Müntzer, "The Prague Manifesto," in *CWTM,* 360.
33. Müntzer, *Revelation and Revolution,* 19.
34. *CWTM,* 46 (letter no. 31).

rulers and grew increasingly bitter as a result.[35] Karlstadt offered to help him find a new post and, eventually, after short term positions in Nordhausen, Halle and Glauchau, Müntzer secured a trial position as preacher at St John's in the New Town in Allstedt in March 1523.[36] That office depended on electoral confirmation and dukes John and John Frederick came to hear him preach. Müntzer's basic Lutheranism had reasserted itself. He looked to the secular authorities to take the matter of Reformation in hand and allied himself to Hans Zeiss, the castellan (governor or keeper) of the elector's castle and to Mayor Nicholas Rückert.[37]

Unlike Luther and Karlstadt, however, Müntzer had no clearly stated political philosophy beyond the basic Lutheran idea that the secular rulers have a serious role to play in the church and in religious affairs. He may be considered radical, however, in that he actually expected the magistrates to perform their duties! All evangelicals believe that the secular authorities held the sword for a reason but Bradstock saw Müntzer's apocalyptic expectations and mysticism informing his political expectations, increasingly post-1523 with calls for the elect to act being made.

Those who are not pro-active in the destruction of the forces of the Antichrist were held as sympathizers and agents of the devil and this became a repeated theme in Müntzer's Allstedt writings. A time of reaping was at hand (in reference to the parable of the wheat and the tares)—the secular sword must take the initiative, lead the way, destroy the tares and clear the way for the elect. He castigated Luther and Melanchthon for their determination to delay reform (so the weak at heart could catch up) but nor did he advocate rapid change (as did Karlstadt). In his first public political statement, *Open Letter to the Brothers at Stolberg* (18 July 1523), he warned against "unjustifiable rebellion"—that is, of trying to force religious, social and political change. There were radical elements in Stolberg advocating violence, unsatisfied that the local reformation effort had the support of ducal representatives. It is important, Müntzer noted, "that we allow God to rule" first (reform of theology) before vast changes could be brought about (e.g., "as yet the world cannot accept this.") He offered a vision of the future under God's rule, however, ". . . then will the assembly of the elect lay hold on the whole wide world, which will acquire a Christian government that no sack of gunpowder can ever topple." The secular lords of this future Christendom would also be among the elect as "no one can

---

35. Gritsch, *Müntzer*, 45; *CWTM*, 50–51 (letter no. 35).
36. *CWTM*, 52–53 (letter no. 37).
37. Rupp, *Patterns*, 185, 201.

rule until he has passed through the time of testing."[38] Müntzer ruled out violence in the short term as inappropriate but acknowledged appropriate future violence was on the cards.[39]

All too soon Müntzer, like Luther, found genuine believers among the political elite hard to come by. He was keen to get people involved in the reform of the church. Early Christians had been much more proactive in their faith and Müntzer believed that the loss of enthusiasm had tarnished the church and led to an illegitimate clerical hierarchy which exercised stolen social and political function—at first because they had to, later because they had become greedy for secular power. In his mind's eye, therefore, secular rulers and magistrates were merely taking back their authority. But there is a fine line between leading a reforming effort and wrong-headed interference with it. While this may seem little more than standard evangelical fare, Muntzer's theocratic vision must be accounted for—Christians ruled by the word of God not by the dead letters found in Scripture. In that context secular rulers enforce and protect the gospel, the word of God, and the spiritual servants of God. They are the bulwarks against the ungodly and non-believers. Their work is central so, should secular lords be found in opposition to the word of God their swords must be turned against them. This was more or less what he boldly asserted in a letter to Count Ernst von Mansfeld.

Müntzer's preaching was powerful and he attracted large crowds, many travelling from outside the town to hear him (including Mansfeld miners). Mansfeld, however, was within the territory of the staunchly Catholic count. Ernst had forbidden his subjects attending Müntzer's sermons and had issued a stern warning to the mayor and magistrates of Allstedt not to encourage them. The miners appealed to Müntzer and he subsequently wrote to the count, portraying him as an enemy of the gospel whose actions were leading him to a sticky end, as unbalanced, and as certainly insane. All this would be exposed to the world should he continue to stand in the way of God's work.

The letter, of 22 September 1523, also gives us the first explicit statement of how Müntzer understood the purpose of princes in his interpretation of Rom 13. Traditionally this text provided a basis of a ruler's expected obedience from his subjects, but Müntzer turned it around into the basis of princely duty; "to rule the people so that they learn to fear God alone." The count was then charged with usurping this natural order—wanting to be feared in the place of God. He advised the count not to act or react in haste,

---

38. *CWTM*, 60–4 (letters nos. 41A & B).
39. Baylor, "Thomas Muntzer's First Publication," 452, 454.

as this would have dire (but unspecified) consequences.[40] No more than a few days later Müntzer addressed his theory on princely duty to the elector himself who, if not a committed evangelical *per se* was at least not a Catholic obscurantist. Müntzer explained his evangelical reform programme as Bible based and largely reflecting Luther's work in Wittenberg (without the unwarranted care for the weak of faith). He also complained how the count had interfered with the peoples' search for genuine spiritual guidance. Müntzer had invited the count (with his choice of spiritual authorities) to attend a sermon and judge him according to the gospel. Instead, the count appealed over the elector's head to the emperor.

Müntzer found the count's actions rather bizarre: "he should have taken his learned people with him and instructed me in a friendly and modest manner. If I had been vanquished then he should have arraigned me before your electoral grace and thereafter forbidden his people to listen to such services." It was not a question of the count's authority to protect his people from heretical opinions, but there were clearly other conditions of duty to be met first—investigation, evaluation—which the count had not met. Herein lay the difference between a concerned shepherd and a tyrant.

The count's actions would seem to transgress both Scripture and imperial edicts (in as much as Müntzer assumed he was preaching evangelical truth). His interpretation of *Romans* followed: "this [the count's actions] will bewilder the people, who should love princes rather than fear them: Romans 13. Princes hold no terrors for the pious." There is certainly very little about this that could not have been extracted from Luther's wider *priesthood of all believers*, if at the edges, but now Müntzer added a caveat hinting at justifiable revolt: "But should that change, then the sword will be taken from them and will be given to the people who burn with zeal so that the godless can be defeated, Daniel 7."[41] Although the message is dire in its implications, the tone of the letter is respectful—the elector is due respect based on his earthly office and his pro-gospel stance—and Müntzer appealed to his higher authority, as his prince, to judge his preaching. All too soon Müntzer would have his public test in the aftermath of the Mallerbach incident.

The Allstedt period was a productive one for Müntzer as both writer and activist and he anticipated confrontation. Over the 1523–24 period he organized a band of the elect—a brotherhood, league or covenant—to protect the word of God and bring down its enemies, and he preached out against whatever or whoever offended his spiritual sensibilities. This included the Mallerbach pilgrimage chapel on the outskirts of the city which

---

40. *CWTM*, 66–67 (letter 44).
41. *CWTM*, 69 (letter 45), referring to Dan 7:26 and the ruling power of kings.

featured a miraculous statue of the virgin.[42] On 24 March 1524 Müntzer's league (with Müntzer watching), with the foreknowledge (and participation) of members of the council, destroyed the chapel as the work of the devil, as idolatrous, and as an affront to their piety. The Abbess of Naundorf subsequently complained to Duke John over the incident, seeking punishment and compensation, and the duke allied this incident with other minor acts of violence in the region. He summoned Zeiss (his castellan), the mayor, and the town councillors to his court at Weimar on 9 May and gave them a fortnight to arrest the iconoclasts. Twenty days later nothing had been done; the affair was considered trivial by the magistrates and Zeiss pleaded for patience, fearing to stir up violence by making too much of the matter. On 4 June Ziliax Knaut (a councilman) was sacrificed to the duke's impatience. A letter was sent to the duke (inspired, if not penned by Müntzer himself) on 14 June justifying the action as a defence against false religious practices and idolatry. A tense situation was made worse when Müntzer's leaguers armed themselves and marched in support of Knaut, even as the elector urged further arrests.[43]

Müntzer did not deny or question the duke's or the elector's authority but he thought they were acting inappropriately and he could not square the pious act of destroying the chapel with the elector's call to punish those pious men. Of course the elector has the right to command and expect obedience and use the sword to "carry out retribution on the evil-doers and the godless," but he argued that the destruction was for the common good. Did the elector really mean to say that the pious should be punished for the destruction of a devilish institution?[44] On Luther's advice the elector reconsidered. Duke John even came to hear Müntzer out (13 July 1524[45]) on the occasion of his sermon *Interpretation of the second chapter of Daniel* (later expanded into a treatise explaining Müntzer's theology and his vision of the elect in the fashioning of the next world).

Leaving his wider theological doctrines aside, it is important to note that salvation for Müntzer depended on a purgation of the self and a whole-hearted connectedness to God. This condition relied heavily on a metaphorical descent into hell and a subsequent crying out for salvation. Salvation was granted to those who thrust themselves finally and unreservedly into the hands of God alone. The ego-centric, self-regarding will of the man (the old Adam) must be abandoned and replaced by the love and

---

42. Goertz, "Karlstadt," 23.
43. Gritsch, *Müntzer*, 63.
44. *CWTM*, 79–81 (letter no. 50).
45. Lindberg, *European Reformations*, 146; Lindberg, *The Third Reformation*, 79.

understanding of God (the new Christ). For the entire community to be so saved, a similar purgation must occur on the wider scale. The godless symbolize the self-regarding will in the metaphor—they must be purged in order that communal connectedness to God can be achieved. For Müntzer, the duty of communal purgation was in the hands of secular lords and magistrates.[46] This was the central message of the sermon preached before dukes John and John Frederick.

Temporal authority is not an accident of birth or right of victory in war; princes hold the sword *for a reason*. To Müntzer, the dukes led astray by impressive, but nonetheless false, Bible thumpers—either the traditional but corrupted Roman clergy or on the new style bookish Wittenberg clergy—and have consequently failed to truly understand the Reformation which was happening all around them. They risked becoming tyrannical in their opposition. The laity, having little or no truck with book learning, has been more open to visionary prophecy. As a result they are more aware of, and better prepared for, the imminent secular and religious changes to come (not to mention more willing to oppose perceived tyranny). That is a new, pro-active Christianity, and Müntzer, as its prophet, assumed the task of preparing the Christian princes for their role in the projected new world order. What is that role?

Secular rulers must ensure that true faith is preached to the people. This is more than mere policing, punishment and censorship of the book trade, however, the prince must be Old Testament! He must become once again the sword-wielding defender of the good and the terrible scourge of the wicked, instilling the fear of God in all of his subjects. The prince led the people toward salvation and the restoration of the church to what it had once been through fear of God, which leads to the mercy of God.[47] To be effective, princes must be more open to the advice of genuine prophets (prophecy which can be tested against Scripture) and must leave behind the often self-serving advice of the bookish as untrustworthy and irrelevant. Masses, clergy and rulers alike must "live by the revelation of God", which requires a new understanding of Rom 13, the standard text of secular power. Not only is there a duty on the part of the subject to obey the true Christian prince but, now, Müntzer emphasized the prince's duty to his subjects—to administer justice and vengeance in equal measure. The time of clemency to non-believers is over—no more waiting for the weak in faith. The princes, as per the *priesthood of all believers*, have been entrusted with a secure authority *over* the elect but also *on behalf of* the elect. They must use the sword or it

---

46. Bradstock, *Faith in the Revolution*, 25.
47. Müntzer, "Second Chapter of Daniel," in *CWTM*, 235.

well be taken from them—false rulers, like tyrants everywhere, should and will come to sticky ends at the hands of the elect.

Müntzer's sermon was provocative. Christendom is in need of reform but the empire is little more than a "pretty spectacle . . . eels and snakes coupling together immorally in one great heap." The spiritual ("priests and clerics are the snakes") co-mingle universally with the secular ("the secular lords and rulers are the eels")—an allusion to Luther's *doctrine of the two kingdoms* perhaps. The rulers of Saxony are, however, half-way to salvation (e.g., evangelical and having left Rome behind) but they need to take the next step; "take up the cause of the gospel boldly . . . for once you really grasp the plight of the Christian people as a result of the treachery of the false clergy and the abandoned criminals your rage against them will be boundless, beyond all imagining." The rage of the princes, however, must be directed *but not after the advice of the bookish*: "for they have made such a fool of you that everyone swears by the saints that in their official capacity princes are just pagans, that all they have to do is to maintain civil order." For Luther the secular ruler is a necessary outgrowth of man's sinful nature, necessary to protect the faithful from the faithless. Müntzer cautioned that this is no time for foolish (i.e., rational) sentiments; princes must be a more positive force than this. Quoting Matt 10:34, "I am not come to send peace; but the sword." This is the role of the prince in the world—to be the sword: "sweep aside those evil men who obstruct the gospel! Take them out of circulation! Otherwise you will be devils, not the servants of God which Paul calls you in Romans 13 . . . ," and indeed, "you are angels when you want to do which is right!" He also warned them that failure to act would result in their loss of power or worse.[48]

Historians have found in this a plea for the protection and support of secular authorities. Müntzer took the classic doctrine of civil obedience, as discussed in countless traditional interpretations of Rom 13, and turned the doctrine on its head with a new interpretation, distilling the message of *Rom* through the words of Dan 2—the apocalyptic story of Nebuchadnezzar and the false prophets. Romans 13 becomes a call to action in the creation of the theocracy to come—princes must use the sword and cut down the enemies of the gospel as God's agents most suited to the task—their goal being the restoration of the pure, primitive church and change in the religious, social and political spheres.[49] The dukes' reaction to the sermon was less than enthusiastic but at least they allowed it to be

48. Müntzer, "Second Chapter of Daniel," in *CWTM*, 243, 246, 247–48, 250, 251.

49. Rupp, *Pattersns*, 203–4; Bradstock, *Faith in the Revolution*, 25–26; Gritsch, *Müntzer*, 69–70. Also see Rothbard, "Karl Marx," 145; or Crofts, "Three Renaissance Expressions," 20–22.

printed and disseminated.[50] What might have come of it is academic; they were all overtaken by events beyond their control.

— § —

Duke George had engineered the capture of Müntzer's followers in Sangerhausen. This, and the elector's indifference to his advice, led Müntzer to reconsider the role of magistrates. Like Karlstadt in the aftermath of the Wittenberg disturbances Müntzer now focussed on the congregation of the elect to pro-actively assert their rights to gospel preaching and pure religion without the aid of political or institutional church leadership. This was expressed in his active encouragement of the formation of covenant leagues. Müntzer was instrumental or at least influential in the formation of "more than thirty leagues and covenants of the elect" across the empire.[51] These leagues would also be used. To the town council of Sangerhausen Müntzer wrote; "I will speak against you, sing against you, write against you, I will do the very worst that I can think up."[52] Where Luther wrote that even tyrants were to be obeyed (God would send a scourge), Müntzer now offered them another choice; "A prince and sovereign lord is put there to have authority over temporal goods, and his power extends no further than that ... he shall have no authority at all over our souls, for in such matters one has to be more obedient to God than to man."[53] Although his attention was turning toward building leagues and bridges between communities of the elect, the pro-active element of his salvation theology was now being taken to mean by many as a call to arms.

— § —

Müntzer had clearly moved in the direction of Karlstadt: they shared a dedication to spiritual interpretation and experiential religion; they had turned away from traditional socio-political norms; and, both emphasized the lower classes in a new way—as somehow purer, unsullied by the bookish scholars. Where they differed was Müntzer's contemplation of a violent re-shaping of society which Karlstadt rejected.[54] Indeed, shortly hereafter the revolting peasants became for Müntzer the only genuinely pro-active

50. *CWTM*, 82–3 (letter no. 52).
51. *CWTM*, 83–85 (letter no. 53); Housley, *Religious Warfare*, 95.
52. *CWTM*, 85–86 (letter no. 54).
53. *CWTM*, 86–891 (letter no. 55).
54. *CWTM*, 91–92 (letter no. 56).

element in pursuit and defence of the gospel. However, even as he extolled the virtues of revolt, Müntzer had not yet given up on princes who were genuine Christians and who pursued genuine faith (according to his own doctrinal assumptions). As far as the new world order is concerned he still expressed respect for princely authority and still counted the magistrates of Allstedt among his supporters, but he now found princely attitudes increasingly frustrating and sought to point out the apparent contractions between the current reality and the world to come. This is the overall tone of the letters sent to Zeiss of late July 1524.

The princes of Saxony were failing the test of true faith. Refugees had begun to pour into evangelical territories but the princes were offering them no protection against forced repatriation, which raised Müntzer's hackles. The Catholic princes, the tyrants (those who opposed the gospel) "ought to be throttled like dogs"—a statement revised in a subsequent letter to "mad dogs."[55] He is raising the stakes for the Christian princes—tyrants need to be actively opposed. "You cannot go on turning a blind eye to other territories, as has been customary. For it has become clear as day that they have absolutely no time at all for the Christian faith. As a result their power is at an end and will shortly be handed over to the common people." If something is not done soon, "no people will trust their own lords . . . the old loyalties will not fit the bill any more at all."[56] Faith and salvation are now being inextricably tied to action—"the person who will not risk his neck for the sake of God in these dangerous times, will not be found vindicated in his faith either."[57] These letters were written on the 22 July. Three days later Müntzer wrote to Zeiss again over the attitude of the Saxon princes who must "begin to do more than peer through their fingers, failing to instil genuine priests in their principality; protecting the wicked and making no plans at all which accord with God's most kindly will . . . our princes maintain an absolute, tight-lipped silence." Although he admitted that traditions like feudal dues and duties be honoured, such an attitude was conditional on the princes seeing to their own duties and obligations.[58] Although Müntzer still had a sympathetic ear in Allstedt pressure from imperial and electoral bodies, and Luther, forced the mayor and magistrates there to officially abandoning him.

This latest betrayal prompted Müntzer's drafting of two related confessions of faith, *The Testimony of the First Chapter of Luke* and *A Manifest*

---

55. *CWTM*, 95–99 (letters nos. 57–58).
56. *CWTM*, 96, 98 (letters nos. 57–58).
57. *CWTM*, 97 (letters nos. 57–58).
58. *CWTM*, 100–101 (letter no. 59).

Exposé of True Faith.[59] Almost identical theologically, the message to the council and the magistrates of the elector's court is clear—tyrants must be faced up to and met with force. Any hope he might once have vested in princely authority was gone—even the evangelical princes are seemingly too timid to act in defence of the elect and the gospel they claim to support. The existing church hierarchy and secular governments need to be purged of God's enemies. Müntzer's conclusion was that only revolt by the humble will finally unseat the godless from their positions of power.

These two works retrace much the same ground as the recent Zeiss letters, restating Müntzer's understanding of the role of princes and secular lords: "princes are not there to frighten men into good deeds but to threaten doers of evil deeds with the hangman. Hence they are nothing but hangmen and jailers; that is the whole scope of their trade."[60] This is certainly a long way from his earliest political notations, but consistent with his reinterpretation of *Rom*. The greatest problem is that the masses fear the secular lords ("unintelligent rulers who offend against all equity and do not accept the word of God") more than they fear God. Faith has become nothing but pretence. In order to recapture the true Christian fear of God, the reality of the church and political society must be destroyed: "tear the godless from their judgement seats and raise up humble, coarse folk in their place." These new secular lords will then look after the poor and deal with them in the way that good shepherds should do—making provision "in word and deed" for genuine faith. This is how princes should act, as opposed to how they do act:

> and those that should stand in the vanguard of the Christian people—which are called princes for that reason—prove conclusively, every time an issue or plan crops up, their lack of faith by fearing, because of their fellow princes, to do right. They imagine they would be driven out if they were to stand by the truth, which they only pretend to accept because it has not brought any persecution upon them. They like being called the best Christians of all, but they juggle around to find a way to excuse their godless fellow-princes, and declare barefacedly that if their subjects were persecuted by their neighbours for the sake of the gospel they would not spring to their defence. They want to be good, sturdy jailers and executioners of common thieves, that is all.[61]

---

59. Münzter, "Testimony" and "A Manifest Exposé" (on facing pages), in *CWTM*, 253–323.

60. Münzter, "A Manifest Exposé," 282.

61. Münzter, "A Manifest Exposé," 286, 286–88, 316.

In other words, political leaders, rulers and princes want the power God has mandated them but without the subsequent responsibilities toward the salvation of their peoples. They have instead pursued their own worldly desires and thus perverted the natural order of creation, subjecting man to other created beings rather than to the divine. Müntzer was also clearly offended by the inactivity of the Saxon princes in particular with regard to the refugee situation and with their commitment to the needs of faith. By the time he left Allstedt his patience had clearly been exhausted. His expectation of princes to serve and protect the elect and the gospel had been dashed for the last time. It was high time the world recognized the "bigwigs" for the false Christians and hypocrites they really were: "He has torn down the mighty from their seat, since they presume to exercise authority over faith and to subject it to their will, although they themselves have not learned how faith comes about. Yet they set about condemning everyone . . ."[62] Sometime before mid-September, Müntzer arrived in the imperial city of Mülhausen, where the Reformation was under the leadership of the radical former priest, Heinrich Pfeiffer.

Mülhausen was a city divided between classes and political tensions (a patrician council of magistrates opposed the representatives of the city districts—the Eight—who represented the artisan interests) and this tension served as a backdrop to Müntzer's follow up treatise *Vindication and Refutation*. As the title indicates it was both a defence of the ideas expressed in the *Expose* and a criticism of Luther's recent *Letter* with his encouragement of wrong-headed political, social and religious ideas. It is also a political statement in broad terms in that the themes of the two previous treatises are further developed, merging other divergent ideas. Rather than the politically charged Rom 13 or Dan 2, the proof text here is John 8, where the theme is persecution—Christ's by the Pharisees, Müntzer's at the hands of Luther. But he also wanted to remind Luther of the wider implications of his *priesthood* doctrine (as filtered through Müntzer's experiential salvation theology) in which the power of the sword rests with the entire community of the elect (i.e., the church) and so is only wielded by the secular lord on the behalf of the people and in service to justice and equity. "From the passages in Daniel 7[:27], Revelation 6[:15*ff*], Romans 13[:1] and 1 Kings 8 I pointed out that the princes are not lords over the sword but servants of it. They should not act as they please, but execute justice."[63] Luther has become a toady to princely ambitions, allowing them to wrestle the sword from the community and use it to serve their own worldly drives. In this

---

62. Münzter, "Testimony," 283.
63. Münzter, "Vindication and Refutation," in *CWTM*, 334.

way the church is just as ill served by him as it is by the traditional Roman hierarchy. Indeed, thanks to Luther, no one really monitors princely use of the sword or complains about them at all. Justice can only be failed in such a situation; insurrection against such princes will put matters right again and the elect will rule as they should. To that end he and Pfeiffer put forward a proposal in Mülhausen for the dissolution of the existing council and for the formation of an "eternal council" which would execute God's word, justice and defend the Reformation.

For Müntzer, the church and the community of the elect are one and the same thing and leadership of the community still takes the form of necessary secular rulers on the one hand and religious leaders (priests, prophets) on the other. But with the *Peasants' Revolt* in full swing, more radical voices were emerging. Thomas Grebel of Zürich, for example, wrote to Müntzer on 5 September 1524 to make common cause but also to express a different opinion on this issue of the secular authority and the church. "One should not," wrote Grebel, "protect the gospel and its adherents with the sword, either, nor should they protect themselves . . . True believing Christians are sheep in the midst of wolves, sheep for slaughtering." We shall examine Grebel, the Swiss Brethren, and Anabaptist sectarians (as Bible literalists) shortly. In his effort to energize Reformation fervour among the masses Müntzer and Pfeiffer produced and distributed the so-called *Eleven Mühlhausen Articles*, which were also sent out to the peasants in the city's environs to raise further support.

If nothing else *Articles* tell us that secular government for Müntzer is necessary for the church to function properly. The city government in Mülhausen, however, were sorely lacking having not been elected with the fear of God in mind.[64] Luther and the other magisterial reformers had created a "half-baked mixture of those outside and those inside" the true faith. The *priesthood of all believers* is a good starting point, but the community must then actually choose its own leadership. To ensure this magistrates would have no fixed term in office so that they could be turned out in practice (not just in theory) if this became necessary, and unjust councillors were to be executed. No one is to be compelled to govern against their will, and they were to be paid a sufficient wage to protect against greed. Moreover, public records were to be kept of all their decisions and actions and all decisions would bear the common seal, developing an idea of transparency in government. *Articles* attracted considerable popular support within the city but was rejected by the patrician council on 19 September, resulting in

---

64. Münzter and Pfeiffer, "The Mühlhausen Articles," in *CWTM*, 455.

ineffectual violence in the environs of the city.[65] Müntzer and Pfeiffer were expelled. Much the same thing happened to Müntzer in Nuremberg.

Müntzer wandered for a time only to return to Mülhausen in February 1525. Pfeiffer had returned earlier and succeeded rousing support for Müntzer's reorganization of the city government. On 17 March 1525 the "eternal council" was elected and began a city-wide reorganization, taking a defensive posture. We already know the result.

Müntzer, and Karlstadt, as noted, started with the essential evangelical position on the necessity of secular rulers in accordance with Scripture and natural law. In much of this Luther had set the tone with his *priesthood of all believers*, unwilling though he was to see it through to its not unreasonable conclusions. Zwingli had taken the issue in another direction, forgoing the division between the two kingdoms, establishing instead a theocracy in which secular rulers and religious leaders worked in tandem for the good of the church and society both. He divided tasks, however, between the spiritual and political offices. Müntzer united these underlying philosophies, removing the artificial divisions between the kingdoms, emphasizing the duties of the secular rulers in both the earthly and spiritual realms—rulers elected out of the elect community and subject to its oversight and discipline by that community. The sword became a symbol or badge of office in a more significant way than even a crown, and was subject to removal, even violent removal, if the secular ruler did not do his specific Godly duty. Nonetheless, radical, mystic or magisterial reformer aside, secular rulers did have a clear authority within and over the church because they had a divine mandate as God's sword-bearer. The Swiss Brethren and Anabaptist communities, extreme Biblicists among them, disagreed with all of them.

Anabaptists:
The Staff Bearers and the Sword Bearers

"Anabaptist" is a label applied to a broad collection of localized groups. Some were extreme Biblicists, others were apocalyptic mystics. They

---

65. *CWTM*, 132–4 (letter 70).

sported some limited common beliefs, but were fragmented by many disagreements (amongst themselves and with the magisterial reformers). Chief among these variances was the extent of cooperation with secular governments, participation in government, and the extent of secular influence over church matters.

At one end of the spectrum of doctrinal commitment were the so-called *stäbler* Anabaptists (or the "staff bearers"), adherents of a belief-system worked out by Grebel, Sattler and the *Schleitheim Articles*. They were separatists; their church of the elect was isolated from the wider society entirely. Grebel would go so far as to hold that genuine believers could not be magistrates at all (that is, they could not engage in any government-related work) and, in corollary, no magistrate could possibly be a genuine believer because of his involvement with the world and its many temptations. Eventually this doctrine was agreed as normative for many groups, and it was embodied in article six at Schleitheim. At the other end were the so-called *schwertler* Anabaptists (or the "sword bearers"). They followed thinkers like Hubmaier into a non-separatist tradition where going to war and paying special war taxes was acceptable for believers in support of the government.[66] For them, although rare certainly, magistrates could be genuine believers and *vice-versa*, and Hubmaier argued strongly that Christians should participate in government—"just" government (that is, where the word of God held sway). Thinkers like Marpeck, Simons and Denck generally fell somewhere between these two extremes, while those like Hut embodied a violence-orientated position.

Where most agreed, among themselves and with the magisterial reformers, was the belief that no matter what else might be in evidence secular government was a divine creation and thus had a divine mandate to rule over the physical world for the purpose of dealing with the wicked. What they wanted to do, however, was redefine the role of secular authority according to their own varied doctrines of the church. Luther's *doctrine of the two kingdoms* had influence. Most Anabaptists agreed that secular government was created by God to perform specific functions of an earthly nature—to protect and reward the good (i.e., genuine Christians, the elect) and punish the wicked. The government keeps order in the world with the sword, with human laws and traditions, and will do so while non-believers exist. Many Anabaptists also made a distinction between heretics and dissenters on one hand and criminals on the other. This was a distinction the magisterial reformers rarely made and consequently used the power of

---

66. For discussion of the distinctions, see Bender, "The Anabaptist Vision," 51; and Houde, "Anabaptism," 252.

the state inappropriately (in Anabaptist's eyes) as a moral arbiter (e.g., the marriage court and synod of Zürich). Putting aside Müntzer's late tendency toward violence and bloodshed (trying to force the issue), the various Anabaptist groups more or less sought to extract from the civil authorities freedom of worship within their own congregations. They wanted to worship without interference from secular authorities (how they understood *priesthood of all believers*).

— § —

Grebel and the Swiss Brethren: Separatism

The Swiss Brethren parted company with the magisterial reformers (in this case with Zwingli specifically) over questions of what qualified as specifically scriptural matters (i.e., matters of faith alone), those not subject to state controls and civil authority. The simple desire to separate their church and their faith from state interference was not necessarily an indictment of the state or an insurrection *per se*—the Anabaptist groups generally shared a desire to worship free of secular coercion—but in the era of the *Peasants' Revolt* anything could be made to look more radical than it actually was. In essence, however, the Swiss Brethren movement grew out of disaffection with Zwingli's tendency to delay complete reform until he was sure of public opinion and his habit of deferring to the magistrates for discipline, final decisions, and implementation of new doctrines or approaches.

Harold Schaff traced the origins of Anabaptism to the second Zürich disputation of 26 October 1523. There, Grebel had charged Zwingli with only a half-realized *sola scriptura* on the issue of the Mass, and Simon Stumpf raised questions on civil participation in church matters.[67] Hubmaier was a witness to this disagreement. An argument could be made for the earlier origin, however, in the tithe disputes which developed in the small villages around Zürich but, whichever is the case, both matters involved questions over the extent of secular power in subjectively religious issues.

The issue of the abolition of tithe assessments—a tax which supported clergy in the city—was taken up in a petition in six rural villages. The complaint was less about the money and more about the fact that the canons of the Grossmünster misappropriated the funds and consequently failed to provide evangelical preaching in the villages. Zwingli was a key protester as early as 1520. He preached that tithes were not scriptural and therefore should

---

67. Schaff, "The Anabaptists," 37.

be voluntary within the community as a moral obligation in support of preachers (i.e., a sufficient wage) but, as was his habit, he then waited for the parishioners themselves and the magistrates to test and act upon the issues raised. When a parishioner of Stumpf, in Höngg, did act on the proposed principle of voluntary payments, by reducing his grain tithe contribution, the council put the objector in prison. Soon other parishioners were petitioning the council for relief from their own obligations.

In a letter of 17 June 1523 Grebel was also awaiting a decision from the council. His was handed down on 22 June upholding tithe payments. Adding insult to injury, Zwingli consequently preached a sermon arguing that, while on the level of divine justice, tithes and interest payments were wrong-headed, on a purely human, material, and social level, everyone should pay as the government commanded it for the good of society. He had designated tithes as a material rather than divine issue, and thus within the secular mandate. Grebel, however, equated the decision with tyranny and was disappointed by Zwingli's capitulation.[68] Stumpf and other rural priests meanwhile called for resistance to further payments both as a protest against the established Roman hierarchy and in support of local spiritual needs, calling for a self-directed community Reformation.

The question became whether tithing was a religious or secular issue and the three men found themselves at odds. Zwingli sided with the government; Grebel and Stumpf siding with the rural congregations. Both sides claimed the support of the gospel. According to Stayer, the tithe issue would later become a rallying point for the violence which followed in the spring and summer of 1525; in 1523, however, it merely simmered in the background.[69] With regard to the other basic Reformation issues, nothing had officially been carried out for several months after the first disputation and, as revision was postponed and re-examined, demonstrations of public frustration mounted. The second disputation (26–28 October) took place in a tense atmosphere.

As an introductory statement Zwingli let it be known that the disputation had been assembled solely to discern the Word of God on the issues which had cropped up (e.g., the use of images) in the nine months since the first assembly. He warned that they were not assembled to discuss how their findings were to be implemented, as this was the prerogative of the magistrates. Here then was the very issue which had disturbed the consciences of some of his students and disciples—just what were the boundaries of the council's prerogative on issues which affected the church? Should the magistrates have

---

68. Harder, ed., *Grebel*, 207–13.
69. Stayer, "The Anabaptists and the Sects," 119–20.

anything to do with religious issues, like images and the Mass, issues determined by the church interpreting Scripture under the influence of the Holy Spirit? Some heated debate ensued between Zwingli and Stumpf in the presence of Grebel and Hubmaier—the men who would emerge as the leaders of the breakaway church in Switzerland and southern Germany.

Putting aside the utility of images, on the second day of the disputation Grebel raised the issue that priests should be given instruction on changes to the Mass. In context he was doing no more than asking the magistrates not to delay further instruction in the matter. Zwingli repeated his opening remark: "Milords will discern how the mass should henceforth be properly observed"—in other words, the assembly would discern the scriptural teachings and the practical applications of that discernment would be in the hands of the council. Stumpf objected; "Master Huldrych! You have no authority to place the decision in Milord's hands, for the decision is already made: the Spirit of God decides. If therefore Milords were to discern and decide anything that is contrary to God's decision, I will ask Christ for his Spirit and will teach and act against it." Stumpf rejected participation by the secular authorities in the decisions of the church as crossing a barrier between earthly and divine matters. Zwingli agreed that there was a barrier of sorts, the magistrates do not "decide about God's Word," but reminded his friend that this was not the point of the assembly. Once the meaning of Scripture was discerned the assembly and council would together try to find the means to act without causing disruption and "uproar."[70] It was the magistrates' duty to keep the peace (how to implement the Reformation fell under that category).

With regard to basic reforms nothing was officially done for several months as numerous revisions were proposed and postponed and demonstrations mounted. Grebel's disillusionment was fully expressed on 18 December 1523. In a letter to his brother-in-law he outlined the growing schism in Zürich between declarations of principle and implementation of decisions by the council and Zwingli. He and Stumpf hatched a plan for a separatist church and presented it to Zwingli a few days later (as Zwingli recounted in his *Refutation* a few years later).

They proposed a separate church of the elect, faithful to scriptural principles and out of which a new council was to be elected—a Christian magistracy—to implement its required changes. In essence this sounds ominous and revolutionary; since the faithful would be isolated from the temptations of mixed society they would eventually reduce the need for civil authority altogether. Grebel actually meant no more than that the faithful

70. Harder, ed., *Grebel*, 242.

(i.e., the congregation) would elect its own church council or a *council of the elect* to make and implement its own ecclesiastical decisions. Zwingli, however, took this suggestion as a wilful misunderstanding of Scripture and as an attempt to replace the secular town council with a puppet institution. Grebel later argued that there had been no question that secular authority was to be obeyed but that church specific issues (i.e., matters of faith) would best be made and carried out by the faithful themselves—it was to have been a distinctive church within secular society.

Although this was in line with wider evangelical thinking Zwingli counselled against what he understood as a separation of the church—a real schism—while Grebel/Stumpf meant only a separation from the magisterial church *per se*. Their opinion was that the church of the believers would grow and prosper as the magisterial church fell into decline as the people became genuinely Christian. The one would eventually replace the other. All secular issues remained in the hands of the magistrates as they protected the entire process. Zwingli believed, however, that the magisterial church would itself grow and change as the Word was promulgated and understanding spread among the masses. There was no need to force the issue, and he also feared for the confusion two churches would cause, envisioning chaos. So the hiving off of a separatist church had little to do with obedience to secular authority *per se* but rather to a division over the extent of magisterial authority in strictly religious matters (and which specifically were those solely religious matters). Over time some Anabaptist leaders began to conceive of the church as an alternate society just as the early Christians had rejected the norms of Roman society. Following the *Peasants' Revolt* and subsequent persecutions they would finally also reject the norms of European society (e.g., Münster in the early 1530s).[71]

By 3 September 1524 Grebel had been silent long enough. He began writing letters—famously to Müntzer, but also to Karlstadt and some others. It is clear that waiting on the decision of the council to act was his main bugbear. "Look at the reason for all my audacity; I have waited, and they have not spoken." He would base his actions on *sola scriptura*. Two of his letters to Müntzer present a vision of a separate believers' church, free of state supervision and pacifist by design: "do not protect the gospel and its adherents with the sword, either, nor should they protect themselves . . . True believing Christians are sheep in the midst of wolves, sheep for slaughtering . . . They use neither worldly sword nor war, since killing has ceased with them entirely."[72]

71. McGrath, *Reformation Thought*, 219.
72. Harder, ed., *Grebel*, 283–84, 290.

By *worldly sword* historians think Grebel meant civil government. He was taking matters of faith completely out of the secular world and influence. He and his Swiss Brethren had also abandoned the idea of the genuinely Christian magistrate. Once a separatist church of believers had been mooted (without the interference of civil powers in matters of faith), the reality of it was swift, leading to such doctrine as believers' baptism and debates over discipline, the ban, the Lord's Supper and many other divisive issues, not least of which was socio-political isolationism. In many ways the dispute over the involvement of secular authorities in matters of faith, which issues this encompassed, the foundation of a separatist church and Zwingli's (mis)understanding of the Grebel/Stumpf proposal shortly became caught up in their decision to defy the council on the issues of infant and adult baptism and, of course, the *Peasants Revolt* tarred them all as revolutionaries. Officially, however, the *städler* Anabaptists did not hold a revolutionary position, but they were on the extreme.

— § —

The Schleitheim Articles: Non-Resisting Separation

In the aftermath of the *Peasants' Revolt* and with their leaders being arrested and executed as extremists and revolutionaries, millenarian or "end of the world" beliefs started to form a major element in Swiss Brethren thinking. Anabaptists of the Grebel tradition envisioned a world in which earthly rule had been swept away along with the unbelievers. With the second coming of Christ, the saved—the elect—would obviously have no need of magistrates or secular authorities as material concerns would not be an issue. At that point scriptural appeals to obey the law and render unto Caesar would also be quite meaningless. This was the world anticipated by Sattler and the formulators of the articles (one that Müntzer wanted to force into existence). Until that world was a reality, however, a base obedience would be rendered if the demands of government were not in conflict with the teachings of Christ. Anabaptists should, however, separate themselves from the evils of the world now so as to avoid anything which might stain their spiritual salvation later. To some *Articles* became a "radical articulation of a strict separation of church and state," rejecting service (as a magistrate), wielding the sword or swearing oaths—all of which obviously had secular repercussions.[73]

73. Urry, *Mennonites*, 19–20.

This in mind *Articles* addressed Anabaptists of the non-separatist tradition with an explanation of both doctrine and principles.

First and foremost, however, Sattler made plain that the formulators of *Articles* were not antinomians, like some of the more radical sectarians. They did not use their spiritual beliefs as justification for disobedience or violence, since secular authority was also divine in origin and due obedience. He then explained what their doctrinal beliefs were in anticipation of that glorious world to come. The fourth article presented an extreme view of the Lutheran *doctrine of the two kingdoms* juxtaposing the two as "good and evil, believing and unbelieving, darkness and light." Although secular government was not yet mentioned specifically, abandonment of the sword and the obligation of using it and all violence was rejected in article six, using *Matt* 5:39 ["You should not resist evil"] as a proof text. Civil government, "the sword"—specifically the secular power of coercion—was certainly of divine creation but was to be directed at specific earthly purposes—protect the good, punish the wicked—and was not a matter in dispute. But, as a disciplinary device in and over the church, secular coercive authority had to be rejected.

This was a little self-serving; Luther, Zwingli (and later Calvin) were all quite willing to turn the power of the government against religious dissenters, and the church handing heretics over for secular punishment was a mediaeval norm. For Sattler, within the church, within the "perfection of Christ", the ban was sufficient in dealing with the sinner and the heretic. Here is a tacit call for toleration—heretics only harm themselves and those willing to be harmed by their views will be punished by God. In any case, the Christian may not use the sword against the wicked (as that was the charge of the secular power), nor serve as a judge in worldly courts, nor hold a government position (as that way worldly temptations lay). They would be obedient but they would not participate.

Articles takes as a starting point a pure community of the Spirit to be separate from but, (currently and necessarily) existing within the world of the flesh (just as the soul resides trapped within the body). There are obvious political overtones in *Articles'* conclusion against the swearing of oaths as well. The basis of rejection is that human flesh is weak so that an oath may later be forsworn under some external pressure. Only God can swear an oath and be eternally unswerving, so swearing of oaths was to be rejected as pointless.[74] For Sattler it did not matter if the magistrate was a Christian (given the conditions he was laying down it seems unlikely he could be).

---

74. Baylor, *Revelation*, 175–79. Also see, Eno, *Subjects or Citizens?*, 3–5.

Although *Articles* stood in direct opposition to Hubmaier's doctrine, with Grebel's support it became a staple of Anabaptist sectarian belief.

—— § ——

Balthasar Hubmaier: Cooperation with the Secular Power

Hubmaier had witnessed the brief but heated exchanges between Zwingli, Grebel and Stumpf at the second disputation and he became a sincere Zwingli adherent as a result. Except in one small area, however, there is little to distinguish his and Zwingli's opinions. The exception was over images (a hot topic). Hubmaier noted that, given the clear word of God, the genuine value of images would be recognized, "then a whole parish congregation will gather and decide unanimously without any disorder that the images shall be moved out and laid to sleep."[75] This reads like Zwingli's wait and see position but it could also be an early hint in support of something like Grebel's council of the elect. Although Hubmaier thought of himself as a Zwinglian, his subsequent writings indicate a growing association with the Brethren well before his own baptism into the sect by Reuchlin. However, he also came to express different opinions to Grebel and Sattler on the possibility of the genuinely Christian secular authority and on the use of the temporal sword. Zwingli's *Sixty-seven Articles* (articles thirty-five to forty-three) was Hubmaier's base-line on temporal power.

Zwingli made Scripture and sound Christian moral principles the twin nexus of secular oversight of the covenantal commune. Thus, if a ruler were to base his rule on the word of God, little appears to lie beyond the scope of his power. He could be opposed or replaced only in the event that he started to rule or act contrary to "the guiding principles of Christ."[76] Zwingli's *Articles* was the basis of Hubmaier's own *Eighteen theses concerning the Christian life*, published as the basis of a Zürich-like disputation he hosted in Waldshut. For very different reasons, however, the civil authorities in the Austrian town were not invited to act as judges as had "Milords" of Zürich. Yet it seems clear that some common understanding with Grebel had been made.

In Hubmaier's thirteenth article, for instance, a reference to the obligations of the "fellows of the congregation" included support of the preachers, evoking the idea of the establishment of a council of the elect and articulation of its duties. His point here, unlike Grebel's, was the elimination of

75. "Statements at the Second Zurich Disputation," 26.
76. Noll, *Confessions*, 44.

benefice-seeking "courtesans"—that is, priests more interested in economic or political advancement—than in the hiving off of a separatist church with hand-picked pseudo-magistrates defending it. Hubmaier thought that the "fellows" would only aid in the encouragement of local dedicated shepherds. In this way, "pensioners, members of *collegia*, absentees, and babblers of lies and dreams" would all be discouraged. This is not a long way off, however, from Grebel's plan for the corrupted church to die off through attrition.[77]

A short time after the publication of *Eighteen theses* rumours and incidents of rebel violence spread. Waldshut initially adopted a mediating position between the peasants and the nobles, but there was sympathy for the evangelical movement. This was a result of Hubmaier's preaching, which clashed with the Catholic beliefs of the Austrian rulers. While Hubmaier was personally prepared to man the walls, pike in hand on guard against Catholic forces, others were less willing to risk destruction. He moved to the more accommodating nearby evangelical Swiss town of Schaffhausen for political refuge in early September 1524. A question of extradition, however, was raised by the nearby Catholic cantons. The basis of an arrest warrant was that Hubmaier had preached against tithes, interest rates, and rents, and that he had rejected the norms of feudal society and rule.[78] Although the Schaffhausen magistrates did not act upon the warrant, the charges would hang over him as these same issues were taken up by the peasant rebels. Hubmaier wrote out a series of appeals to the local magistrates against an impending arrest order and extradition, putting his views into context.

Among other clearly Zwinglian statements he outlined two relevant political beliefs. The first was a generally positive view of government *per se* as the creation of God. The second was a desire to take the ultimate control of religion out of the hands of the state—a freedom of religion position of the *two kingdoms* variety—placing it firmly in the hands of the congregation. In this way, for instance, an Austrian would owe Archduke Ferdinand fealty and service of the body and goods but would admit to no control over his soul and conscience. Hubmaier placed himself under the judgement of the local magistrates: "But if I should be found to be in the wrong, your Honours have sword, fire, and water that can cut, burn and drown here as well as elsewhere; in accord with the circumstances of the offence you should then not let me go without punishing me with prison and death"—a common, general statement of the magisterial duty to protect the church from heterodoxy.[79] Hubmaier recognized the secular lords' rights to judge: "He calls judges servants

---

77. Hubmaier, "Eighteen Theses," 34.
78. Scott, "Hubmaier, Schappeler and Hergot," 20.
79. Hubmaier, "An Earnest Christian Appeal," 39, 41, 47.

of God who are to sit and rule on Earth in God's stead," provided God's word was the baseline of their judgements and their final authority. This was in line with Zwingli's view of magisterial responsibility to judge disputations and implement decisions.[80] Subsequent experiences, however, forced Hubmaier away from the Zwinglian baseline position.

In his treatise *On heretics and those who burn them*, for instance, we find Hubmaier casting some limited disapproval. Articles twenty to twenty-four form a block dealing with questions of secular authority and its limitations. While he agreed that it is the secular power's duty to protect the good against the ravages of the wicked and the evil, this duty no longer included the punishment of unbelievers, dissenters and heretics—the "godless"—as they are the exclusive responsibility of the church. Either they are to be corrected in their spiritual beliefs (i.e., the Rule of Christ) or to be ignored as outside of the church (through the ban). The church should no longer hand heretics over to the state. Christians use the word of God against non-believers (which is the spiritual sword so often designated), while the state exercises justice against the wicked. The tacit assumption was that non-believers and heretics are not also necessarily wicked by secular definition. Hubmaier was taking the generally accepted division between the *two kingdoms* and re-examining the boundary.

In essence he was saying nothing more than that the wicked (those who wreck physical damage to their neighbours) are not of the same condition as sinners and heretics and, so, need to be treated differently. The reasons are outlined in article twenty-two. Evil-doers cause bodily harm and material damage against uncooperative or unknowing victims while unbelievers or heretics cause harm only to someone willing to be influenced away from the gospel. The secular authority cannot reach into the conscience—into the heart and soul—of each person (as only God has that power) so cannot know the entire truth of the matter and cannot force change through sword, fire or water. In article twenty-four he affirmed that it was possible that God could turn the evil of heretics and unbelievers to some good through preachers, teachers and patient instruction in the Bible, all of which secular authorities cannot do (although they can provide and support the preachers and teachers who do so).[81] All Hubmaier is really doing is re-thinking the common mediaeval equating of the heretic with the rebel; by implication he was making a case for toleration and religious liberty.[82] Association with the peasant rebels, however, when placed beside pleas for religious freedom on

---

80. Hubmaier, "An Earnest Christian Appeal," 44.
81. Hubmaier, "Heretics," 63–64.
82. Estep, *Revolution within the Revolution*, 28–30.

their behalf and a move in the direction of a believers' church and adult baptism made life rather difficult for Hubmaier in Catholic Austria. Although he maintained that the people of Waldshut were prepared to render the Austrian authorities the obedience due them, he put in the proviso that their religious freedoms be recognized. It was not long after this that Hubmaier was condemned by Zwingli as an adherent to re-baptism, and that Waldshut fell under the archduke's microscope. Hubmaier fled the town, to reduce the danger to his congregation, turning up in Zürich on 5 December 1525. Fearing that his appearance would stir up sectarian trouble he was taken into custody by the town council on Zwingli's recommendation.

Hubmaier was imprisoned but after a disputation with Zwingli (in the presence of members of the council) he recanted his theology before the Small Council and subsequently before the Two Hundred. His rehabilitation was marred, however, when he recanted the recantation before a large congregation audience in which Zwingli was present (29 December). Hubmaier was seized in the pulpit and dragged off to Wellenberg—the island prison set aside for the housing of Anabaptists, where he had plenty of time to write and reconsider his doctrine (between torture sessions). Under these conditions a second recantation was secured; this time it was written out and subsequently published (a few days after he left Zürich for Moravia).

— § —

Hubmaier had been accused of leading an insurrection. In his *Recantation*, however, Hubmaier denied the charge that he barred Christians from government: "Ever and always I have said that a Christian can be in government, and that the more Christian he is, the more honourable he would rule."[83] In this way he denied association with some of the more radical Swiss Anabaptist sectarians, and he was allowed to leave Zürich for the far more tolerant city of Nikolsburg. Hans Hut was based there and it did not take long for the two men to divide the Anabaptist community between their rival ideals. Hut, a follower of Müntzer's apocalyptic and millenarian views, championed the use of the sword as a cleansing device against the "godless." He somehow united under his banner advocates of extreme non-resistance, non-cooperation (e.g., those who refused to pay taxes), and those who were violence orientated. Against this majority view Hubmaier upheld both the legitimacy of secular government (as divinely mandated) and the state (which alone was mandated to wield the sword), thus departing from both the non-resistance and violent revolutionary themes. They

---

83. Hubmaier, "Recantation at Zürich," 152.

agreed, ideally, that all spiritual matters would be under church authority exclusively, but their divisions occasioned many rival treatises. Key to our understanding of Hubmaier are two—*A Brief Apologia* (June 1526) and *On the Sword* (June 1527).

In *Apologia* Hubmaier reconsidered many of the issues which had finally brought him to Nikolsburg—the charges and accusations which had dogged him since Waldshut and his related theological and scriptural exegesis. Among many things said about him, "I am a revolutionary and a seducer of the people; I preach that no one should obey the government, nor pay interest or tithes"[84] (perhaps confusing him with the followers of Sattler), and he was often accused of wishing to tear down the system of feudal obligations, quite apart from leading peasant insurrections (like Müntzer). Hubmaier answered back:

> No preacher in the areas I have been has gone to more trouble and labor in writing and preaching than I in order that people should be obedient to the government. Since it is of God, who hung the sword at its side, one should without contraction render to it tolls, duties, tribute, honor, and respect . . . on the other hand I have also told the government to wield the sword according to the order of God for the protection of the righteous and the punishment of the evil, or God will take away its mandate and mete out to it the same measure . . . never in my life have I taught that subjects should not fulfil the duty and obedience due to their government. Rather, when even heavier burdens are imposed upon them that are not contrary to God (whom one should obey more than people) they are to take them up willingly and carry them with patience as their cross.

For Hubmaier, godliness and justice should clearly determine the limits placed on the obligations of the poor. On the tithe issue he noted that "a Christian does not quarrel or fight, rather he gives a fifth or a third, not to mention a tenth of his goods. Yes, he also lets his coat go with his cloak, Matt. 5:40." Later in the same work he spelled out the duties of government: "learn to do good, practice justice, help the oppressed, judge for the orphan, render assistance to the widows . . . hear everybody and do not sentence and condemn anyone uncharged, unheard, yes even unseen, only on the basis of false witness." It seems, for Hubmaier, that nothing falls outside the oversight of the secular power. Having said that; "if a cause were too difficult for the world government and would concern the faith of the Christian Church, then one

---

84. Hubmaier, "A Brief Apologia," 298.

should immediately refer it to Moses, that is, to the Scripture."[85] He shared with Zwingli the opinion that government is involved in all matters, but in matters of faith it needs to be well advised or even to turn over the issues to the church. Hubmaier noted that secular government, acting in good faith, could expect God would supply righteous preachers and teachers for their cause.

We have examined Zwingli's doctrine in chapter two and noted above his more radical-minded disciples taking exception to his magisterial-led reform movement. They questioned whether secular authority (local or national) have the right to implement Reformation and raised questions about a separation between the church or the congregation or even the individual Christian and the secular power. Some followed this up with a question of whether or not a Christian could legitimately wield the sword on behalf of the government and, if so, should he so do. Clearly, the Swiss Brethren and *Schleitheim* view was pacifist. Christians do not wield the sword or cooperate with secular powers in order to avoid associated worldly temptations like greed. They practice non-violent resistance and should be prepared to suffer for their beliefs. Hut, echoing Müntzer, took another view, however. The elect must sometimes grab the sword away from apathetic secular figures and actively resist the wicked for themselves. Hubmaier expressed a minority viewpoint—he had a positive understanding of the role and authority of secular government (he kept appealing to rulers for support) like Zwingli and Luther, and a positive position on a Christian's use of the sword in co-operation with the civil authorities (as a divine command clearly evident in Scripture). All he asked in return was that the secular authority be prepared to base its judgements on the word of God and turn over to the church clearly spiritual matters over which the magistrates had no real mandate to rule. This was the central message of *On the Sword*, directed against the majority view of non-cooperation and opposing both Hut's more violent stance and the passivity of the Swiss Brethren.

Here, Hubmaier considered the scriptural passages used by his opponents in justification of their positions and highlighted where they were being unrealistic, overly idealistic, or where they had taking the Scripture too far out of context. In this way, where Grebel or Sattler portrayed the world and the church as mutually exclusive (and even hostile), Hubmaier could present them instead as separate but complimentary entities. The church is in the world and, tasked as it is with the reconciliation of fallen mankind to

---

85. Hubmaier, "A Brief Apologia," 303–4, 304–5, 311–13.

God must work closely with worldly powers to that end, redeeming them eventually from the world. To paraphrase Mabry, the church nurtures man back to righteousness before God and, in this way, the kingdom of the world becomes the kingdom of Christ (without Grebel's separatism or Sattler's isolationism)—which was more or less Zwingli's position.

In the meantime, the church is in the evil world. The state must protect it so the church can perform its divine mandate. In return for protection the church prays for the state, supports it, and cooperates with it in the performance of its own divine mandate. They are not opposed; the world is not entirely evil and the two kingdoms can closely cooperate quite effectively. The church and state, clearly, are better off when they concentrate on their own tasks but this can be done without building a wall between them.[86] So, for example, in his exegesis of the first passage often used—John 18:36—Hubmaier admits that Christ may very well say that his kingdom was not of this world but clearly none of his still mortal followers can legitimately make the same claim: "help us out of this kingdom, we are stuck in it right up to our ears . . ."[87] Since Christians are in the world and subject to its temptations until they finally leave it they had best deal with it! Nowadays we might say something like *meeting the problems head on* or *beating the enemy at his own game*. This being the case, *Matt 26:52–4* is not an admonition against Peter for carrying a sword but rather for his wanting to use it inappropriately: "One should not stop protecting and guarding all righteous and innocent people . . . therefore the rulers are obliged for the sake of the salvation of their souls to protect and guard all innocent and peaceful people until a sure voice of God comes" to let them know their duty is finished. The secular rulers have many such protective duties, "therefore God has hung the sword at the government's side and has made it to be his servant."

The majority sectarian opinion (following Sattler) is that passages such as Luke 9:54–56 or 12:13ff support a claim that Christians cannot act as judges. This is based on the idea that Christ claimed for himself another mandate—the fulfilment of the Word. For Hubmaier this is not a rejection of the office *per se* but merely the recognition that he, personally, had no calling or mandate to act as a judge. Men have elections and thus summon judges, mayors, burgomasters and all sorts of secular rulers to their various offices and those summoned perform the office as almost a moral obligation. Indeed, it should always be the case that Christians, when they do require a judge, bring their issues to another Christian. To take his case to an unbelieving judge, in fact, Hubmaier considered quite

---

86. Mabry, *Balthasar Hubmaier's Doctrine of the Church*, 188–89.
87. Hubmaier, "On the Sword," 497.

wrong-headed: "If then, a Christian, by power of the divine word, may and should be a judge with the mouth, he may also be a protector with the hand of the one who wins justice and may punish the unjust. For what use would the law, court, and judge be if one were not allowed to carry out and enforce the punishment of the evil-doers?"

In the seventh passage he made an important distinction between secular punishments and the use of the ban (that point raised at Schleitheim) and based on the Rule of Christ in *Matthew*. The ban deals with only the unworthy and non-believers. Recall that Grebel thought the ban sufficient replacement for the governmental sword in all causes (as did Sattler in his sixth article). For Hubmaier they are simply two different, specific commands for two different issues, leading into his exegesis of Rom 13:7: "hand over tribute to whom tribute is due." Perhaps had sin not come into the world with the fall laws, sword, fire, etc., would be unnecessary. God had provided the ban for those sins which the sword cannot discern. Here we return to a distinction between physical crimes against persons or properties and issues like heresy or apostasy. The secular authority has the right or the duty to intervene and judge matters for their own good even where the disputants did not want it because it is also for the good of society as a whole. This segues nicely into the tenth passage—2 Cor 10:4ff—which the Brethren use as proof of Christians using for weapons only their faith and the Word. Again, Hubmaier makes a convincing deconstruction of the arguments distinguishing between two swords—the scriptural and the physical—both of which have specific and unique applications. In places Paul too clearly wrote of the physical weapon and elsewhere of the spiritual. Both are necessary. Hubmaier also dismantled the received meaning of Luke 22:25ff in his thirteenth passage.

The texts were often used as admonitions against earthly rule. Clearly, however, it was meant in context as an admonition against those who preach taking part in worldly affairs: "The passage does not forbid the government to Christians, but teaches us that we should not quarrel, fight, and strive about it, nor conquer land and people with the sword and with force." Preachers do not strive for the honour and dignity due to worldly princes and lords (as Roman bishops were apt to do). In the fifteenth passage Hubmaier focussed on the sectarians' basis for non-resistance (e.g., Eph 1:22-23 or Col 1:18) and drew an allusion to the physical as opposed to the spiritual.

Nature and the fall have determined that man is not a member under the head that is Christ except by virtue of his faith and, even so, we are clearly not all of the same office. This is reminiscent of some of the implications of the *priesthood of all believers*: "one should go forth with teaching; the other protecting; the third cultivating the earth . . . ," and he made a distinction between the spiritual and temporal realms reminiscent of Luther's. Finally, Hubmaier's exegesis of Rom 13:1ff as "confirmation of the government."[88] He was not suggesting blind obedience. The government has clear duties but it is also required to base its rule on the word of God and good citizens and subjects need to be aware of this. Where the government acts for the right reasons (that is, according to its divine mandate), "then help, counsel, and sustain it, as often and as much as you are commanded." However, for governments not acting according to its mandate (as tyrants perhaps), three options are left to the Christian—passive resistance, flight or sufferance.

The issue that put resistance to, or cooperation with, the secular power into the spotlight was the war against the Turkish threat to Austrian territory and Lord Leonard von Liechtenstein's levying of a dedicated war tax to finance the Moravian burden of defence. Hubmaier had a good personal relationship with the von Liechtenstein brothers, the "principal members" of his Moravian congregation, and he needed the continued protection of the non-Catholic Moravian aristocracy against the threat of being handed over to Archduke Ferdinand. From *On the Sword*, therefore, we see that it is the duty of the elect to aid the secular ruler however he can, provided the ruler is serving God's word. Hubmaier may have seen the defensive effort against the Turk in line with the ruler's duty to protect the church. As Stayer noted, however, this might have been a more cynical exercise then it appears and many Anabaptist refugees from Catholic Austria had much less positive experiences and, consequently, rejected positive views. Hut, in his apocalyptic fervour, rejected Hubmaier's pro-government stance out of hand. He saw the Turk as God's scourge of the non-elect and his group resisted both taking up the sword in service to the government and paying the war tax. He also denounced the *Schleitheim articles* which, therefore, became a bone of contention between sectarian groups from this point on.[89] In this way a less prominent concern of Swiss and South German Anabaptism was taken up by the largest sectarian immigrant-refugee community from 1527 and thereafter exported out again when the Austrian rulers tightened their grip over their Moravian subjects. We see this kind of pacifist, limited association, for instance, in Menno Simmons's work, in what Stayer termed the beginnings of "*apoliticalism.*"

---

88. Hubmaier, "On the Sword," 499, 507, 517, 520.

89. Stayer, "Anabaptists and the Sword Revisited," 117; Stayer, "The Anabaptist Revolt," 59.

Melchior Hoffman:
Anabaptism after Schleitheim

In the aftermath of the Schleitheim conference, and as a result of Hubmaier's Moravian experiences, Anabaptist exegesis on secular authority split into two dominant, rival, understandings. Growing in popularity was the Sattler model of pacifist separatism from the worldly authority, the other, growing less popular, was the Hut-Müntzer violence orientated, resisting, non-separatist, apocalyptic model. This second, millenarian in scope, was sub-divided between those who saw government in friendly (i.e., fighting on behalf of the elect) or unfriendly terms. Otherwise, only a very small percentage followed Hubmaier's model of cooperation with "Christian" governments (friendly or not), which was viewed suspiciously by many.

Hans Denck, for instance, noted in his treatise *Concerning True Love* (1527) how odd this minority position was. Yes, government is divine (in that it serves the wrath of God) but the Christian should never desire harm to another. Thus "a friend of God should not be in the government but out of it . . . subject to none but the Lord."[90] A true-believer cannot serve both God and man (i.e., two kingdoms doctrine). In 1532 Pilgram Marpeck, advocating the *Schleitheim Articles*, wrote *Confession*, approaching the issue in a different but familiar way.

> I admit worldly, carnal, and earthly rulers as servants of God in earthly matters, but not in the kingdom of Christ . . . to them rightfully belong all carnal honour, fear, obedience, tax, toll, and tribute. However, when such persons who hold authority become Christians . . . they may not use the aforementioned carnal force, sovereignty or ruling in the kingdom of Christ.[91]

The Sattler model of pacifist separatism came to represent a majority view as Anabaptism made its way into Northern Europe, leaving apocalyptic expectations behind but not forgotten (and increasingly desperate in its loss of advocates). Many historians consider Hut, for example, as the apogee of apocalyptic fervour. Paradise would be ushered in when the elect would draw "the sword of vengeance" against the enemies of God. For Hut and his followers violence was anticipated and approved in the long term rather than practised in the short—a perhaps too subtle line for most civil authorities.[92] As we shall see, Melchior Hoffman and his disciples at Münster rejected even this much subtlety, taking up the sword to usher in the apocalypse. He

---

90. Denck, "Concerning True Love," 249–50.
91. Marpeck, "Confession," 251–2.
92. Stayer, "Swiss-South German Anabaptism," 85.

was at the true summit of the Müntzer school of thought but, after Münster, it burned out. After Münster, passive non-conformity with the secular powers became the rule as Anabaptists were then viewed only as disruptive, non-cooperative, potential political and religious dissidents (whatever the truth of the local sect's belief system).

In the mid-to-late 1520s Hoffman was an obscure missionary of Zwinglianism in northern Germany, the Low Countries, and in Scandinavia. Zwingli's Eucharist doctrine was unacceptable in Luther-dominated regions. Complaints and persecution forced Hoffman south, finally to the Imperial city of Strasbourg in 1529. He was accepted, initially, because he shared with Martin Bucer and Wolfgang Capito (the local religious leaders) a view of the church as a complete community, as a moral force, and as the arbiter of clerical discipline. Hoffman agreed with both Hubmaier and Bucer that the pious magistrate could further the cause of the church by opposing false religion. A Christian, therefore, could be an office-holder and remain a Christian in his view so long as he was fulfilling the divine mandate to protect the good and punish the wicked. Although this would seem to echo Luther's *two kingdoms* doctrine, Hoffman placed limitations on the magistrates. For instance, if the prince tried to order his subjects to do something contradictory to the word of God, obedience was no longer a duty.

In a no longer extent treatise, *On the Sword*, Hoffman opposed Hubmaier and sided with Denck and Marpeck by allowing no place for the temporal sword *within* the church *per se*. When a prince attempts to impose a false faith on his subjects, for example, their duty to cooperate ended. Under normal circumstances the two kingdoms need never interfere in each other's functions. Hoffman agreed that the sword existed to punish the wicked and protect the church, but this was from *without* the congregation. Hoffman's theology otherwise was less well received as increasingly radically spiritualist which pushed him into the orbit of the local Anabaptist sectarians.

Hoffman carefully developed a view which saw church history in three stages: the earliest apostolic times; the period of papal tyranny; and, finally, the period of the Reformation. It was into this third (contemporary) period that the two witnesses of the end times would appear—Elijah and Enoch—precipitating violence, destruction of non-believers by the Turks and, finally, the return of Christ. It is certainly possible that such writings were attractive to the apocalyptic visionaries of the Hut school just as their basic piety, Biblicism, and mystical ideas were attractive to Hoffman. He met the visionaries Lienhard and Ursula Jost, collected and published their visions, and made himself a nuisance by presenting their case for a separate church and equal rights in a petition to the council, becoming a member of the sect himself in 1530. Unfortunately for him, this was a time when the Strasbourg clergy were at loggerheads with the magistrates over the very issue of a reformed church organization.

The magistrates advocated a slow and cautious move forward and resisted as long as they could seeing an established church into reality. Up to 1529 public opinion was not unified on the issue of what the church should be, and so the magistrates were willing to tolerate non-threatening sectarians in their midst (so as not to discourage their tolerant image and the many trade and industry benefits this brought). The last thing they needed or wanted, however, was a Grebel-like plan for a separate church in their midst. The Strasbourg council wanted to retain a final ecclesiastical authority. This had been wrested from the Roman bishop. Nor did they want to risk offending their temporal overlord, the Catholic emperor, by advertising or succumbing to their large sectarian community. An imperial mandate had been issued against the Anabaptists on 4 January 1528. As a city based on trade they did not want to lose the cosmopolitan feel which finally subscribing a religious view would threaten.[93] Magisterial toleration, however, allowed Anabaptism to flourish but offended the Strasbourg religious leaders (e.g., Bucer and Capito), who advocated anti-sectarian mandates and worked tirelessly to have the more famous sectarian leaders exiled. They had already seen off Sattler, Denck, Reublin and Marbeck prior to 1528. The presence of radical sects also tended to impede regular church services; infant baptism was down, congregations were thinning out. On 24 September 1530 the council's anti-sectarian mandate (of 1527) was renewed coincidentally with Hoffman's ill-timed petition. He avoided arrest by running away.

Hoffman returned north a committed Anabaptist, founding groups in and around Emden, while his Strasbourg disciples, known as "Melchiorites", were being rounded up. He did what he could to give succour to his followers in the city, even making surreptitious return visits. According to his biographers Christian Neff and Werner Packull, sometime between his Emden/Strasbourg round trips Hoffman had time to write and publish an exposition on *Romans* in which he rejected Christians carrying the temporal sword but insisting upon unconditional obedience to the secular authorities. With apocalyptic fervour on the rise, Hoffman came to see himself in the role of Elijah, with Strasbourg as the New Jerusalem to come.[94] Returning

---

93. Kreider, "The Anabaptists," 101.

94. Neff and Packull, *GAMEO*: http://www.gameo.org/encyclopedia/contents/

to Strasbourg in 1533, he was finally captured in May, having surrendered to the council. He foresaw the coming slaughter of the non-believers and hoped to sit out the massacre from behind the walls of the prison and under the protection of the magistrates who would, in the aftermath, use the secular sword to protect and/or establish the true faith again. Hoffman was treated well at first, allowed to write, receive guests, even attend council disputes and lecture occasional disciples but, over time, the conditions he was kept in got more and more severe and the predicted end times never came. He expected to be exiled again eventually, but when Melchiorites in Münster led that city to disaster (united Catholics, Lutherans and Reformed evangelicals in common cause against them) his fate was sealed.

In prison, Hoffman developed a doctrine of the church which placed "apostolic messengers" at the apex of a four tier hierarchy (over prophets, pastors and people). As the prophets could not be certain whether their dreams and visions were divine or diabolical, like the pastors and masses they too needed to be subject to some interpretive spiritual authority. As the messengers were guided by the Holy Spirit, in effect, the entire community was subject to the pronouncements of the messengers. They had "almost royal power" and were able to "enforce excommunication" as well.[95] Hoffman had clearly parted with *priesthood of all believers* and *two kingdoms* doctrine for an extreme version of Hubmaier's *fellows of the congregation* in opposition to the "congregational democracy" of *Schleitheim*. He also foresaw two pious kings emerging to protect the elect from the ravages of the emperor (which he wrote about in *On the pure fear of God*). In the treatise, King Solomon represented temporal authority and King Jonah represented spiritual power. Together, the two kings would usher in the second coming; as a prelude, Solomon would establish the "theocratic kingdom of peace."[96] Although Hoffman saw the Strasbourg magistrates in the Solomon role, his more radical Melchiorite disciples (led by Jan Mathijs and Jan van Leiden) determine the New Jerusalem was not Strasbourg, but Münster.

From the point of view of the sword and secular authority, Hoffman had momentarily occupied a theoretical middle ground between Hubmaier and Sattler. In his philosophy the elect played supporting roles to their magisterial defenders. The elect would pray, dig trenches, stand

H646.html.

95. Deppermann, *Hoffman*, 265.
96. Issak, "The Struggle for an Evangelical Town," 79.

guard duty, and man sentry positions on the walls but would not engage in actual killing (as this was a temporal duty). From prison Hoffman taught that the sword was in the hands of the secular ruler only and that Christians were not to hinder the government in their duty. If believers fill some position in government, and perform in accordance with God's word, he may also fulfil his function if this includes wielding the sword (an echo perhaps of Luther's functionalism and separation of man and office). Melchiorites in the north, however, under constant threat from their Hapsburg overlords dreamt only of the world to come, the expected two kings, and how to hurry this along.[97] They became theoretically more Hut than Hubmaier. Hoffman, for a time, endorsed the view that the victory of the saints' protectors would usher in an "earthly theocratic interregnum" prior to Christ's return, but some aspects of his message were vague and open to interpretation. The ungodly should be/will be (?) destroyed; the elect will rule, impervious to harm, injury, and the effects of sin; the founding of a theocracy will happen; and, the messengers will detail God's meaning to the masses. All that was needed was a charismatic leader.

Bernhard Rothmann and the Münster Debacle, 1530–1535

Rolf Klötzer examined events in Münster in order to explain them without reference to too much related propaganda (e.g., internal sectarian pamphleteering or hostile external reports). In his view, what might otherwise have been a moderately controversial example of magisterial-type Reformation—a Luther sympathetic council and its clash with a Zwingli influenced popular preacher—turned into something far more bizarre, featuring apocalyptic fervour, militant Melchoiritism, and rampant sexual incontinence.

Like many important cities of the day tensions existed between key groups. Within the city, on the one hand were aristocrats (who dominated the council) and, on the other, the leaders of the powerful trade guilds (who acted as aldermen and petitioned the council on behalf of the population). Both groups sought greater freedom from external episcopal control. Münster was both a key member of the Hanseatic trade league and the seat of an important prince-bishop of the empire.[98] As elsewhere, but amplified,

---

97. Fingers, *A Contemporary Anabaptist Theology*, 297; Stayer, "The Anabaptist Revolt," 66.

98. Stayer, "The Anabaptist Revolt," 66.

anticlerical tensions existed against both the local monasteries (monks were charged with the usual faults) and episcopal rule. The authority of the bishop was fragile; although important, Münster was considered more a stepping stone on the ladder of a greater episcopal career (no less than three bishops had been created in rapid succession by the 1530s). Demands from the guilds against monastic manufacturing had been accepted by both the council and the Cathedral chapter which hinted at agreement on other socio-political issues and evangelical religious reforms. The potentialities were never fully realised, however, as the uncertainties created by the *Peasants' Revolt* clouded the issues.[99]

At St Mauritz (a church on the outskirts of the city) Rothmann was spreading basic evangelical doctrine and attracting large crowds from the city and the vicinity, while also taking occasional study trips to such places at Wittenberg and Strasbourg. His was a co-mingling of Lutheran and Zwinglian doctrine which alarmed the leading Catholic figures. He was finally forbidden to preach in summer 1531. This action raised tension between Catholics demanding an Imperial order be processed against him and the guilds, aldermen, and citizens rising in his favour as one of their own. As a block, the latter pressured the council to back the preacher against the Catholic establishment. The parishioners of St Lambert's, in a provocative act then installed Rothmann as their pastor on 23 February 1532, defying both bishop and civic mandates.

The appointment, *ad hoc* though it was, came on the back of a confession of faith in thirty articles which had just been published by Rothmann a month earlier. He supported the right of the congregation to select its own pastor, mixing in other elements of the *priesthood of all believers* and *sola scriptura* doctrines but with a Zwinglian spiritual understanding of the sacraments. Rothmann was that rare breed of reformer: friend and confidante of Luther, Melanchthon, Bucer and Capito; inspired equally by Zwingli's *Fidei* and Melanchthon's *Loci*—powerful but contrasting confessions. Initially an advocate of Lutheran *two kingdoms* doctrine, Rothmann separated the spiritual and physical realms but, as the evangelical movement gained more traction he incorporated Zwinglian covenantal doctrine. In other words he moulded a wider, communal view of religious matters which set the community above the individual and expanded the role of the political leaders into the spiritual realm for the good of all. As elsewhere, timing also had a role to play in the emergent storm.

As Rothmann was settling in to his tenure at St Lambert's new council elections brought to dominance a pro-Luther party which snubbed the bishop

---

99. Klötzer, "The Melchoirites and Münster," 223.

and installed evangelicals where they could in the other urban parishes.[100] As a result, outside the city the bishop raised an army in an attempt to reinforce Catholic obedience while within a citizen band (with some professional soldiers) assembled to defend their gains. The bishop's pitifully small army was bested and Philip of Hess himself intervened to mediate a compromise (14 February 1533). The parish churches would retain their evangelical preachers while the Cathedral and cloisters would remain Catholic. Luther wrote the council too, warning them off Rothmann (now the leading figure) and his radical Zwinglian doctrine. Despite the council's pro-Luther position they considered Rothmann as an ally, sharing as they all did anti-Anabaptist views. Instead of distancing themselves from him, the council asked Rothmann to write up a new church order (April 1533) for the city.

As a model of church reform Rothmann confined himself to works of Bucer in Strasbourg and Zwingli in Zürich, holding with the latter on the sacraments and thus offending the ruling Lutheran party's desires. Landgrave Philip intervened again; this time he insisted that the sacrament statements be changed to reflect a Lutheran understanding, but the combined tension of external pressure and internal conflict had already moved Rothmann toward a separatist "Grebel-Sattler" model as a replacement for the magisterial state church format the council wanted. The separate church would see to its own community but, as a concession, would obey the council in earthly matters. Into this delicate situation came emissaries from Hoffman's Haarlem disciple Jan Matthijs.

Matthijs's Melchiorite emissaries were attracted to Münster as a more tolerate location for a base of operations, standing as it did just outside the Habsburg-dominated Low Countries. Matthijs had already assumed a role as one of Hoffman's missionaries and witnesses to the end times (i.e., the "Enoch" to his "Elijah"), and his influence was gaining ground in Holland. Over the course of these early years more and more Melchoirites arrived from communities in Emden and Amsterdam to test the generally tolerant religious climate of Münster's northern Rhine/Westphalian setting. Matthijs was charismatic; he offered Rothmann support and an expanding congregation, and led him away from Zwinglianism. Soon enough Rothmann began to advocate the separation of believers from the godless, expelling all non-believers from the city. In this way a new element entered the Swiss church model—the voluntary church of the militant self-identified elect.[101]

---

100. Klötzer, "The Melchoirites and Münster," 225. Also see, Neff et al., "Rothmann, Bernhard," in *GAMEO*: http://www.gameo.org/encyclopedia/contents/ R6852.html.

101. Littell, *The Anabaptist View of the Church*, 30.

The pro-Lutheran party in the council turned to the Landgrave and the *Schmalkaldic* league for support, while Rothmann and the evangelical preachers (spiritual-minded and attracted to Swiss ideals) were supported by the guilds, a large percentage of the citizens (many armed), and the growing (and millenarian) militant sectarian community. Rothmann was ousted at St Lambert's, participated in public disputations (7–8 August 1533), and was reinstated by October (but forbidden to preach).[102] As the central figure around who religious, political and social tensions swirled, Rothmann was increasingly drawn into the sectarian camp and subsequently opposed a new council sponsored church order (of November 1533). He was at odds with the council, with the Landgrave, with the bishop, and with Lutherans and Catholics alike, but found relief (after a formal baptism into the Melchoirite sect on 5 January 1534) in an alliance with Matthijs and Jan Bockelson (also known as John of Leiden) who were both in the city by mid-February. Not long thereafter Rothmann was writing in support of further change, going so far as to advocate the destruction of "ungodly" government. Lutherans and Catholics fled the city and, in essence, the siege began.[103]

Rothmann became the voice of Münster sectarian extremism, popularizing Melchiorite doctrines including those on the relationship between secular power and the church. *Restitution* (October 1534), for example, was a re-interpretation of history (based on ideas embraced by Hoffman in Strasbourg) in which Rothmann outlined a cycle of continuous fallings away from the church followed up by returns to God. The cycle would end, however, with the new King David preparing the kingdom one last time for the new Solomon (i.e., Christ)—Bockelson (now known as King Jan van Leiden) was Rothmann's embodiment of David. The treatise was dedicated to the restoration of the early Christian Church, echoing Hoffman's understanding of the duties of the civil power in the end times.

In the following citation, for instance, Rothmann explained his understanding of *Romans* on the issue of government and the temporal sword: "[a true Christian government] is a servant of God, the protector of the innocent and the righteous, an avenger of evil, having received power from God on earth to use it accordingly." A problem exists in that government can sometimes be oppressive (i.e., opposed to righteousness). In Rothmann's estimation, Münster has thrown off demonic influences, re-establishing "government among

---

102. Klötzer, "The Melchoirites and Münster," 228.
103. Stayer, "The Anabaptist Revolt," 66.

us according to his Word . . . this is the kingdom and the throne of David, in which, through the sword of righteousness, the kingdom among us is to be cleansed and extended from now on. Thus the true and peaceful Solomon can enter it and possess it."[104] The sword was to be used; governments which abandon their proper functions would be dealt with by God. While the implication is clear, the means is vague. Rothmann's treatise *On Vengeance* spelled out the means more clearly—aggressive force.

This treatise was to have been a clarion call to the elect to take up arms and punish the godless wherever they were, while another, *On Earthly power* (never published) was aimed at hostile foreign powers. This was a fairly standard treatment of the theme that temporal power existed to punish the wicked and was not to be used as a scourge upon the righteous. Rothmann applied apocalyptic imaginings and said that God's will, from the time of creation, was that men obey only Him. Human sin and rebelliousness led to the creation of rival earthly powers and governments and God allowed it as a means to protect the good. These earthly powers, wicked from the start, however, only grew worse over time. Historically, Rothmann thought, for the better part of 1400 years temporal power had been misused and was an enemy of God, allied as it was so firmly with Rome.[105] The new Kingdom of David would bring down all other worldly powers and all their treasures and authorities would be divided in the end by the true believers.[106]

In any case, on the day of the sectarian dominated council's first meeting (24 February 1534) the prophet Bockelson addressed the gathered crowds and told them to obey the civil authority (i.e., the council) fearing neither pope, emperor, prince, bishop or any other external force. He was trying to fuse the entirety of the community together in a way the separatist church was meant to do, and he advised that the non-baptised—clearly those who doubted the church—should be sent into exile, removing a distracting influence. Bockelson had already assumed a position of authority between the people and the magistrates (perhaps as a "fellow"). He also took charge of the watch—all members were to be armed and man the walls as the bishop's forces were already again encamped around the city. What emerged in these early days is an interesting political dynamic in which government was exercised by a combination of council, prophet and preachers working as one—fusing together the physical (the council drawing up new Reformation orders) and the spiritual (the prophet and pastors working to unite the community into one metaphorical body of

---

104. Rothmann, "Restitution," 253–54.
105. Klötzer, "The Melchoirites and Münster," 253.
106. Allen, *A History of Political Thought*, 46.

Christ). Orders for the needs of the newly arrived and the underprivileged were made alongside collections of money and food from all members for the commonality. This may have been the realization of Hoffman's theocracy, but someone would have to emerge against the time when clashes of authority would inevitably take place. By mid-March 1534 the prophet and the emissary—Bockelson and Matthijs respectively—had consolidated their leadership but authority would have to somehow be made sure in order to resolve the many internal conflicts already coming to the forefront (e.g., between natives and outsiders, between rich and poor).

In essence, the metaphorical stage was set for what happened next. As the Enoch to Hoffman's Elijah, the next step in the celestial drama was, according to *Rev* 11, Christ's return after the deaths of the two witnesses. Hoffman was fading away rapidly in a Strasbourg prison, so Matthijs took matters into his own hands and led small groups out of the city to confront the bishop's forces directly. It was a win-win scenario for him. Should he triumphed it would surely be a signal of God's favour and should he be killed it was the fulfilment of divine prophecy.

In the event—5 April 1534 (Easter Day)—he was killed. Accordingly, the first king—the new David—now revealed himself as Bockelson. He assumed power as King Jan and swore to lead the true believers and prepare the way for Solomon with the sweeping away of the godless and the wicked. King Jan, prophet and king, combined the two kingdoms under one leader—sometimes reading from the Bible to groups of followers and at other times training fighting men in the Cathedral square.[107] Christ would be returning but, argued the king, to what kind of city? Münster was to serve as a model for the world. There was still therefore much to be done, including the inflicting of punishment on the godless and strengthening of communal bonds. Punishment of the wicked took centre stage, discipline and correction passing from the temporal to the church and from protection of the church to a social function meant to intensify congregational unity. As such, the separate elected council of the city became redundant.

The council and the guilds were subsequently dismantled and twelve Elders were named in their place—symbolically representing the twelve tribes of Israel—selected to represent all elements and interests in the city, including a reflection of social status and ranks of citizenship (from outsiders to former magistrates). For Klötzer this was an "institutionalization" of the prophetic office, or the passing on of the temporal sword to the community as a whole. Logically, it was also the final stage of priesthood of all believers doctrine (that final step in the Grebel plan for the council of the elect he once

---

107. Fingers, *A Contemporary Anabaptist Theology*, 297–98.

proposed to Zwingli). The Elders, in ways only hinted at by others, handled any and all issues—justice, discipline, social order, executions and all secular matters as well as oversight of the church, pastors and all spiritual situations. Münster was on a war setting in all ways—defensively against incursions, offensively against the siege, and spiritually against apostasy, heretics and doubters. Drawing the community together into one homogeneous body became the next step, and this accounts for many of the actions which in the eyes of outsiders and non-believers seemed inexplicable—simple clothing for all, the collection of all money and food into a common pool, polygamy for men (the surplus of women would be under someone's loving care)—but there was also compulsory education and Bible study.

In theory this should all work out as Grebel once assumed—the separate church would grow and eventually Christianize everyone as the old false churches died out. The new David would hand over a once violent world to the peace-loving king when he finally arrived. As violent, opposing false princes were eliminated by action or rehabilitation, and peaceful princes brought on board, soon, Jan said, the world would be prepared for the next stage. Rothmann's treatise On Vengeance outlined the theological justifications. The experiment was brought down as supplies ran out and the blockade succeeded.

King Jan did what he could. He replaced the twelve Elders directly from his own household and married sixteen women of aristocratic and guild backgrounds. These actions gave the city's leading families not only a unity, but a new stake in the city's survival. He also adopted a new standard which featured both the temporal and spiritual swords; an Old Testament and a sword leading his progresses and appearances as he personally assumed the task of punishing the wicked and protecting the good. The king chaired the justice system, administered the army, and performed executions while, as prophet, he interpreted the word of God to his people.[108] As the shortages grew more severe, however, so too did the king's suspicions, sword rattling, and execution of non-believers with the king and the city's prophet backpeddling on previous prophesies, making declarations of vengeance, and casting out non-believers into the hands of the surrounding troops. April 1535 saw the explosive end of the first sectarian experiment.

—— § ——

In the aftermath of Münster, Anabaptist sectarianism had two strikes against it—the recent debacle and the *Peasants' Revolt*—which left it inextricably

---

108. Klötzer, "The Melchoirites and Münster," 243–45.

associated with violence, bloodshed, and socio-political disruption. In truth, militant isolationism had largely been burned out of Anabaptism. In the Low Countries, the emerging dominant philosophy was now pacifist, of limited association between the church and the civil powers and, as Stayer termed, apolitical. This new attitude was explained in 1539 by Menno Simons, the dominant voice of the sectarians, in *A foundation and plain instruction of the saving doctrine of our Lord Jesus Christ*.[109]

Simons dealt with a range of subjects in a treatise intended as a means of countering all the misunderstandings surrounding Anabaptism since Münster. In the portion titled "A Christian and affectionate exhortation to all in authority," for example, he tacked the questions of civil authority and how Anabaptists are to respond to it. First, he disentangled the Dutch community from the recent disaster:

> Here I well know that we have to hear of Munster, dominions, polygamy, sword, theft, murder and of the like abominations and disgrace, which, you always assert, result from baptism; and under this pretext you reprove everything the mouth of the Lord commanded, and what the holy apostles taught and practised, and for this purpose you cite some seditious sects and factions, that the cry of the learned and your blood-shedding may be sanctioned.

Simons pushed for a return to Hubmaier's or Sattler's vision, describing Anabaptists as everything the extremists of Münster were not. They are peaceful:

> We teach and confess that we know of no sword, nor commotion in the kingdom or church of Christ, other than the sharp sword of the Spirit, God's word, as is abundantly shown in our writings, which is sharper and more piercing than any two-edged sword . . . but the sword of worldly policy we leave with those to whom it is committed.

Anabaptists are respectful of marriage—"We acknowledge, teach, and approve of no other matrimony than that one, which Christ and his apostles publicly and plainly taught in the New Testament, namely, one man and one woman, Matt. 19:4, and that they may not be divorced except in case of adultery, Matt. 5:32 . . ."—nor are they violent—"We know of no murdering, much less do we teach or permit it; for we truly believe that a murderer has neither lot nor part in the kingdom of God, Gal. 5:21 . . ."—nor do they covet

---

109. Quotes taken from the online version, found at http://www.mennosimons.net/fulltext.html. This is the edition found in *The Complete Works of Menno Simons*.

secular power—"We acknowledge, teach and seek no other kingdom than that of Christ, which shall endure for ever, in which there is no pomp, splendor, gold, silver, meat and drink, but righteousness, peace and joy in the Holy Ghost; we confess with Christ, that our kingdom is not of this world." Simons tried to impress upon his readers that the Anabaptists want to serve as a model, "a pattern to all the world, with our doctrine, life, blood and death, that they might reflect, awaken, repent and be saved, for this is the nature of pure love to pray for persecutors, to render good for evil, to love the enemy." With regard to the power of the secular authority, Simons was equally clear and equally traditional in his exegesis.

Anabaptism is apolitical. Simons wanted to make it plain that there are two separate kingdoms: "We also write the truth in Christ and lie not, that spiritually, we acknowledge no king, neither in heaven above nor upon earth beneath, than the only, eternal and true king, spiritual David, Christ Jesus, who is Lord of lords, and King of kings . . . ," although, "according to the flesh, we teach and exhort to be obedient to the emperor, king, lords and princes, yea, to all in authority, in all their transactions and civil regulations, so far as they are not contrary to the word of God, Rom. 13:1–3." He acknowledged, however, a sad commonplace among evangelical thinkers that princes who were also true believers were few and far between, but nonetheless, they have a duty to perform in punishing the wicked and protecting the good. The wise king "disperseth the ungodly . . . you are to chastise and punish, in the true fear of God, with all equitable and just discretion, the open evil doers; such as thieves, murderers, sodomites, adulterers, debauchers, menslayers, the violent, fornicators, sorcerers, robbers . . . ," protect the poor and ignorant and establish the true church. Simons advised that the basis of sound government was, of course, the Word of God: "love righteousness, do justice to widows and orphans, judge rightly between man and man, fear no man's highness; despise no man's littleness, hate all avarice, chastise with discretion, suffer the word of God to be taught in liberty, prevent none to walk in the ways of truth . . ." He re-emphasized in the treatise the separation of the two kingdoms, "do not interfere with the right and kingdom of Christ; for he alone is the Ruler of the conscience, and beside him there is none other, let him be your emperor, and his holy word your edict, in this matter; and you will soon be satiated with raging and murder." The Anabaptists would be part of the world, a model for it, but would do so in a pacifist, apolitical manner—a model for all.

4

Secular Authority in the Works of the Second-Generation Reformers

THE REFORMERS OF THE first generation (e.g., Luther, Zwingli, and Karlstadt) established certain doctrinal principles with regard to the theoretical and practical relationships between the church and the state. The working out of the meaning of *priesthood of all believers*, of *sola scriptura*, and of salvation theology had spiritual ramifications for both ruler and ruled and these had to be explored and worked out in practice. Both Luther and Zwingli acknowledged that the state, the secular authority, however this was configured by man was, nonetheless, of divine origin. God created the civil powers, gave them a purpose (to protect the good and punish the wicked) and gave them a means for doing so (the sword). The reformers of the first generation decried the way that the temporal sword had been usurped by religious authorities in Rome, and they developed theologies explaining what the differences and connections between the two kingdoms should be, should have been all along.

In the most general of term, they imagined the earthly kingdom of civil authorities dealing primarily with physical matters—money, property, laws, war, and justice, indeed anything which affected physical relationships between people. They imagined the spiritual kingdom dealing with the soul—the gospel, salvation and faith. Only God could know truthfully whether a man was saved or not, of course, but matters which touched upon holiness (such as preaching and teaching of the word) fell to the clergy and the church as its rightful custodians. Undeniably, however, there are matters that do not fit perfectly into one kingdom or the other, like church property or the necessary upkeep of clerics. The magisterial reformers, over the course of the early Reformation, argued that such issues were civil matters at the discretion of the community, and this came to also include religious ceremonies and most other external, non-salvific, matters (e.g., whether candles or roods are to be used or not). In such ways the two kingdoms were made exclusionary.

The ramifications of Luther's *priesthood of all believers* doctrine, however, seemed to fly in the face of this separation. Those priests whose task was to rule were still considered priests. As noted, many reformers tried to explain away the apparent contradiction. While Erasmus simply reminded Christian magistrates that they were Christians first and should therefore rule in a Christian manner, Luther worked out a solution based on functionality. A ruler was a Christian by virtue of the gift of justification, but a ruler according to office and duty. By taking the man out of the office, however, Luther introduced the idea that a king or mayor or any magistrate need not be a Christian to command obedience from Christians. Zwingli went in another direction based on a communal understanding of the relationship between church and state (as well as his humanist education).

Zwingli acknowledged that rulers had a role to play in leading the church (by virtue of their divine mandate) but held that they needed to work in tandem with priests, preachers, prophets and pastors (who were the custodians of the church). The civic leaders must be advised as to what is the true meaning of the word of God (advice provided by the clergy) and then act upon it (i.e., translate it into legislation for the good of every member of the community). For Zwingli, therefore, a close association must develop between the secular authority and the church, whereas for Luther there was a clearer division, one rarely crossed except in emergency situations. Metaphorically, we might think of it as the difference between a firm embrace and a handshake.

How did the reformers who followed in the footsteps, or who worked in close association with the first generation adhere to the thinking of the masters? Did Melanchthon (Luther's closest friend and associate) agree with Luther in all things? Did Bullinger and Calvin adapt or adopt Zwingli's thinking? How did the great compromiser, Martin Bucer, find a formula accommodating both Lutheran and Reformed parties? Was Oecolampadius more influenced by Zwingli or by Erasmus? What were the positions of Martyr, and Laski, and Beza on the issue? These are the reformers of the second generation who stirred the work of the masters from the dynamic into the doctrinal period.

— § —

Philipp Melanchthon:
The Prince as Steward of the Church—
Peace and Order (to 1530)

James Estes described the relationship between Luther and Melanchthon as collaborative (although cooperative might be a better term). The two men understood and respected each other's opinions and, while not always entirely in agreement there was a degree of mutual influence. They agreed on the separation of the kingdoms of church and state and understood the *"cura religionis"* of the magistrate similarly as something special—the prince having a duty of care toward the church as a whole. Their philosophy was different enough, however, to make a brief examination of Melanchthon's thinking worthwhile.

For Melanchthon, the godly magistrate had a dual function which, up to the period of the *Augsburg Confession*, he saw as custodial. The magistrate, at whatever level, was the custodian of temporal society responsible for justice, defence, and good order as well as supportive of true religion. Luther gave the secular ruler religious obligations by virtue of his *priesthood* in common with all the other *priests*—a kind of equality under God. At this point we have seen the doctrine de-constructed and re-built in a number of ways—some quite logical and convincing—and Melanchthon also found within it a different understanding. He also gave the secular ruler religious obligations by virtue of his *priesthood—and—*by virtue of his position as the foremost member of the particular church.

It was a subtle difference based on the fact that Melanchthon was not a priest but a scholar, from a family of scholars, destined for a career in the court of the Elector Palatine (following in his father's footsteps). Service to a prince had been, for Melanchthon, the highest form of public duty. He had been influenced by the Erasmian formulation of the Christian state headed by the Christian prince—appointed by God and tasked with the spiritual and moral education of his people—as found in his *Institution of the Christian Prince* (1516).[1] For Luther, God had created the magistrate to protect the church from the wicked and from the ramifications of false doctrine. For Melanchthon (and Erasmus), God created the magistrate for that purpose *but also* for the next logical step—the prince was to establish and maintain true religion. Historians characterize Melanchthon as the scholar who popularized and streamlined Luther's theology. With regard to theories of secular authority, he added to and altered aspects of Luther's thought[2], tak-

---

1. Estes, *Peace*, 54–55.
2. Estes, "The Role of Godly Magistrates," 464.

ing a more positive view of the magisterial office than the Luther formulated doctrine of *the two kingdoms* allowed.

In the 1520s, that period of Luther's greatest productivity on the issue (e.g., *Address to the Christian Nobility, On Secular Authority*), Melanchthon's doctrine largely only reflected Luther's own, exchanging Erasmus-inspired humanist philosophy with Luther-inspired evangelical perspective. He took up the *priesthood of all believers* shifting decision making authority from Rome and the Catholic hierarchy to the community on its own behalf (e.g., selecting its own pastors). Moreover, he accepted the changing interpretation of ceremonies and other externals from salvific necessities to non-salvific human additions. The church became for him a community of *priests*, including those priests who rule, and Melanchthon reflected the functionalism of Luther's doctrine as well as the separation of the Christian between his duty as a Christian and his duty as the holder of some office (e.g., cobbler, candle-maker, or councillor).

The doctrine of *the two kingdoms* established the divine nature of secular office while also isolating its function from the other kingdom. For Melanchthon, the Word of God was the basic guide and final arbiter for all practices. He agreed with Luther that personal faith was a private matter beyond the influence of other people but provided the heterodox did not try to influence others Melanchthon left him in peace. Later, due to changing political circumstances, secular lords became more central to Luther's program of reform (as bishops and other church leaders failed to make the necessary changes). Secular rulers were, for both men, to be concerned with all matters which touched upon public peace and order, including aspects of ecclesiology—conditions in and practices of the church—and they agreed that with the rising tide of sectarianism this mandate included combat of blasphemy and factionalism (as threats to peace and order and to be dealt with as such). Melanchthon exercised considerable intellectual latitude, however, in his attempts to popularize and disseminate "Lutheranism." Nowadays we might call him a public relations officer.

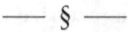

Melanchthon created a simpler, more straight-forward version in the early 1520s as Luther's influence replaced Erasmus's. For Luther, the state was divine but was of the wicked world, the physical realm, and need not necessarily be Christian to still be legitimate (and he had already expressed serious doubts about most princes' status as genuine believers). For Melanchthon, the state, a divine creation, must also have some religious purpose beyond punishing evil-doers. Luther assigned the state some incidentally religious function (where such matters as marriage issues crossed into the secular realm or where otherwise spiritual matters became threats to peace and order) but still, largely secular. For Melanchthon, the state was both secular and spiritual. Luther separated the man from the office-holder; as Christians, all men have a spiritual role to play, but magistrates were limited to secular matters (except where religious authorities refused to act). For Melanchthon, the magistrate also had a duty to concern himself in the fostering and development of true religion by virtue of being a leader of men. His was the logical position. We find it first expressed in February 1521 in his treatise *Oratio pro Martino Luthero theologo*—an *apologia* against the polemics of emerging Catholic opponents.[3]

The *Oratio* was aimed as those princes (e.g., leaders of communities and rulers of states) who were contacted by papal agents to act as enforcers of papal mandates against Luther. Melanchthon explained to them that the prince has the duty of removing those things adjudged (after careful consideration of the Scriptures) to be superfluous to salvation (if the community deems they be removed), and those things otherwise considered abuses based on his authority as prince. Here we see Luther's *priesthood of all believers* and aspects of his *Address* appended to remnant Erasmian thought.

This must be done in an effort to clean up and reform the church to a more wholesome, pure, original condition. Frederick the Wise is held up as an example of the kind of prince they should all aspire to be, that is, a ruler who recognizes that he has been established and maintained in his position by God, and who therefore has set himself on the path (with sound advice) to liberate the church from merely human traditions and papal abuses. Since the community regulates its own ecclesiastical environment, the prince has a leading role as a leading member of the community. He therefore must uphold the gospel, restore true worship, re-establish fundamental practices, promote Christian piety and learning, abolish idolatry, and combat factionalism.[4] This is clearly a greater role that Luther allowed the secular authority, but not overwhelmingly so and not enough for Luther to object. Princes stand in for God in the world and, therefore, have a duty to lead the church to the ends God created it for—spread of the gospel, liberation from

---

3. Estes, "The RRle of Godly Magistrates," 467; Melanchthon, *Didymi Faventini* can be found online in the original Latin.

4. Estes, *Peace*, 58–60.

false practices, the teaching and understanding of the Word. For both men these were the duties of the church in the totality of its membership and, for Melanchthon, this concerned magistrates as princes among men. Of course, not all princes (however Christian they may claim to be) act appropriately. Luther had doubts about all of them but, nonetheless, those who set earthly matters above the gospel needed to be re-educated. That was one goal of Luther's *Address* and of Melanchthon's *Oratio*.

Although not squarely in agreement there was no animosity between the two friends. Sitting in the Wartburg, at the mercy of secular powers, Luther took time to examine the issue closer at Melanchthon's urging. It seems that Melanchthon was concerned at the lack of specific gospel affirmations for Christian participation in government. He was researching what would become the relevant passages of his new treatise, *Loci Communes*—sections entitled "*de humanis legibus*" and "*de magistratibus*"—and had come to define the sword in *Romans* as both civil regulation and whatever institutions had been established for the punishment of the wicked—that is, courts of justice, the military, the executioner. He had been searching the gospel for evidence that Christians were permitted to participate in worldly government—to carry the sword, hold office or maintain law and order—but found no specific positive passage. Without scriptural support it was a contentious issue. In a letter of 13 July 1521 Luther affirmed he could find no specific commandments either. No Christian had been specifically ordered to take up the sword on behalf of the government but he could also find no specific objections. A reading of Scripture made the idea commendable but not compulsory. They agreed that if everyone just acted in a good Christian manner there would be no need for secular authority. Christians participating in government is a voluntary, non-salvific matter, neither commanded nor forbidden by Scripture so wholly within the mandate of the community.

Civil government is clearly necessary to protect the church, and certain passages in Scripture imply acceptance of this necessity—Luke 3:14 indirectly recognized military services; 1 Tim 2:1-2 commended prayers on behalf of princes and magistrates. More directly relevant are the usual sources cited on behalf of governmental power—Rom 13; 1 Pet 2:13-4. For Luther, civil government was an earthly matter, in the hands of the effected community, and the Bible instructed Christians in proper behaviour toward secular power. The only relevant objection was regarding immoderate behaviour.[5] Melanchthon adopted this position in *Loci* (published first in December 1521) and never strayed far from it thereafter.

---

5. *AE*, 45:256–63 (letter no. 85); Estes, "Godly Magistrates," 468–69.

— § —

Loci Communes had grown out of Melanchthon's lectures and writings on Pauline texts over the course of the early 1520s. Secular authority is considered in two brief and unexciting chapters. In the earlier chapter on "human laws", the emerging evangelical norm that civil laws "which magistrates, princes, kings, and cities sanction in the state" are divine in origin and authoritative for laity and clerics alike was acknowledged. Magistrates have special purposes in the punishment of the wicked. Romans 13:1–3 is given as the familiar exegesis, limited by Acts 5:29 regarding laws or orders contrary to divine and natural law.[6] The meat of this chapter is, however, a polemic against "pontifical laws"—that is, clerical involvement in civil affairs and the creation of canons which effect civil matters. Melanchthon equated this with tyranny of a sort as it strayed well beyond gospel norms and blurred the divisions between civil authority and spiritual works. In the latter chapter "on magistrates", his and Luther's considerations on civil authority and the work of the magistrates were repeated.[7] Over the Lutheran commonplaces, however, Melanchthon added a case against ecclesiastical magistrates—that is, bishops who act outside of their gospel-based duties to preach and pastor.

Prince-bishops, for instance, cannot legitimately exercise magisterial authority if the boundaries of secular authority are set within the Rom 13—Acts 5 limitations. There is nothing explicitly innovative here, but there are interesting inferences. Estes argued that Melanchthon had indirectly incorporated his alternative exegesis on the role of the magistrate *as custodian of the church and true religion* into his discussion of the three types of law—human, natural and divine. He did this by first drawing up clear interrelationships between them (in that civil or human laws must be constrained by divine and natural laws or be disobeyed) and second, drawing up the relationship between natural and divine law as noted in the commonplace arrangement of the *Decalogue* into two tables. The first table incorporated the first three commandments on the worship of God and the second table incorporated the remaining commandments on morals and human dealings. Although there is no explicit statement of the magistrate as custodian of the two tables of the law the implication is there.[8] These two, lean, chapters of the first edition of *Loci* were later augmented by further considerations. For example, Melanchthon's *Themata ad sextam*

---

6. Pauck, ed., *Melanchthon and Bucer*, 62.
7. Pauck, ed., *Melanchthon and Bucer*, 148–50.
8. Estes, *Peace*, 63.

feriam discutienda (or *Theses for the Friday disputation*) led to changes in the 1523 and 1525 editions of *Loci*.

Themata featured twenty-four theses drawn up for a debate on 25 July 1522 on questions differentiating spiritual and temporal government. Luther was not yet ready to concede that non-salvific matters were necessarily in the secular mandate but Melanchthon was ready. External matters (which touched the church) were of physical concern and therefore subject to civil authority for the good of the community. Recall that Luther's *doctrine of the two kingdoms* held civil authority as merely corporal (touching only earthly matters). Melanchthon expanded the role of the civil power. His first thesis was "Government is twofold: spiritual and physical."[9] In thesis twenty-two he noted that "ecclesiastical traditions are civil laws, of some value pedagogically, but pertaining in no way to spiritual government."[10] In thesis five he made more explicit the connection between civil authority and the two tables of the *Decalogue*, and theses twenty-five and six make additional negative statements—that is, what spiritual authority is not. So as "the ministry of the gospel is plainly a spiritual realm" and "because this ministry proclaims nothing but the righteousness of the Spirit, it lays down nothing about the external control of affairs"—clearly therefore these are civil matters. Where Luther vigorously separated the two kingdoms into self-contained realms, Melanchthon was able to make a case where the secular power had both civil and spiritual authority (limited by the gospel and to external matters). Later, Luther came around to Melanchthon's position that church property and material provisioning for the clergy were also secular responsibilities as were the threats of false worship and sectarianism.

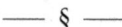

By 1527 Luther and Melanchthon agreed that the secular authority had a decisive role to play in the maintenance of true and unified worship and correct doctrine. As noted, Luther came to this conclusion as a result of the religious authorities failures to act to counter problems (like the increasing popular Swiss view, the rise of radical sectarianism, or in the construction and enforcement of much needed new church orders). He was willing to concede only that secular authorities acted in emergency situations, urging a general visitation of the churches be undertaken by the Saxon princes (Luther and Melanchthon were both subsequently designated as visitors). Where Luther accepted that the magistrate must

---

9. Melanchthon, "Themes for the Sixth Holiday," 89.
10. Melanchthon, "Themes for the Sixth Holiday," 90.

oppose false doctrine, Melanchthon added that the magistrate must also recognize and implement true doctrine. Luther thought of these as two separate matters, whereas Melanchthon logically held them as two sides of the same coin, and his correspondence with the electoral officials highlight the range of problems around Thuringia they needed to address, including disputes over baptism and errors in the Eucharist doctrine. Elector John issued orders to combat these lapses, taking, and sometimes softening imperial mandates thereby acting in a fashion both Melanchthon and Luther approved. Melanchthon took up the arguments against sectarians and their insistence on isolationism or non-cooperation as misunderstandings of Scripture. Certainly a Christian could serve as a magistrate or in any number of secular offices—justice, soldier, councillor.[11]

—— § ——

Philipp Melanchthon: The Prince as Steward of the Church— The Glory of God (post-1530)

The events of the 1530s had a marked impact on Luther's *doctrine of the two kingdoms* not least of which was bishops and clerical officials continuously ignoring his advice. Orthodoxy and ecclesiastical organization were key issues in light of the visitation and in the era of the Diet of Augsburg decisions were forced upon secular rulers, particularly between Catholic or Protestant adherence. Evangelical governments needed to impose well defined doctrinal and faith statements—Confessions—to counteract both Roman Catholic and sectarian opposition. Catholic and sectarian theologians were just as capable as the magisterial reformers to quote Scripture and apply basic evangelical doctrines like *priesthood of all believers* and *sola scriptura* to their own ends, so the Lutherans needed some statement putting clear blue water between them. Melanchthon, companion of Luther and correspondent of Bucer, Erasmus and many others of varying viewpoints, was perhaps the best person to collate the evidence and write the statement which became the *Augsburg Confession* and its subsequent *Apology* (statements meant to unify rather than divide). This in mind, two articles are particularly relevant to our current theme—sixteen and twenty-eight, aimed respectively at the sectarians and the Catholics.

11. Oyer, *Lutheran Reformers*, 142–54.

In the former, civil authority is recognized as divine and Christians are assured that they can rightfully hold office, property, be soldiers, take oaths, etc., limited only by the strictures of Acts 5:29 (in that they cannot be lawfully commanded to disobey God). The latter article (on ecclesiastical authority) revisited the issue of churchmen in positions of secular authority. To Melanchthon's regret, the Catholic authorities rejected the *Confession* and the emperor commissioned a response (which in turn influenced Melanchthon to emend, up-date and continuous re-vamp). The two key articles remained largely unchanged throughout, although additional scriptural supports were added, and the work was augmented by further treatises. For instance, in 1532 Melanchthon published *Commentaries on the Epistle of St Paul to the Romans* wherein magistrates were referred to as "gifts and ordinances of God." Melanchthon stated that St Paul meant that "magistrates must be obeyed by everyone." In 1535, a new edition of *Loci* reflected this harder stance.[12] *Apology*, the culmination of new research and augmentations, was officially accepted by the Schmalkaldic League in February 1537.

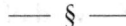

Apology was the product of new considerations resulting from the experience of face-to-face confrontations with Catholic negotiators (at Augsburg) and the witness of sectarian influence (in the Saxon visitations). Melanchthon defended his doctrine of the magistrate's spiritual function as both Christian and magistrate against those who argued that this violated the separation of the two kingdoms and against those who argued for the tolerance of unorthodox opinion. Historians characterize the work as "catechism"; Melanchthon moved beyond guidelines to the reading of *Romans*.[13] In the era of the *Peasants' Revolt* and Eucharist crisis it was no longer wise to simply allow those who tacitly objected their liberty of conscience. Enforcement of peace and stability now rested on the enforcement of religious correctness. Melanchthon maintained a crucial connection to his humanist roots, however, writing that the state was for him, as for Erasmus and Zwingli, a religious entity—Christian—and it had a God-given religious purpose. He still tried to set this within Luther's broad *two kingdoms* framework, but changed emphasis to the positive obligations of the prince to preserve the true church and oversee the true faith for the sake of peace and order and the advancement of the glory and honour due to God.[14]

---

12. Skinner, *The Foundations of Modern Political Thought*, 2:202.
13. Kolb, *Bound Choice*, 84.
14. Dixon, "The Politics of Law and Gospel," 45.

Melanchthon now made the salvation of their subjects' souls of paramount importance to civil authorities, toward which heresy and blasphemy were clearly disruptive influences. Moreover, the previous arguments about non-salvific external matters (like ceremonies or images) were subsumed under an argument that secular authorities—as combining both temporal and religious influences—were to establish and maintain true religion through the active removal of all old abuses. This was a princely divine duty; "fear of the wrath of God" for not performing it. Temporal authorities were responsible for secular discipline (i.e., justice, policing), were to provide for the church (i.e., ensure appropriate preaching and spread of the gospel), and were to ferret out and eliminate unorthodoxy, finally calling for a death penalty for blasphemers.[15] From the 1559 edition: "the authorities must watch over the second table of commandments and the first even more so. For the rulers have to serve the honour of God above all things. They are the guardians of the church. And whoever has taken the name of God in vain, he should be punished by death."[16] Obviously, only truly Christian magistrates would do. Rulers were "obliged to accept the holy gospel, to believe, confess, and direct others to true divine service." The authority can still be heathen (and still be legitimate and beneficial in many ways), but as such must also be considered somehow "out of order" or incomplete.[17] Luther still doubted the existence of genuinely Christian magistrates (in an era when both Catholic and Protestant authorities secularized former Catholic Church properties for personal gain. Melanchthon's view of the magistrate has been called a "stewardship without independent authority"[18], formalized in 1539 by *De officio principum* (or *On the office of the prince*) which stressed civil authority as guardian of both the first and second tables of the *Decalogue*. While Melanchthon augmented the work of Luther, Oecolampadius did much the same for the work of Zwingli.

— § —

Oecolampadius: Church Discipline and the Council of Elders

For Zwingli the church and the civil community were one and the same thing—the church was the community and the Christian was the good

---

15. Dixon, "The Politics of Law and Gospel," 47; Dixon, *Protestants*, 74–75.
16. Dixon, "The Politics of Law and Gospel," 47.
17. Estes, "Godly Magistrates," 476–7; Dixon, *Protestants*, 75.
18. Keen and Melanchthon, "Political Authority and Ecclesiology," 13.

citizen. The magistrate, therefore, was the supreme earthly authority and equivalent of an Old Testament king. There could be no ecclesiastical jurisdiction apart from, or independent of, the civil authority. The magistrate was equally concern with the piety of the masses, with their behaviour, and with the protection of the church/commonwealth. Success in all three depended on discipline.

For Zwingli this meant checking evil, preventing or punishing crimes, and of keeping order in the community—in the church and among the citizenry. The focus on these issues harkened back to abuses in the traditional clerical establishment which had produced clerical tyrants and baseless rules. The purpose of discipline was not to "purify the church"; for Zwingli this was not possible on earth as it would always be a mixed community of wheat and tares (true and false believers). When we consider his ecclesiology, providential, sacramental, and justification theologies, this view of the relationship between church and state makes sense. When the Swiss Brethren presented an alternative view in the mid-1520s Zwingli developed (with Bullinger) an answer in the doctrinal framework of the covenant which, among other things, strengthened the idea of the magistrates as the rulers of society in its entirety—civil and religious issues all considered.[19] We have seen the Anabaptist response to Zwingli; Oecolampadius presented a related but alternative view.

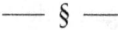

Oecolampadius led the reform effort in contemporary Basel; his uphill battles there were due to the presence of a bishop and cathedral chapter, solidly Catholic, as well as with a core of confirmed Catholics on the inner council of the magistracy. His position was somewhat privileged, however, in that the council protected him against Catholic attacks and against the pronouncements of the papacy, using him as a kind of political tool to enhance their own power at the cost of these Catholic institutions and to exult their own authority in matters of the developing Reformation of the church.

The council walked a fine line between religious parties, however, due to its refusal to give up any particular advantage or power. Basel was the location of many profitable printing presses, it was an imperial city, a member of the Swiss Confederacy, a bishop's seat, and the home of Erasmus so, no matter which direction they eventually turned something valuable was at risk. Oecolampadius used the opportunities his position accorded him to do what he could to further the evangelical cause, but

---

19. J. Wayne Baker, "Christian Discipline," 108.

he could only rely on the usual route of evangelical reform—appeal to the magistrates—with limited expectations of success.[20] In other cities reformers appealed to their councils as the final arbiters of religious practice to exercise authority and enforce preaching from the Bible and spread of the word of God. Appeals to the council in Basel, however, were met with only half-hearted interest and limited execution due to political and economic circumstances. An ordinance of May 1523 illustrates this, stipulating only that preaching was to be Scripture-based and preachers were to avoid unwarranted accusations of heresy and *ad hominem* attacks.[21] New liturgies were introduced, but nothing much came of it. The two religious parties were evenly matched—Oecolampadius had support in the city and in the wider Basel environs but so too did his Catholic opponents—and the council tried to maintain a neutral stance.

Oecolampadius used the council's stance where he could: new ideas were presented to the council for approval; some licence was given to some reformers; Mass ceremonials were adapted in some churches. Oecolampadius was happy to fulfil his preaching and pastoral responsibilities and experiment with alternate rites for marriage, baptism and communion; his publication schedule was impressive. Needless to say perhaps this neutral position could not last what with Lutherans, Zwinglians, radicals and Catholics competing inside the city and the Catholic and Protestant cantons competing politically in the Confederacy. On 16 May 1527 the moment came; the magistrates called on the two parties to submit position papers. Little came of the effort as the Catholic authorities opposed magisterial interference in spiritual matters. A compromise of sorts was settled later; Catholic ceremonies and Reformed services were set in select locations about the city or scheduled for specific times. Things only began to change when the end of the year guild feasts invited only evangelical preachers to attend and, the following month, when 400 citizens appealed to the council for a firm statement. But little appeared prior to the Baden and Berne Colloquies, after which evangelical momentum was running so high in the other Swiss cities that the Basel council had no choice but to finally act.

The magistrates were then faced with the full array of evangelical sermons, treatises and pamphlets pouring out of the Basel printing houses; Oecolampadius pressed them to exercise their authority and direct the effort. Even at this point, however, the most the council seemed willing to do was release a much anticipate edict (February 1528) which amounted

---

20. Poythress, 31–40, presents a useful overview. Also see, Poythress, *Reformer of Basel*.
21. Rupp, *Patterns*, 30.

to little more than this pithy statement "*every man should abide in his own faith.*" Oecolampadius persisted; partaking in frequent consultations and urging the view that magistrates should led the way and protect the spiritual health of the community. With the spectre of iconoclastic violence and demands from the guilds rising in the background, finally, in January 1529, the council came around and took renewed action; they determined to enforce the mandate of 1523. On 6 January 1529 the gates of the town were opened to those who wished to leave (Erasmus choose so to do) and a disputation would be held on the issues in June. Masses were discontinued in some churches. Riots continued to rage, however, until the council finally declared their hand and dismissed the Catholic members, officially abolishing the Mass and removing images. On 18 February a lay commission was established to draw up a new ordinance and Oecolampadius submitted memoranda and position papers outlining the relationship between the church and the civil authority.

The new ordinance duly appeared on 1 April and it certainly checked all the right evangelical boxes, having been largely written by Oecolampadius himself. The parameters of reform were to be set by the Word of God—the framework upon which all else hung. Sermons would be based on the gospel "purely, plainly and clearly, to the honour of God and the planting of brotherly love," forming the heart of the church service. Otherwise, excommunication would be used responsibly; synods were established to examine the doctrine and morals of the pastors, preachers, and teachers while also allowing them a forum to discuss problems in the parishes and present grievances and suggestions to the council; a marriage court was set up after the example of Zürich's magisterial court; education became a central focus; and, church lands and properties were to be secularized. The new ordinance stipulated that sinners should get two fraternal admonishments before excommunication and that the power to excommunicate be vested in the pastors and deacons, which gave the church a means to influence lay piety. The magistrates baulked at this last point seeing in it a prelude to the same kind of clerical tyranny they sought to eliminate. Oecolampadius was not, however, investing discipline solely with the clergy but with the church as a whole. What does this mean?

Oecolampadius, in his early career, had briefly served the church as a penitentiary (c.1518–1521). It had been his role to hear confessions and assign penances. It was a system almost designed to nurture tyranny (in the hands of an unscrupulous priest). In an early treatise he presented an alternative penitential system based on fraternal confession and admonishment as both scriptural (e.g., *James* 5:16) and less burdensome on the penitent. Nothing came of that, but in 1525 he returned to the discipline issue. In his new *Missal*, Oecolampadius considered exclusion as a Scripture-based disciplinary device, limiting excommunication to extreme cases of anti-communal behavior—the rebellious, those who disobeyed the secular authority, those who disrespect the sacraments and the Word.[22] The goal was purity of the church and the community. The magistrates feared that this would develop into clerical tyranny. Elsewhere in Protestant Switzerland councillors, as leading members of the congregations, took on shepherding roles and public and private morality was subject to investigation by the council. Oecolampadius recognized that it was the duty of the civil authority to protect the church, safeguard the lives of the people, and assist and promote the faith and the gospel, but putting discipline exclusively in the hands of the secular authority risked a different kind of tyranny.

A solution to the conundrum of effective discipline came in May 1530 when Oecolampadius was commissioned to draft a new position paper. He parted with Zwingli (and his successor Bullinger), who understood excommunication as a civil duty, maintaining instead that it was a church issue employing what Baker termed a "variant understanding" of Zwinglian covenant theology. The Zürich theologians emphasized the unity and continuities between the Old and New Testaments (which consequently determined the role of the magistrate as based on the model of biblical kings) whereas Oecolampadius theorized that instead of continuity the old covenant must give way to the new, recognizing that of course this would impact doctrine.[23] He presented his conclusions to the spring meeting of the Basel synod in *Oratio de reducenda excommunicatione* (or *Oration concerning the fact that excommunication ought to be reinstated*). Of interest to our purpose here is Oecolampadius's opposition to the long standing tradition that obstinate sinners be handed over to the civil authority for discipline and punishment.

Discipline was a church matter, for Oecolampadius it was part and parcel of the pastors' pastoral function; it was an interior spiritual matter, not an outward issue of correct practice. As such, temporal fines and punishments (e.g., prison, death) might never prove enough to make the church (the commune) more wholesome; excommunication and cutting off from the religious community of those persistent sinners, however, could make all the difference in the effort to purify the church. Oecolampadius was unwilling to hand the power of discipline over to clerics or councillors, but the

---

22. Graham, *The Uses of Reform*, 10–11.
23. Graham, *The Uses of Reform*, 36–37; McCoy and Baker, *Fountainhead*, 22–23.

congregation—the church as a whole—could also not effectively wield disciplinary power as women and children were part of that assembly. Presbyters and elders, however, wise men of good repute could wield that authority on behalf of the church as a whole.

For Oecolampadius, unlike Zwingli, the church and the state were not the same and could not, therefore, legislate for each other. Christ had instituted excommunication in the church in order to amend the lives of the believer and purify the church and this led him to the necessary innovation (or long overdue re-introduction) of a separate church court of twelve elders or censors (a mixed body of pastors, magistrates and parishioners) to judge sinners according to the rule of Christ (in *Matt* 18) and to exercise discipline over them—taking this body as an updating of the primitive church's *presbyteroi*. The board of elders could not be a temporal body; sin (impurity of doctrine and moral misdeed) was dealt with by the church, and crime (transgression of human ordinances) was dealt with by the courts. Oecolampadius was drawing a line between members of the church and members of the civic community in that the latter could very well also include Jews, heathens, Anabaptists and Catholics. While he was certainly willing to work with the council on a number of moral issues he wanted the autonomy of the spiritual authority recognized in this way. He said that in so doing society would benefit as pious and blameless Christians would be moulded by the church for the city. His proposal was aimed, he thought, at reducing the potential of both political and ecclesiastical tyranny.[24]

Oecolampadius cast a wide net to attract support. He appealed to the secular leaders of the Protestant cantons (addressing the *Christian Civic League* at Aarau in September 1530) and corresponded with Zwingli, Bucer and Capito among other religious leaders. He presented his different covenantal thinking this way—the church was a single Christian commonwealth (after Zwingli) with two substrata (spiritual and temporal) existing in parallel with each other rather than conjoined (as Zwingli held). Zwingli acknowledged that Oecolampadius had a point. "The Christian man [he wrote] is nothing other than the faithful and good citizen; the Christian city is nothing other than the Christian church" and Oecolampadius held the magistrates responsible to produce the good citizens while the church produced "pious and blameless Christians."[25] The upshot was that man existed under two polities and magisterial discipline was insufficient. Offenders

---

24. Poythress, 67; Rupp, "The Reformation in Zürich," 105; Spijker, *The Ecclesiastical Offices*, 219–20.

25. Baker, "Church Discipline or Civil Punishment," 6–7.

could still enjoy fellowship and the sacrament in the church, therefore exclusion under the church's control was essential to societal purity.

For Oecolampadius the power of the keys had been given to the church and, while the papacy (as a body of clerics) had abused that power this did not change the essential matter that excommunication was an ecclesiastical device. He warned his assembled colleagues that even the best magistrates, as Christian as they may be would still be distracted by secular matters and, consequently, ecclesiastical matters would not receive sufficient attention. For him, excommunication was the remedy for sin, while civil punishments were remedies for crimes—sin and crimes being two different things. The church was to act with love, for correction, and for spiritual edification and the magistrates act to punish offences. Furthermore, the purposes of excommunication were interior and spiritual, aimed at amending the ways of the sinner and to purify the church.

Oecolampadius's plan for a separate church court would logically mean that one bad person might become subject to two separate courts—the magisterial tribunal and the clerical court—should he disrupt the peace and profane religion. This scenario was one of the many fundamental causes of anti-clericalism. Oecolampadius explained to his audience at Aarau that the Reformed Church was neither, in his eyes, fully reformed nor genuinely yet a church, being without the keys to enforce discipline, piety, and true belief on its own behalf as the body of Christ on earth. It was the duty of magistrates, as good Christians he said, to do their duty and hand back discipline to the church.[26] While this verges on Luther's fundamental position of two separate kingdoms, Zwingli did not immediately rubbish his friend's idea even as the Zürich council opposed it at Aarau, effectively killing it off. Oecolampadius did not ultimately get his way in Basel either. After a six month trial period the proposal was modified (in his absence) by a Council mandate of 14 December 1530. There would be no centralized ecclesiastical body but instead excommunication committees in each parish. Two members of the council sat with a lay member to oversee the morals of the parish and if those sinners judged did not seek restoration within the month, civil penalties were imposed with the council having the final disciplinary power. After Oecolampadius's death, this scheme was also shelved in favour of a

---

26. Baker, "Church, State, and Dissent," 151.

system of self-regulation overseen by the church but regulated and directed by the council (with a few censors appointed in March 1531).[27]

Oecolampadius had tried, in Rupp's words, "valiantly to set up safeguards against a possible tyranny of the godly magistrates," providing a device which Bucer and Calvin (separately) later re-developed.[28] His successor, Myconius, had a much clearer Zwinglian view on the cooperative partnership of church and state and a permanent body was established by September 1532—a *kirchenrat* of four executive council members, four senior pastors, and twelve members of the synod which met quarterly and had oversight of the synods and all church business. By 1534 lay members of the *kirchenrat* dominated the synods at the expense of the pastors and reduced the meeting to an annual event. While Oecolampadius's conception of the church/state relationship was shelved in Basel, as noted, Bucer, Calvin and Beza all pursued it later as the better option. Bullinger followed Zwingli.

— § —

Heinrich Bullinger:
The Magistrate as Overseer of the Covenantal Community

In much the same way that Melanchthon developed and re-packaged Lutheran doctrine for a wider audience, Bullinger did for Zwingli. Melanchthon had found a need to make Luther's two kingdom's doctrine more appealing due to the threat of Catholicism on the march and because Protestant princes inexplicably ignored their spiritual obligations. Bullinger had the on-going threat of radical sectarianism to confront which, to him, contravened, and was the greatest threat to, the eternal divine covenant.

By way of review, Bullinger specifically, and the Swiss reformers generally, saw their commonwealth as a collection of people gathered together in a society based on a scriptural covenant or the federal principle. This means that the church *was* society, and both pastor and magistrate therefore had divinely specified roles to play. Over the course of the 1520s some of the ramifications of this thinking had already been worked out. The magistrates of Zürich set the norm for evangelical Switzerland in making this understanding a reality with the creation of a Reformed community in which all the powers of discipline and oversight rested in the hands of the council. Zwingli's covenantal thinking (a by-product of his predestination theology,

---

27. Sunshine, *Reforming French Protestantism*, 120; Spijker, *The Ecclesiastical Offices*, 222 (no. 525).

28. Rupp, *Patterns*, 37–39, 45; Nelson–Burnett, "Kilchen ist uff dem Radthus?" 50.

his Erasmian-humanist influences and his anti-Anabaptist disputes) meant that he held the local community and church as one sacral entity (entered into *via* infant baptism) and so, naturally, the *cura religionis* was in the hands of the leaders of the community—the magistrates. We noted the development of the marriage court in 1525 and the synod in 1528 as evidence of his position and his influence with the council. Quickly, the marriage court evolved into a morality court for the citizens, setting out penalties for immoral behaviour with the council acting as the only court of appeal from its judgements. The synod (under the leadership of the mayor and the antistes—or highest church official) shepherded the pastors, looking to the council for legislative and disciplinary measures (including excommunication) when necessary.[29] Zwingli influenced all matters in the church and council through a combination of sheer charisma and prophetic drive. The roles of both the church and state in his sacred communal system were the results of Zwingli's thinking and work with the state officials, and this influenced reformers in both Bern and Basel as the Zürich system was exported and its influence spread. After the Protestant defeat at Kappel (11 October 1531) at the height of the Confederacy's civil war, all might have been lost to Zürich if not for Heinrich Bullinger.

The Zürich Reformation effort faced existential threats in the aftermath of the civil war. The victorious Catholic cantons had emerged in a superior political position within the Confederacy while, in terms of doctrinal influence, Lutheranism made great strides across southern Germany. Zürich's spiritual leadership was also threatened by defections; from its theological position and from colleagues in Bern, Basel, Schaffhausen, and even within its own environs denying former allegiances. Historians familiar with the matter suggest that itinerant sectarian preachers and Catholic or Lutheran advocates convinced the rural folk (and some town folk) that the recent war had been the fault of the Zürich clergy (particularly Zwingli) interfering in political matters beyond their understanding and training. The Zürich magistrates had their scapegoat for past and recent mistakes and used it in rebuilding their credibility. They made assurances that clergy would by kept out of politics and under the control of the council; they assured the people that there would be no more Zwinglis.[30]

---

29. Baker, "Church, State, and Dissent," 135.
30. Ella, *Bullinger*, 89; McCoy and Baker, *Fountainhead*, 11–20.

What this meant in practice was that the clergy would no longer have the freedom to make political commentaries in their sermons or speak on incendiary matters (as determined by the council) stirring up the masses. The Church of Zürich would be re-moulded into another institution of the state where it would occupy a still important but inferior position.[31] For men like Bullinger the attitude of the magistrates was the first hurdle in a three-year struggle to have Zwingli's understanding of the church's relationship with the state—one aspect of the covenant—spelled out and accepted. When he addressed the gathering of pastors and magistrates as the new antistes on 13 December 1531 he promised that the clergy would be loyal to the political authority but also insisted that they must have the right to condemn error wherever they found it. This was their prophetic obligation, carried out through notes, meetings, and sermons if needs be, sermons being the very cornerstone of the church and its main method of educating the flock. Their sermons would be fettered, he said, only to the Word of God and not to the word of any man, and he explained that the pastors did not support the notion of a state run by the church or of a church run by the state but they did see Zürich as a united sacred entity—a Christian state ruled over by Christian magistrates. This central principle would persevere beyond the *Second Helvetic Confession*—the very nature of the covenantal community was determined by the character of the magistrate himself (or themselves as the case may be). Bullinger agreed that the clergy would not, therefore, be involved in political affairs (inasmuch as these could be separated from religious affairs) and that they would be subject to magisterial discipline. The magistrates were satisfied with this proposal (Bullinger threatened to quit otherwise) even if they did not fully understand its theological ramifications.

Bullinger had obligated the clergy, as shepherds, to point out wrongdoing (that is, to pinpoint acts contravening Scripture) wherever they found them, and the implications of this obligation occupied much subsequent debate and discussion.[32] He worked closely with the magistrates (as the chief pastor rather than as a "Zwinglian" partisan) to safeguard the changes inspired and implemented by Zwingli, to reinforce them, and to protect the reform effort from opponents foreign and domestic. For example, Zwingli's ordinances were strengthened by Bullinger's new church order (approved by the Great Council) of October 1532. The role of the clergy (under the synod) was therein re-defined in terms of special civil office; pastors became officers

---

31. Nelson–Burnett, "Kilchen ist uff dem Radthus?" 49.
32. Mühling, *Kirchenpolitik*, 147; Ella, *Bullinger*, 121.

who preached and performed pastoral duties, safeguarding true religion as determined by the synod and enforced by the magistrates.[33]

Having examined his ecclesiology elsewhere[34], and putting other doctrines aside, it might be sufficient to conclude that Bullinger's opinions about the church's relationship with the civil authority did not differ significantly from Zwingli's. He had turned to and expanded upon the master's understanding of the covenant only in order to get a better handle on the roles of the church and the magistrates. In post-war Zürich, however, survival necessitated a greater concentrating on communal unity, and this came to occupy a much more central position in his writings than it had in Zwingli's.

By way of summary, for Zwingli and Bullinger the covenant community, the Christian commonwealth (or visible church), was laid out in Scripture as a mix of saints and sinners (true, merely professed, and non-believers) akin to civil society. Zwingli had used such a definition against the Anabaptists from 1525. The conditions of the covenant—God's relationship to his people—applied to both church and state. Erasmus and Melanchthon held the civil authority as an essentially Christian body and, now Bullinger agreed, calling it a covenantal institution (like the church). Therefore it was imperative for him that the pastor and the magistrate cooperate for the good health of the community. The pastor was to interpret the meaning of the covenant in his sermons, condemn and confront evil practices and opinions, ferret out wickedness. The pastor was the shepherd of the flock but, in a similar way Bullinger also spoke of the magistrate as a minister of God. Even though the pastor and magistrate worked within the same structure clearly their offices were not identical. We noted that the pastor's role was spiritual in essence—the evangelical norm—with no role as ruler or judge and subject to the magistrate where this did not interfere in the spread of the gospel or cross the Word of God. The magistrate was to safeguard all the conditions which allowed the gospel to be spread by the pastors, to keep peace and societal order, and to administer justice. In 1534 Bullinger wrote a treatise entitled *De testamento seu foedere Dei unico et aeterno* or *The one and eternal testament or covenant of God* as explanation and guideline.

In the second part of the treatise, in the section discussing civil and judicial law, Bullinger outlined the importance of civil authorities:

---

33. Baker, "Church, State, and Dissent," 137.
34. Chibi, *The Wheat and the Tares*, 224–46.

> The judicial or civil laws provide rules for the maintenance of peace and public tranquillity, for punishing the guilty, for waging war and repelling enemies, for the defence of liberty, of the oppressed, or widows, of orphans, and of the fatherland, and for the making of laws of justice and equity relating to the purchase, the loan, possessions, inheritance, and other legal subjects of this sort. Are not these things also included in that very condition of the covenant which prescribes integrity and commands that we walk in the presence of God?

He understood the basic framework of the covenant stemming from *Gen* [17:1–14]. God promised to be God, sufficient to all the needs of his people and in return they agreed to uphold the covenant by being faithful and morally upright (e.g., love thy neighbour). For Bullinger this covenantal agreement was the focus of both the Old and New Testaments; the moral laws were a restatement of the Abrahamic covenant. In 1530s' Zürich, therefore, prophets taught the covenant while magistrates enforced the necessary conditions. Together, the church and secular authority nurtured "purity of the soul, sincerity of faith, and love of virtue and the neighbor"[35] or piety—the *sine quo non* of true faith. The internal and external conditions of the community must be properly ordered; the latter was the responsibility of the magistrate.

"What is more strange," Bullinger wrote, "than the insanity that drives those who exclude the magistrate from the church of God, as if there were no need of his functions, or who consider his functions to be of the sort that cannot or ought not to be numbered among the holy and spiritual works of the people of God?"[36] Later, in his second *Decade*, he phrased it this way:

> Who is ignorant, that the magistrate's especial care ought to be to keep the commonweal in safeguard and prosperity? Which undoubtedly he cannot do, unless he provide to have the Word of God preached too his people and cause them to be taught the true worship of God, by that means making himself, as it were, the minister of true religion.[37]

We will examine the *Decades* in due course.

Although the 'Zürich understanding' of the covenant was under threat from the Catholic cantons, the greater threat was Anabaptist sectarianism. As noted, Zwingli and Bullinger both held the visible church and the community as one and the same united sacred entity. Similarly, for both, schism

---

35. Bullinger, "The One and Eternal Testament," 113.
36. Bullinger, "The One and Eternal Testament," 114.
37. Bullinger, *Decades*, 2/vii, 324. Also see, Raath, "Covenant," 1001–3.

and separation from the church and its theological underpinnings was both high crime and heresy.[38] The Anabaptist program of an isolated church and non-cooperation with the civil authorities was therefore a threat to social peace, order and piety. In 1531 Bullinger wrote *Von dem unverschampten fräefel ergerlichem verwyrren und unwarhafftem leeren der selbsgesandten Widertoeuffern viergespraech Buecher* (or *Four books to warn the faithful from the shameless disturbances, offensive confusion and false teachings of the Anabaptists*), emphasizing especially issues of genuine Christian and ethical behaviour to counter the rising Anabaptist menace.

Recall that Grebel and Stumpf had presented a plan for the church which they believed would help members achieve a moral perfection *through separation from earthly temptations.* Since they did not involve themselves in civil matters, the sectarians also thought themselves exempt from the constraints of civil authority (anticipating Münster). While Zwingli and Bullinger agreed that if everyone was perfectly pious there would be no need for secular authority such was just not the case. Sinful humans dwell alongside the good and, consequently, the good need protection from the wicked. The wicked need to be restrained, brought to justice, and punished for their acts. Anabaptists were *the* threat to the physical unity of the church but they were not the only philosophical menace. Caspar von Schwenckfeld, for example, influenced many pastors and parishioners away from the basics of magisterial reform and, inadvertently perhaps, away from the underpinnings of the "Zürich understanding."

Schwenckfeld was a nobleman, a former Lutheran, an itinerant preacher of the mystic/spiritualist school of thought and, like many of his colleagues he believed that while the civil authority *was* of divine creation it was created *solely* to order human society with no mandate to interfere in religious matters. In this way he dismissed the importance of the visible church. In 1532 he countered Bullinger's *Four books* with *Difference between the Old and New Testament* wherein he fully rejected the authority of the Old Testament over believers (as some kind of Judaic legalism) as well as any claimed continuities with the New Testament (e.g., infant baptism was not a reinterpretation of circumcision).[39] In a letter of 3 March 1533 Schwenckfeld explained that the magistrate has authority only over human justice and temporal matters as *per* the *two kingdoms* theology of Luther.

38. Oyer, "The Reformers Oppose the Anabaptist Theology," 206.
39. Gordon, *Swiss Reformation*, 211.

In essence he wanted to remove the office of the magistrate and the kingdom of Christ—separate as these are—from all Old Testament association. It was steeped in legalism, outward righteousness, and written laws which emphasized the letter rather than the spirit. If it was the case that Christianity was dictated by outward regulations then, yes, the magistrate would be the inheritor of the Old Testament kings and would have the authority to regulate religion and punish religious offences with the sword. But, according to Schwenckfeld, this was not Christianity. Christianity is faith and interior righteousness and freedom of conscience and, as such, is beyond the authority of the magistrate. He hinted that magisterial reform was really nothing more than a new type of popery (tyranny).[40]

Leo Jud (a disaffected Zwinglian) echoed some of this and put forth a plan (similar to the Grebel/Stumpf plan but influenced by Oecolampadius) which transferred disciplinary authority out of the hands of the magistrates and into the hands of an ecclesiastical morals court manned by church members exclusively elected out of the congregation. The court would be independent of the magistrates and would have the power of excommunication. Oecolampadius had made a similar representation to Zwingli. In March 1532 Jud notified Bullinger that the time was right to put clear blue water between the church and state—each with distinctive laws, jurisdictions, courts and enforcement.

Such ideas obviously ran counter to the "Zürich understanding" and Bullinger reminded Jud that a magistrate was also a servant of God. The idea of a Christian magistrate was by no means contradictory, explaining moreover, the basic duties of the pastor and the magistrates in terms any evangelical could accept. Jud held that a magistrate could be involved in church discipline as an elder rather than as a magistrate *per se*, while Bullinger argued that the Christian magistrate ruled the church (commonweal or community) as both a leader of the civil order and as a premier member of the visible church. If the rulers are diligent and Christian, the ethical improvement of the members should follow. Jud's preaching threatened the delicate balance Bullinger had achieved and he took it upon himself to face down anything which threatened the "Zürich understanding."

— § —

What did Bullinger do?

He created another synodic structure for the territorial churches and drafted letters and treatises and sent these to the Bernese disputants at

---

40. Baker, "Church, State, and Dissent," 144.

Zöfingen (in 1532), adopting a hard line against Anabaptists (including the death penalty) and stressing the continuity between the covenant of the Old Testament (with Israel) and the New (with Christians), with magistrates taking the position of the Old Testament kings. As the Bernese theologians debated with the Anabaptist leadership the definition of the church, excommunication, and the magistracy, Bullinger coached them on how to make the case for Old Testament evidence. He also sketched out a paper on the duty of the magistrate in the church which clearly linked the covenant with magisterial discipline and authority over religious matters. The sketch, entitled *What the duty of the magistrate is in the church of Christ, who lawfully defends it against the seditions of heretics and the attacks of tyrants'* has six points and provides a succinct overview of "Zürich understanding." There is one God, one testament and one spirit of both the old and the new people. Consequently, the religion, the faith and the church of the ancients and ours is also the same. Here, Bullinger made the stipulation that a very few things have changed due to consideration of the people and the times. As for the magistrates, since there was a magistracy in the ancient [church], it follows logically that it has not been annulled and, furthermore, it is the duty of the magistrate to restrain blasphemy, to forbid heresies, and to take care of discipline. The magistrates "guard the evangelical truth and its worshippers with arms, if necessary, against the godless ones" and if the magistrate neglects this [duty], dealing [only] with civil justice and the like, he is impious and less than perfect [since he neglects religious matters]. It is unclear whether the magistrate can then be overthrown.

Despite the fact that Anabaptism was in decline in Zürich territory Bullinger did not drop his guard and subsequent events at Münster inspired him to propose to the Zürich synod harsher anti-Anabaptist decrees. He submitted a draft—"*Whether it is the duty of the honorable magistracy to punish in honor, body or goods men who lead astray or who have been led astray from the faith*"—dealing with such ideas as forcing faith and the death penalty for heretics. Forcing faith was characterized as the driving out of evil influences. While there was no denying that faith was God-given, for Bullinger, toleration of heresy was akin to allowing everyone free reign to do whatever they liked, which clearly upset both the church and the state aspects of the commonweal. Forcing someone away from evil and error must be profitable to both the individual and the community but, of course, not every case warranted death. Moderation and clear deliberation needed to be the normal approach in all cases. After passing the synod the draft was forwarded to the council. In Bullinger's construction of the covenantal community Anabaptist theology and practice offended and disrupted peace, order and true religion.[41] The "Zürich understanding" was taken to Basel in 1536 (out of which meetings the *First Helvetic Confession* was produced) and was largely repeated in the *Second Helvetic Confession* thirty years later.

— § —

We need not devote much space to these Reformed confessions. Of the twenty-seven articles of the *First* only two dealt with issues of temporal government. Article twenty-five dealt with the treatment of apostates, heretics and blasphemers—naming the Anabaptists specifically—and recommending they be "punished and suppressed by the supreme power" [the magistrate] for the wider good of the church. Article twenty-six repeated Bullinger's formulation of the "Zürich understanding." The civil power promotes and protects "the true honor of God and the proper service of God by punishing and rooting out all blasphemy . . ." as well as promoting sound teaching and preaching of the word, education of true religion, discipline, support of the poor and of ministers, turning over church possessions to these purposes. All good Christians must be prepared to play a role in government when called upon to do so, including all those things to which sectarians object, like serving in the military or swearing oaths.[42] The later confession of 1566 expanded upon this, envisioning the magistrate as holding the Word of God in his hands, shielding both it and the people from contrary materials, moulding the community toward godliness (or worldliness if he was not a true Christian). When the magistrate is a Christian, his laws are made according to the Word, he judges, protects and punishes according to its terms, draws the sword against "all malefactors, seditious persons, thieves, murderers, oppressors, blasphemers, perjured persons, and all those whom God has commanded him to punish and even to execute." The magistrate stands between the good order of the properly fashioned church and the chaos inspired by sectarians, blasphemers and heretics—as a father to his people—who all obey "for he who opposes the magistrate provokes the severe wrath of God against himself."[43]

— § —

41. Baker, "Church, State, and Dissent," 140, 148, 150.
42. Cochrane, "The First Helvetic Confession," 110–11.
43. Cochrane, "The Second Helvetic Confession," 301–2. Also see Raath, "Covenant," 1003–4, for additional examinations.

The *Second Helvetic Confession*, important as it is, drew on Bullinger's most influential work, the *Decades*—five books of ten sermons each outlining the totality of his theology; the "Zürich understanding" of the covenant holds it all together.

As noted earlier (and as particularly in the sermons of the second book and referenced in the third[44]) the two tables of the divine law (or moral or natural law) provide Bullinger's firm evidence of God's promise as guarantor of the covenant and man's duty as beneficiary.[45] There are special considerations, however: sermon six exempts the magistrate from "thou shalt not kill" in particular circumstances, distinguishing types of magistrates, and the necessity of obedience; sermon eight considers the work of judges; and, nine the issue of warfare. As to our main theme, the relationship between the magistrate and religion, sermon seven was Bullinger's most detailed statement.

The office of the magistrate revolved around three basic points—order, judgement and punishment; his ordinance, his rules or decrees, were made for "maintaining of religion, honesty, justice, and public peace: and it consisteth on two points; in ordering rightly matters of religion, and making good laws for the preservation of honesty, justice, and common peace." From this he concluded:

> The catholic verity teacheth, that the care of religion doth especially belong to the magistrate; and that it is not in his power only, but his office and duty also, to dispose and advance religion . . . Who is ignorant, that the magistrate's especial care ought to be to keep the commonweal in safe guard and prosperity? Which undoubtedly he cannot do, unless he provide to have the word of God preached to his people, and cause them to be taught the true worship of God, by that means making himself, as it were, the minister of true religion.[46]

As such, his authority includes the "trial of doctrines," which translates as oversight of the synod's work and passing of the death sentence on heretics and schismatics. While both the pastor and magistrate were ministers of God dedicated to the well-being of the covenantal community, Bullinger distinguished their offices in a way reminiscent of Luther's functionality. He would not have a king preach or baptise, nor have the pastor judge murder cases. There were many offices in the church but "God is the God of order,

---

44. Bullinger, *Decades*, 1:298–393. Sermon six (298–322); sermon seven (323–44); sermon eight (345–69); and sermon nine (370–93).

45. Baker, "Retrospective," 364.

46. Cochrane, "The First Helvetic Confession," 223–24.

and not of confusion . . . the magistrate of duty ought to have a care of religion, either in ruin to restore it, or in soundness to preserve it; and still to see that it proceed according to the rule of the word of God."[47] The covenantal sacred community is based firmly on the law of God. For Bullinger this is placed into the hands of the king by the pastors (through preaching and teaching) so that he, in turn, is aware of God's will in regard to both church and state matters—"by which law he had to govern the whole estate of all his realm." It is a heavy burden to bear; even more so than the ecclesiastical estate. The prince is responsible for the entire health of the whole community. Bullinger has weaved together the two kingdoms into one tight knit unit which checks and balances worked into it. "The politic magistrate is commanded to give ear to the ecclesiastical ruler and the ecclesiastical minister must obey the politic governor in all things which the law commandeth" according to the final authority of the Word of God.[48]

Bullinger and Zwingli opposed Anabaptism in the mid-1520s developing the "Zürich understanding" of the covenant as a framework mechanism which could be used against it. For Zwingli, the covenant provided a useful explanation for the continued importance of infant baptism and for the power of the magistrates in the Reformation process. It was a unifying vision—one God, one people, one historic church—with some remaining hints of bilateralism (e.g., two kingdoms). Bullinger, whether in consultation with Zwingli or no in the later 1520s[49], made the covenant the central plank of his theology, developing a unilateral vision which subsequent theologians drew upon and applied to their own circumstances.

Martin Bucer:
Church and the Civil Authority as Co-terminus Entities

From his first treatise of 1523 to his last of 1550, Bucer sought a means to "Christianize" all aspects of human life, instilling sound moral values and godly public conduct as a matter of course into all members of the

---

47. Bullinger, *Decades*, 1:329.
48. Bullinger, *Decades*, 1:329–30.
49. McCoy and Baker, *Fountainhead*, 21; *Swiss Anabaptism*, 333 (begins Bullinger's recording of meetings and disputes).

community. He was a scholar, a diplomat and practiced a spiritual statesmanship as once irenic and controversial. His reputation as a mediator led to frequent travel, temporary re-location, and a growing talent for devising ecclesiastical ordinances. In Bern, Ulm, Augsburg, and in Hesse he perfected his plans for Strasbourg *via* a focus on the transformative applications of Scripture and divine law.[50] The first he applied to religious practices (to eliminate Roman abuses) and the second he applied to society (in terms of regulation, discipline and practice). Like Zwingli, Oecolampadius and Bullinger, Bucer wanted to inspire the building of a new, improved Christian society through the founding of the "state church"—a church which had the support and protection of the temporal authorities *but* which also had some independence of action and control of moral discipline. His doctrine has been called a *co-terminus vision*. What does this mean?

Bucer developed irenic statements of theology (that is, he found useful compromise between the major influences) and his church/state thinking reflects this stance. He discounted Luther's *two kingdoms*; he did not recognize two mutually exclusive (but occasionally overlapping) hierarchies, although he recognized two authorities and there is a hint of functionality about his approach. He also passed over the "Zürich understanding" of the covenant, although Zwingli's unilateral covenant theory gave Bucer context (that is, the community is the church).[51] For Bucer the church had a function independent of the state. He equated the earthly expression of the kingdom of Christ (eternal and heavenly) with the church membership as a "fellowship" of the Lord's Supper rather than as the specific people of God, and it was the fellowship which was supported, moulded, and purified by the work of magistrates (clerical and temporal).

The two entities of church and state were aimed at the same goal of a heightened Christianisation of society, and Bucer held them as part and parcel of each other—mutually subordinate according to their particular roles supervising individual secular duties and spiritual obligations.[52] That is to say, for Bucer, pastors also had a secular role and magistrates (and laymen in general) also had religious duties—they are both quasi-religious and quasi-political in function. A body of lay wardens, therefore, could be considered an ecclesiastical body rather than merely a political one. Bucer's ultimate goal was to transform the church into a God-fearing community which demonstrated its faith pro-actively through concern for both

50. Eells, "The Contributions of Martin Bucer," 35.
51. McCoy and Baker, *Fountainhead*, 22–23.
52. Van Drunen, *Natural Law and the Two Kingdoms*, 116; Spijker, *The Ecclesiastical Offices*, 191.

the spiritual and physical well-being of all of its members. The necessary means to achieve this was the re-introduction of a purer Christian discipline, placed in the hands of the church itself. Recall that Oecolampadius had sought to implement much the same situation in Basel. Although Bucer feared giving rise to an over-zealous church authority, like the one he saw developing under Oecolampadius, the Strasbourg council sought to stifle any effort which gave the church too much independence.

Bucer envisioned a self-contained system of education (on-going, lifelong learning to enrich the on-going sanctification process), public confession of faith and obedience, the Rule of Christ, moral oversight by the pastors and lay elders in a church body (adopting Oecolampadius's idea) and, at the extreme end, public penances and excommunication under clerical authority.[53] His lay elders, however, unlike Oecolampadius's, were not laymen participating in an oversight capacity, but ministers of the church (after the example of *Ephesians* 4:11-2)—that is, officers of the body of Christ but not preachers of the Word.[54] Like all the magisterial reformers Bucer recognized and looked to the magistrates as key to the success of the Reformation, but he faced an array of difficulties; the effort in Strasbourg stalled due to magisterial anti-clerical scruples, general apathy, and the fact of so many different and competing evangelical groups vying for official attention. Moreover, his fundamentally Zwinglian approach often clashed with some of the ideas of his partner Wolfgang Capito, with Lutherans, sectarian groups, and, of course, with traditional Catholics still in the city. To avoid the pitfalls of egregious debate Bucer developed church orders and designed ecclesiastical disciplinary bodies abroad to be subsequently implemented in Strasbourg.

When the city of Ulm joined the *Schmalkaldic League* in early 1531 the magistrates there were forced to look more seriously into Reformation issues. The council appointed a special committee (including the mayor, four patricians, and four guild masters) dedicated to the creation of a new church order but, due to inexperience this failed. They subsequently sought the direct aid of three familiar correspondents, Bucer, Oecolampadius, and Ambrosius Blaurer. Blauer is an interesting figure here. As the leader of the Reformation in Konstanz he sought to combine Lutheran and Zwinglian influences and had already implemented a system in which every citizen

---

53. Burnett, "Church Discipline," 438–40.
54. Graham, *The Uses of Reform*, 14.

took a turn enforcing moral orders on the city as a member of a supervisory council. The three men arrived in Strasbourg on 21 May.

Bucer almost immediately presented a plan to the council for the appointment of parish wardens. He had presented the plan in Strasbourg on 25 February 1531, but expanded it now with eighteen constructive articles, including plans for a magisterial marriage court, a board of church wardens and yearly synods—ecclesiastical and social renewal were at the heart of the proposed order. Of these articles the final four dealt with the rights and duties of the civil authorities with regard to the re-organization of the church and with the full establishment of Bucer's basic and familiar social renewal vision. With his two colleagues and a local reformer—a Zwingli disciple name Konrad Sam—Bucer formulated and submitted a declaration of principles entitled "*Christian doctrines, ceremonies, and life; composed by the preachers, along with the advice of my appointed Lords.*"[55]

The Ulm government was tasked to fill vacant preaching posts with men who as near as possible "approximate the apostle's standards" (that is, Paul's requirements in his pastoral letters), but also with the examination of their faults, to provide for their livings, and to dismiss them should new faults be uncovered later. Placing the pastors under the magistracy was also a boon to them; it gave them an additional level of protection against slander—a kind of board of appeal against vicious reports. Bucer proposed a number of Zwinglian innovations as well, like the creation of a committee—magistrates with experience in church affairs working with superior members of the pastorate—to examine candidate preachers and oversee the disciplinary process. A general board of church wardens would supervise the churches, overseeing general needs and moral direction, while twice yearly synods were meant to enhance the life of the church, manned by all the preachers (urban and rural) and delegates from all the parishes ("wise and devout men"). The congregation would receive synodic instruction through the delegates and would, in turn, act *en masse* and in common as a kind of bishop with regard to visitations, censure, and excommunication. In common the wardens and ministers would carry out an annual visitation of the rural churches, investigating especially reports of "strange doctrine."

As elsewhere, discipline was a key question. In Ulm authority was to be handed over to a "board of eight esteemed, devout, God-fearing, wise and diligent men"—three magistrates, three members of the congregations, and two ministers. Each member was responsible for one district of the city (recall Oecolampadius's idea of a council of elders). Congregations would take their concerns for the admonished, but still unrepentant, sinner to this

---

55. Greschat, "Church and Civil Community," 21.

body, at which point the general order of the Rule of Christ would be followed with the council acting as the ultimate tribunal, deciding punishment or banishment, following which the preachers were to make announcements in the pulpits (which might nowadays be termed *naming and shaming*). In theory, unchristian conduct would become anathema throughout the entire church/community of Ulm and indeed most of the guilty were charged with moral offences (e.g., adultery or theft).[56] Bucer shared with Oecolampadius the idea that while the magistrates could clear the sinner of his particular crime—overseeing public morality in this way—it would be in the hands of the eight "ministers of discipline" (representing the congregation) as to whether he was subsequently readmitted to the fellowship of the church. Such responsibility necessitated a meticulous selection process with emphasis on "special zeal, wisdom and, aptitude in Christian conduct." The council delegated four members (from the four guilds) and they selected the members of the board on the advice of the pastors. The board would have weekly meetings and membership would change on a kind of on-going rota system where two members are replaced and two members remained. Bucer's ideals of moral reform also stretched to the magistrates themselves, to whom he proposed a board of discipline assembled to punish offenders within the government. This translated out to the community as a need, consequently, to elect to government only "God-fearing and upright men."[57] The Ulm magistrates ultimately baulked over two of Bucer's eighteen proposals when the order was announced on 16 June.

Unfortunately, the two dropped proposals had been central to Bucer's complete Christianisation endeavour. With regard to the appointment of ministers Bucer wanted the opinions and needs of the congregation considered (*priesthood of all believers*) but he had not presented a concrete plan of practical implementation—he only articulated the principle. The council removed it from the final formulation leaving appointments and examinations in their own hands with the aid of the wardens and the appointment of a process supervisor. Authority over preaching was not shared with any particular church body. Neither would discipline be outside total magisterial control. Any final decisions were to be theirs; Bucer's board of discipline would be comprised of four councillors, only two men of the congregation, and two preachers. The board would oversee the whole congregation, admonish and warn, but would not have any power over excommunication. There would be no dividing of responsibilities by district, the council would

---

56. Spijker, *The Ecclesiastical Offices*, 191–92. Also see, Freudenberg, "Catechisms," 92; and Coy, *Strangers and Misfits*, 82.

57. Spijker, *The Ecclesiastical Offices*, 193.

have the final word on excommunications, and the preachers' sermons would include whatever announcements the council choose to allow. Disappointing as this must have been for Bucer the end product did reflect his proposed structure, his ideals of "good Christian living," and "all sinful, unchristian vice" was to be exposed and eradicated—moral reform *via* preaching sermons, catechisms, and visitations.[58]

The new church order proved unpopular with the clergy. Opponents emerged, some treatises were written, and a dispute was held on 17 June, by which point the effort had been rendered academic. Although Bucer, Oecolampadius and Blaurer stayed on to oversee such familure activities as changes to the Mass and removal of images, none of them remained in Ulm by July.[59] Bucer visited Memmingen and Biberach on his way back to Strasbourg, writing *General Announcement* as justification of the Ulm reform effort, attaching subsequent published versions of the Ulm church order. His next summons came from Augsburg.

Bucer was a correspondent of the Zwinglian pastor there, Michael Keller, who had drafted and posted a number of doctrinal position papers. As in Strasbourg, however, the council of Augsburg was reform-leaning but faced with powerful competing obstacles (e.g., location in Catholic Bavaria, a sitting bishop named Christoph von Stadion, social class division, antistranger xenophobia, and competing religious parties). In January 1534 a newly elected council with a powerful mandate for change implemented a series of minor reforms (e.g., removal of images) inviting Bucer to visit and provide practical guidance. He stayed for a month in the first instance, 6 November to 9 December, to shore up the initial effort, producing a draft of ten articles for the endorsement of the pastors. Again, the power of the magistrates was an important aspect of these articles, placing the care and direction of the church under council auspices and stressing the obedience of the clergy to the civil authority. Bucer returned in February 1535 and negotiated an agreement with the preachers enabling the magistrates to enter into negotiations with the *Schmalkaldic League*. The power of the temporal authority was underlined by two treatises of some interest to us here. Bucer wrote supplementary material (*On the office of government*) for Wolfgang Musculus's translation of Augustine's letter to Count (sometimes

---

58. Spijker, *The Ecclesiastical Offices*, 195; Coy, *Strangers and Misfits*, 82; Greschat, *Bucer*, 108–9.

59. Greschat, *Bucer*, 109–10; Close, *The Negotiated Reformation*, 92.

General) Boniface, as well as a treatise on civil authority entitled *Dialogues or Discussion*. A new church ordinance, however, was not completed until his next visit of 18 May 1537.[60]

Bucer drew out of the saint's letter a number of correspondences between its ancient setting and contemporary Augsburg. Boniface, a civil administrator in Rome's African province, often wrote in defence of the many imperial laws, edicts and harsher actions issued and enforced against continued but dying Donatist resistance to the solution of the council of Carthage. Augustine, himself a convert to Christianity, approved harsh action against heretics and schismatics "passed for the protection of God's truth." For Bucer, chapter eight of the letter-treatise was key; that held out both sermons and imperials edicts as the means of gathering the church together.[61] *Dialogues* followed up on similar Augustinian themes in the form of a discussion between a Zwinglian, a spiritualist, and a man in the middle, juxtaposing the decisions of sound secular authority against idolatry and blasphemy (shots fired at the Roman clerical establishment).

For Bucer magistrates are the "chief shepherd and superintendents of the church," whose duty is to protect and reform it according to sound evangelical doctrines. His language can be harsh; there are explicit calls for fire, the sword, and even strangulation of the heretic's family. Theologians make their arguments to the magistrates giving them the necessary justifications for implementing the reform movement. Once the falsity of the popish religion has been stamped out, the magistrates serve as watchdogs thereafter, the wrath of God hanging over the community.[62] In Bucer's wider theology, faith remained the gift of God and sanctification was an on-going project with the aid of the Holy Spirit. No man can be totally free of temptation and sin, so each needed the civil power to aid him through education (the top priority), admonishment, advice, punishment and correction. Everyone benefited when the civil power scrupulously performed its duty—the sinner was corrected, the lax were encouraged, the congregation (the fellowship or body) was purified, and society emerged as a moral entity. In an empire of course, local magistrates are not entirely at liberty as they are subject to territorial rulers and the emperor. Bucer added that the Word of God is a touchstone against which to test all secular commands (hinting at a justification for necessary disobedience).[63] On the local level it is a paternal

---

60. Greschat, *Bucer*, 113; Close, *The Negotiated Reformation*, 96–97.

61. Augustine, *Retractions*, 226–27. This can be found online at http://www.newadvent.org/ fathers/1102185.htm (presenting the text found in *NPNF*, 1).

62. Jaussen, *History of the German People*, 5:290–92.

63. Greschat, *Bucer*, 115.

vision; magistrates act out of concern and obligation, warding off trouble as a father in a household. The council is the totality of "father", making up for the negligence and mistakes of any and all individual fathers.

Whether father figure or exemplar of Old Testament ruler, the magistrate had power over the reform of religion and discipline as a quasi-spiritual figure. Bucer drew distinctions, however, between state and ecclesiastical spheres (i.e., exterior and interior themes) in a way that Oecolampadius had not envisioned. For Bucer, the magistracy acted in their capacity as pseudo-ministers rather than in their capacity as lay politicians (which granted related but different authorities). In Ulm and in Augsburg he had gone to great lengths to have these principles recognized. As ministers (not of the Word) magistrates are involved in all efforts to purify the church (i.e., the community). None of this theory (outlined in letters, mandates and treaties) held much sway with the Strasbourg council, however, which was unwilling to delegate ecclesiastical authority to clerical counterparts. Bucer's reforms were both appreciated and encouraged but the magistrates did not sanction everything.

For example, the council mandate of 25 August 1529—enforcing moral discipline—was never strictly enforced. Moreover, the new magisterial marriage court (established *via* mandate 16 December 1529) did not feature pastors in any decision making or advisory capacity; the church warden system was established (30 October 1531) safeguarding magisterial authority rather than congregational participation. Bucer followed Oecolampadius's vision of a body of elders which, in Strasbourg, would have decentralized corrective power out of the hands of an already over-burdened council. Each parish would be responsible for its own discipline. Instead, the Senate appointed three wardens—a magistrate, an alderman and a parishioner—for each of the newly reorganized seven parishes of the city to supervise morals, discipline, correct doctrine, and to assist the pastors in every way they could (including doctrinal exegesis).[64] The wardens oversaw the church on behalf of the council—attending meetings of the pastors' convention, consulting on pastoral matters. Bucer had envisioned the elders system as a prelude to a self-contained, self-regulating community fellowship, not as an end in itself, but he chose his battles carefully.[65] Here, at least, the clergy had some influence. What he really wanted was for the council to give up tolerance of Anabaptists as a necessary pre-condition to real change ... mostly.

64. Rott, "The Strasbourg Kirchenpfleger," 122.
65. Spijker, *The Ecclesiastical Offices*, 197.

Bucer was of two minds on the sectarians. He conceded that they presented a model of good Christian piety, practicing the kind of caring brotherhood he wanted to instil in all members of the fellowship. As greatly as they embodied the internal aspects of an ideal moral life, however, they offended and threatened the external domain of the magistrates. A threat to one aspect was a threat to both; Anabaptism endangered the unity, faith and piety of the entire community.[66] Bucer appealed to the council to enact anti-sectarian legislation, but the magistrates resisted, wanting evidence of a unified public opinion on the Reformation, a fully tested church order which guaranteed the council's retention of full ecclesiastical authority, and proposals which would not irk the emperor. Bucer succeeded in getting a renewed anti-sectarian mandate (24 September 1530) but it was enforced no more closely than the previous mandate).[67] A little later, presentations to the council on 30 November 1532 achieved a little more. Preaching of the gospel had achieved only so much. More was possible, but toleration of non-conformist views had to end (*via* the sword if necessary). A commission (of four laymen) was created which subsequently proposed (12 April 1533) the establishment of a city-wide synod (presided over by the commissioners), a set of doctrinal principles (in sixteen articles drafted by Bucer) to be subscribed by all, and procedures for the examination of sectarian leaders and rural pastors. The synod first assembled on 3 June—four commissioners, the twenty-one wardens, and all the preachers and teachers of the city.[68]

The early signs were positive: Bucer's articles were revised and endorsed; the pastors gave voice to long-standing grievances; the rural pastors were examined and all of them endorsed the articles (10–14 June). For perhaps obvious reasons the sectarian leaders would not endorse the largely anti-sectarian regulations and the magistrates failed to enforce subscription. Disputations with the sectarian leaders did take place—sometimes official sanctioned, sometimes not—and clerical pressure was brought to bear.[69] In the meantime the synod turned to the creation of a new church order, drawing upon previous statements and presentations.

The new draft, known as *Deliberations* (or *Considerations*), was subsequently modified by the council to invest all final decisions therein, including the supervision of doctrine and appointments, the oversight of committees, meetings and synods, the board of wardens, discipline, as well

---

66. Rott, "The Strasbourg Kirchenpfleger," 117; Kroon, "Martin Bucer and the Problem of Tolerance," 160, 164.

67. Kreider, "The Anabaptists," 106.

68. Greschat, *Bucer*, 121.

69. Spijker, *The Ecclesiastical Offices*, 115; Selderhuis, *Marriage and Divorce*, 78.

as other moral issues like sumptuary laws and provisions for civil marriage ceremonies. Also included was oversight of a weekly meeting of a church council of preachers, assistant preachers, and government representatives, but publication was delayed to January 1535.[70] A more decisive magisterial commitment was achieved, however, on 28 January 1534 when the preachers threatened to resign *en masse* over further delay (after news from Münster became wider known). The exile of non-conformists and sectarians began on 3 March 1534; a new mandate accepted Bucer's modified sixteen articles and the city subscribed the *Tetrapolitan Confession*. This was the Zwinglian/Swiss document (written by Bucer and Capito) as a means of aligning the Reformation efforts of Strasbourg, Konstanz, Memmingen, and Lindau. Anabaptists fled the city and harsher mandates for the Strasbourg environs forced sectarianism out altogether. This was Bucer's only real success; his plans for the church as a body with certain autonomous powers were never realized, and subsequent articles of confession only largely reflected earlier attempts.[71] While moral reform and discipline was never abandoned (in theory) the council did not budge from its position of pragmatic delay and its refusal to consider an autonomous ecclesiastical authority. By 1540 Bucer was appealing directly to the congregations to force the council's hand.

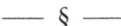

The Protestant states of the empire had been rocked doctrinally, militarily and politically. There was renewed dispute over the meaning of the sacrament, a general council of the church was on the horizon (i.e., Trent), and the Protestants had lost a war to the Catholic states. According to a biography, Bucer saw these set-backs as divine punishment for their postponements in the founding of a true covenantal church. The Christianization of society could not, Bucer thought, be achieved while the magistrates and ecclesiastics remained at odds. His solution was a doubling-down on the *co-terminus* endeavour. Christian fellowships would combine magisterial action (in the form of public mandates enforcing public discipline and morality) with parochial action (in the form of local systems of penance and church discipline). A new treatise entitled *Regarding the abolishment of church vices*, emphasized the duties and responsibilities of the civil authorities while, at the same time, berating them for having failed to enforce existing law. Moreover, members of the covenant, so-called committed Christians, had also failed to act, both to submit themselves to church discipline and to meet

---

70. Selderhuis, *Marriage and Divorce*, 78; Greschat, *Bucer*, 122.
71. Spijker, *The Ecclesiastical Offices*, 204–5; Burnett, "Church Discipline," 441.

their responsibilities for the moral correction and admonishment of others. The council agreed to set harsher punishments and revive old disciplinary mandates (including a new disciplinary ordinance in 1548) but, predictably, it did not approve the idea of any more congregational autonomy. The fellowship idea was abandoned *via* a mandate of 31 October 1547 despite Bucer's rear-guard actions of publications, discussions and suggested unilateral action for the congregations.

The magistrates simply put no stock in the idea of autonomous clerical authority and, although the clerical establish did, they would not act. The situation prompted Bucer to publish a new treatise, *On the Church's Defects and Failings* (1546), in which he now tried to differentiate temporal and clerical authority in some clear cut, unanswerable way. He took up the now-standard external and internal divisions, placing banning and excommunication in the internal category of church responsibilities, underlining in this way the need for the fellowships scheme: "the worldly authority restrict[s] itself to its own sphere and arrogate[s] to itself no greater power than is imposed and ordered by God, in other words, that it have no desire to hinder the concerns of the church."[72] This was not a departure from his earlier theories and beliefs; the two entities were still *co-terminus* and interrelated and, so, they needs must cooperate. The magistrates were simply not living for their neighbours. Those who took their faith, salvation, and membership of the church and covenant seriously must be allowed to come together and persuade the rest by their example. The magistrates feared, however, that this would introduce a schism in the parishes no less serious than that visited upon them by the sectarians. The self-recognized morally superior groups would form an elite body within the larger congregation. Bucer countered this by seeking out some organizational structure which would encourage the fellowships to work alongside the pastors and wardens and avoid such a schism, but the real question was how these fellowships were not, in fact, a prelude to another isolated believers' church? Bucer could not overcome magisterial opposition or censorship of the writings before *Interim* put paid to further action.[73]

A change of scenery gave Bucer one final chance to put his *co-terminus* vision into practise, in England, at the beginning of the 1550s.

---

72. Greschat, "Church and Civil Community," 3, quoting *Defects*.
73. Greschat, *Bucer*, 213–17; Burnett, "Church Discipline," 448.

For Bucer, England suffered the same want of social and moral stability as found in the Protestant cities of the empire. Yes, the magistrates (in the form of a king and council) had already wrestled the kingdom out from under the tyranny of Rome, but the realm remained barely reformed. Bucer sought to ingrain his Christianisation plan, but he was never officially consulted on how this might be achieved, but he did write about it. On 21 October 1550 he passed his latest manuscript, *De Regno Christi* (*The kingdom of Christ*), over to a friend to present upwards as a new year's gift to the young Edward VI. Although the book was not actually published in the lifetime of either Bucer or Edward, and nor would it appear in English translation until well into the eighteenth century, there is some clear evidence that both the king and others knew its contents.

Bucer's familiar vision, the Christianisation of society (i.e., all of life brought under the Rule of Christ) was rehearsed for this new audience. He emphasized a properly administered discipline by suitable ministers fitted to the task—ministers of both the church and the state upholding the autonomy of the church for the good of society as a whole. The king was to lead the effort—Bucer showed him how—and God's good order was to be established by the royal government. The English would be improved internally by the work of the Holy Spirit and externally by the work of the magistrates. The two authorities set the stage for Bucer's salvation by lifelong sanctification doctrine).[74] Bucer understood salvation as a process by which God gathers his own and wills them to be subject to worldly authorities—whether civil or ecclesiastical—which exist to assist in the purging of sin. In book one of *De Regno Christi* Bucer made a point of outlining, for Edward, the ways in which the two earthbound authorities interact (in seven points of comparison). It is a compelling discussion, each point supplied with convincing biblical examples, and this goes a long way toward making it clear just how each kingdom is bound, in ways subordinate or superior, to the other.

The first point is that both kingdoms—of the world or of Christ—are ruled by a sole authority (whether king, council or parliament) which, nonetheless, delegates ruling function to other lesser figures. While Christ is able to be all things to all men He nonetheless uses ministers and other officers for specific ends while, clearly, the civil power cannot be all things to all men and must delegate of necessity. The two kingdoms are also the same (second

---

74. Greschat, *Bucer*, 243–44.

point) in that each "ought to establish and promote the means of making their citizens devout and righteous who rightly acknowledge and worship their God and who are truly helpful toward their neighbours in all their actions . . . for the building of faith and salvation." In other words they have the same goal but differentiated approaches to its final achievement. The magistrate cannot see into the hearts of men. He can, however, remove the obviously wicked and obviously impious in order to keep the flock pure and untroubled, "prepare them for the reception of the word of God . . . for they are ministers of God"; genuine piety and righteousness is in the hands of Christ Himself.[75] In this way the kingdom of the world is subordinate and a helper to the kingdom of Christ.

Both kingdoms (third point) tolerate the wicked up to the point where they openly reveal themselves and subsequently remain obstinate in their wickedness. For the temporal authority the use of the sword was given to ensure peace and tranquillity whereas the kingdom of Christ deploys the Word, penance, and exclusion. It is appropriate that the magistrate kill the perpetually offensive in the worldly kingdom while the church's disciplinary authority ends with excommunication. The fourth point is that both kingdoms use certain external means to bind the people to the kingdom more firmly—covenants, oaths and sacraments—administered through the officers of the kingdom. Here Bucer used the familiar passages of *Ephesians* to differentiate ecclesiastical functions. Both kingdoms (point five) are responsible for the education of their members so that each genuine citizen or member of the church can be useful to the rest. In the church Christ provides all the necessities, administered through such functionaries as overseers and deacons, whereas in the world the king must ensure that each of his subject's needs are met, delegating responsibility to his officials. Given these responsibilities, Bucer noted (point six) that each kingdom was at war with evil men and evil spirits for which they employ appropriate weaponry (either carnal or spiritual). Finally, and perhaps most importantly (point seven), was that the two kingdoms are mutual subordinate.

Christians are subject to the powers of the world, to "just princes" or "terrible tyrants" alike. Here Bucer discussed all the normal aspects of civil obedience—paying taxes, obeying the laws, using the court system, the meeting of personal obligations. Magistrates (kings and kingdoms) are themselves subject to Christ and to "developing piety not for themselves alone, but they also seek to lead their subjects to it," including the acceptance of clerical admonishment for themselves and the performance of

---

75. Bucer, "De Regno Christi," 180. This is also discussed in Graham, *The Uses of Reform*, 225.

genuine and public acts of repentance, if necessary, to set good examples for their people.[76] It was here, of course, Bucer and the reformers in general faced their greatest opposition. To many it looked like the old, severely abused, papal penitential system. Bucer argued that individual clergyman were not acting as anything other than as a functionary of the church, and "such princes yield finally not only to the public ministers of Christ and the pastors of the churches, but also to the churches in their entirety."

In this way he hoped to establish a system of checks and balances in the relationship between the kingdoms, making it clear how the civil authority fully participate in the creation of the "Christocracy", where the social order is dependent upon a church formed and organized around clear scriptural principles. Once this church is established by the king all give it their allegiance—this is the final Christianisation of society. The civil authority brings the church to pass, protects it, and nurtures it through the provision of suitable priests. The question of elders comes up later in the treatise as Bucer considered more fully the church, the kingdom of Christ, as a means of giving aid to the preachers and pastors. To conform to the English tradition, the senior elder would be called a bishop. Elders too are ministers of Christ but in a "mediocre way"—teachers, models of prudence, administrators rather than ministers of the sacrament. They are "ministers of the discipline of life and manners."

This brought Bucer full circle back to his original regard for the life and well-being of the neighbour outweighing that of the self. Where a man might have two or three neighbours, these elders care for and advise everyone else as a neighbour, should anyone in the parish fall out of the moral life (as described in the Scriptures—the Rule of Christ set out in *Matthew*)—and living for others. Elders were to be appointed in proportion to the entire population, must be well acquainted with all the people of the parish, must observe their lives, and admonish their faults.[77] In this way Christianisation was to become a total community effort from king down to lowliest labourer.

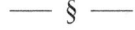

---

76. Bucer, "De Regno Christi," 181–87.
77. Graham, *The Uses of Reform*, 231, 241.

John Calvin: Realization of the Oecolampadius-Bucer Community Vision

Over the course of the dynamic period of the Reformation and into the confessional stage, the attitude of some urban magistrates seems confusing. Why did they obstruct the efforts of their own particular reformers when it seemed that they were themselves the chief beneficiaries of a new, emerging power structure? The late mediaeval tensions that had existed between the church and state authorities over matters of control had been eased with the throwing off of papal power (in some places) and with the easing in of new doctrine, certainly, but replacing them were threats of violence, radical sectarianism, and new, sometimes confusing, contemporary political alliances. All those who subscribed the *priesthood of all believers* ideal placed the appointment of pastors and preachers into the hands of the leaders of the political community (thereby in theory avoiding the clerical tyranny of the papal variety) to whom the ecclesiastical officers were subsequently to be as obedient as any other citizen in all outward, external, human matters (including the external organization of the church itself). All the evangelicals were equally anxious to avoid anything that smacked of clerical privilege (like immunity to prosecution or benefit of clergy). It seems counter-productive that the magistrates then, with appointments and structuring issues in their hands, should subsequently refuse to allow the pastors to take the lead in purely spiritual issues or over matters of social morality and discipline. Why was the mediaeval tension between the two institutional bodies still an issue?

The simple answer is that having thrown off the yoke of papal obedience (viewed as clerical tyranny by some) and having taken on the mantle of anti-clericalism to the benefit of the civil community, they were loath to slip into another yoke voluntarily, even the kinder, gentler yoke of Christ, no matter how necessary to their own salvation. Calvin tried to explain to the French king in the dedication of his great treatise that, as king, he should focus his mind to the following points: "how the glory of God is to be maintained on the earth immaculate, how the truth of God is to preserve its dignity, how the kingdom of Christ is too continue amongst us compact and secure." Calvin, like Luther, recognized God as the supreme authority over the two kingdoms. Having made the king (the magistrate by whatever name) his earthly agent (lieutenant or deputy), He expected the world to be "ruled . . . by his divine word."[78] It followed that ministers of the church

---

78. Calvin, *Institutes* (1541), 7.

must have some autonomous means of bringing this about, working with, not for, the civil authorities who work toward the same goal through their own means. This is the focus of Calvin's political doctrine in a nutshell—magistrates should be focussed on spreading the glory of God and the word of God in ways suitable to their role much as the ministry does the same. By 1536 and the first edition of *Institutions*, however, Calvin was fully aware of the tensions that still existed between spiritual and civil authorities, and he could not have been unaware of the array of theories, solutions and explanations on how these tensions were to be overcome.

Other doctrinal positions aside, both Luther and Oecolampadius, for example, recorded obvious differences between the two authorities and noted that only one of them could ensure purity in the church—the body of Christ—ascribing the other a protective and supporting role. Initially, Calvin held a conventionally similar view based on his predestination theology. Because the church—the invisible fellowship of the elect under the headship of Christ—could not be discerned by mortal means civil government could not directly impact upon it, although it could take a generally protective role against the obviously wicked. Zwingli and Bullinger postulated a different view, drawing no difference between the authorities, and placing the civil authority of godly magistrates at the head of the Reformation effort for the entire community (the covenantal congregation). Bucer stood between Luther and Zwingli finding the two authorities aimed at the same goal (e.g., the glory of God, the spread of the gospel) but tackling them in different but complimentary and co-dependent ways. Calvin maintained all the commonplace assumptions: he postulated the divine origin of the state and of the civil authority; he extolled the magistrate's role in the protection of the good and punishment of the wicked. In his earliest writings, however, he was willing to go further, to expand the role of the magistrate into the spiritual kingdom, combatting idolatry and proactively quashing blasphemy wherever it was found. For Calvin, the role of the magistrate was safeguarding "a public form of religion ... visible among Christians and that humanity may exist among human beings." Luther accepted civil government as legitimate but peripheral; Bullinger tried to arrange a cooperative establishment; Calvin would move the magistrate to centre stage.[79]

As of 1536, however, he was still unsure how to explain the necessity for doing so, spending three years exploring the parameters of the Reformed Church's visible/invisible paradigm. Familiar evangelical doctrine was that the magistrate orders religion properly (in externals) because the elect (i.e., true believers) as well as the merely professed need a visible forum where

---

79. Höpfl, *The Christian Polity of John Calvin*, 45.

all the true marks of the church can be readily observed. Calvin's theology makes great use of God's sensual gifts to man (anything which affects the senses) as a means of illustrating divine principles in an accessible way. These could be applied to the church–state relationship as well—the magistrate is necessary to aid the human journey.[80] When he first set foot in Geneva, however, Calvin observed that the reality was far from his ideal.

— § —

In the Geneva of the early to mid-1530s ministers of the church had been reduced to little more than minor civil servants licensed only to preach with little or no real pastoral power to affect change or improve society. The church barely existed as an institution and did not even own the buildings set aside for its use. There was also no clear understanding of the church as the body of Christ, no means of controlling or characterizing the membership of the church, and no officers subject to church authority (rather than to state control). Although sympathetic to the Reformation the magistrates were lacklustre in their oversight of religious matters, while ministers, pastors and teachers had no direct access to the decision making process (e.g., so grievances went unheard). As the ministry was almost entirely composed of strangers to Geneva (French émigrés like Calvin escaping conditions in France) they had no official status in the city. So, the ministers were evangelical, the council was sympathetic, and the word of God was acknowledged as the sole source of truth but that was as far as Reformation had gone. There was no agreed creed or confession or pastoral organization.

Having thrown off the yoke of both Rome (in the form of the Bishop of Geneva) and the political power of the Duke of Savoy, the Genevan magistrates were not keen to yoke themselves or the city to anything other than their own hard-earned authority, safeguarding their hard-won liberties against anything which hinted at restriction of their idea of Christian liberty.[81] When Calvin agreed to take on a pastoral role beyond his university lectureship a few months after his arrival, however, he determined to give the church some essential starting points—a clear confessional definition and the power to enforce and defend it. Like other reformers, however, he needed the cooperation of the state to make it happen and to avoid charges of clerical tyranny. This in mind he submitted a confession of faith to the council on 10 November 1536 as well as a series of articles defining a new ecclesiastical order. The *Genevan Confession* gives us a brief glimpse of what

---

80. Calvin, *Institutes* (1541), 658; Calvin, "On Civil Government," 49.

81. Foster, "Calvin's Programme for a Puritan State," 403.

Calvin and his partner William Farel (another leading French émigré) intended to do with the church, including taking it out from under the control of the temporal power.

The underling theory is conventionally similar to Luther's doctrine (*two kingdoms*). Calvin recognized humanity's existential duality—inner spiritual being and external physical being under the sovereignty of God. The two kingdoms ideally should be ruled over by different rulers, regulated by different laws, understood and examined separately by authorities established by God for that specific purpose. *Confession* acknowledged the evangelical norm of the civil magistrate as an office ordained by God for the preservation of peace and good order in the state, to which all should be obedient within the bounds of the Word of God, but two articles (nineteen and twenty-one) introduced new features.

Excommunication was given a new prominence by Calvin as an ecclesiastical measure granted to the church by God. This was granted to protect the integrity of the congregation of the faithful as well as the purity of the Lord's Supper (around which the fellowship would be more obviously structured in subsequent writings). Excommunication, seen in this light, also played a key role in the amendment or rejuvenation of the life of the sinner. Calvin wanted men of impure conscience removed so as to spare the potential contamination of good men. The magistrate, according to the latter article, was acknowledged as a divine vocation to which all owe obedience within the parameters of the Word of God and within the bounds of the temporal, external sphere, but his concern was the public good and the punishment of those who would disrupt it or those who would threaten the church. This disruption is equated with "infidelity towards God" (i.e., disobeying the magistrate is therefore to disobey God); civil obedience is religious duty.[82] Ministers of the Word were given a heightened dignity than that afforded them in the first edition of *Institutions*, however, which made the Genevan magistrates suspicious that an authority other than their own was hidden in the details. That Calvin and Farel wanted the articles subscribed to weed out political and religious undesirables may have been perfectly reasonable, but to the magistrates this reeked of clericalism and was heavily resisted. Calvin subsequently adopted a more informal orientation starting not at the top but at the grassroots level.[83] In theory, future magistrates would be more open to Calvin's reforming principles.

This in mind, a new and very detailed draft ordinance for the church was submitted by the ministers to the council on 16 January 1537 (followed

---

82. Calvin and Farel, "The Genevan Confession," 31–33.
83. Höpfl, *The Christian Polity of John Calvin*, 61.

up by a new catechism to begin the education process). The ordinance was based on the ministers' understandings of the Word and their judgement as to what was necessary for Geneva. There is clear appreciation here for the work of Oecolampadius on the key issues of excommunication, discipline, and the role of elders as designated, church controlled, officers.

Calvin argued that excommunication was exclusively an ecclesiastical disciplinary device, a means to safeguard the integrity of the Lord's Supper (as differentiated from the papal Mass), and purity of the fellowship of the congregation built around that true sacrament. He was drawing a connecting line between social behaviour and religious behaviour, setting the Rule of Christ firmly into a social context and drawing out evangelical norms that placed clear blue water between their own and papal usage. Excommunication had been nothing but a tool of Roman tyranny beforehand, but it could be (or should be) a tool of Christian love in the proper hands. This understanding was crucial because Calvin was investing much more importance into sensual, external signs than Luther had done as a means by which God graciously catered to human weaknesses. He consequently appealed to the magistrates to select good, faithful and strong-willed men out of the congregation to oversee Christian living in the city as a first step toward necessary grassroots moral improvement.

It is a familiar process: selection was in the hands of the magistrates; these "certain persons" have oversight of the life and governance of behaviour in the quarters of the city; they bring ministerial attention to bear on vice and disorder; they apply the Rule of Christ to determine disciplinary responses, and so on. Initial failure to reform would mean pastoral censor and an announcement to the congregation against the miscreant. Failure to reform again would lead to a decree of excommunication. Calvin made no specific mention of who pronounced the excommunication, but the inference is that it was an ecclesiastical device. The banned member would be excluded from fellowship but was expected to listen to sermons in hope of repentance. The magistrate had no official role in this parish level discipline, but does determine the fate of the unrepentant. For Calvin as for others the church does not engage in punitive or coercive physical punishments (beyond exclusion), while the state guards the church against whatever blemishes may come.[84] Here is a hint of Bucer's *co-terminus* doctrine. Magistrates safeguard the unity of the church and the honour of God from without, while ministers do so from within. The church enforces discipline up to the point at which the sinner is denied a place within the fellowship of the Lord's Supper. Afterwards, magistrates ensure, with punishments and/or exile, that the unrepentant

---

84. Calvin, "Organization of the Church," 47–55; Graham, *The Uses of Reform*, 24.

cannot tar the reputation of the community. Although here Calvin theorized a support role for the magistrates, a more co-dependent relationship was suggested for a new matrimonial court.

The upshot of the proposed draft was threefold: membership of the mixed visible church of true and professed believers would be established *via* creed and subscription; future members were to be educated to an acceptable level *via* catechism learning; and, membership was to be pruned based on discipline and morality. As noted, Oecolampadius or Bucer would have added a body of wardens (dominated by the council) to oversee the process.

Because Calvin failed to develop that Reformed motif there was also a problem of rival jurisdictions. In essence the draft articles established the church (with its autonomous power of discipline and governance) as akin to a state within the state. In theory this should not have been a problem; obedience to the ministers of the church as a civil duty was equated with obedience to the magistrates as a religious duty, but none of Calvin's writings as yet explained clearly how that obedience to the magistrates worked out in practice. New syndic elections ironically worked against him even as Calvin was inspired to clarify magisterial authority in the new 1539 edition of *Institutes*.[85]

The structure of the chapter on civil authority had, as in the 1536 edition, incorporated a three-fold discussion of magistrates, laws, and obedience. Magistrates were portrayed as deputies of God to whom had been assigned a familiar, limited, role in the defence of the good and punishment of the wicked, but to this now was ascribed a heightened importance, not unlike Oecolampadius's reorganization of Basel.[86] Calvin began to emphasize the unity of the covenantal community as both a civil cooperative and a Christian fellowship, but made no real distinction between types of polity noting only that external conditions influenced local variations. Like Oecolampadius Calvin emphasized two covenants—a spiritual, new covenant and a carnal, old covenant, both of which had existed from the time of Adam (when the carnal dominated), the spiritual becoming clear only with the coming of the Christ and the possibility of redemption. The elements of the old—good works, rules, regulations and ceremonies—must give way to the

---

85. The four syndics (elected yearly) oversaw all domestic responsibilities on behalf of the entire citizenry. They also choose the members of the Small Council from the aristocratic families (the first syndic acting as head of the Small Council).

86. Calvin, *Institutes* (1541), 639, 656, 658–66.

elements of the new—true sacraments. Although not the dominant theme of his theology, like Zwingli's, Bucer's and Oecolampadius's, however, the covenant was the framework upon which Calvin's doctrines now hung.[87] Oecolampadius's influence is also clear (Calvin had lived in Basel in 1535–6) with a new emphasis on clerical discipline (including excommunication). In the 1539 edition Calvin also more precisely defined the "certain persons" (of 1536) as elders (or church officers) into whose hands specifically St Paul had placed church governance (as in 1 Cor 12:28); magistrates were the *sine quo non* of godly society.[88]

Without godly civic rules and regulations, and without the good being protected from the wicked, chaos and anarchy would ensue; the elect would be unable to find each other and the glory of God would never be properly serviced. The godly magistrate assures that the conditions are conducive to the existence of the true marks of the church. Obedience to the godly magistrate therefore, and the magistrate's dedication to equity in all his works, determines the success of society. This obviously has clear ramifications for the external elements of the church. Calvin may have had the radical sectarians (and events in Münster) in mind for much of this new discussion and for that which followed, considering not only necessary obedience but war, taxes and tribute, as well as the uses of law courts as normative for Christians. The only limitations on magisterial power were the law of God and the public good. The magistrate must resist the temptations presented to him, however, and remember that he acts in God's name in the preservation of the godly society. He has been presented the sword of punishment for that very purpose.

These were commonplaces elsewhere but Geneva needed re-educating. Calvin was not writing for the magistrates, but for Christians who needed to understand why civil authorities must be obeyed. With regard to the laws of human interaction Calvin noted that, "the law is a silent magistrate and the magistrate a living law," giving them much the same importance. More specifically, however, he drew upon Melanchthon's discussion of the law and the two tables of the *Decalogue* in his discussion of moral, ceremonial and judicial law-forms. Moral law honours God in faith and piety and instils love of the neighbours in the heart—in essence God's sovereign will is the base guideline. While ceremonial law is dismissed as Judaic and pre-Christian, judicial law (i.e., justice, equity or living in harmony) Calvin equated with natural law (after Melanchthon). His conclusion was that "people cannot resist magistrates without resisting God," but the magistrate ought to be

---

87. McCoy and Baker, *Fountainhead*, 22–23.
88. Höpfl, *The Christian Polity of John Calvin*, 83.

clearly dedicated to the law of God too and, "a father of the country which he governs, a shepherd of the people, guardian of the peace, protector of justice and preserver of innocence."[89]

— § —

The new syndics (elected on 3 February 1538) removed ministers from the marriage court, forbade pastors from getting involved in political matters from the pulpit, and restricted the liturgy to the Bern usage (e.g., outlining ceremonial practices and sacramental doctrines in line with those of the city that protected Geneva against its many external enemies). While the magistrates may have had little choice there, restricting the pastors in their preaching violated Calvin's understanding of the true marks of the church and Christian liberty. He sought to give the church clear definition and autonomy in disciplinary matters in order to safeguard its own character but this depended on magisterial compliance. Farce ensued; pastors refused to administer the sacrament at the Easter service and ignored the new preaching prohibition while Calvin (and Farel) were sacked and exiled. As a mere *habitant*—foreign resident—Calvin had no legal recourse.

Calvin took a position as pastor to the French exile community in Strasbourg assisting and observing Bucer and Capito. By the time he was invited back to Geneva in 1541 his opinions had firmed up, and his theoretical debts to Oecolampadius and Bucer had become much clearer. He had observed what could be done with all the elements of godly society working together—magistrates supporting the work of a board of wardens (elders)—even if it was not quite perfect. During his Strasbourg exile Calvin assisted Bucer in trying to establish an autonomous church discipline (exercising the power of the keys) and exported Bucer's (and Oecolampadius's) organizational principles to Geneva. Like the Swiss reformers Calvin came to recognize a positive role for the (godly) civil magistrate in God's ordering of society and the church. Elements of Bucer's *co-terminus* position (emphasis on the four ecclesiastical offices created by God to direct the visible church) were combined with Oecolampadius's system of discipline and excommunication. With the subsequent development of the Consistory, Calvin clearly expected to achieve an autonomous ecclesiastical authority.[90] It was also while in Strasbourg that he began to put into practice the organization of the congregation around the Lord's Supper, keeping this pure by having people apply to his judgement on their suitability before admission to it. It

---

89. Calvin, *Institutes* (1541), 667, 674.
90. Bouwsma, *Calvin*, 204–13; Baker, "Bullinger and Calvin," 110; Spijker, *Calvin*, 55.

took fourteen years before a proximate doctrine was accepted by the council in Geneva, and even then it was dependent on Calvin's dominant personality and hard work rather than statutory status.

McGrath paints a disturbing picture of a Geneva where religion, society and politics had descended into near chaos. Calvin was summoned back as a kind of saviour; he was promised a great deal of autonomy in his creation of a church order too, the only stipulation being that the council's civil authority was in no way compromised.[91] Calvin took away from Strasbourg Bucer's *co-terminus* view of the two authorities in the glory of God, but overlaid it with Oecolampadius's view of the essential differences between the two polities and his determination that they should not interfere in the sphere of the other (except in supportive roles). Jettisoned was Bucer's view of magistrates as quasi-religious and ministers as quasi-political, but Calvin needed them committed to the same causes. Such had been the purpose of Calvin's *Ecclesiastical Ordinances* (1541) and it had almost succeeded. It was officially sanctioned on 20 November, but close negotiation had denuded Calvin's independent authority for the church of any true autonomy. It is no less interesting for all that.

Calvin had tried to establish governance of the church as a separate institution *via* recognition of the four scriptural offices[92], in the detailing of their duties, their selection, and in the establishment and detailing of the duties of an overarching Consistory. Geneva had political consistories (twenty) already established to oversee morality (led by *capitaines*) and Calvin sought to apply a similar structure to the clerical establishment. The Geneva ministry would, in theory, apply moral authority and enforce godly order, self-regulating to ensure worthy ministers. Objections centred on the implication of special clerical status (in denial of the *priesthood of all believers* standard). Calvin conceded that policing of the ministry was the role of the magistrates, so the Consistory was established, finally, as a mixed body of ecclesiastical and lay leaders. It was an institution which spoke with the voice of both polities for the benefit of the whole community; clericalism was avoided in that the civil council acted as the final court of appeal.[93]

Calvin's intent had been that the Consistory, as a clerical institution, be dedicated to the policing of religious orthodoxy and social morality,

---

91. McGrath, *Reformation Thought*, 215–17.
92. For details, see Chibi, *The Wheat and the Tares*, 244–75.
93. Hillerbrand, *Division*, 450.

standing as the guarantor of Christian discipline. Its primary function was safeguarding the purity of the fellowship of the church. It was structured as a board of pastors (nine in the first instance)—the Venerable Company—sitting with twelve elders and a council clerk to record its works and give it an initial public legitimacy. The magistrates, however, came to see it as another instrument of government and organized it accordingly. So it was headed by a layman, one of the city's syndics, and the elders were re-drafted as government deputies commissioned for specific moral functions. The twelve elders—two men of the little council, four of the council of sixty and six of the council of two-hundred—were "men of good and honest life, without reproach and beyond suspicion, and above all fearing God and possessing spiritual prudence."[94] There were many experienced magistrates to choose from—*capitaines* and former *capitaines*—and ministers were also drafted in as technical experts. We need look no further than Oecolampadius's or Bucer's board of wardens to understand the Consistory's functions and responsibilities in the parishes (boundaries which overlapped the twenty political consistories).

As with similar bodies in Basel, Strasbourg, and Zürich, the Geneva Consistory did not have an autonomous power of excommunication and it was further ordained that any issue which could not be resolved in the Consistory would be passed *upward* to the magistrates and, moreover, that any judgements passed by the Consistory in the course of its day-to-day work were also to be reported *upward* for adjudication. Calvin fought long and hard at the time, including with other pastors against this more civil conception, but came to accept the restrictions as the best "our day can bear."[95] The Consistory was denied any effective compulsory power or jurisdiction as any summonses would need to be carried out by a council officer designated for the task.[96] It did have a clear function in the oversight of moral behaviour and orthodoxy for the ministry (*via* the investigation of reports of crimes or clerical incontinence), however, as part of a well-structured system of institutions and practices all of which had been incorporated in other cities to varying degrees of success. So, for instance, weekly assemblies of the urban and rural ministers were suggested to discuss Scripture; doctrine would be discussed among the ministers, subsequently in association with the elders, with differences of opinion submitted to the magistrates (in essence recognizing their powers of dismissal). Calvin envisioned a ministry

---

94. Calvin, "Ordinances," 63.
95. Spijker, *Calvin*, 73; Höpfl, *The Christian Polity of John Calvin*, 138.
96. Calvin, "Ordinances," 63–64, 70; Foster, "Calvin's Programme for a Puritan State," 423; Graham, *The Uses of Reform*, 25.

which was self-regulating, supported by a Strasbourg-like commitment to education and he had *almost* achieved it.[97]

If it is true, as some historians suggest, that Calvin was trying to create a "city of God" after Augustine's great work, that is, a truly godly, Christian commonwealth, he still had a long way to go, but he had made a start. In pursuit of this, in the *Ordinances* and in the 1543 edition of *Institutes* he presented some very clear ideas about the organization of the church, ecclesiastical self-regulating government (through disciplinary institutions and excommunication), and the relationship between ecclesiastical and civil polities as different but complimentary, *co-terminus* institutions. He had clear ideas on the work of the ministry with regard to morality, orthodoxy, and social order, and he recognized that magistrates had, by necessity, an important role to play in the establishment of the true marks of the visible church and in the directing of society. His writings concentrated on offering justifications for the uniqueness of the ministry in a way that denied papal clericalism but showed how, collectively, it was the key to the creation of that city of God on earth. His political doctrines *per se* had not changed since 1536—he still saw distinctions between the two polities—but his work changed after his return to Geneva and the passing of the *Ordinances* to the practical implementation of his theories. This is why it would take a further fourteen years to complete (and success was only achieved when Calvin's supporters among the citizens finally formed a majority control of the councils) and, even so, contests with the magistrates never fully ended.[98] The best he could hope for was a balance between the two kingdoms and recognition of the common goal of a purified fellowship.

Theodore Beza: Maintaining the Balance of Power

In Calvin's Geneva a kind of equilibrium had settled between the ecclesiastical and civil authorities based less on official ordinances and rather more on Calvin's dominant personality and his ability to coerce agreement. It was a

---

97. Höpfl, *The Christian Polity of John Calvin*, 93–97.
98. McGrath, *Calvin*, 114–23.

precarious balance; magistrates found in it a too severe regimen, verging on legalism, while ministers held it as too lax. The church did exercise autonomy over excommunication and moral discipline of the population, over its internal governance, and over the determination of correct doctrine, but this was grounded on Calvin's longevity and personality rather than his claims of scriptural correctness. There was no officially agreed limitation on magisterial interference in ecclesiastical matters (and their superiority over the ministers was accepted) but respect for the wishes of Calvin held sway. Could Theodore Beza command the same respect?

Burgundian by birth, Beza was a familiar figure to the church establishment in Geneva having settled in the city around 1558 *via* previous work in Lausanne. His writings were popular enough (see below); he had a clear doctrine on the relationship between church and state (similar to Calvin's but leaning more in the direction of magisterial authority); and, he had experience with Calvinist reform (which he had failed to instil at Lausanne). Under Calvin, Beza was Moderator of the Venerable Company of Pastors from 1563 and after Calvin's death Beza became *de facto* head of the Reformed movement in Europe. He did not share Calvin's force of personality, however, and with regard to the balance between magistrates and ministers dominance tipped in the favour of the former. Beza adopted a conciliatory stance between the groups having harboured doubts about Calvin's disciplinary system all along. Beza's doctrine emerged over the course of three treatises—*De haereticis a civili magistratu puniendis (Concerning the Duty of Punishing Heretics by the Civil Magistrate* (1554), *Confession de foi du Chrétien (The Christian Faith)* (1559), and *Right of Magistrates* (1574) which all deserve some attention.

In *De haereticis* Beza advocated the commonplace doctrine that heretics and blasphemers were subject to punishment (and even death) at the hands of the civil authorities.[99] This viewpoint was contentious in the 1550s, however, due to the case of Michael Servetus, polymath scholar and nontrinitarian theologian (i.e., he believed that the three persons of the trinity were not distinct but rather differing aspects of the one God) who had been captured and burnt at Geneva on 27 October 1553 after denunciation and imprisonment in Vienne (from which he escaped). Calvin had discovered Servetus in Geneva and denounced him to the magistrates, setting his trial and execution in motion. Inexplicably, this event proved a

---

99. Beza, *De haereticis*. This can be found in *Tractationes theologicae*, 1:85–169.

kind of anti-Calvin *cause célèbre* in European religious circles. Although widely condemned, by Luther, Melanchthon, and throughout the Swiss cantons (Reformed and Catholic), as a Spaniard Servetus was legally subject only to exile. Moreover, Calvin had often hinted at toleration in editions of *Institutions*. While Calvin's involvement was limited at best, he bore the brunt of condemnation. Beza defended the actions taken and the magistrates' rights and duty to act, however, as necessary to the health of the church, society, and true religion, but these were unpopular views at a time when toleration was the more fashionable view.

There were three pillars to toleration theology—that heretics should not be punished for their views; that they should certainly not be punished by civil magistrates; and, finally, that they should not be put to death—doctrine supported by a weaving of wide-ranging scriptural and philosophical evidence. In essence detractors argued that no one should be compelled to belief and, besides which, heresy was hardly a crime on a scale with murder, so why do heretics warrant the harshest of all penalties? These writers, chief among them Calvin's former friend Sebastian Castellio, used the parable of the wheat and tares to good effect, showing magistrates usurping God's own power in their acts against heretics. Beza took the antithesis position to each of the three pillars.[100]

In his reflections on contemporary thought, biblical exegesis, and sacred history Beza placed heretics into a distinctive category of criminal, defining them as those who follow their own judgements in defence of doctrines already proved false from arguments of Scripture. Heretics are not ordinary criminals; they threaten the very fabric of the church, its peace, and unity. He described heretics as a cancer or poison in the system which must be prevented from spreading by the simply means of cutting it out as soon as it was uncovered. So, all heretics are to be punished, and by civil magistrates (of whatever formation), who do not act in their own knowledge but who execute the right judgements of the church. As the divinely appointed guardian and governor of human society (the chief end of which is the honouring and worship of God) magistrates secure the true worship and protect the true church. The magistrate could not conserve and protect true worship without coercing and punishing those who spread false doctrine, attract disciples, and establish sects. Unchecked, dozens of small, competing sects would result, confusing everything.

Beza used the term "external discipline of the church," which must be consigned either to the magistrate or to the minister and, since it cannot be assigned to the minister (who exercises the power of the keys not the

---

100. Baird, *Theodore Beza*, 52–53, for a useful overview.

power of the sword) it must logically be assigned to the magistrate should ecclesiastical persuasions, excommunications, and advocacy fail to cure the cancer. Even if the magistrate was a tyrant, Beza defended his right to act because even tyranny is better than anarchy. The avoidance of anarchy became a major theme in Beza's works thereafter. The godly magistrate must not be persuaded away from his duty.[101] With regard to the ultimate punishment Beza found it axiomatic that the first principle of punishment must be to act as a deterrent for others. Moreover, whereas murder and robbery are crimes measured against ones fellow men, heresy willingly and knowingly pursued is a crime against the glory of God (which is the ultimate purpose of life itself). He equated heresy with stubborn contempt for the Word, glory of God, and of the church. "For the majesty of God should be held to be of such moment among all men, through the everlasting ages, that, whoever scoffs at it, because he scoffs at the very Author of life itself, most justly deserves to be put to death by violence."[102]

Beza expanded on such motifs providing much needed clarification in *Confession*. Starting with the thirty-second chapter, he explained his doctrine with regard to such key issues as ecclesiastical jurisdiction, elders, excommunication and, finally, with two chapters dealing with the work of civil magistrates echoing Calvin and commonplace Swiss Reformed positions. For instance, he took Calvin's interpretation of *Corinthians* as the correct view, describing elders as ecclesiastical governors appointed by God to regulate a necessary ecclesiastical discipline, part and parcel of the congregation. Elders preside but do not rule; their office is spiritual in nature and must be conceived of in a way that does not conflict with the physical office of the magistrate. Beza noted that both offices affect believers in the community, and both are scriptural, but there can be no denying that they are separate and necessarily distinct authorities.[103] "Ecclesiastical jurisdiction," he noted at the start of chapter thirty-three, "tends to one end, that the entire body of the church, in general and each of its members in particular, be maintained in edification according to what is maintained in the Word of God." Beza was mainly concerned with proper order and divided ecclesiastical jurisdiction into two principle aspects.

---

101. Hall, *Genevan Reformation*, 216–17; Zagorin, *Religious Toleration*, 123.
102. Beza, *Tractationes*, 1:155.
103. Beza, *Confession du Foi*, 99–100.

The first establishes doctrine, morality, and external discipline (i.e., the sovereign power of God) while the second determines appropriate punishments for transgression of the regulations (i.e., the power of ecclesiastical governors). Turning to elders in chapter thirty-four he assigned them a duty "to elect fit persons" for the other ecclesiastical offices. What becomes an issue here is just who these elders are and what the details of their election are specifically. Beza, writing with France and Huguenots in mind, wanted to dismantle the vast and complicated patronage networks and benefice systems which had allowed the doctrinaire Catholic Guise family to rise to prominence and influence. Pastors, for instance, must be elected with the consent of the whole (particular) church rather than planted in the local church by some distant benefice owner. Beza understood that this congregational election did not mean each and every member casted a vote, however. Instead, he envisioned selection as a necessary duty of elders and godly magistrates (on behalf of the whole). Turning to the power of excommunication, like Calvin and Bucer, Beza took this as an aspect of the church's exercise of the power of the keys (vested in the Consistory). The godly magistrate has a vital role in ensuring that these godly practices are carried out properly.

With regard to the magistrates specifically (chapters forty-four and five), Beza presupposed that the magistrate, as a Christian, would want to rule according to his beliefs rather than his personal desires. So it seems axiomatic that the godly magistrate's attention is focussed on the correct worship of God as the keystone of any sound political program. Well-ordered churches, the punishment and elimination of heresy and false prophets are to be his goals. This view is, of course, conventionally evangelical; realization of the true marks of the well-ordered church is the greatest commendation a godly magistrate can have. Putting aside arguments from *De Haereticis* (repeated throughout *Confession*) the magistrate is constrained only by two issues—the Word of God and the needs of the particular location. This means that rules will vary in detail from place to place but they will all rest finally on God's law. Beza found, however, that it is not enough to merely ascribe obedience (as per Rom 13:1); a wider statement was necessary, hinting at resistance (in support of the Huguenots). An imposter king could be repressed, for example, by lesser magistrates as a duty to their people, but Beza denied the common Christian any right of revolt. Resistance here is against the man (the holder of the office) rather than against the office *per se*. In this case the rightful king, even if he is a tyrant, must be obeyed (recall he found anarchy the worst political situation). He might not have explored the resistance motif any further save for the St Bartholomew's Day massacre.

— § —

In brief, from about 23 August 1572 (and lasting several weeks) Huguenot congregations and their political leadership in France were targeted for destruction seemingly on the orders of the king or the king's mother. In the cities, town and rural areas, angry Catholic mobs slaughtered as many as 30,000 Huguenots, including their principle noble Gaspard de Coligny (on 24 August). Beza had replaced Calvin as the spiritual leader of the Huguenots and subsequently shifted his position toward a more hard resistance doctrine in *The Right of Magistrates* along with a less exulted view of magisterial power.[104]

Beza set out a series of key questions on the extent of magisterial authority weaving together the evidence of Scripture, sacred history, rational argumentation and theoretical opinions to move the basis of magisterial authority out of the divine sphere and into a more human, earthly sphere. The very first answer to the first question—"Should magistrates as well as God be unconditionally obeyed?"—gives us clear evidence of the shift in Beza's thought. Of course, if the magistrate was always the voice of God's commandments "they too would warrant unconditional obedience," but all too often this was not the case. He looked at both "irreligious" (i.e., opposed to the law of God and the first table of the *Decalogue*) and "iniquitous" (i.e., against sound Christian behaviour) measures as standards against which people gauge their responses.

Calvin had always advised the masses do not question or make too determined an inquiry into the reasons magistrates make the orders they do; assume "the best reasons" instead, and offer prayers to guide their leaders. In the second question Beza changed this stance. Should the subject merely assume that their leaders are acting for the best reasons or, if they have trouble consciences, should they not seek to know the reasons, and started to tie resistance (i.e., disobedience) in with the nature of magisterial rule.[105] What does this mean?

If a tyrant ordered something which God had forbidden (some irreligious act) then simple disobedience is enough—no more is expected of the Christian man. Should the tyrant forbid an act that God commands, however, the individual must disobey his master and follow God. While this is not an entirely new aspect in Beza's thought (there had been hints before) here it is spelled out fully, along with what the evangelical norm of obeying God first actually means in practical terms. So, for instance, the people can resort

---

104. Zagorin, *Rebels and Rulers*, 1:69.
105. Beza, "Right of Magistrates," 101.

to the law itself, moderately, and in proportion to the harm done to them if a magistrate wronged them somehow but force of arms was restricted to other lesser magistrates. The more telling shift in his thought, however, was in reducing the exulted nature of magisterial authority: "people do not come from rulers; that peoples, whether they have chosen to be governed by a single prince or by a number of elected notables, are older than these rulers; and that peoples, accordingly, are not created for rulers, but rulers rather for their peoples."[106] In other words the power of the magistrate does not come from God directly but indirectly and based on the institution and collective will of the people themselves—and then with particular conditions of service and qualifications understood. If this sounds familiar, you can review early sixteenth-century conciliarist political theory.[107] If the magistrate becomes tyrannical the people have the right to disobey and pro-actively seek to remove him. In his treatise Beza pursued two related ideas—the response to the usurper of another's rightful authority and rightful rulers who illicitly expand the boundaries of their own rule—and he also reconsidered those lesser magistrates who have the right to actively resist.

When he writes of lesser magistrates (in France, below the king), he differentiated so-called "officers of the crown" from "officers of the king"—separating the man from the office. Officers of the royal household, for instance, work for the king directly whereas "dukes, marquesses, counts" and the like, because their positions were once conferred by general consent and only since had become hereditary are officers of the crown. Here too were lesser urban and rural elected officials—like the syndics. Such officers hold power "not of the sovereign but of the sovereignty." Beza used them to argue that a kind of political contract existed between king (the man) and the officers of the kingdom. If one side or the other of this check and balancing system were to fail to perform their duty with regard to the sovereignty of the realm, the other side has the duty (obligation) to correct or resist, through force of arms if necessary. Beza placed a corrective power within the collection of lesser officers of the state (i.e., "the legislative power").[108] This refers to parliament in England or the estates in Aragon or France.

> The chief duty of a good magistrate is to employ all the means that God has given him to make sure that God is recognized and served as king of kings by the subjects whom God has committed to his care. To this end, accordingly, he should use the weapon of the law against disturbances of the true

---

106. Beza, "Right of Magistrates," 104.
107. A useful study is Oakley, "Almain and Major," 673–90.
108. Beza, "Magistrates," 112.

religion who will not listen to the admonitions and censors of the Church and his military arm against those who cannot otherwise be halted.[109]

In other words, the right of deposition does not lay with the people in general but with the lesser magistrates acting on their behalf. After the massacre, however, Beza discarded the mediaeval norm as well as the usual evangelical practices and turned to a position which held that subordinate governmental officials had been given legitimate authority to depose tyrants (where certain specific conditions had been met). Otherwise, the two polities remained in balance with a common goal in spreading the Word and honouring God. In this way resistance doctrine was added to the co-terminus theory. Knox, another Calvin disciple, took the new idea to a dangerous extreme.

— § —

John Knox:
Rulers, Lords and People of the Covenanted Nation

Knox followed Calvin's doctrine very closely in terms of theology, politics, and in his understanding of the relationship between the two polities. While *Institutes* was his starting point he quickly moved beyond Calvin and Beza over resistance theology and the authority of lesser magistrates. Calvin had gone only so far, ascribing lesser or subordinate magistrates a role in governance of a country where a sole ruler or supreme council existed, perhaps advising or even rising up and restraining the ruler should that prove necessary. Beza, as noted, allowed these lesser magistrates to step in and remove the corrupt or corrupting ruler, keeping Calvin's restrictions against the commonality in place but giving them a limited right to seek answers while, still, praying for the tyrant and resisting irreligious and iniquitous orders. Knox would go further still; he would ascribe to the people of the covenanted state a voice in its government and the right of pro-active resistance.[110] Long before he knew Calvin, Beza, Bullinger, or other Reformed theologians on a personal level, however, Knox was already familiar with conciliarist theory (as a student of John Mair at St Andrew's University) and its applications against claims of papal supremacy. Reid noted the establishment of bands of nobles, bound together through oaths, was a long standing feature in Scottish

---

109. Beza, "Magistrates," 133.
110. Reid, "John Knox's Theology," 529.

political affairs so it was not a huge leap from such organization to the covenant arrangement. The combination of familiar experience in the ways and means of Scottish politics and Reformed covenantal thought produced Knox's theory of the covenanted state where the people as a whole (including all classes) agreed to serve God as a collective, faithful whole.

This was how he expressed the covenantal idea it in a letter-treatise written for the benefit of his congregations: "This is the league between God and us, that He alone shall be our God, and we shall be his people: He shall communicate with us of his graces and goodness; we shall serve him in body and spirit: He shall be our safeguard from death and damnation; We shall seek to him, and shall fly from all strange gods."[111] This harkens back to Zwingli and the role of the people of God to swear to keep the one true faith and follow or preach the one true Word. The commune was obedient in matters of religion, recognized one body, ruled by one law, and adversarial to "all sorts of idolatry." In his mind England had proven itself a covenanted nation through acceptance of the Reformation and the throwing off of papal practices, especially idolatry, and he had hopes that Scotland might soon follow suit. England under Edward VI had met the criteria as Knox saw it, but that of Mary I broke the covenant. Was there anything that could be done to rectify that situation?

On 8 May 1554, from exile, Knox wrote a letter-treatise back to the faithful in England giving a full account of his opinions and advice. In *A Godly letter* he summed up the situation as a turning away from right religion. At least this was the case of their leaders. The people of the covenant, the faithful, could turn back before it was too late. For Knox, a great part of this was a simple recognition of duty. Preachers must be prepared to preach as they see the situation developing (as he was doing in his writing and had done in the early days of Mary's reign as a royal chaplain) and avoid preaching only what they think the monarch wants to hear. "Let a thing be here noted, that the prophets of God sometimes may teach [what some may call] treason against kings." He acknowledged that while such words may well offend the king, they are not offensive to God (based as they are on the Word) and he predicted that the English would suffer the fate of ancient Judea unless there was a major course correction.

First, the faithful should be prepared to leave the country. Second, the officers of the kingdom, "princes and nobles" should be prepared to defend the faithful against the wicked; "but how many of the nobility within England boldly speaks now in the defence of God's messengers, is easy to be told!" Here, clearly, was Beza's similar appeal to subordinate magistrates in

---

111. Knox, "A Godly Letter of Warning," 190. I have modernized the language.

France. Pastors, now in England, had no freedom to preach in maintenance of the doctrines of God, and the duty of monarchs to support and maintain the preachers was ignored. By remaining silent, however, the people of England, the subordinate magistrates and the pastors all tacitly connived with the priests of Rome and other wicked persons as well as with the tyrant on the throne. Knox would have them speak out, object, and separate from the so-called idolaters even if it meant their deaths. He advised the people to rise up, but he stopped short of given them the power of life and death. The duty to slay the idolaters was in the hands of the civil magistrates. The people of the covenant, to whom the letter was addressed, he advised "to avoid participation and company of their abominations, as well in body as in soul."[112] Knox could not resist hinting that Mary be assassinated.

After his letter-treatise was sent and subsequently published Knox went on a pilgrimage of sorts to Geneva and Zürich, looking to Calvin and Bullinger (among others) for advice on the resistance issue—specifically against hereditary monarchs, minors, and female rulers. Bullinger advised him that there were no specific scriptural objections to these, provided certain other conditions were satisfied (largely to do with local laws and customs). With regard to resistance and subordinate magistrates, however, Bullinger agreed with Knox, "Holy Scripture not only permits, but even enjoins upon the magistrate a just and necessary defence" of the faithful against the irreligious ruler.[113] Bullinger noted that specific cases needed to be examined carefully, however, and that he was not prepared to support open rebellion against rightful rulers (even tyrants). He conceded that death was preferable to idolatry and agreed that the faithful could attach themselves to subordinate magistrates (i.e., nobles) in their uprisings against unfaithful rulers. Calvin told him much the same thing—local political conditions had to be satisfied.[114] When Knox returned to Geneva after the chaos of Frankfurt (in which his faction was exiled), his writings took on a more clear, basic Calvinist view on the relationship of church and state and their relative authorities. But Knox was not known as a patient or conciliatory man.

In *A faithful admonition to the professors of God's truth in England* (July 1554), for instance, and extreme vehemence aside, he did not write to stir up rebellion so much as to urge the faithful to obey the queen in all things that did not contravene the Word of God. *Admonition* sought instead to strengthen their resolve and the perseverance of the faithful against succumbing to idolatry (the returned Catholic Mass); Knox warned of the

---

112. Knox, "A Godly Letter of Warning," 179–80, 188, 194.
113. Bullinger, "Answers," 224.
114. Knox and Healey, "Waiting for Deborah," 373.

dangers the faithful were being led into by the queen's intention to hand the kingdom over into the hands of a stranger: "an open traitoress to the Imperial crown of England, contrary to the just laws of the realm to bring in a stranger, and make a proud Spaniard king, to the shame, dishonour, and destruction of the nobility."[115]

That was 1554 when Mary was not long on the throne. Five years later, before he knew of her death, his patience had been exhausted. He wrote *A brief exhortation to England* in which he raged that having accepted Mary and having turned their back on the Reformation the people as a whole (not just the devil's priests of the previous treatise) were guilty of a rebellion against God. Knox made appeals to the subordinate magistrates of both England and Scotland (after Calvin's or Beza's example) to step in now and reform the church in a way the queen's themselves (Mary Tudor or Scotland's French regent Marie of Guise) clearly would not. It is interesting that Marie, acting on her daughter Mary's behalf, had practised some toleration of Protestant nobles but refused Knox's overtures toward commitment to the faith herself. As these women had turned their backs on God, Knox thought the only remedy was their removal. Before any rebellion could be stirred up in England, however, Knox discovered Mary's death and he turned his attentions to his native Scotland.

He first addressed a letter to the regent and, when this failed he turned to the Protestant nobles to carry out the task of Reformation—in cooperation with the government if possible but, failing that, with protest against anything that contravened the Word. In Scotland, at least, this appeal resulted in the formulation of the so-called "Lords of the congregation." For Knox, the lesser magistrates had a covenantal duty as officers *of the kingdom* to prevent injustice and steer reform of the church in the proper direction, seeing as the ruler failed to do so.[116] If this required active disobedience so be it. A subsequent letter to the nobles, to this effect, was followed up by a letter to the commonality, to which he now ascribed the right to take action (should the lords fail their duty). He famously went further, of course, writing against female rule itself (in *First blast*) as an abomination of natural law, and planned a treatise against hereditary rule (a *Second blast*) to strengthen his case. Knox had developed a doctrine that public office could now legitimately only be held by members of the covenant and that tyrants have no basis in legitimacy at all—no oath or promise could bind a subject to such a ruler, and the people clearly had the right to depose and punish the tyrant themselves. The power of the state over both polities had been moved down the social scale.

115. Knox, "A Faithful Admonition," 287, 295.
116. Reid, "John Knox's Theology," 534.

5

Civil Authority and the Church in Tudor England

REFORMATION IN EARLY MODERN England was a uniquely top-down movement; a politically influenced imposition on the realm which served dynastic agenda rather than spiritual need. There was interest in religious change independent of the crown, but change was controlled and regulation by the changing dynastic needs of the monarch. Henry VIII, for example, officially turned away from Rome for political expediency. Radicals in the 1520s, to whom the king had turned for support, saw Luther as a viable religious influence (perhaps because of certain doctrinal similarities with the native English Lollardy), but by the mid-1530s his pre-eminence had given way to Bullinger and the international commonwealth of letters centred at Zürich. The Swiss reformers were read by such highly placed men as Cranmer, Hooper and Grindal, relations were encouraged by Bullinger dedicated books to Henry VIII and Edward VI, and English support was further cultivated through the works of such gifted writers as Tyndale and the immigration of such notables as Bucer, Martyr and Laski (all personal friends of Bullinger's and of Calvin's). True, given more time Mary Tudor may well have subsumed Protestant doctrine under a humanist influenced Catholicism then in development in European circles, but that was not to be. Her religious policies drove the cream of English theologians and polemicists into Swiss arms, which allowed Elizabeth to reap benefits in the development of an essentially Reformed settlement. By the end of the Tudor century, however, Bullinger's non-resistance to civil magistrates had given ground to Calvin's and Beza's limited resistance theory (Knox acting as an agent). While the last Tudor lived, however, the royal ecclesiastical supremacy which she inherited from her father and half-brother brooked no resistance and men like Richard Hooker tried to formulate doctrine which could accommodate both Puritanism (i.e., Geneva-centric Protestantism) and Anglicanism.

When we discuss issues of civil polity and ecclesiastical governance in England in the early modern period it is inevitable that we turn in the first instance to the royal supremacy as it developed in and beyond the 1530s—what led to it and what it meant? The answers to these questions are very much the same as developed in Saxony, Zürich and Strasbourg. As elsewhere, in England by the mid-1530s, ecclesiastical authority had been transferred from the pope to the chief magistrate (in this case Henry VIII) who was recognized by both parliament (a political body approximating Beza's mid-level magistracy) and convocation (which could be thought of as a consistory) as supreme head of the church in England and the source of all spiritual and temporal jurisdictions (much like Luther's emperor figure between God and man). The king had taken into his hands control of the institutional apparatus of the church, its judicial and financial offices, supervision, and the determination of correct doctrine very much as ruling magistrates had elsewhere. In Protestant eyes, however, the king and his subordinate magistrates had only taken the process half-way. A vernacular Bible had been approved, presented, and then denied once again to the vast majority of the people; doctrine was at best only half reformed; the king and his subordinate magistrates were (all too often) less than godly role-models. The opportunity to steer a better course was provided by God when Henry was succeeded by a boy. Protestant thinkers saw a chance to influence full reform: godliness could be ingrained into Edward in anticipation of the day when he would come into his own; the subordinate magistrates would be encouraged to act as their scriptural counterparts had acted, that is, with the focus on the creation of the Christian commonwealth; the English, as the people of the covenant, would finally come into their own. Much of this failed and Mary added insult to injury by returning the realm to papal obedience and inflicting a foreign king upon it, leaving Elizabeth finally to pick up the pieces amidst competing and much more radical alternatives.

Henry VIII and the Establishment of the Royal Ecclesiastical Supremacy

Ostensibly, the changes of the 1530s were superficial; it was a small shift in a long-term arrangement which saw the royal will almost always met by the pope in a beneficial partnership almost unique in European politics.[1] The king very much determined the nature of clerical leadership in England as there was a well-worn path to the top of the church and, while the clergy had the *de iure* right to gather in convocation to discuss ecclesiastical government and legislation at any time they wished, for whatever purpose they wished, they *de facto* met only if and when the king summoned them to do so (exactly as did their lay counterparts in parliament).[2] It would be a mistake to claim that England had never faced such church *v.* state tensions as existed elsewhere in Europe. The revolt of the barons, *Magna Charta*, the assassination of Thomas Becket, the statutes of *Praemunire* and Provisors (in the fourteenth century) sat atop those events which otherwise influenced a denigration of papal authority across Christendom. From the start of the Tudor period (1485) no papal canon which conflicted with existing English law was recognized but, at the same time, most governmental and diplomatic positions were filled by senior church officials. The dynamics of the relationship between the two polities was crystal clear: "By the ordinance and sufferance of God, we are king of England, and kings of England in time past have never had any superior but God only."[3]

This, the most famous expression of Henry VIII's thinking on royal sovereignty, was augmented by the royal attitude during the English occupation of the French city of Tournai. Henry made several claims of exclusive authority, going so far as to isolate the clergy from French ecclesiastical patronage networks. "We having the supreme power as lord and king in the regalie of Tournai without recognition of any superior owe of right to have the homage fealty and oath of fidelity as well of the said pretended bishop by reason of his temporalities which he holdeth of us as of other within the precincts of the same territory."[4] Henry VIII recognised no superior authority in any of his territories. Indeed, a clerical dispute over testamentary jurisdiction between Bishop Richard Fox (Winchester) and Archbishop William Warham (Canterbury) in 1510 set another precedent for future action.

In southern convocation (the assembling of the province of Canterbury) the senior clergy failed to resolve an issue. Fox and Warham built up alliances and appointed proctors at Rome (to argue their cases)[5] but, in

1. Eppley, *Defending Royal Supremacy*, 5.

2. Chibi, "Had I But Served God," 75–136.

3. Ogle, *Lollard's Tower*, 152–53. *Praemunire* forbade the appeal of cases outside the kingdom where the king's court had jurisdiction, and *Provisors* curtailed papal power to provide or confer benefice in England.

4. PRO, SP 1/13, fol. 127v; BL, Cott. MSS. Vit. B iii, fol. 122v, as quoted in Mayer, "On the Road to 1534," 21.

5. BL, Add. MSS., 48012, fol. 22.

March 1512 the pope authorised the king to settle the matter in England, wanting it resolved on the scene. Henry, more than willing, wasted no time assigning the matter to "certayne of our counsel."[6] While the pope sought only convenience, this set a precedent for the king's power to judge the clergy on so-called spiritual issues. The precedent was subsequently re-enforced as a result of the Kidderminster/Standish dispute (the context of the first royal quote).

Henry VIII expected to be obeyed by his subjects, whether lay or clerical, foreign or domestic, an expectation based on precedent—a legal position. In the late 1520s, however, the pre-existing tensions between the two polities, as elsewhere, needed only an additional spark to blow up into something far greater; in England the issue of the royal marriage crisis provided it. A dynastic existential predicament was made worse by the papacy's unhelpfully (and entirely beyond his control) entrenched position. As he could offer no immediate solutions, the king's own scholars and political councillors forged a new path, establishing new boundaries for papal and regal authority which, ultimately, excluded the papacy. The process was a simple one but the ramifications were far-reaching.

The Abrogation of Papal Authority, c. 1529–1534

Henry VIII's divorce campaign is so familiar to modern audiences that only the political, diplomatic or theological minutiae are not commonly known. The Tudor dynasty was threatened because Henry VIII did not have a legitimate male heir (after two decades of marriage). In public the king was stoic but in private he was frantic. Experts were brought into the king's immediate circle to examine the issues and specialists were sent to a number of universities to gauge, engage, and assemble academic opinion as to whether a theoretical marriage (which suspiciously matched Henry VIII's own circumstances) transgressed divine law, whether the pope could dispense divine law, whether the case could be determined in England itself, and whether the pope could actually summon the king to a court in Rome. These proxies sought to establish the boundaries of papal jurisdiction as it impacted upon these key issues.

Some important French and Italian universities, including Paris and Bologna, determined that the marriage did transgress divine law and that

---

6. *BL, Cott. MSS. Vit. B ii*, fol. 22; Wilkins, *Concilia*, iii, 656; *Literae Cantuarienses*, 3:430.

the pope could not dispense for it.[7] These arguments and more were assembled into a little Latin book, *Censurae*, and an English translation, *Determinations* (1531) to strengthen the king's case and reputation for righteousness, but the pope remained politically and militarily entrenched.[8] With the scholarly opinions also came a massive collection of subsidiary documents, historical citations, legal evidences, and polemics, all subsequently edited into the *Collectanea satis copiosa* (literally, a collection of sufficient weight). The takeaway is that the king was not only justified but duty bound to take whatever action was deemed necessary to resolve the issue. The research also hinted that the crown of England enjoyed a kind of sovereignty over the domestic institutional church, that the domestic church had certain provincial prerogative rights, and that a royal marriage was within that jurisdiction. As the pope remained entrenched, however, a dismantling of papal authority in England was initiated. It was an *ad hoc* process which lasted about five years.

Over the course of the so-called Reformation Parliament (1529–36) the political and religious establishments brought pressure to bear on both the papacy and the domestic church, while parliament provided a useful forum of national discussion of the issues (as well as new legislation). The pope's presence in the ecclesiastical governance of the English Church was, ultimately, whittled away *via* a spontaneously evolved two pronged attack.

The pope's chief representative in England, Cardinal Thomas Wolsey (Archbishop of York) was tried in 1529 in King's Bench for *praemunire* offences (adding weight to the precedent of the king's right to judge clerics), and success here allowed for the expansion of the effort the next year when fifteen important clerics were threatened under the same *praemunire* statutes. The implications were obvious; fear was palpable. The livings and the lives of all the clergy were in the king's hands awaiting judgement. While the implications of this sunk in, new treatises based on the massive *Collectanea* archive were introduced into convocation and parliament propping up the pro-divorce lobby and highlighting anti-clerical, anti-papal allegations. Two new claims are of particular importance. One was a theoretical claim that the king could perform clerical functions himself and the other was a more clear-cut claim for certain administrative and judicial authorities which gave him moral and disciplinary sanction (but no actual sacerdotal function). With the threat of *praemunire* hanging over them, convocation capitulated, recognized the king as their supreme

7. Bedouelle, "The Consultation of the Universities," 21–36.

8. *Censurae* (STC 14286) and *Determinations* (STC 14287) can be found in *The Divorce Tracts of Henry VIII*. A study of the material can be found in Chibi, *Bishop John Stokesley*; and Murphy, "Literature and Propaganda," 135–58.

head, and accepted his jurisdictional and administrative authority over the domestic church. Over the next few years papal claims to judicial, legislative, and financial entitlements were transferred to the crown *via* parliamentary legislation. The effort culminated in the *Act of Supremacy* (1534). Although doctrine had not been changed, the king had been exposed to many theories from a diverse set of continental theologians, anglicised by English scholars and adopted to English circumstances, out of which the king could pick and choose. Here we will concentrate on the crown's control of the church and religion and the justifications. Without doubt, the most influential of the English scholars was William Tyndale.

Tyndale and Obedience Theology

Tyndale was a man ahead of his time and thus something of a pariah. His treatise, *The obedience of a Christian man*, for instance, provided one of the earliest influences on Henrician *caesaro-papist* doctrine. This was a term coined in the late nineteenth-century to describe a claim which maintained that the king held both secular power and spiritual authority by divine right. Understood this way, of course Henry would declare this previously condemned treatise "a book for me and for all kings to read."[9] *Obedience* was a "sweeping assertion of the rights and duties of princes and their claim to the undivided allegiance, body and soul, of their subjects . . ."[10] but whether he actually read the treatise himself is debated to this day.[11] There is no denying that Thomas Cromwell, managing the king's political programme, knew what the treatise contained. Beyond obedience theology (a keynote of the royal religious settlement), Tyndale defended a range of radical evangelical doctrines, many of which Henry would never support but which Cromwell deemed crucial to the crown's public relations/propaganda effort.[12]

As a basis for extensive royal power, however, Tyndale's book had considerable value, particularly to those who might be developing a theory of royal authority as a bulwark against over-inflated papal licence, but this was not its sole or even its major theme. The real topic of discussion was

---

9. Strype, *EM*, I:i, 172. *Obedience* can be found online at http://www.godrules.net/library/tyndale/19tyndale7.htm.

10. Scarisbrick, *Henry VIII*, 287.

11. E.g., Elton, *Reform*, 126; Haas, "Martin Luther's 'Divine Right,'" 317–25; Rex, "The Crisis of Obedience," 865–67, 872.

12. Rex, "The Crisis of Obedience," 865–67, 872.

the need for obedience in light of *sola fide* theology and the popular stance that good works had no *salvific* value (a doctrine which Henry disregarded as heretical and which explained the treatise's indexing). Theologically, Tyndale set out to counter Roman claims (voiced by such figures as Bishop John Fisher, Sir Thomas More, and even the king himself) which upset a true and righteous church, state and society. Tyndale illustrated many instances where Rome had usurped temporal power and where it had twisted existing power relationships to its own advantage, echoing many common anti-papal tropes. A correctly observed salvation doctrine did not abrogate social responsibility, quite the opposite in fact. Wrapped up in this (and anti-Catholic, anti-papal vitriol aside) was a guideline for how Christians should live their lives, a great part of which was an expectation of duty on those who hold office in the temporal hierarchies and obedience to those in authority based on the fourth commandment of the *Decalogue*.

Tyndale's exposition of Rom 13, for example, had tremendous propaganda value as the reformer determined that kings were placed into their positions by God and given the sword to protect the righteous, punish the wicked, and defend the church. One does not obey the magistrate simple out of "fear of vengeance," however, "but also because of conscience." Such was the basis of paying tribute—magistrates and ministers serve the same purpose and must both be supported fully. For Tyndale, temporal authority had not been ushered in due to the Fall (as some Protestants assumed) but was and is a necessary aspect of creation itself. Unlike other evangelicals, who thought if everyone would only act in a Christian fashion there would be no need for government, Tyndale held that there had always been a need; the Fall merely changed outward conditions.

Even the most basic social unit—the family—had a necessary hierarchy with the father seeing to the health and prosperity of the whole and counting on the obedience of the subordinate members. Tyndale expanded the terms outward and upward allowing no right of resistance either to the king or to his subordinate magistrates (the king being a subordinate magistrate to God alone). For an inferior to resist the superior was to usurp God's authority (based on Deut 32); to rebel was to take up the sword, which removed God judicial authority. "God hath made the king in every realm judge over all, and over him is there no judge. He that judgeth the king judgeth God; and he that layeth hands on the king layeth hand on God; and he that resisteth the king resisteth God, and damneth God's law and ordinance." Just as the king is an agent of divine justice, the king's officers are also divine agents, relatively speaking. This honouring of the king applies to tyrants as well (equally agents of divine justice) "for a tyrant, though he do wrong unto the good, yet he punisheth the evil, and maketh all men obey, neither suffereth any man to poll but himself only." There is something worse than the tyrant, and that is the "passive king" or the "king that is soft as silk, and effeminate"—that is, a ruler too ready to give in to his vices and obsequious favourites.[13]

Thus, as a basis for extensive royal power *Obedience* appears to provide the king, who was considering a very unpopular divorce and a movement away from papal authority, a neat case for unquestioned submission. Sadly, for Tyndale's chances at rehabilitated into the royal service and forgiveness for his unorthodox opinions, we have only here read half his argument. Unquestioned obedience depended on the fulfilment of popular expectations of service. There was an element of reciprocation, of mutual dependency, and a Luther-like theory of functionality in the treatise. It was the *office* of the king which was owed obedience as God's chosen officer; the *person* of the king was still just a man like any other, with the duties and obligations as any Christian (i.e., a servant to all others). The king's function was to ensure the prosperity of a community of equals under God. "The most despised person in his realm is [also] the king's brother, and fellow-member with him, and equal with him in the kingdom of God and of Christ." The king takes on the "person of God," his office, only when absolutely necessary, at which point he is merciless, "the sharp law of vengeance," but as a man he is mother and father, "bearing every man's weakness, teaching, warning, exhorting, and ever caring for them, and so tenderly loved them, that he desired God either to forgive them, or to damn him with them." In office, "let kings take their duty of their subjects: and that that is necessary to the defence of the realm. Let them rule their realms themselves, with the help of lay-men that are sage, wise, learned, and expert."[14]

The treatise is also a recording of complaints against the intrusion of bishops and other ecclesiastical officers into temporal affairs. This material is familiar as Luther's sharp separation of the two kingdoms. Henry VIII was the king in the temporal sphere, but a Christian man in the spiritual sphere, as subject as any other to ministers of the church. Tyndale differed from Luther; church and state were not mutually exclusive regiments. Rather, he pre-dated Bucer; church and state were over-lapping, mutually dependent, parallel kingdoms—*co-terminus*. Recall that Tyndale saw the temporal regiment as an original creation ordinance. All kinds of societies (from the family unit to the state) need some form of government, whether over the sinful, or over the saints—the godliness of the people did not mitigate the need. The spiritual regiment and the covenant was created by the Fall in that

---

13. Tyndale, "The Obedience of a Christian Man," 208–9, 212, 214.
14. Tyndale, "The Obedience of a Christian Man," 238, 242.

while all of humanity, by virtue of living together, need, and are part of the temporal kingdom, those who call themselves Christians are part and parcel of a spiritual regiment, both the elect and the damned together.[15] Tyndale's distinctive construction of the two regiments was developed in *An exposition on the fifth, sixth and seventh chapters of Matthew* (1533).

Exposition is a diatribe against Rome's wrong-headed co-mixing of the temporal and spiritual authorities to which too many magistrates had been complicit in service to their own base desires. "They have so ruffled and tangled the temporal and spiritual regiments together, and made thereof such confusion, that no man can know the one from the other; to the intent that they would seem to have both by the authority of Christ, who never usurped temporal regiment unto himself."[16] Tyndale's purpose was to disentangle the regiments but strengthen the concept of Christians living under both regimes. His argument is thought-provoking and worth quoting at length:

> Ye must understand that there are two states or degrees in this world; the kingdom of heaven, which is the regiment of the gospel, - and the kingdom of this world, which is the temporal regiment. In the first state there is neither father, mother, son, daughter; neither master, mistress, maid, manservant, nor husband, nor wife, nor lord, nor subject, nor man, nor woman. But Christ is all, and each to the other is Christ himself. There is none better than the other, but all alike good, all brethren, and Christ only is Lord over all. Neither is there any other tiling to do, or other law, save to love one another as Christ loved us. In the temporal regiment is husband, wife, father, mother, son, daughter, master, mistress, maid, manservant, lord, and subject. Now is every person a double person, and under both the regiments. In the first regiment, thou art a person for thine own self, under Christ and his doctrine, and mayest neither hate nor be angry, and much less fight or avenge. But must, after the example of Christ, humble thyself, forsake and deny thyself, and hate thyself, and cast thyself away, and be meek and patient, and let every man go over thee, and tread thee under foot, and do thee wrong; and yet love them, and pray for them, as Christ did for his crucifiers. For love is all, and what is not of love, that is damnable, and cast out of that kingdom . . . In the temporal regiment thou art a person in respect of others; thou art a husband, father, mother, master, mistress, lord, ruler; or wife, son, daughter, servant, subject, &c. And there thou must

15. Werrell, *Theology of Tyndale*, 156-65.
16. Tyndale, "Exposition," 131.

do according to thine office. If thou be a father, thou must do the office of a father and rule, or else thou condemnest thyself. Thou must bring all under obedience. Thou must have obedience of thy wife, of thy servants, and of thy subjects; and the other must obey. If they will not obey with love, thou must chide and fight, as far as the law of God and the law of the land will suffer thee. And when thou canst not rule them, thou art bound, in many cases, to deliver them unto the higher officer, from whom thou didst take the charge over them.[17]

A king, the highest magistrate, like all men is of both regiments. He is God's agent of rule in the temporal regiment—his office is of divine origin—and a man in the spiritual regiment and thus subject to its officers. That is, to be taught by preachers, to be admonished by elders, to be subject to discipline, etc. Henry VIII could certainly find much to recommend in Tyndale's works as a justification of royal sovereignty, and he could use Tyndale as a testament to unquestioned obedience, and his ministers and lesser magistrates began doing so in the early 1530s.

—— § ——

The Henrician Obedience Campaign, c. 1531 Onwards

The major policy initiative of the Henrician government from 1531 was the dissemination of obedience doctrine. That is, emphasis on the king's sovereign authority and the obedience due to him based on God's law (as in the fourth commandment). The king's duty, a familiar refrain, was to bring peace and prosperity to his realm. A solution to the marriage crisis, therefore, an existential threat, became part and parcel of that effort. Hammering the divine precept of due obedience into the hearts and minds of the literate public was deemed the most fruitful approach to resolving the divorce dilemma, as well as to the evolving process of dismantling papal authority in England. It was presumed, for the sake of argument, that obeying the pope (who opposed the king's process) was akin to obeying man's laws over God's own. Domestic treatises of the period highlighted these motifs—obedience to the king above all as a divine commandment—which some writers attempted to co-op for other purposes (e.g., as an ingress for full on Protestant reform).

—— § ——

17. Tyndale, "Exposition," 177–80.

One such writer was Robert Barnes. Barnes delineated a range of Lutheran doctrines in the first edition of *Supplication* (1531), including *sola fideism*, the sacrament in both kinds, images, and the keys but for our purpose here his sixth essay is crucial. There he deconstructed Luther's *two kingdoms* and adapted it to English conditions. Barnes first presented a lengthy condemnation of the English bishops for having censured Tyndale's translations of the Bible, appealing to the king and clarifying the differences between human and divine law. His goal was to prove how the papists had subverted the natural order. The epistles of Paul and Peter provide ample scriptural evidence and the basics are Protestant commonplaces. Temporal power, for instance, the preserve of "kings, dukes, earls, lords, barons, judges, mayors and reeves and to all other ministers under them" employs the temporal sword to order the commonwealth, allot worldly goods into proper ownership, correct transgressors, "where unto belongs any outward ordering or any corporal pain. In this power is the king chief and full ruler, all others be ministers and servants." Barnes explained how tyrannical rulers must be endured (so long as divine law and gospel truth are not rejected) but rejected resistance theology, leaving prayer, earnest appeal, and flight should all else fail. Those who cannot flee must face the music stoically. Barnes then repeated Tyndale's condemnation of the English bishops, turning to the genuine authorities of the spiritual kingdom, the preachers and the pastoral shepherds. Real priests govern the soul and minister the spirit having "nothing to do with the external justice and righteousness of the worldly." They preach and teach the word of God; they do not sit in parliament and perform the functions of the magistrates.[18] Cromwell saw in Barnes high potential and protected him from the recriminations of Lord Chancellor More.

Alongside such figures as Barnes was an official government propaganda program under the direction of Cromwell. They employed useful evangelical commonplaces (after Barnes) as well as the conclusions of *Determinations* and the *Collectanea* to produce a treatise of September 1532 called *Glasse of Truthe*. A divine and a jurist (both partisans of the king) review the vast array of divorce-related materials and arguments as well as the many papal abuses of its wrongly assumed authority, abuses which had both delayed settlement of the marriage crisis and confused the true meaning of divine law. Twice in the course of the work "obedience theology" is stated as

---

18. Barnes, "Supplication" (1531), 629, 630–32, 636. The English has been modified.

fact.[19] The dialogue hit all the key points: it was illegitimate for the pope to summon the parties away from England; the weight of evidence supported the lawyer's contention that the case must be resolved in England; the divine opined that the English people will support the king, whatever his decision, out of love, recognition of justice and "according to their duty." To do otherwise was to yoke themselves to the purely human laws of a foreign power (which was against the word of God and *praemunire*). The king's actions were equated with the divine role ascribed magistrates by most evangelical reformers, that is, the peace and prosperity of the realm and his duty to protect the realm against destabilizing influences. The king's role was peacemaker; he commanded the faith and trust of the people; king, parliament and convocation would resolve the crisis; and the masses obey as a divine commandment.[20] There was, as yet, no hint of schism; the divine and lawyer acknowledge a genuine papal jurisdiction still, but the groundwork is being laid against that day when the country would be asked to either support the king or a foreign power (anticipating a forthcoming excommunication).[21] That point came and went.

Over the course of the Reformation Parliament the vast array of papal authorities was legislated away and transferred to the supreme head, included the determination of doctrinal standards and the visitation and correction of religious houses. Thomas Swinnerton's *A Litel Treatise ageynste the mutterynge of some papistis in corners* reviewed, explained, and lauded the entire process, focussing less on scriptural evidences (e.g., Rom 13, 2 Pet 2) and more on the social and economic burdens that had plagued the country under the burden of papal obedience (e.g., taxes, dues and fines). The array of papal abuses was reviewed and a golden future was in the making provided the masses now obey both God's law (now that we are properly aware of it) and the king—who was nothing less than a Godsend, a saviour sent to restore the realm to good order and ensure Christian liberty. Where Swinnerton did employ the scriptural verses (noted above) it was to describe a hierarchical structure of the civil regiment where everyone is beholden to someone above them (lifted from Tyndale?)[22] and where obedience is due to the prince and to his subordinate magistrates, "demene ourselves like lowly and obedient subjects, whether it be to the king himself as the most chief and excellent of all or else to the dukes and governors that are set by him . . .

---

19. Rex, "The Crisis of Obedience," 878. *Glasse of Truthe* can be found in *Pocock*, 2:385–421. A good (but disputable) examination is Haas, "Henry VIII's Glasse of Truthe," 353–62.

20. *Pocock*, 2:385, 409–10, 418–19.

21. Rex, "The Crisis of Obedience," 878–79.

22. Swinnerton, *Litel Treatise*, 550–1. Also see, Rück, "Patriotic Tendencies," 6–7.

because he is the minister of God, and doth represent and occupy the place of God here in earth." Even if God did not demand it . . .

> how much more then are we bound to love, to obey, to honour and aid our most gracious prince with all our very hearts which specially for our sakes taketh so great pain and that so diligently doth seek the means how to rid us out of bondage, out of misery, out of need and vexation, that we be brought unto by the covetousness of the bribing bishop of Rome (the which by that name of Pope polleth and pilfereth away the riches of this realm), and that so much mindeth to restore us to all our old wealthiness and liberty again.[23]

Swinnerton mixed religious ideas, pseudo-nationalist motifs, and economic arguments to illustrate how popes had subjected England to any number of miseries and how Henry VIII, in defiance of Rome and for the good of the realm (and certainly not out of personal interest!) restored good order, peace, prosperity and Christian liberty to his people. Obedience theology became such a dominant theme in the 1530s and so useful that few government sponsored pamphlets and treatises failed to mention it. Perhaps the best use, however, was Thomas Starkey's *An Exhortation to the People instructing them to Unity and Obedience* (c. September 1535). This was a defence of royal supremacy and another demolition of papal supremacy commissioned by Cromwell, but Luther was now taking a backseat to the irenic principles of Melanchthon's latest treatise, *Loci communes theologici*.[24]

Starkey began with a few commonplace observations on royal duty, good order and peace. Tyndale had recently published a prologue to his translation of *Romans* and asserted that temporal power was created to further the commonwealth, maintain peace, punish the wicked and protect the good. Starkey took this up and added that the civil polity was only of material importance, having no *salvific* value *per se*, a not unknown position. However, both men asserted that the temporal sword must be respected; without it the masses would suffer both social and moral confusion. Obedience to the chief magistrate (and Starkey allowed that this could be a king or a Republican senate depending on the particular nature and needs of the people) is both a political and a spiritual duty for the individual Christian.[25]

---

23. Swinnerton, *Litel Treatise*, 551.
24. Elton, *Reform and Renewal*, 51–52.
25. For Tyndale, see Greaves, "Concepts of Political Obedience," 24.

Melanchthon had adapted Luther's initially rigid *two kingdom* doctrine in the hopes that spiritual unity would follow, replacing the disunity caused by papal dominion with a unity grounded on the wider gospel foundation with local variations understood for what they were—indifferent external alternatives. Starkey followed Melanchthon where he noted that the two tables of the *Decalogue* cannot be divorced from a reliance on natural law (both stressing the key fourth commandment).

Starkey also introduced Melanchthon's ideas of *adiaphora* (i.e., things indifferent) into the English canon. He placed determination of external matters into the list of royal duties, including ecclesiastical governance, the determination of holy days, clerical marriage, papal primacy and, initially, reading the Bible in the vernacular. Papal primacy may be a surprise inclusion, but Starkey was making the argument that too much reverence paid to a human institution was a clear path to spiritual disunity. As the papacy (as an institution) had no gospel support, whereas secular rule did, it was obvious that God intended all external aspects of the church to be in the hands of secular magistrates. The spiritual and temporal spheres also had interdependence for Starkey in the same way they had for Bucer.

The sum of the Christian life was to love thy neighbour. Such behaviour was the external expression of the on-going sanctification some Protestants advocated. For Bucer and Starkey, this required regulation and ordering as much as any other social work. The spiritual here depended for proper and necessary expression on the temporal. Starkey also explored issues of regionalism and particularity, recognizing that while the heart of all social regulation is God's law and the gospel, specific laws, customs and practices are unique to specific places so that a universal authority like the papacy could not be legitimate in natural law. With regard to the settlement of religious doctrine Starkey was clear that there was a necessary process.

Churchmen and theologians, spiritual officers, gather in councils, synods and convocations to debate and decide doctrine based on their superior understanding of the gospel, but the sovereign magistrate must approve their findings before they are disseminated to the nation at large. Melanchthon had placed both theologians and magistrates into the council of learned men but nonetheless took execution of policy out of the council's hands and placed this into the hands of the magistrate alone. Presumably this was meant as a safeguard against heresy (from which the king must protect his people) and so the magistrates must be able to recognize true doctrine in order to approve it. This brings us back to the intertwined dependency of the two polities.[26]

---

26. Mayer, *Thomas Starkey and the Commonweal*, 216–27. Also see, Zeeveld, "Thomas Starkey," 183–84.

Along the way Starkey limited the opportunities for rebellion against tyrants and even against a tyrant who might enforce non-gospel religious policies as there is some good in all of God's works.

Recall that Marsiglio of Padua's great political treatise *Defensor Pacis* was discussed earlier. Marsiglio had sought to separate civil polity from the assumed papal political authority as a curative to Christian internecine warfare. He placed into the hands of the magistrate (which he imagined embodied the collected will of the people) coercive powers to enforce civil behaviour and religious orthodoxy. He allowed the papacy to interpret the Scriptures and define doctrine but shifted ecclesiastical authority over to general councils as summoned and legitimized by temporal rulers. Marsiglio was obviously a firm influence on subsequent treatises on the two regiments and the extent of civil authority over ecclesiastical issues, and Cromwell commissioned William Marshal (a court lawyer and translator of Bucer) to transform *Defensor Pacis* into English. In theory this would give royal supremacy thinking further *gravitas*, connecting it to Renaissance philosophy. I say "transformed" because Marshal could not use the original theory of royal power as an expression of popular will, changing that to an emphasis on obedience to the king as a divine precept. Moreover, his evangelical credentials had been established in his earlier *Godly Primer* (1534). There, Marshal argued against good works as having salvific value but rather as indicative of true faith, but he noted that among the best of the good works was "to be obedient in all things unto kings, princes, judges and other such officers, as far as they command civil things."[27] A few years later Richard Morrison, in *Lamentation* (1536), elevated obedience from good work to badge of the true Christian man.[28]

More detailed political theory aside, Marshal was tasked to define the relationship between the ruler and the ruled in a way useful to the new Henrician understanding of royal authority and obedience doctrine.[29] Marsiglio had argued that the health of the political nation depended upon how well the magistrates represented the collective will of the people in law, in the creation and enforcement of law, and in the punishments of transgressors. As noted, Marshal needed to reduce any suggestion of

---

27. Rex, "The Crisis of Obedience," 882; Butterworth, *The English Primers*, 52–62, 279–85; *Three primers*, 72.

28. Morison, *Exhortation*, sig. B2r (as quoted in Rex, "The crisis of obedience," 883).

29. Lockwood, "Marsilius of Padua," 93.

popular will and replace it with a principle of hereditary rule, turning parliament (Tyndale's subordinate magistrates) into the institutionalized expression of the will of the people for the creation of human laws. The king, however, alone or through delegation, exercises a coercive force behind the law. Parliament is a participant in the creation process only, having no autonomous power of legislation (the king approves or vetoes all bills) or of assembly (the king summons the representatives of the people to him)—the king authorises its works, signifies or rejects its discussions, and approves or disapproves its rulings. This actually brought *Defence of Peace* into line with contemporary continental evangelical thinking. As for resistance theology, Marshal agreed that correction might be necessary (the king is also a man) but it is not clearly spelled out how this correction might come about except perhaps as some divine act.

In the first part of the *Defence of Peace*, therefore, Marshal forwarded a Lutheran understanding of the two kingdoms and applied it to the English case. In part two he considered the spiritual kingdom and its ecclesiastical offices (with the necessary subtext of the elimination of papal interference in English affairs and the English Church). Since the only source of power is God, and God picked the king—presumably a good Christian—the second phase of the argument is nearly self-evident—the clergy of England owe no obedience to the pope but only to their king. The king summons convocation, delegates authority to his ecclesiastical magistrates (officers of the church), who collectively have the authority to define doctrine and orthodoxy based on Scripture. Scripture, God's Word, divine law, we see now are at the heart of both the clerical and temporal establishments. The clergy, like their civil counterparts have no coercive powers or any independent power to gather in synods or councils and, like the subordinate civil officers the subordinate ecclesiastical officers are also dependent upon royal election (which can be delegated to a bishop or a dean). Otherwise, the king has power over the temporalities of the church (which led to the dissolution of the monasteries) and, while he does not exercise sacerdotal function he does judge heretics as part of his duty to protect the realm from the wicked.

If Henry VIII could be convinced that Protestant writers offered the best support for his royal supremacy (and his control of the country's religious direction) maybe the king could be convinced of the rightness of Protestant doctrine as well. Barnes, Tyndale, Swinnerton, Marshal, Morrison and Starkey pursued a means of explaining how evangelical doctrine was not a threat to domestic security, emphasizing obedience doctrine. Conservatives were not slow to see the possibilities and the threat, writing justifications of the royal supremacy which also emphasized obedience doctrine, but in a more traditional Catholic context. Stephen Gardiner, the Bishop of Winchester, had initially opposed the king's headship of the church but subsequently came around. His *De vera obedientia* (or *Of true obedience*, 1535) brought him back into the king's good graces, appealing as it did to the conservative-minded king.

Gardiner justified the royal ecclesiastical supremacy through a one-kingdom argument (not unlike covenantal theology), and opposed the Lutheran heresy (i.e., *sola fideism*) through a carefully worked exposition of traditional justification theology and how it was fortified by obedience. Rather than presenting obedience to the law as would an evangelical—as perhaps an external outpouring of interior faith (non-*salvific* but still necessary after a fashion)—nor as had Tyndale—as a necessary condition of God's plan of creation itself—Gardiner showed obedience to the law as to be the highest necessary good work (similar to the argument used by his fellow jurist Marshal) but with a traditional Catholic doctrinal understanding.

Gardiner was crafty and subtle and anti-Lutheran. He used the letter of Lutheran obedience theology (e.g., the magistrate as the highest temporal authority) against the spirit of Lutheran justification theology (which like most Catholics he thought of was antinomian), appending now familiar appeals to the *Decalogue*. Like his king, Gardiner had abandoned papal supremacy (as disobedience to the law) but affirmed Catholic salvation doctrine. He thought that God ascribed good works a certain minimal *salvific* value and helped man through cooperative grace. Obedience to the higher powers was the pinnacle of the law, not only as a divine precept clearly found in Scripture but also as the advancing of sound Christian liberty (i.e., the final exemption from over-burdensome papal impositions).[30] Obedience was the modern-day equivalent of Old Testament "slain sacrifices and offerings" which signified "sincere and pure service and honour." Gardiner's thoughts are clear; those ancient sacrifices illustrate "how much more clearly he [God] esteemed obedience, he [God] had manifestly declared in many places of the Scriptures that he [God] sets more by obedience than by all oblations and sacrifices."[31] Who could doubt that Christ embodied this perfectly; he offered himself in perfect obedience to God. Obedience to magistrates, high and low, has already been equated with obedience to God (e.g., human magistrates as earthly agents) and so it

---

30. Rex, "The Crisis of Obedience," 886–87.
31. Gardiner, "Oration of True Obedience," 73–75.

becomes the highest of spiritual imperatives and a necessary condition in man's salvation. Gardiner the renowned jurist came more to the fore when he writes of the king's title as supreme head.

Like some Protestant theorists, Gardiner too equated the people of the realm (the political nation) with the people of the church of the realm (the spiritual nation) so he can present the king, as the head of the former, necessarily as head of the latter. While the particular church in England is part of a wider, universal church under God and Christ, each local institution is bounded by legal and/or geographical constraints as well as by points of national tradition and custom. This practical argument was bolstered by a rejection of *two kingdom* doctrine. Gardiner noted that although some great minds maintain a distinction between the temporal and spiritual kingdoms, it is a false dichotomy. "The good men [of Rome] were afraid lest any king should wax too holy . . . they wanted a fine device, thinking it a witty part, to appoint a king his office so as he take no thought whether his people be good or not," but it must be the king's duty "to see that they steal not, nor murder, and that the lay folk oppress not the good peoples."[32] Gardiner ascribed both temporal and spiritual authority to the king as God's agent in England. The king is the head of the realm in its entirety. Gardiner stopped short of ascribing the king sacerdotal function, but he did attribute coercive authority in support of good doctrine. It was a supervisory position; the king took advice, observed disputations, critiqued and, finally, authorized the publication of treatises and confessional statements.

The best evidence of the king's supervisory role in the direction of the English Church was the fact that he actually performed this function. Henry VIII summoned clerical assemblies tasked to produce confessions of faith which met his own understanding of necessary doctrine. Obedience theology and Bucerian *two kingdoms* doctrine (the *co-terminus* model), unsurprisingly, featured. In 1537 the so-called *Bishops' book* (or *The institution of a Christian man*) was published. Alongside explanations and exegesis (on the *Apostles' Creed*, the seven sacraments, the *Decalogue*, the *Pater Noster*, the *Ave Maria*, justification and purgatorial doctrine), royal supremacy was detailed across sections discussing the sacrament of orders and the fifth commandment (a re-positioning of the fourth commandment).

On the question of orders, *Bishops' book* recognized two divinely ordained authorities—one a governing temporal authority (the "power of the

---

32. Gardiner, "Oration of True Obedience," 87–88, 105.

sword") and the other, within the church militant, officers who exercise the power of the keys. This is worth quoting in full.

> Certain other ministers or officers, which should have special power, authority, and commission, under Christ, to preach and teach the word of God unto his people; to dispense and administer the sacraments of God unto them, and by the same to confer and give the graces of the Holy Ghost; to consecrate the blessed body of Christ in the sacrament of the altar; to loose and absolve from sin all persons which be truly penitent and sorry for the same; to bind and to excommunicate such as be guilty in manifest crimes and alms, and will not amend their defaults; to order and consecrate others in the same room, order, and office, whereunto they be called and admitted themselves; and finally, to feed Christ's people, like good pastors and rectors, (as the apostle calleth them,) with their wholesome doctrine; and by their continual exhortations and admonitions, to reduce them from sin and iniquity, so much as in them lieth, and to bring them unto the perfect knowledge, the perfect love and dread of God, and unto the perfect charity of their neighbours.[33]

The ecclesiastical office was limited to spiritual functions, staffed by preachers and teachers whose purpose is edification and spiritual health. What are the practical limitations?

Regarding the bishops (the highest ministers) there are a few. For example, "all punishment which priests or bishops may, by the authority of the gospel, inflict or put to any person, is *by word only*, and not be any violence or constraint corporal." The power of excommunication is spiritual but the power of coercion and punishment is temporal. The powers of appointments, admission and approval of qualifications were spiritual while presentation and nomination to office, as a human ordinance in recognition of the customs and traditions of the realm, was temporal. *Bishops' book* also prioritized a distinctively English way of doing things. Spiritual officers could "devise and prescribe such necessary and convenient ceremonies and ordinances unto the people" as they found necessary, but always under the royal supervisory authority. This conclusion was tied to a nuanced take on no less a theorist than Marsiglio of Padua. The conclusion was that before there were Christian princes, priests and bishops made their regulations and ordinances "with the consent of the people" and afterwards "with the authority and consent of the said princes and the people."

---

33. *Formularies*, 101–2.

This element of popular consent explains how certain divine absolutes (e.g., the *Decalogue*) are sometimes met differently across different realms. England's particular set of spiritual regulations and ordinances, for instance, are not necessarily laid out and organized in the same way as France's. But, while differences can be ascribed to the unique expression of the temporal kingdom, the power of the magistrate is always similar.

> Insomuch that kings and princes, after they had once received the faith of Christ, and were baptized, considering the same to tend to the furtherance of Christ's religion, did not only approve the said canons, then made by the church, but did also enact and make new laws of their own, concerning the good order of the church, and furthermore did also constrain their subjects, by corporal pain and punishment, to observe the same. For it is out of all doubt that the priests and bishops never had any authority by the gospel to punish any man by corporal violence; and therefore they were often-times moved of necessity to require Christian princes to interpose their authority, and by the same to constrain and reduce inobedient persons unto the obedience and good order of the church: which the Christian princes, as God's ministers in that part, and for the zeal they had to the establishing of Christ's religion, not only did gladly execute, but did also give unto priests and bishops farther power and jurisdiction in certain other temporal and civil matters, like as by the laws, statutes, immunities, privileges, and grants of princes made in that behalf, and by the uses also and customs of sundry realms and nations, it doth manifestly appear. And therefore it was and shall be always lawful unto the said kings and princes, and their successors, with the consent of their parliaments, to revoke and call again into their own hands, or otherwise to restrain all the power and jurisdiction which was given and assigned unto priests and bishops by the licence, consent, sufferance, and authority of the said kings and princes, and not by the authority of God and his gospel, whensoever they shall have such grounds and causes so to do, as shall be necessary, wholesome, and expedient for the weal of their realms, the repressing of vice, and the increase of Christ's faith and religion.

In England, Luther's solid line between the powers of the two kingdoms was ignored; ecclesiastical authority could extend into the temporal realm *if the king so orders* (e.g., English bishops still sit in the Lords). On the other side of the coin the power of magistrates also extends into spiritual sphere, "specially and principally to defend the faith of Christ and his religion, to conserve and maintain the true doctrine of Christ, and all such as be true preachers and setters forth thereof, and to abolish all abuses, heresies, and idolatries, which be brought in by heretics and evil preachers, and to punish with corporal pains such as of malice be occasioners of the same." It was not a question of sacerdotal function—"we may not think that it doth appertain unto the office of kings and princes to preach and teach, to administer the sacraments, to absolve, to excommunicate, and such other things belonging to the office and administration of bishops and priests"—it was a question of proper oversight with emphasis on obedience—"God hath also commanded the said priests and bishops to obey, with all faithfulness and reverence, all the laws made by the said princes, being not contrary to the laws of God, whatsoever they be." This was an outgrowth of *Bishops' book's* exegesis of the (now fifth) commandment to *honour thy father and mother*. Obedience was joined to a kind of familial fidelity—subject to prince as child to father—so not just disobedience but any resistance becomes unthinkable and a crime against God.[34] In 1543, the *King's Book* reformulated the discussion; magistrates were not like parents, rather, parents were like magistrates.[35]

The Henrician theorists justified royal ecclesiastical supremacy in terms of necessary obedience—to God's law and word, to the king as God's agent, to magistrates as the fulfilment of covenantal and spiritual principles. The abrogation of papal supremacy was justified as a long coming reconnection with natural and divine law. The king was God's agent (partaking of His authority) and his subordinate magistrates and ecclesiastical governors were in turn royal agents (partaking of the king's authority). England was a microcosm of the divine order in which everyone knew their place, fulfilled their role, and loved their neighbours in the Christian liberty that the king had won for them in his challenge to, and defeat of, papal forces. It was the divine duty—based on the word in Rom 13 and 1 Pet 2—of the masses to obey all the king's impositions because God worked through him. The king, however, as a flawed human being might sometimes forget his duty and give in to temptation. At this point the people were allowed to engage in passive resistance to bring him back to his senses, but armed revolt was out of the question—and tyranny was better than anarchy.

34. *Formularies*, 112, 113–14, 119–22, 152–55.
35. Rex, "The Crisis of Obedience," 891.

Edward VI:
Projecting Godly Magistracy and Christian Commonwealth

The conceit of English theorists, evangelical and conservative, was that the king was a godly magistrate dedicated (with his subordinates) to the creation of a godly church and commonwealth. They were very clear on questions of obedience, the king's duty to spread true religion, and advancing the covenant, but Henry VIII's actual measures were half-hearted. In the 1530s he approved a vernacular translation of the Bible but then in the 1540s severely restricted its use. Lutheran doctrine was dismissed as *antinomian*, Swiss doctrine was dismissed as *sacramentarian*, and the king never found his ideal *via media* between Rome and Zürich. Nor did Henry VIII embody an ideal vision of a godly magistrate. He was greedy, prideful, gluttonous, lustful, and violent, and his subordinate magistrates were no better (a pack of jackals shadowing a lion for scraps). His bishops and ecclesiastical governors were hard pressed to satisfy both the king's religious scruples and the needs of the people—try as they might.[36] His death and the succession of a boy was seemingly a reward to reformers, a gift from God, a chance to fix what had gone wrong and return to the path from which Henry VIII had strayed. English Protestants dreamed of now putting the covenant into good order.[37]

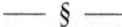

To realize the vision of the covenant and Christian commonwealth the king's handlers (humanists and evangelicals) needed to ensure domestic security (at a time of war), order (at a time of bad harvests) and unquestioned obedience to the new regime (of a boy). Thomas Cranmer, Archbishop of Canterbury and respected theologian, began immediately revamping the homilies project he had begun in the previous reign. Homilies are useful as a means of both edification and education. They are an aid to preachers in writing sermons, in understanding basic theology, and in evaluating sacred history. So inspired, preachers can, in turn and in theory, motivate their parishioners to read the Scriptures and/or live more Christian lives. By July 1547 a complete *Book of Homilies* was published featuring twelve sermons featuring instruction in moral guidance, Christian living, *sola fideism*, and the sacraments, among key doctrinal themes toward the revival of a righteous covenant.[38] As

---

36. For an example, see Chibi, "State v Church," 77–98.
37. Davies, *Religion of the Word*, 140–46.
38. Wabuda, "Bishops and the Provision of Homilies," 564.

for the Christian commonwealth the sermons touched on themes of royal ecclesiastical supremacy, the importance of civil magistracy, and obedience to God's law. For our purposes here, however, the tenth sermon, *An exhortation concerning good order and obedience to rulers and magistrates*, provides the focus.[39] This was a sermon in three parts.

Cranmer's task was daunting; a boy king and an aristocratic council of (frankly grasping) nobles squabbling for dominance. Edward and the regency council both had to be educated in their duties while the people needed to be taught why obedience to (sometimes less than ideal) magistrates was an absolute spiritual necessity. They needed to learn that while human conditions change the covenant is immutable. Preachers were to emphasize that the perfect natural order of heaven was still reflected on earth in God's appointing of magistrates (rulers) who ruled in expectation of order. England without temporal leaders would be a dire place; "take away kings . . . no man shall ride or go by the high way unrobbed, no man shall sleep in his own house or bed unkilled, no man shall keep his wife, children, and possessions in quietness . . . there must needs follow all mischief and utter destruction both of souls, bodies, goods and commonwealth." It is incumbent, however, upon rulers to rule properly; learn the gospel, the Word, and the laws of God—"here taught diligently to apply and give themselves to knowledge and wisdom, necessary for the ordering of God's people to their governance committed." That God's agent was a boy, and that the king's subordinate magistrates were not known for their righteousness, made no difference; God still ruled through them. Clarifying the power of magistrates was the first part of the sermon. The second part was to disabuse rebels of any assumed right of resistance.

There is no God-given right to resist or rebel against the king. This theme was built around a lengthy exposition of biblical texts but Cranmer added warnings to the magistrates against abusing their positions or commanding "us to do anything contrary to God's commandments." Prayer and patient sufferance was the order of the day. The cynical might think that, as the Lord Protector was keen to carry on a costly war with Scotland exhortations to obedience and non-resistance had more than spiritual importance attached to them. Despite a boy king and warlike magistrates, however, he and they were still the rightful and divinely appointed defenders of both God's order and society and the church. Part three, therefore, featured a lengthy diatribe on the theme of papal usurpations and the problems that

---

39. Cranmer, "Exhortation Concerning Good Order," 95–108. This sermon can also be found online at http://www.anglicanlibrary.org/homilies/bk1hom10.htm/.

disordered system had brought to God's chosen in England.[40] Popery was associated with sin and disorder. The covenant theme—God and his people—had clear resonance, but it was the obedience argument which was stressed as *the* necessary foundation stone to good order. While Cranmer's was the official voice of reform exegesis, others weighed in to influence the effort. John Hooper, over the course of his career Bishop of Gloucester and of Worcester, brought with him from a continental exile a much more focussed Swiss understanding.

We have noted the stress the Henrician theorists of the 1530s had placed on the *Decalogue*, situating it, and obedience theology, at the heart of both the catechising process and the covenantal understanding of society and the church. Hooper, on his return to England, tied this in with the archbishop's homilies teaching. Two fundamental ideas were brought together.

The vision of kingship presented in the *Homilies* was both conservative and radical (for the English anyway). It was conservative in that the preservation of a hierarchical society predicated upon order and obedience was the goal; it was radical in emphasizing the king's personal responsibility for the imposition of religious change and the spread of Gospel truth. Hooper, in his exposition on the *Decalogue*, picked up a covenantal vision from Bullinger and folded into it Cranmer's homilies teachings, using the parallels between England emerging out of papal bondage and biblical Israel emerging out of Egypt to illustrate his points. God had gathered his people and delivered them out of oppression, bringing them out of captivity to a new homeland, and he gave them ten laws by which to live in a contented society. As in previous exegesis, each of the two tables of the *Decalogue* has a clear, related purpose; God showed his people the proper method of worship (governing their spiritual lives) and also how to live (governing their physical lives) in a godly fashion—how to let God be their God and how to live their lives accordingly.[41] Clearly neither table could function properly if the other was not correctly adhered to. As the writers of the 1530s had found, the first commandment of the second table was the linchpin. But married to this was another necessity—educating both a boy not yet experienced of worldly temptations and an aristocracy too dedicated to their own passions.

---

40. Cranmer, "Exhortation Concerning Good Order," 97, 99, 102–3.
41. Hooper, "Declaration," 351.

Familiar evangelical ideas were revisited before Hooper turned to the important consideration of the prince's office, duties and rewards. Taking Deut 17:14 as a prooftext, and in keeping with the covenant theme, he advanced his own understanding: "thou shalt take him that I choose in the midst of thy brothers (understood that now all kings, be they good or bad, are put in their authority by God); thou canst make no stranger king over thee." The natural order of the commonwealth depended on a ruler who was a natural part of it. Because the king (albeit a boy) is like a father to his children, his purpose must be to advance and safeguard the life of his people even over his own. Hooper explained, for instance, that "the king there is forbidden to multiply horses," which is to say that he must refrain from self-glorification. The message was to trust in God rather than in man. To trust in a king who is a mighty warrior (i.e., who has many horses) is in fact merely trusting in the flesh of man above the wisdom of God. That such a message would be taken to heart in the court of a marshal Protector and war-loving nobles is doubtful, but it may have had some resonance in the mind of a king steeped in humanist education. It was shown to Edward that a king must live a life of prudence and modesty and must adhere to divine law even as he ensured that others were living godly lives and protecting them from the wicked with godly justice. He must ensure that the people are instructed in the first table and its related precepts (through teachers and preachers in the church) not excluding himself from their teachings and guidance.

Turning to *Ps* 101 Hooper wrote of the establishment of the king's household and subordinate magistrates: "They must lead the people and themselves by the law, and not against the law; to be ministers of the law, and not masters over the law . . . ," and not be offended when they are reminded of their duties by ministers. The historian might ask whether a group of faction ridden, greedy, aristocrats would (could?) take Hooper's message to heart. Hooper and his associates, Cranmer, Latimer, Ridley and others considered their writings and sermons as preparatory works, however, against the glorious day when the king reached his majority. In the meantime Hooper addressed the aristocracy, such as they were, in hopes that the natural leaders of society (i.e., the king's subordinate magistrates) might remember their place: "In time past men were accounted noble for virtue and justice . . . the nobility now-a-days is degenerate. It applieth no study to follow the wisdom, learning, and virtues of their predecessors but thinketh it enough to have the name, without effect."[42] The good of the commonwealth must be at the heart of the vision of the king and the magistrates.

42. Hooper, "Declaration," 363.

When it is, then they are worthy of their offices and the obedience owed to them. Hooper would go on to revisit these themes in a *Confession* (1550) and in an *Exposition on Romans* 13 (1551). Hugh Latimer, a former Bishop of Worcester, also made use of the themes of godly kingship and civil obedience in his Lenten sermons at court in 1549.

Latimer had recognised two truths; the succession of a clever and studious boy could greatly benefit English Protestants, but the church faced destabilization as internecine evangelical squabbles were exacerbated by a faction riddled royal court and government. He used the Lenten sermons in hopes of remoulding the court and educating the king and his governors in good Christian virtues—a godly king and godly magistrates would, in turn, mould a godly church and commonwealth. In the first and most important of the sermons (2 March 1549) Latimer took an advisory tone. God in his wisdom had provided the English two useful things—a true king and his Word—and in these two was all that was needed to deliver the covenant out from under the captivity of Rome. How the king was to rule, live, and what to avoid were key themes, emphasizing the Word of God and a modified doctrine of the two swords.

> For in this world God hath two swords, the one is a temporal sword, the other a spiritual. The temporal sword resteth in the hands of kings, magistrates, and rulers, under him; whereunto all subjects, as well the clergy as the laity, be subject, and punishable for any offence contrary to the same book. The spiritual sword is in the hands of the ministers and preachers; whereunto all kings, magistrates, and rulers, ought to be obedient; that is, to hear and follow, so long as the ministers sit in Christ's chair; that is, speaking out of Christ's book. The king correcteth transgressors with the temporal sword; yea, and the preacher also, if he be an offender. But the preacher cannot correct the king, if he be a transgressor of God's word, with the temporal sword; but he must correct and reprove him with the spiritual sword; fearing no man; setting God only before his eyes, under whom he is a minister, to supplant and root up all vice and mischief by God's word: whereunto all men ought to be obedient . . . Therefore let the preacher teach, improve, amend, and instruct in righteousness, with the spiritual sword; fearing no man, though death should ensue.[43]

---

43. Latimer, "The First Sermon," 85–86.

Turning to the office of the king, Latimer picked up the covenantal overtones of Hooper's understanding of Deut 17:14.

The king, set down by God, is a man of the nation over which he rules (not a stranger to the land) warning the king against over indulgence in worldly temptations and displays (e.g., not too many horses, not too many wives, not too much wealth) as these tend to become ends unto themselves rather than means to advance the godly commonwealth. As for the "nobles", Latimer echoed Bucer in preaching that the king and his officers must embody Christian morality and not live merely for themselves. The king embodies God; subordinate magistrates must embody the king to the masses:

> To extort and take away the right of the poor, is against the honour of the king. If you do move the king to do after that manner, then you speak against the honour of the king; for I full certify you, extortioners, violent oppressors, ingrossers of tenements and lands, through whose covetousness villages decay and fall down, the king's liege people for lack of sustenance are famished and decayed, they be those which speak against the honour of the king. God requireth in the king and all magistrates a good heart, to walk directly in his ways, and in all subjects an obedience due unto a king. Therefore I pray God both the king, and also we his people, may endeavour diligently to walk in his ways, to his great honour and our profit.[44]

The English commonwealth had been given a gift—a fresh start. The honour of God (embodied by the king and reflected by the ruling classes) was not to be found in the accumulation of great wealth but in good leadership and advancement of the commonwealth.[45] Toward this end Latimer highlighted intertwined concerns—the obedience due to the king, his duty, and the state of the nation as created by the irreligious, immoral life of the aristocracy. He pinned his hopes on educating the king in his duty to the commonwealth and to the creation of the covenant (in the second sermon of 15 March) emphasizing the continual "setting forth of God's word, and profit of the commonwealth."[46] The king was both a student and an expositor of God's word; his life was not his own; he must oversee the clergy and ensure that they too are doing their own duties.

In the remaining five sermons he sometimes considered related issues like the abrogation of papal authority and continuing papal influences in England. In the fifth (5 April) for instance, he asked and answered the

---

44. Latimer, "The First Sermon," 93–94.
45. Latimer, "The First Sermon," 99–100.
46. Latimer, "The Second Sermon," 117–18.

question of *what should a king take upon him to redress matter of religion*—making the case for good order and natural law. In the sixth (of 12 April) he emphasized the difficulty of the king's work: "for I know no man hath a greater labour than a king. What is his labour? To study God's book, to see that there be no un-preaching prelates in his realm, nor bribing judges; to see to all estates; to provide for the poor; to see victuals good cheap."[47] Historical judgement is that Edward was well on the way toward embodying the ideal of the righteous king . . . selectively.

Edward concerned himself with purely religious matters only in so much as these touched upon issues of royal supremacy and sovereignty. For instance, in editing the king's papers Jordan found him pious, but more interested in "control of the structures of ecclesiastical power" than in doctrinal debate.[48] The king took note, without comment, of the creation in parliament of a new oath for episcopal consecrations and the execution of Joan of Kent as an Anabaptist and anti-Trinitarian. He noted the establishing of the *Strangers' Churches* under the supervision of Peter Martyr Vermigli, Hooper's appointment as Bishop of Gloucester, and the councils' order for the removal of altars. Edward wanted his half-sister (and heir) Mary to amend her religious practices; "It was said I constrained not her faith but willeth her (not as a king to rule . . .) but as a subject to obey."[49] Edward set forth the word of God, punished offenders against true religion, and encouraged true religion by seeing to it that his own preachers, six royal chaplains (including John Knox) were regularly dispatched to the more conservative portions of the realm. The king also commissioned thirty-two persons to "examine, correct, and set forth the ecclesiastical laws," leaving it to be directed by Cranmer and Vermigli.[50] Edward was certainly aware of the major Protestant themes, as evinced in the first of his collected political papers, *Discourse on the Reform of Abuses in Church and State*.

The king recognized the evangelical norm of two overlapping kingdoms and that his sovereignty extended over both, but it is clear that his interest was really in the temporal sphere. He understood governance of the spiritual kingdom to exist in three actions: "setting forth the word of God, continuing the people in prayer, and the discipline," and he took a very brief

---

47. Latimer, "The Sixth Sermon," 215.
48. Edward VI, *Chronicle and Political Papers of Edward VI*, xxii.
49. Edward VI, "Chronicle," 55, 80.
50. Edward VI, "Chronicle," 110.

portion of the *Discourse* to expand upon these points. He wrote that "the setting forth of the word of God consists in the good discreet doctrine and example of the teachers and spiritual officers," that is, the setting forth of sermons and teaching through preaching the word. There was scant notice of the homilies project and prayer book projects as fulfilment of the second consideration, although there was a little more attention paid to disciplinary measures. Some element of continental Protestantism can be seen in the selection of elders, as "those that should be the executers of this discipline were men of tried honesty, wisdom, and judgement." Edward saw this as the role of bishops, and he was determined that his subordinate governors should see to the lives and morals of all newly appointed bishops (and preachers) so that these elements are met.[51] We can only speculate on what may have happened had Edward reached and surpassed his majority.

— § —

Mary Tudor: Papal Supremacy and Resistance Theology

Two leading reform theorists of the previous reigns, Gardiner and Cranmer, have been labelled as "Anglo" (–Catholic and –Protestant respectively).[52] From their opposing viewpoints they regarded England as the fulfilment of those special circumstances or covenantal qualities that the Israel of the Old Testament had failed to fulfil. The English king could, or so it was thought, reflect ancient kings in reasserting control of both secular and ecclesiastical spheres (for the good of his people) hinting, as Cranmer and others had, that kings possess even priestly powers. For conservatives like Gardiner it was assumed that the king could offer better leadership and protection for the church than had Italy-centric popes in far-off Rome. Those Old Testament rulers in mind, the divine right of kings became their theoretical platform. The succession of a boy in 1547 forced the addition of a new element. Subordinate magistrates were said to share in the king's ecclesiastical powers (while he was still a minor). As the king was the agent of God, these men were agents of the crown. Propagandist and public-relations men forwarded legal arguments, unique to England (e.g., king-in-parliament, statutes and precedents), as well as commonplace evangelical explanations to reinforce conclusions for the literate elite. The idea of Mary succeeding her brother (as the legally correct option) was viewed as problematic.

51. Edward VI, "Discourse," 159–67.
52. Danner, "Resistance and the Ungodly Magistrate," 472.

For example, political theories on the supremacy of king-in-parliament and statute legislation were muted and closely re-examined (some wondered if a sovereign queen was even a legitimate idea in England) and Protestant theology would have to be abandoned. The crisis year 1553 saw "godly" magistrates turning against the true succession (trying and failing to parachute the Duke of Northumberland's daughter-on-law on to the throne). The covenantal realm of England faced an existential crisis in the coming of a queen who favoured Spanish customs, a Spanish husband, Catholicism, and papal allegiance. For some, like the conservatives Gardiner and Edmund Bonner (Bishop of London), the regime change was a welcome boast to their personal fortunes (and doctrinal beliefs) while for the evangelicals, like Hooper, Cranmer and Latimer, it presented far less favourable options. Some remained, prayed, and tried to persevere while others left, wrote, and hoped that those who remained did not lose faith in the strength of the fellowship and the covenant. To aid those who stayed behind, the exiles produced in-depth explorations of Swiss resistance theology, taking their questions and themselves to the sources.

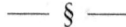

As a quick recap, Bullinger recognised the power of the civil magistrate to determine questions of religion. He had expressed no opposition to the royal ecclesiastical supremacy (as developed under Henry VIII and Edward VI) and he wrote that even ungodly rulers had to be tolerated as better than anarchy (echoing Beza). For Bullinger, magistrates were ably assisted and guided by the advice of prophets and evangelists for the betterment of the covenantal state (i.e., the godly commonwealth) wherein the church and state were partners. Officially Bullinger never emphasized a separate ecclesiastical power of discipline or excommunication, though, which was enough to prevent the civil authorities of Zürich from viewing their ecclesiastical counterparts as any kind of real threat. This also helped the clergy maintain moral authority as men of integrity within the civil realm (unlike the nitpicky and interfering Catholic clergy).[53] Calvin wanted a more autonomous ecclesiastical institution with more clear-cut divisions of authority between the civil and spiritual powers. Calvinists developed a resistance element against ungodly rulers; Bullinger opposed such a development. Those few Marian exiles who took refuge in Geneva adopted and adapted Calvin's resistance element. For men like John Ponet and Christopher Goodman, for

---

53. Moots, *Politics Reformed*, 51–52.

whom the Marian regime offered only the archetypal vision of ungodly rule, resistance theology finally included tyrannicide.

The restoration of Catholicism proved an arduous task as nearly twenty years of anti-Catholic, anti-papal propaganda had conditioned the literate public to view it (and the rule of a woman) as against natural law and covenantal theology. Mary would become bloody (after a series of set-backs, frustrations, health scares and disappointments) but her reign began in the spirit of her humanist training. She was determined not to force the Mass on her subjects (hoping that making it available would entice some, and the anticipated groundswell of support would influence others), nor did she intend to force people to act against their consciences (as she had so often been pressured to do under her brother and father). Catholicism would be restored and the Mass would be made readily available, but this was not a return to the fault-ridden late mediaeval practice. The Marian regime would be progressive; the queen envisioned an evangelical, humanist-inspired Catholicism, modelled more on Erasmus than on Eck. She even accepted the title of supreme head and governor of the Church of England (for the short term) but intended, with the advice and consent of parliament and convocation, to restore supremacy (and its associated authorities) to the pope. This was accomplished over the course of her first three parliaments in 1553 and 1554. The Edwardian Reformation legislation was repealed as was much of the Henrician legislation of the 1530s. In all ways that mattered, the English Church returned to 1529 (that point just before Henry's pursuit of a divorce from Mary's mother started the dominoes tumbling). All previous heresy legislation was re-enacted to set religion back on a steady course and the church into its familiar position as an adjunct of royal government. Preaching was suppressed in the first instance to allow cooler heads to prevail while the terms of constituted religion were reworked.

In the short term Protestant theorists were flummoxed; Mary seemed to be the epitome of the civil magistrate they had always wanted. Leaving doctrine aside, the queen consulted her subordinate magistrates gathered in parliament and in convocation; heretics were identified by lay authorities and turned over for examination and judgement to religious authorities, who turned them back over to the temporal authorities for punishment if they refused to recant or submit. The bishops in convocation—the elders of the church in Edward VI's eyes—assembled and pro-actively debated and discussed the issues of doctrine, reform and ecclesiastical canons—leading the supreme head through their conclusions. Mary did not throw the English Church into the hands of Rome blindly; this was a return to 1529 when *praemunire*, Provisors, and a powerful monarch ruled the nation recognising no superior authority.[54] Mary, her council, her chancellor (Gardiner) and her Archbishop of Canterbury (Reginald Pole) set out to emphasize Scripture (a new authorized English Bible was on the cards), teaching and education (catechising children and adults), the importance of preaching and pastoral work (new homilies were soon issued), and they planned for the moral improvement of both the clergy and the laity through regular episcopal visitations and injunctions. Indeed, many of the elements of Catholicism so reviled by Protestants were de-emphasized or ignored altogether—saints, pilgrimages, relics—as was priestly power and the theory of a divinely ordained papal authority. Mary seemed to be looking for her father's *via media*; Erasmus was her touchstone. Externals and material piety was curbed; internal spiritual development, Scripture and obedience was endorsed.[55] Mary engineered a return to the time just before all her personal troubles began, hoping to return the kingdom to a firm setting and proceeding from that point again along the road of Tridentine Catholic reform (examined next chapter). Bishop Bonner was pleased; men like Goodman and Ponet were not.

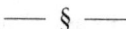

Bonner was a canon and civil lawyer, an advocate of the royal supremacy, and he held moderate but Catholic reform views. He had written both the preface for Gardiner's *De vera obedientia* and a homily on charity for Cranmer's collection of 1542 (emphasizing the important role of magistrates and the power of the sword) as well as favouring vernacular Bible projects. Edward's subordinate magistrates took Bonner's bishopric away from him and charged him with treason although he never opposed the king's supremacy or his right to try a man in orders. Bonner had objected only to the pace and extent of religious change, recognizing that too much of it was in the hands of a small group of self-interested men with a political rather than social or spiritual agenda; he was not willing to participate in the spread of doctrines he found radical. He was restored to London under Mary and became a key figure in the regime's attempts to eradicate heresy as a keen participant

---

54. Alexander, "Bonner and the Marian Persecutions," 159; Mann, *Supremacy and survival*, 42–4.

55. Haigh, *Reformations*, 217.

in re-education efforts.⁵⁶ Two important treatises stand out from Bonner's publications of the time. *A profitable and necessarye doctrine* (1554) revised and expanded upon the arguments of *King's Book* while *Homilies sette forth by Eddmune byshop of London* (1555) collected together thirteen sermons to help preachers re-educate their parishioners in the basics of Catholic theology, emphasising transubstantiation and papal doctrinal supremacy. Two of the sermons were written by Nicholas Harpsfield (a returned Edwardian exile) which blamed much of the religious chaos prevalent throughout contemporary Germany as evidence of the problems inherent in too much co-mixing of the two kingdoms.⁵⁷

John Ponet (a married priest) was a humanist scholar who had served Cranmer as a chaplain and Edward VI as Bishop of Rochester (1550–1) and of Winchester (1551–3). Although he had not been involved in the crisis events of 1553 he also would not submit to the Marian regime. His bishopric was returned to Gardiner and, following the failure of Wyatt's rebellion, Ponet fled to Strasbourg from where he entered into regular correspondence with Bullinger, keeping him abreast of the Frankfurt prayer book implosion. Christopher Goodman, an Oxford don, left England at about that same time but went to Frankfurt and subsequently to Geneva. Their different experiences produced different writings and allow us a good comparison on what choices were being offered the English evangelical community.

Ponet's *Short treatise of politike power* (1556) is a hard and contradictory treatise which went on to become of staple of seventeenth century Puritan political theory while Goodman's *How superior powers ought to be obeyed* (1558), which started as a sermon, has a better articulated central message. Goodman's value was ultimately limited, however, by the fact that, like Knox, he bitterly attacked the rule of women in general rather than remaining focussed on the rule of one woman in particular. David Wollman examined both treatises and found that, in different ways, they arrived at much the same conclusion of a necessary pro-active resistance to ungodly authority, and that even rebellion by lesser magistrates (and even by the masses if it cames to that) can be lawful and godly under certain very specific circumstances (although neither man took the ultimate step of calling for another general uprising against Mary).

Ponet rehearsed many of the basic evangelical conclusions about the role of the civil magistrates and the expression of ecclesiastical authority. These include the divine institution of government, the importance of harmonizing natural positive human law, the necessary priority of love for

56. Macek, *The Loyal Opposition*, 23.
57. Cooper, *Propaganda and the Tudor State*, 228.

God and fellow man, obedience as the foundation of order, the state's duty to punish the wicked and promote the worthy, and the importance of location determined specific laws created, however, ultimately in line with God's Word. Unlike other evangelicals, however, he did not oppose the Marian regime solely on doctrinal principles, or on Mary's perceived failure to maintain true religion, or her perceived failure to meet many of the necessary qualities of the prince of the covenant state (despite his great annoyance over her favouring of foreign princes—the pope and the emperor). Throughout the treatise he sought to set these commonplace theories within the English situation and ascribed additional conciliarist and constitutional ideas against the queen—the will of the people to be ruled; the role of lesser magistrates as determined by the ruled; the need for the chief magistrate to be checked by some common representative assembly. For him, the Marian regime failed to match the required human duties of the covenant.

Ponet's standard for the church/state relationship was akin to Luther's *two kingdoms* doctrine. In reflection of the two aspects of man, Ponet set the higher spiritual aspect over the lower physical aspect (which he gave no authority over the other) and equated the two aspects to the political and spiritual realms, recognising that there must, however, be some kind of balance between them. Where Luther made allowances for princely power, however, Ponet asserted the power of the state (i.e., the commonwealth) over that of the prince—placing patriotism just after love of God in a true believer's priority. Patriotism, love of country, must outweigh the love of any particular member thereof as no single member is more important than the whole realm. The commonwealth can certainly exist and the covenantal state can last without a prince, but the prince depends entirely for his office and authority on the acceptance of the commonwealth. According to his exegesis of Samuel and because Mary failed to understand and support this truth, the queen was due no obedience or recognition as a lawful ruler.

From a neutral point of view Ponet's argument was neither whimsical nor baseless. The queen wanted to restore formerly appropriated church property. After nearly two decades of selling off ecclesiastical assets, however, this was all but impossible. Mary secured a papal dispensation which allowed all the land now in private hands to remain so (she was not unrealistic), but she restored those lands still in the control of the crown. This was the nub of Ponet's opposition. That limited restoration created a hole in royal finances which she expected parliament to fill *via* subsidies, loans and taxation (in essence passing an unnecessary debt on to the nation at large). Such perceived mismanagement, along with the queen's determination to also give up ecclesiastical revenues, gave weight to Ponet's complaints of ungodly rule, particularly when she tried to force those in exile to return to England on pain of loss of their properties (which would have impoverished Ponet himself).⁵⁸ The democratic principle inherent in Luther's *priesthood of all believers* also informed Ponet's thinking. He wanted the crown to ensure that each subject was gainfully and appropriately employed and were accorded equality before the law, a reflection of spiritual equality in the commonwealth. Before the law there is (or should be) no recognition of persons—kings and magistrates enforce the law as a matter of office and not of person; as persons they are subject to the law. Ponet applied this principle to property (in conflict with contemporary feudal ideals and the widespread patronage and clientage networks in existence throughout Europe), and observed that Mary had forced the commonwealth to act against the will of the people (e.g., her taxation and religious statutes) seeking her own profit rather than the advancement of the covenant (wherein private ownership should be recognized and consequent charity practised). He called on the assembly (i.e., parliament) as representative of the will of the people to replace the head of the body politic with a new head, one more conformable to their duty and the collective will (as Wyatt, after a fashion, had tried to do with Ponet's support).

Anti-Catholic, anti-Spanish and anti-papal rhetoric aside Ponet argued that English theologians had somehow arrived at a misunderstanding of the role and authority of magistrates, particularly princes, based on a misreading of the relevant Scriptures (not entirely unlike the way the papacy had misunderstood those passages used to underlay the authority of Peter as "the rock"). Obedience to the prince and magistrates was clearly important in the maintenance of public order, but obedience very much depended on the orders of the prince meeting certain limiting criteria, which Mary's orders did not. They must contribute to the general benefit of the commonwealth (which return of former church property clearly harmed), they must follow God's laws (which the queen's religious policies did not), and they must conform to the laws of nature (which, as a female ruler, Mary subverted), not to mention subjecting the realm to the rule of two/three foreign princes (i.e., the pope, the emperor and Philip of Spain).⁵⁹ Mary became the very model of a tyrant; "an evil person coming to the government of any state, either by usurpation, by election, or by succession, [who] utterly neglecting the cause why kinges, princes, and other governours in common wealths be made (that is, the welthe of the people) seketh onlie or chiefly his owne profit and pleasure."⁶⁰ Such a ruler is open

---

58. Peardon, "The Politics of Polemic," 41.
59. Peardon, "The Politics of Polemic," 45.
60. Ponet, *A Short Treatise*, 98–99, as quoted in Wollman, "Biblical justification," 34.

to dethronement despite the understanding of Rom 13 or 1 Pet 2 toward absolute obedience to civil authorities.

Ponet did not equate tyrannicide with a disavowing of political duty; it was actually a confirmation of obedience. The Christian's ultimate duty was to the commonwealth (i.e., the sovereignty of the covenantal state) rather than to the monarch (as a member of that state). To overthrow the monarch, who was a tyrant and ungodly, was equated with an affirmation of the covenant (obeying God). The process of removing the tyrant was to be led by the nobility and lesser magistrates, or the assembly (i.e., parliament), working on behalf of the commonwealth and not for their own purposes or power. If they failed to act, the onus moved to ministers exercising the power of the keys—excommunication—which removed the offending prince from the fellowship of the Lord's Supper and from the commonwealth/covenant. Ponet went so far as to suggest that even a private person may set things right again if he had God's commandment or the compliance of the assembly, but conceded that this was a rare and special case. Most individuals can only fall back on prayer, perseverance or flight. One historian suggested that this reasoning was the basis of Ponet's support of Wyatt (that rare and special individual).[61]

By the mid-1550s, the thrust of evangelical thinking (as evinced by Calvin) had been that passive resistance in the form of prayer and self-exile were the options open to those who opposed the rule of the prince for reasons of conscience. Goodman and Knox (as noted) both accepted the ungodly magistrate—even the tyrant—as an instrument of God's will. Around this time, however, religious tensions were growing in France (Catholic v. Huguenot) inspiring resistance theology in the Reformed school, and Ponet moved away from the evangelical norm into this new territory. He did not accept the idea that God was the author of evil or that the tyrant was an agent of God (as Tyndale had written), installed for the punishment of the wicked population, relying instead on a wider application of the key words in the major passages to arrive at more radical conclusions. His reading had Paul command every soul (every person from prince to pauper) to obey higher authorities—be subject to their rulers—with rulers as much subject to God's laws as anyone else, and he placed the onus on each level in the political hierarchy to punish the wicked and the sinful wherever this was found (even if at a higher level).[62] Extrapolating from Old Testament sources he concluded that the killing of tyrants was beneficial to the people

---

61. Beer, "John Ponet's Shorte Treatise," 380; Greaves, "Concepts of Political Obedience," 25.

62. Ponet, *A Short Treatise*, 111–18.

and righteous in the eyes of God, even if no one particular citation justified the act itself (falling back on godly mandates instead). Here he also fell back on arguments from reason. Rulers are subject to natural law and those particular positive human laws (those which agree with divine and natural laws). Ponet had been moved by broad political principles more so than by religious considerations. Goodman's sermon-treatise approached the same conclusions through a more strict and literal understanding of the relevant Scripture.

Goodman interpreting the key Bible passages as relating to godly magistrates and godly rule specifically, rather than to magistrates and rules in general. He extrapolated certain contemporary conclusions from the historical situation of the early Christians as well, although he was careful to avoid the conclusion (so often charged) that freedom from the law necessarily meant lawlessness, as some early Christians (and contemporary Anabaptists) falsely assumed. Obedience was due, therefore, to governments and magistrates who carried out their God-given duties to defend the good and punish the wicked. He attacked the queen and those who supported the regime as having abandoned their duty to God in exchange for the temptations of the flesh—they obeyed man rather than God. Mary, of course, could be dismissed as an illegitimate ruler first because she favoured Spain as a model state, Spaniards as opposed to Englishmen, Catholicism as a religion, the pope as a spiritual advisor and the emperor as a personal mentor (how could she be thought of as English at all?), second because the rule of women offended natural law principles.[63] Goodman bound this to a covenantal argument that the ruler must be "one of their brethren"—the chosen people—because strangers (the Spanish?) bring "oppression and idolatry." England, he argued, was now overrun with strangers (who can never really be brethren), "but chiefly to avoid that monster in nature, and disorder amongst men, which is the Empire and government of a woman." Goodman provided very literal scriptural interpretations (worth quoting in full):

> saying expressly: From the midst of your brethren shall you chose a king for yourself, and not amongst your sisters. For God is not contrary to Himself, which at the beginning appointed the woman to be in subjection to her husband [Genesis 3:16], and the man to be head of the woman (as the Apostle says) who will not permit so much to the woman, as to speak in the Assembly of men [1 Corinthians 34-35; 1 Timothy 2:11-12], much less to be ruler of a realm or nation. If women are not permitted by civil

---

63. Danner, "Christopher Goodman," 62-63.

policies to rule in inferior offices, to be Counselors, Peers of a realm, Justices, Sheriffs, Bailiffs, and such like: Make yourselves judges, whether it is mete for them to govern whole realms and nations? If the word of God cannot persuade you, by which she is made subject to her husband, much more to the counsel and authority of a whole realm, which word also appoints your kings to be chosen from among their brethren, and not from their sisters: who are forbidden as persons unmete to speak in a congregation: be judges yourselves, and let nature teach you the absurdity thereof. And this much have I of purpose noted in this matter, to let you see to all our shames, how far you have been led besides your common senses and the manifest word of God, in electing, anointing, and crowning a woman to be your Queen and Governess, and she in very deed a bastard, and unlawfully begotten. But be it that she was not a bastard, but the kings daughter as lawfully begotten as was her sister, that godly Lady, and meek lamb, void of all Spanish pride, and strong blood: yet in the sickness, and at the death of our lawful Prince of godly memory King Edward the Sixth, this should not have been your first counsel or question, who should be your Queen, what woman you should crown, if you had been preferred of God's glory, and wise counselors, or naturally affected towards your country. But first and principally, who had been most mete amongst your brethren to have had the government over you, and the whole government of the realm, to rule them carefully in the fear of God, and to preserve them against all oppression of inward tyrants and outward enemies. Whereby you might have been assured to escape all this miserable and unspeakable disorder, and shameful confusion, which now by contrary counsel is brought worthily upon us.

That damage had been done.

Like Ponet, Goodman took passive resistance as a weak response, requiring the godly to be pro-active and public in their resistance, and he placed a particular onus on subordinate magistrates to take the lead in opposing "blasphemie and oppression." He agreed with Ponet that even private persons are charged to have a care for the laws of God.[64] Goodman strayed into a more dangerous territory, however, by allowing individual consciences the right to determine for themselves whether the magistrates fulfilled their

---

64. Wollman, "Biblical Justification," 35, 37. Goodman's *How Superior Powers Ought to Be Obeyed* (1558) can be found online with updated English at http://www.constitution.org/cmt/goodman/obeyed.htm#chap4 (used here).

roles correctly, relying on Acts 5:29 as a proof text.[65] To submit to an ungodly female sovereign was to be equated with rebellion against God.

For both men the meaning of the popular citations in *Romans* and *1 Peter* were not written to the advantage of the ruler but to that of the ruled—that is, the properly ruled. Goodman's purpose was to de-construct the quotations to fit his own exegesis. Paul, therefore, had been writing to a sect at Rome which very much anticipated the contemporary Anabaptists, holding a similar disregard for temporal office, oaths, and the payment of taxes and tithes. But he went beyond what was written, extrapolating the secrets hidden beneath the actual words.

In chapter eleven, for instance, he acknowledged that "all men are bound to obey such Magistrates, whom God has ordained over us lawfully according to His word, which rule in His fear according to their office." To Goodman this meant only those rulers "orderly and lawfully instituted by God," otherwise it would seem to be that God "approve all tyranny and oppression . . . wicked and ungodly rulers . . . disorders and subversions in commonwealths." Such cannot be God's ordinance. "For He never ordained any laws to approve, but to reprove and punish tyrants, idolaters, papists, and oppressors." That being the case, disobeying tyrants is not resistance but righteousness. "And in disobeying and resisting such, we do not resist God's ordinance, but Satan's, and our sin, which is the cause of such." For Goodman, therefore, that which was due to magistrates was due only insofar as the magistrate had clear godly support and a divine mandate for his (gender specific) rule. Likewise, he read into *Peter* a distinction between patiently obeying the prince who was "rough and forward" as opposed to that one who was "wicked and ungodly." A Christian must bear with the former and accept harsh treatments (as a master may treat a servant at times) and still serve faithfully for the sake of God so long as the ruler remained (if only outwardly) within God's laws (e.g., punishing transgressors, defending the innocent). It is not for the individual to judge the ruler. However, "if without fear they transgress God's laws themselves and command others to do the same, then have they lost that honor and obedience which otherwise their subjects did owe unto them: and ought no more to be taken for Magistrates: but punished as private transgressors . . ."

From here, Goodman turned his attention to Christ's order against Peter's use of the sword and the *two kingdoms* organization this suggests. Clergy use spiritual weapons to defend the gospel and the laity material weapons to defend the godly, the gospel and Christendom as a whole, the point being

---

65. I.e., "But Peter and the *other* apostles answered and said: 'We ought to obey God rather than men.'"

that lesser magistrates can therefore lawfully oppose higher powers if they attempt to impose wickedness on the state.

With chapter eleven Goodman began drawing conclusions, first placing an onus on all magistrates, subordinate magistrates and commoners alike to ensure that princes are "subject to God's laws." Rebellion against an ungodly ruler, therefore, becomes a divine duty after this interpretation—disobedience to the ungodly ruler is a clear and public demonstration of true obedience to God. Both Goodman and Ponet had turned to the text of Samuel [e.g., 1 Sam 14: 43–5] among others in the Old Testament to find examples which supported their interpretation and which nominally matched the situation in England. Mary, either directly or indirectly, became the living embodiment of either the wicked, ungodly monarch or the punishment sent by God for the sins of the nation in turning its collective back on the covenant. The solution was tyrannicide; it was scripturally justifiable. Both men called upon the lesser magistrates to perform this necessary duty on behalf of the covenantal state. In essence, disobedience to the ungodly ruler had become, for them, a divine precept.

Neither writer ultimately called for a rebellion though, instead falling back on the common evangelical assertion of prayer, perseverance or flight. Both make the assumption that Mary was sent by God as a punishment for the sins of the commonwealth (in not finding and properly supporting a godly ruler after the death of Edward), both found that repentance and Christian behaviour will now resolve the issue—both giving voice to other evangelical norms. In many ways, Ponet, Goodman and others, like Knox, were defying many aspects of evangelical belief as well as distinctive English theological developments. As we have seen here, the theory, in development long before Luther, was that kings and magistrates were the agents of divine law, natural law, and positive human law—they were as gods themselves in this sphere (as officers rather than as human beings). This being the case, if the magistrate was evil and abused his authority it was because God wanted him to do so as a punishment of the people he abused—obedience was still due. If the tyrant ruler, the heathen king, the tempted magistrate made rulings contrary to the Word of God, prayer, perseverance and death were the options to those with offended consciences (although some allowed fleeing the nation as a less arduous alternative, but one which came with its own set of problems). If, however, someone had a clear godly mandate to do so then killing the tyrant was acceptable (both men were rather vague on the details, however). By the time Goodman's polemic was published, however, Ponet was dead and the situation in England had already partially resolved itself. Goodman had been so hostile to female rule, however, that he was never fully able to rehabilitate himself. Both men helped develop (in their way) new theories—resistance theology and the covenant—which plagued Elizabeth.[66]

— § —

Elizabeth: Royal Ecclesiastical Supremacy Resumed

Since 1529 and the start of the so-called "Reformation Parliament", constituted religion (i.e., ecclesiastical government and doctrine) in England had been determined by a process of crown-in-parliament, the monarch working through the established machinery of a legislative equation in which crown, lords and commons cooperated in the creation of statute law. As only that exact cooperation could establish the highest temporal law, only that cooperative effort could subsequently change or abrogate it. Over the course of the crisis period in Tudor history, however, the reins of power within the equation had been stretched and pulled in different directions. Edward's subordinate magistrates, for instance, moved constituted religion much further toward Switzerland than Henry VIII could ever have imagined, while Mary and hers pulled it back to a point almost out of the popular memory, restoring papal "supremacy" and Catholic doctrine while maintaining a Henrician administrative control. This means that after nearly thirty years of accumulated precedent, in 1558 the new queen had little choice but to work through parliament in order to re-constitute religion as she thought appropriate—re-establishing a royal ecclesiastical supremacy in law which brooked no interference from abroad or from outside ecclesiastical channels. Queen-in-parliament established legislation which determined accepted doctrine (theology), determined heresy (punishments) and tying together the crown, parliament and the convocation of the clergy in the process of ecclesiastical government. Elizabeth rather sharply brought the church to a standard of practice co-mixing late-Henrician and Edwardian norms, officially accepting Scripture as the principle source of doctrine and practice, but not entirely resting on that standard. By the mid-1560s this brought the queen into conflict with some of her subjects—Catholic and Protestant—over questions of the church, constituted religion, and magisterial authority.

66. Wollman, "Biblical Justification," 38–41.

§

The new supremacy legislation of 1558–9 re-affirmed loyalty to God's sovereign authority before any merely human authority in the determination of orthodoxy.[67] This was the central message of *Thirty-nine Articles*, a reformulation of Cranmer's proposed *Forty-two articles* which had reflected Swiss Reformed theology. *Articles* was accepted and authorized by the queen for widespread use (with a few further changes) in 1563. In 1571 it was reaffirmed by the bishops (with the changes approved by the queen) and given legislative mandate by parliament, thereby establishing the doctrine of the church, its liturgy, and its polity firmly in positive human law. Elizabeth thereafter adopted a position in protection of the established church—as guardian or defender of the faith—and the major occupation of theologians passed from definition of the faith to exhortations on obedience and order. It was at this level, however, that the previous two reigns had raised issues which would dog Elizabeth now. For many Protestant polemicists the previous two reigns had raised serious questions—covenantal practice had been subverted by Mary (who transferred the supreme headship outside the realm) and by a combination of Crown and subordinate magistrates in both previous reigns. Elizabeth also offended natural law principles as much as had her half-sister. The mid-Tudor crisis in religious reform led to a serious schism in the Elizabethan era, and much of this had to do with the extent of magisterial control over the church, as practised by the queen and her bishops exclusively.

In terms of the Swiss Reformed faith, the prince or chief magistrate working with subordinates had not been enough to guarantee the supremacy of God's own will in the determination of religious or doctrinal truths in England. Indeed, under Mary, the crown, parliament and convocation had more or less subverted God's will entirely according to some. Not only had the ruling magistracy failed to enforce and engender Christian teaching, they had also failed to constitute true religion, and failed to prevent a breach of natural law. To more radical Protestant thinkers this raised serious questions on the viability of the usual legal and constitutional processes at work. The Elizabethan *Act of Uniformity* [1 Eliz. 1, c.2] admitted that mistakes had been made in the past "detrimental to the honour of God."[68] For some this begged a question of whether English magistrates could be trusted with the usual powers ascribed to them by Reformed theology. Had the office of the crown worn out its welcome; could magistrates be

---

67. Eppley, "Royal Supremacy," 145.
68. Elton, *Tudor Constitution*, no. 195.

trusted (let alone absolutely obeyed); could the queen unite such a spiritually divided people? As under her father, the queen relied on the precepts of established obedience theology.

Elizabeth had the advantage that most Protestant writers tended to distance themselves from the radical theories of active resistance and tyrannicide which had been developed by the likes of Knox, Ponet and Goodman in the 1540s and 1550s and Calvinist theology supporting the rights of the lesser magistrates to overthrow an ungodly or tyrannical prince had yet to be fully explored. Certainly the idea that an individual (mandated by God or not) could move against the crown was discarded. Instead theorists moved back to the early Tudor obedience theology (of pre-1553) which stated that to obey the crown was to obey God's sovereign power. Whether the prince was a wicked tyrant or a godly magistrate, obedience was due and resistance disallowed, according to scriptural truth. The question became which doctrinal position to resume: that of the late Henrician/Edwardian era of simple submission to divinely ordained powers (i.e., to suffer even a wicked magistrate rather than to disobey, showing compliance with the will of God); the later theology of Calvin/Beza on the right of the lesser magistrate to depose a tyrant; or, the Knox-Ponet-Goodman view, pro-active in accessing the godliness of the ruler and their rule and then acting upon the evaluation? The more radical options were disregarded as Anglicans (a useful but anachronistic term) adopted a more conservative stance on the relevant issues.

John Whitgift, scholar and later Archbishop of Canterbury, advocated a view that there was a godly duty of submission to civil powers, the only stipulation being that these powers were themselves Scripture-compliant. In 1574, in polemic dispute with Thomas Cartwright, Whitgift wrote that no matter how tyrannical civil law or rule became, the prince was still to be obeyed, for "disobedience to the prince in civil matters is disobedience to God,"[69] albeit the ruler was wicked or infidel. We will examine the Whitgift v. Cartwright dispute further in due course. For Anglicans, or conforming Protestants, disobedience was allowable (but the consequences inevitable) only when an order was explicitly against Scripture, and they drew the line at open rebellion. With regard to theories we have already examined it is clear that conforming Elizabethan Protestants fit into a covenant position like Bullinger's, one which held no difference between the two kingdoms of church and state,

---

69. *Works*, 2:50.

seeing instead only one united Christian commonwealth under the rule of God's earthly agent. For them, questions of discipline, liturgy, ecclesiastical government and religious customs were all *adiaphora*, not specified in Scripture and therefore subject to the magistrate whose rulings need only fit the parameters of natural law and particular custom. If they did not order anything contrary to Scripture, the ruler must be obeyed. As far as rebellion was concerned they generally accepted that a godly man could gently rebuke a magistrate, if his conscience had been offended by a ruling, but vehement protest, disorder, and violence were out of the question.

Instead such a man must turn to a lesser magistrate for protection against iniquitous laws (to an MP perhaps).[70] Puritans, those advocates of the Geneva system, generally agreed with their conformist brethren over obedience questions, provided magisterial rule was limited to indifferent matters and in no way contrary to divine law or Scripture. A problem developed when radical Puritans (i.e., Presbyterians) differed over the extent of *adiaphora*, seeing such issues as ecclesiastical government, liturgy, and discipline firmly in the domain of the autonomous spiritual kingdom (over which the temporal magistrate had no office but, as a mortal was still a member). Generally they were willing to obey the civil magistrate as a divine office in control of the earthly, political kingdom, going only so far in opposition as praying that ungodly or wicked rulers would be quickly overthrown, otherwise advocating perseverance or self-exile over issues of conscience. Even separatists advocated nothing more than passive resistance. As one might anticipate, polemic dispute tended therefore to revolve around questions which one side took as *adiaphora* and which the other side took as somehow *salvific*. Here we will briefly examine the works of the Puritan polemicists Fields, Wilcox and Cartwright and the conforming Protestants Whitgift and Hooker.

Serious tensions had been building since the reign of Edward over certain issues of which the question of vestments became the most theologically charged. Then, Cranmer and Hooper quarrelled back and forth until the issue was formulated in terms of godly obedience, to which Hooper eventually capitulated. Clearly, the scars had not healed over and the Vestiarian controversy was repeated in 1565 when the queen noted that some of the clergy were not wearing the vestments ordered in the settlement statutes. Some had even tried to use parliament as a means of redress (an appeal to

---

70. Greaves, "Concepts of Political Obedience," 26–28.

lesser magistrates) and the queen ordered Archbishop Parker to settle the matter. Because the queen and bishops subsequently demanded subscription of the *Prayer Book* and the *Thirty-nine articles*, some radicals became disillusioned with the Elizabethan settlement altogether. They questioned the existence of bishops, other "popish" remnants, royal ecclesiastical supremacy, and even its foundations in Scripture. In their eyes the queen and bishops had failed to progress the Reformation; there was no emphasis on a preaching ministry and a lack of godly discipline at the parish level. They looked toward a Presbyterian system (as they saw in Geneva) as a preferred system of ecclesiastical government. Royal ecclesiastical supremacy, as supported by an episcopal hierarchy, became the focus of discontent and criticism in and out of parliament. One of the leading critics of the regime was Thomas Cartwright.

Cartwright, a Cambridge don, led the criticism from the lectern through a series of divinity lectures in 1570 which focussed on the *Acts of the Apostles*, contrasting the English Church with that of its New Testament predecessor. Although he was not raising original objections, and those he did raise were not particularly radical, his words were offensive enough (e.g., threatening both episcopacy and royal sovereignty) and it cost him his position at the hands of the then vice-chairman of the university, Whitgift. Patrick Collinson detailed some of Cartwright's conclusions, and they are familiar—an ecclesiastical system of pastor, elder and deacon, a loose binding together of autonomous congregations through apostolic authority, autonomy from state controls obviously contrary to the Elizabethan settlement of royal authority and episcopal support. When he looked at the bigger picture it seemed to Cartwright that the queen's goals of obedience and social order were ill-served by the current church system in which ecclesiastical officers were more bureaucratic than pastoral, more secular than spiritual.

He saw in the English Church little real individual freedom of conscience and also found discipline quite lax but burdensome too. He postulated that local church discipline would improve both social behaviour and bring purity to the church which the appearance of popish remnant practices disrupted, and he advocated certain evangelical norms—the three ancient offices, congregations electing their own pastors, *sola scriptura*.[71] This academic controversy, and the subscription crisis which preceded it, led two of Cartwright's disciples (the London clergymen John Fields and Thomas Wilcox) to write an *Admonition to parliament* in 1572, making the assumption that as the royal ecclesiastical supremacy was legislative in

---

71. Collinson, *The Elizabethan Puritan Movement*, 45.

formulation, parliament could subsequently alter the church settlement to their own satisfaction.[72] This was followed up by a *Second Admonition* from the pen of Cartwright himself. The professed objective was a call to arms, calling on parliamentarians to legislate away remaining superstitions. Their real objective, of course, was to advocate and popularize the Genevan system of church government—pastor, deacon and elder—using this as a replacement for the ungodly, unscriptural, and frankly corrupted, English episcopal hierarchy. Fields and Wilcox were at the radical edge of Puritan and non-conformist opinion which generally sought only to modify the liturgy and doctrine of the church rather than foster rebellion. Such hard line Presbyterians as they, however, sought to undermine the royal ecclesiastical supremacy itself.[73] Whilst Fields and Wilcox were imprisoned their polemic found a widespread audience and inspired subsequent Presbyterian polemic, although nothing changed. The queen ordered Parker to settle this matter too. Non-conformity was to be suppressed, uncooperative clerics were to lose their livings, and Whitgift was to be co-opted into public relations (i.e., writing propaganda).

—— § ——

The Admonition: Consequences, Supporters, and Critics

From the start of the reign Elizabeth treated parliament and convocation much the same—they were subordinate ministers to her supremacy—and she kept her subordinates of the one sphere out of the business of the other. This would seem contrary to established legislative precedence, however, and ecclesiastical bills continued to be formulated in the commons, much to the queen's dismay. Puritan leaders, frustrated by the bishops' opposition in the Vestianary controversy, sought to render change through parliament, but the bills were inevitably quashed by the queen's officers in the house or by royal veto. *Admonition* sought to outline a solution to the issues and was timed to appear just as the 1571 session was ending in late June (in theory therefore claiming a parliamentary free speech protection for the authors). The tract was not really addressed to parliament, however, but rather to the literate public, and it proved popular.

The treatise is, in fact, two separate essays, both anti-episcopal in scope. The first examines such issues as preaching, sacraments, and ecclesiastical

---

72. Fields and Wilcox, "Admonition to the Parliament," 1–40.
73. Doran, *Elizabeth and Religion*, 33–34.

discipline, none of which in its view conformed to the strictures of Scripture and were, therefore, ungodly and not binding on Christian consciences. A number of objections and recommendations were raised against the current establishment, proposing a tripartite ecclesiastical government of pastor, deacon and elder having joint rule over the church instead of the current hierarchy and system of discipline. The second essay, following closely the structure of the first, highlighted "popish" abuses still extent in the English Church, focussing especially on the weaknesses of the prayer book, questions of externals (like apparel), and the constituted articles of religion. The main objection men like Fields and Wilcox raised was that in recent experience it seemed that faith was being coerced by civil punishments rather than reformed and spread through appropriate systems of ecclesiastical discipline. They wanted to move toward a more clearly Genevan system in which ecclesiastical discipline was in the hands of ecclesiastical bodies overseen by clerical officers, focussed on the congregation and parish, and replacing the system of supreme head and episcopal hierarchy which featured in England.

The *Admonition*, in the first essay, advocated a central focus on a preaching ministry supported by church-based ecclesiastical government and discipline as a means of achieving sound spiritual reform and appropriate social behaviour. On the face of it, they wrote, the doctrine of the English Church is sound, but the church fails by comparison to that of the ancients. The appointment of ministers is neither scriptural nor particularly equitable and, thereby, the congregation is being spiritually short changed; "neither the ministers thereof are accordyng to Gods worde proved, elected, called, or ordayned: nor the function in such sorte so narrowly loked unto, as of right it ought, and is of necessitie required." A picture was being painted of an ideal primitive church's superiority over its modern counterpart:

> whereas in the olde church a trial was had both of their abilitie to instruct, and of their godly conversation also: now, by the letters commendatorie of some one man, noble or other, tag and rag, learned and unlearned, of the basest sorte of the people (to the slander of the Gospell in the mouthes of the adversaries) are freely receaved. In those daies no idolatrous sacrificers or heathenish priests were apointed to be preachers of the Gospel: but we allow, and like wel of popish masse mongers, men for all seasons, Kyng Henries priests, Kyng Edwards priests, Queene Maries priestes, who of a truth (yf Gods worde were precisely folowed) should from the same be utterly removed.

The English Church was not so much reformed as confused by a chaotic variety of opinions and practices. This was partially the result of the queen's and the bishops' denial of the congregations' inherent authority (as taken from *priesthood of all believers*) to examine and elect its own ministers and administer discipline through its own churchmen. The result was a serious indictment of English conditions: the learning of the ministers was inadequate ("then the ministers were preachers: now bare readers") and appointment was by grace and favour of distant nobles or officials rather than by vigorous examination by local leaders as once had been the case— "Then no minister placed in any congregation, but by the consent of the people, now, that authoritie is geven into the hands of the byshop alone, who by his sole authoritie thrusteth upon them such, as they many times aswel for unhonest life, as also for lacke of learning, may, & doe justly dislike." Moreover, some congregations had no pastor, and working pastors were subjected to official licensing, non-scriptural regulations, and instead of being allowed to preach freely from Scripture must instead navigate around homilies, articles and injunctions.[74] Fields and Wilcox appealed to the scriptural division of church offices—elder, deacon and pastor (or minister) as God's own requirement for the governance of the church and the practice of discipline. The office of the elder (called "seniors" here) was "to governe the church with the rest of the ministers, to consulte, to admonish, to correct, and to order all things apperteigning to the state of the congregation." Their complaint was that the English Church was still organized and governed much as was the Roman Catholic Church—a bishop with too many congregations in his charge necessarily assisted in his work by a slew of lesser officers, none of which had been needed in the primitive church and none of whom actually preach. Fields and Wilcox called for an "equality of ministers" to replace bishops and archbishops and a "lawful and godly seignorie" in each congregation, removing that entire range of lesser clerical offices. The whole regiment of the church, they advised, was to be invested in elders, deacons and pastors—this would resolve any problems. What seems like a denial of the authority of the civil magistrate was, the authors argued, merely a change of focus. They wanted to see a strict separation of the two kingdoms, each recognizing God at its head and with no other co-mingling. Indeed, they argued that given their way the prince's authority would be all the more appropriately lauded, respected and obeyed. Is that not what the queen wanted? They did not wish to "take away the authoretie of the civill Magistrate and chief governour" but only to restore Christ, God's word and church discipline. As a result, "the Prince may be better obeyed, the realme more florish in godlines, and the Lord himself more sincerely and purely according to his revealed will served

---

74. Fields and Wilcox, "Admonition to the Parliament," 8, 9, 10.

then heretofore he hath ben, or yet at this present is."[75] Accordingly, discipline (including excommunication) was devised after the Rule of Christ and to be taken out of the episcopal court structure and moved back to the congregational level. Whitgift responded to the *Admonition* with *Answere to a certain libel* in 1573 (amended subsequently to take into account Cartwright's *Second Admonition*), to which Cartwright responded with *Replye* shortly thereafter, a systematic examination of the controversy. The next year saw Whitgift's *Defense of the answere* as well as Cartwright's *Second replie* which had been written from exile and which was supplemented in 1577 with *The rest of the second replie* (which was largely ignored).

—— § ——

How did Whitgift defend the royal ecclesiastical supremacy and discipline of the Elizabethan Church? The answer would appear to be badly and with too many assumptions. The dispute was unlikely to be resolved through polemics in any case. Whitgift and Cartwright were arguing from opposed positions not only in terms of what constituted *adiaphora*, how God constituted society (two exclusive kingdoms or one covenanted commonwealth), and what the role of the civil magistrate actually was, but also (and most importantly) they were arguing over conflicting interpretations of Scripture and the relationship between Scripture and the church. The upshot of Cartwright's Presbyterian position was plain—Scripture (self-interpreted) contained within it a perfect guide and rule for ecclesiastical government and discipline (echoing Fields and Wilcox, as well as Calvin and Beza). Whitgift, conversely, argued that Scripture (interpreted by constituted authority) left a great deal of freedom to civil magistrates in the establishment of the visible, earthly government and institution of the church—matters indifferent to salvation—and therefore it was right to leave these details to the supreme governess and her subordinate magistrates (i.e., her bishops). He charged the Presbyterians with, at one and the same time, the errors of the Roman system (which denied to secular rulers their proper authority) and the Anabaptist sectarians (which denied a need for and cooperation with magisterial authority).[76]

In his *Replye* (or sometimes *First Reply*) Cartwright objected to the inclusion of Presbyterians in the camp of the radical sectarians. The Presbyterians were prepared to not only accept and acknowledge the legitimacy of magisterial power and also to obey their commands "in the Lord, and for the

75. "Admonition to the Parliament," 15, 18.
76. Whitgift, "Defence," 3:298–300.

Lord"—that is, provided the commands were commiserate with Scripture and individual conscience.[77] With regard to royal ecclesiastical supremacy, the debate between Cartwright and Whitgift revolved around the usefulness of Scripture as an exclusive guide to church government and discipline. Whitgift maintained in his *Answere* that while Scripture held a perfect guide to doctrine and faith it made few demands regarding earthly and external matters (like specific forms of ecclesiastical government) as these were indifferent to salvation. Such matters fell within the power of the magistrate to regulate for the commune as a whole. The ministry of the church was, in his conception, therefore subordinate to the civil magistrate (a call back to the Henrician/Edwardian system). Cartwright maintained that Scripture was perfectly sufficient to guide ecclesiastical government.

For Whitgift (arguing from authority—not of Scripture but of learned scholars) the election of ministers was in the hands of the bishops as the officers of the supreme head.[78] Cartwright (arguing from Scripture) noted that election should be in the hands of the congregation (as the church, the body of Christ), maintaining that the hierarchy of bishops was an artificial bureaucracy in the English and popish churches, one not found in the primitive church. He pictured the ancient church as one in which there was one priest (bishop) responsible for each singular congregation in conjunction with a committee of elders and compared this unfavourably with the modern diocesan system of one bishop overseeing dozens if not hundreds of congregations.[79] His argument was that bishops now have a false pre-eminence and power unwarranted by Scripture. This was "popish" in nature as the office of the Archbishop of Canterbury was now comparable to that of the pope in Rome. Whitgift maintained that the church (the visible, earthly institution) was established by human laws commiserate with local or particular conditions, with the proviso that the establishment does not contravene divine law or detract from the glory of God. He equated Cartwright's denial with radical sectarian and Anabaptist error. Cartwright countered that while the magistrate is a power in the temporal, political sphere (in the commonwealth); he is just another man in the church. We may recall the words of Ponet or Goodman here; "The church may be established without the magistrate so as that all the world and all the power of hell cannot shake it, but it cannot expect outward peace and quietness without a godly

---

77. Brook, *Cartwright*, 105. This is an incomplete version.
78. Whitgift, "Defence," 3:435.
79. Brook, *Cartwright*, 119.

magistrate," reducing the magistrate to the regulation of society and protection of the godly and the church.[80]

In *The defence of the Answere* Whitgift recognized that Cartwright had conceived of the church and the commonwealth as two distinct entities requiring distinct governments after the arguments of the Marian exiles. On the issue of the royal headship Whitgift acknowledged that, while Christ is the head of the body of the church invisible (in the spiritual form), he separated this from the external, physical, visible body (of saints and sinners mixed) over which the chief magistrate ruled by virtue of his office. He made a necessary separation between spiritual and temporal matters, arguing that the Christian commonwealth was an external, earthly matter. Cartwright took a more literal view. He argued that Whitgift did a disservice to the prince because if he is the head of the church then he cannot at the same time be a member of it. Cartwright allowed no co-mingling of the kingdoms. As evidence of his vision and the authority of Scripture he cited 2 *Chr* [19:8, 11] as a clear separation of church and state function (e.g., *two kingdoms* doctrine) and Rom 14:23 as the foundation of his position that anything not specifically recommended in Scripture was sinful. Whitgift countered that Cartwright's proof text actually proved his point that government of the church was in the hands of the magistrate. The magistrate placed the Levites and priests, prescribed their duties, gave them authority, singling out Jehoshaphat as the prime example: "Jehosaphat had chief authority and government both in things pertaining to God, and in things pertaining to the commonwealth; but, for better execution of them, the one he did commit to be executed by Amaria the priest, the other by Zabadiah a ruler of the house of Judah." His position was that Elizabeth did much the same thing: "committeth the hearing and judging of ecclesiastical matters to the archbishops and bishops, and temporal matters to the lord chancellor and other judges." To conclude from this scenario that the queen has no power due to these appointments is self-deception. Jehoshaphat and Elizabeth both acted as God commanded, confirming their power over both spheres.[81]

Cartwright noted of the citation in *Romans* that "the place of St. Paul in the xiv of the Romans is of all other most clear, where, speaking of those things which are called indifferent, in the end he concludeth that "whatsoever is not of faith is sin:" but faith is not but in respect of the word of God; therefore whatsoever is not done by the word of God is sin."[82] He took Scripture as the absolute rule and guide for all things and,

---

80. Brook, *Cartwright*, 123.
81. Whitgift, "Defence," 3:302–3 (and no.4).
82. Cartwright, *First Reply*, as quoted in Whitgift, "Defence," 1:190.

while he acknowledged that human reason and wisdom counts for much in the temporal sphere, he could not accept co-mingling of the kingdoms, determining that the church and all things church-related are spiritual matters beyond the competence and authority of civil magistrates (godly or not). Whitgift defended the freedom of civil magistrates to determine and dominate ecclesiastical government and discipline as external matters which Scripture did not address. He wrote that God spread his wisdom not exclusively in Scripture but through natural laws and positive human laws and reason as well. Whitgift rested his case on an appeal to authority—of the queen, of the episcopal establishment, and of the bishops' right to interpreted and translate the Bible, while Presbyterians and Puritans repeated Cartwright's arguments in one treatise after another.

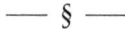

Richard Hooker:
Law, Reason, and Ecclesiastical Polity

Cartwright's polemics of the 1570s gave voice to a strong and convincing position that unless called for clearly and explicitly in Scripture, in the Word, and therefore by the will of God, particular human activities were illicit and to be avoided as sinful. Puritans looked to the Bible for specific justifications for every aspect of their lives and, if they could not find them they took it to mean God forbad it. For Cartwright the Elizabethan ecclesiastical settlement and governance of the church simply ran counter to Scripture. Magisterial control in the spiritual realm, episcopal hierarchy, non-local, non-congregational election of ministers, discipline taken out of parish bodies were not explicitly enjoined so Presbyterians could not fully embrace the settlement in good conscience. For them, the Elizabethan Church settlement, supremacy, episcopal government and discipline were illicit. For Puritans and Presbyterians alike, Whitgift's (and others') pro-supremacy treatises were unconvincing as they appealed to an organizational principle inherent solely in the authority of tradition and learned scholars who had interpreted Scripture and applied it to the English situation but had not shown how that related to divine will. The government and establishment of the visible church were indifferent, they insisted, neither specifically scriptural nor particularly opposed to it. Cartwright, in his unanswered *Second Reply*, and Puritan writers of the 1570s and 1580s continued to argue that human interpretations of Scripture were not reliable sources of God's authority, falling back on the self-sufficient Scripture (ironically, as they interpreted it). They found Whitgift's written responses unreasonable—that is, based on authority—which seemed to render them merely human principles without divine mandate. For such Anglican conformists as Hooker, however, the lack of scriptural explicitness left room for a better argument. As decades of comparative exegesis had not advanced the discussion at all, Hooker turned to natural law (the expression of God's own reasonableness) and the laws of society.

In *Of the Laws of Ecclesiastic Polity*, Hooker's masterpiece, he laid out an argument that law, not Scripture, was the creative force of God. Law was the original source of existence, and it was the organizational principle of all life, angelic to mundane.[83] Obedience to nature and reason was therefore necessarily good because it is in fact obedience to God's will. The English system of ecclesiastical governance (as another society) conforms to the laws of nature and human reason, have therefore a firm foundation in divine wisdom, and has divine origins in both the laws and in human rationality.[84] The examples of nature and reason (both sensual and logical) are available to the church and to society as unwritten (in Scripture) guidance to govern human behaviour. These concepts (unlike Scripture) were not subject to debate and deconstruction. Indeed, Hooker often charged his opponents with artificially extending Scripture into places where it was originally silent simply in order to defend practices they personally found agreeable. In the eight books of *Ecclesiastical polity* Hooker painstakingly (but sometimes tediously) illustrated how reason was the foundation of the settlement and how reason, in agreement with nature, moulded the English Church and how reason was a legitimate source of discerning God's will. His goal was to draw all non-conformists and radicals back into the constituted church settlement.[85]

Hooker accepted the *adiaphora* position of the conforming Anglicans that both church and state organizations were purely human institutions, external, and non-*salvific*. Ecclesiastical and temporal polities were established as means of organizing the sound moral life of the citizen and the believer alike. As such, the chief magistrate of the commonwealth (with the aid of her subordinates in the government of the state and the church) protects the

83. Hooker, "The Laws of Ecclesiastical Polity."

84. Secor, *Hooker*, 254–56.

85. Detailing this purpose was the goal of Almasy, "The Purpose of Richard Hooker's Polemic," 251–70. Here I refer to the edition of *Ecclesiastical Polity* found in *The Works of that Learned and Judicious Divine, Mr. Richard Hooker*. The 1876 Clarendon Press edition of this can be found online at http://anglicanhistory.org/hooker/.

worthy and punishes the ungodly. Magisterial authority was commanded in Scripture and therefore had to be obeyed. Like many others of the conforming tradition Hooker accepted that authority based on piety and reason (that is, in conformity with divine and natural laws) was ideal, that wrong-headed authority could be corrected by reason (perhaps through subordinate magistrates advising the prince) and by the work of the Holy Spirit active in the lives of believers. Hooker discarded Luther's strict separation of the two kingdoms, where the church was in the hands of its members exclusively (the principle Presbyterian position) as well as Cartwright's arguments *sola scriptura* (e.g., government by deacons, pastors and elders, discipline within the authority of the congregation) as mistaken ideals based on a misunderstanding of the primitive church and the influence of history. For him, civil power was divine in nature and intended by God to rule over the external aspects of the church and influence the internal aspects as well. Books one and two of *Ecclesiastical polity* took up this position and highlighted for readers the danger of an uncritical appeal to the primitive church.

Before the written word, God spoke to the primitive church through the laws of nature and through the evidence of human reason. The primitive church was a product of a particular time and place (as is the English Church), the culmination of generations of learned men testing the laws of nature and reason and removing the errors of the past. What remained was good. Scripture was also a product of a time and place and, apart from the foundations of doctrine (in unchangeable or immutable laws), must be supplemented by the laws of nature and human reason to extract the best from it. The meat of book one is a demonstration of these other means of discerning the wisdom and will of God—signs, tokens, "some more certain and some less"—concluding that the most certain is what "the general persuasion of all men to so account it." For instance, as it is generally and widely agreed that theft is wicked, even without an explicit statement of such in Scripture men can know the will of God and not steal. In this way Hooker illustrated that reasonableness, goodness and virtue—what is good for society—is identifiable without explicit scriptural statements. The English system is enforced by the crown because it is good and reasonable, drawing out the conclusion that "the general and perpetual voice of men is as the sentence of God himself. For that which all men have at all times learned, Nature herself must needs have taught; and God being the author of nature, her voice is but his instrument."[86]

Having established that the laws of nature and human reason are genuine means of discerning the will of God, Hooker could readily

---

86. Hooker, *Works*, 1:226–7 (I, vii, 5).

illustrate how the combination leads to the authentic commonwealth. On the one hand "a natural inclination, whereby all men desire sociable life and fellowship" needs to be joined with "an order expressly or secretly agreed upon touching the manner of their union in living together." The commonwealth is animated, held together, and set to work by the combination. Human laws, a result, presumes "the will of man to be inwardly obstinate, rebellious, and averse from all obedience unto the sacred laws of his nature," in order to "frame his outward actions, that they be no hinderance unto the common good for which societies are instituted."[87] God reveals himself through natural laws, and societies formulate because man is a social creature by nature and congregates naturally. However, reason explains that there will always be the wicked or depraved among them so laws regulating relationships are clearly necessary. Hooker extrapolated from this certain general principles on politic society—the need to be governed, the necessary consent to be governed, the microcosm of the household where the father (by nature) rules, to the macrocosm of society where the king is father of all rulers. The ideal society, however, is the product of history and place combined—"the kinds thereof being many, Nature tieth not to anyone but leaveth the choice as a thing arbitrary"[88]—which would explain such variations as kingdoms and republics. The widespread evangelical basis in *sola scriptura* is simply insufficient.

No one would argue that Scripture is unsurpassed as a statement of God's will where some immutable rule is required, as concerning salvation for instance, but all things men comprehend need not be explicitly written out. Learned men have, for example, reasoned out the Trinity and understand the duty to baptize children. Neither doctrine is explicit in Scripture, but the truth of both is understandable as reasonable and godly. Even the fact of the church invisible is based on a reasonable assumptions rather than hard evidences.[89] Laws, therefore, can be immutable or changeable. To illustrate the point Hooker turned to the church, in part another form of human society (in its visible, mutable aspects) but also a supernatural society (in its invisible, indivisible, and mystical aspects). The association can only function with observable laws of reason and of nature in harmony. How people should live and how they should worship God.[90] The visible, earthly form of the church lends itself to bonds of association which men agree between themselves and which human reason and the laws of nature determine as

87. Hooker, *Works*, 1:239–40 (I, x, 1).
88. Hooker, *Works*, 1:243 (I, x, 4).
89. Hooker, *Works*, 1:264, 268 (I, xiii, 1); Secor, *Hooker*, 255.
90. Hooker, *Works*, 1:272–4 (I, xv, 2).

suitable and compliant to God's will (i.e., not opposed to Scripture or nature), whereas the invisible, supernatural society requires that explicit statement of God's will (as found in Scripture). Obviously, Scripture is the base guideline and touchstone for all things, but if some matter is not explicit therein or denied therein we can rest assured that reason and the laws of nature will guide us to good, reasonable and godly solutions. The Puritan and Presbyterian views that there is only one universal form for the governance and practice of the church is thereby shown erroneous. In book two Hooker applied these conclusions against the essential Presbyterian position that any act not explicit in Scripture *must be* sinful.

Cartwright had written (and non-conformists agreed) that Scripture is the sole authority for all human activity, without which explicit instruction all is sin. Hooker deconstructed Cartwright's evidence to illustrate its practical weaknesses. Presbyterians and Puritans place too great and unwarranted a burden on Scripture, "enlarging it further than (as we are persuaded) soundness of truth will bear. For whereas God hath left sundry kinds of laws unto men, and by all those laws the actions of men are in some sort directed; they hold that one only law, the Scripture, must be the rule to direct in all things."[91] In place of scriptural exegesis (often over-stated) Hooker developed four "modes of assurance" by which man can be assured of understanding the will of God: Scripture; "plain aspect and intuitive beholding"; "strong and invincible demonstration"; and "greatest probability." The last mode he discussed as the strongest basis for church polity, arguing that English Church polity is based on nature, Scripture and reason (i.e., greatest probability) in conformity to divine law.[92] The remaining books of Ecclesiastical polity were dedicated to illustrating the point and tearing down Presbyterian and Puritan resistance. It is a complex and complicated argument, but well worth examination.

Starting from generalities and accepted axioms Hooker intended to move to particular issues in order to show that the laws of reason suffice to regulate human interactions and necessary duties. The first discussion was a lengthy criticism of the Presbyterian position that Scripture contains everything good, all that is needed, and what is left out is necessarily illicit as far too narrow.[93] It denies the many and diverse means by which wisdom

---

91. Hooker, *Works*, 1:287 (II, i, 2).
92. Almasy, "The Purpose of Richard Hooker's Polemic," 260.
93. Hooker, *Works*, 1:287–9 (II, i, 4).

is imparted to people (e.g., "the glorious works of Nature", "worldly experience and practice").[94] Cartwright held that every action of men should be directed at the glory or glorification of God but Hooker doubted that Scripture alone showed how this is done, equating glorification with obedience to God's will.[95] *Sola scriptura* is too rigid; "neither food can be tasted, nor raiment put on, nor in the world anything done, but this deed must needs be sin in them what do not first know it approved unto them by Scripture before they do it."[96] He pointed out that the hypocrisy of Puritans not leading their own lives thusly or interpreting Scripture in a way that suited them. This led to the question of *things indifferent—adiaphora*—the issue at the heart of the Elizabethan settlement.

The *sola scriptura* argument denies sensual experiences—the basis of human reason. The Apostle Thomas ("doubting Thomas") needed to see and touch the wounds of Christ for himself before he believed in the risen Christ (John 20:25-29). No one doubts Thomas's faith; likewise faith (or wisdom, or right action, or belief) can be grounded on the assurance of Scripture and persuasions (of others, of reasons, of sensual experiences). The assurance that an act is good and right can be found in Scripture and in reason and sense (i.e., nature), Hooker augmented the weak or impractical basic Presbyterian precept; "in every action not commanded of God *or permitted with approbation*, faith is wanting, and for want of faith there is sin."[97] The source of this approval is observable nature. For instance, people need to eat and cloth themselves, but scriptural restrictions sometimes run counter to observable climatic needs. In the Old Testament God had specifically restricted certain foods to the Jews, and certain dress to their priests, but there are no such commands to the Christian in the gospel. For Hooker, 1 Cor 6:12 sets a good tone; "while 'all things are lawful' . . . all things are not expedient."[98] The standard of expediency was wisdom developed through discretion or, perhaps, through experience and time (i.e., history). Unless Presbyterians meant to invalidate all human life prior to the collecting of the God's word in written form, the lens of human reason is necessary. Moreover, the meaning of Scripture is rarely self-evident despite the many self-assured interpretations. Hooker repeated Whitgift's association of Presbyterians and Puritans with radical sectarians (like Anabaptists) holding that their wild "fancies" need to be countered

94. Hooker, *Works*, 1:290 (II, i, 4).
95. Hooker, *Works*, 1:292 (II, ii, 3).
96. Hooker, *Works*, 1:293 (II, iii).
97. Hooker, *Works*, 1:296 (II, iv, 3).
98. Hooker, *Works*, 1:297 (II, iv, 4).

with "rational persuasions" and/or through conformity with the corporate wisdom of the church as an institution (i.e., its long interpretive history).[99] This was a repeating of Hooker's "greatest probability" position (the touchstone of human reason, the weight of learned opinion) which he then went on to apply in specific instances, like scriptural interpretation or church discipline. Hooker concluded that conforming Anglicans stood between two extreme positions. Roman Catholicism, on the one side, does not sufficiently understand and therefore teaches that the Scriptures are insufficient and need Rome's interpretation and developed traditions in order to assure salvation to believers. On the other side is the opposite extreme of radical non-conformists who deny all knowledge and wisdom apart from Scripture, thereby potentially disregarding actual biblical lessons.[100] Book three begins the deconstruction of the Presbyterian position.

The focus was on *sola scriptura* assertions in regard to ecclesiastical polity, specifically the key points of differentiation between the church visible and invisible and the congregation of saints and sinners. The church visible is explained as another kind of society, human association, or "Christian fellowship, the place and limits whereof are certain"—as in the Church *of England* or the Church *of Rome*. Polity, ecclesiastical government, therefore enters the picture because all associations of men need regulation, the simple fact of human nature which takes into account these *certain* limits.[101] There is no argument that Scripture lays down immutable rules regarding salvation and the sacraments (irrespective of external, earthly divisions) but can any one form of polity (e.g., times and locations, rules of association, discipline) be universally acceptable and immutable? Presbyterians and Puritans thought it could, but we have already seen Hooker's disapproval of such misguided thinking. He isolated from Scripture four general rules: "Nothing scandalous or offensive unto any, especially unto the Church of God" [from 1 Cor 10:32]; "All things in order and with seemliness" [from 1 Cor 14:40]; "All unto edification" [from 1 Cor 14:26]; and "All to the glory of God" [from Rom 14:6, 7 or 1 Cor 10:31].[102] The problem is that there is no singular set of regulations laid down by any of the apostles which fulfil all these precepts; these rules direct the church's action, but without clear external regulation. For Hooker this means that any human regimentation

---

99. For which discussion, see Almasy, "The Purpose of Richard Hooker's Polemic," 255, 256, 265; and Secor, *Hooker*, 260.

100. Hooker, *Works*, 1:335–6 (II, viii, 7).

101. Hooker, *Works*, 1:351–52 (III, i, 14).

102. Hooker, *Works*, 1:361 (III, vii, 1).

is fine, provided it does not break any of the four general rules. Next was the question of immutability.

A favorite argument of the Presbyterians was to compare the primitive church—the laws of its regiment and polity as drawn out of Scripture—with the organization of the Elizabethan Church. Hooker had made note of many examples wherein even the primitive church did not conform to Scripture, concluding that what appears to be immutable law regarding regiment and polity are, in fact, mutable. He drew out the conclusion that laws need to be tested against their proposed purposes as well as against the suitability of the times (echoing Erasmus). For instance, we have the laws given to the Jews by Moses (e.g., moral, ceremonial and judicial) as drawn out of the Old Testament. The moral laws have been adopted to provide the terms of the covenant, but ceremonial and judicial laws are clearly limited in time and place. Moral law (e.g., the Decalogue) is immutable, but rites, ceremonies and ordinances, inspired by God, were fashioned by Moses to meet the specific needs of his people in their current situation. But, "seeing that nations are not all alike, surely the giving of one kind of positive laws unto one only people, without any liberty to alter them, is but a slender proof, that therefore one kind should in like sort be given to serve everlastingly for all."[103]

Hooker concluded from this simple logic that while the church invisible needs nothing more than the Word of God—an external organization is superfluous—the church visible is a society with clear limitations and therefore needs a tailored polity more so than a differentiation of officers as pastors, elders and deacons can provide. Moreover, to maintain peace and order, polity must be imposed on the clerical officers themselves—some must be subordinate and some superior in authority—otherwise faction and schism may arise. In the primitive church the apostles themselves fulfilled the need for superior authorities whereas, in the Elizabethan church, bishops fulfil that need. Hooker concluded book three with the observation that given particular needs (which the primitive church and Scripture could not have or did not anticipate) "that which the Scripture teacheth is not always needful; and much the church of God shall always need which the Scripture teacheth not." This being the case, the teachings of Cartwright and his followers fail in three ways—by omission of necessary (but non-Scripture-based) matters, in requiring doctors, deacons, widows, and such like, as things of perpetual necessity by the law of God (which they are not), and in urging some things by Scripture immutable (which is a faulty interpretation).[104]

---

103. Hooker, *Works*, 1:395 (III, xi, 6).
104. Hooker, *Works*, 1:414 (III, xi, 20).

The main charge of the Presbyterians (and evangelicals in general) was that the settlement left the English Church only partially reformed—little more than an amended copy of Rome. In book four, Hooker turned to the specific problem of ceremonies, some of which looked "popish" in nature and, therefore, hateful to sectarians. The Presbyterians lobbied the queen and parliament continually for the removal of all additions made since the days of the primitive church (thinking thereby perhaps to eliminate all papal abuses). Based on his previous three books, however, Hooker could argue now that the Church *of England*, as an institution, had the right to use or discard any previous ceremony or practice, Roman or Genevan, as its governors saw fit. The church visible had a mission to prepare Christians for salvation and sanctification and, in order to fulfil this function it had the right to establish its own laws and regiment suitable to the culture in which it was set. The typical Tudor response had been to establish a *via media* between the two major continental influences—Catholic and Lutheran or Catholic and Reformed. Some Catholic practices were sure to be preferred in England simply due to the weight of English tradition and long-term association. Englishmen found some of Rome's traditions and practices acceptable (those matters indifferent); that made them good. The very real problem in the evangelical view was that the apostles had rarely commented on *necessary* forms of polity, "so that in tying the Church to the orders of the Apostles' times, they tie it to a marvellous uncertain rule." It was illogical to charge the English Church with hosting unscriptural practices when even the church in Geneva, the very model of Puritan forms, had popish customs still in effect (e.g., god-parents designated in the baptism ceremony).[105]

With book five (the last published in his lifetime) Hooker moved the discussion from generalities to specifics.[106] Books five to eight focus on bishops and elders, episcopal power and the authority of the civil magistrate in order to give evidence that the English Church is a true church. The concentration has also shifted away from Presbyterian concerns toward a comparison with Roman Catholicism and Catholic complaints. He was very critical of the Roman position on, for example, the sacrament of penance, the combined practice of confession, repentance, and satisfaction, hinting that Catholics make too much of these elements and never fully admit God's sovereign

---

105. Hooker, *Works*, 1:422–4 (IV, ii, 2–3, iii), 449 (IV, x). Also see Harrison, "The Church," 305–6.

106. Hill, "Hooker's 'Polity,'" 318.

grace (although some Presbyterian criticisms are addressed in book seven, part and parcel of the episcopal government issue).

Hooker's main focus was the church's execution of necessary and scriptural tasks (as the body of Christ on earth)—propagate the gospel, appropriately minister the true sacraments, and ensure the continuance of divine worship among professed believers. The duty of the bishop is also clear; he is responsible to ensure that these tasks are carried out. Thus, Hooker equated the office of bishop with the position of ecclesiastical governor, using Acts 20:28 as a proof text. Of course, over the span of time and changing of places the office necessarily changed in practice, but not in the essence of ecclesiastical government: "name of a bishop having been used of old to signify both an ecclesiastical overseer in general, and more particularly also a principal ecclesiastical overseer."[107] Presbyterians charged that the word "bishop" does not appear in the Bible or in the ancient church and, thereby, has no place in the true church. True, the word may be a Greek addition, but the office is both ancient and Scripture-based. Hooker defined the bishop as both minister of God (performing the normal sacerdotal functions, like administration of the sacraments), the pastor of pastors; "bishops being principal pastors, are either at large or else with restraint: at large, when the subject of their regiment is indefinite, and not tied to any certain place; bishops with restraint are they whose regiment over the Church is contained within some definite, local compass, beyond which compass their jurisdiction reacheth not."[108]

The two main complaints that Presbyterians had with the office of bishop was the honor attached to the office and the authority granted the holders. The superiority of the bishop over other ministers was given a permanence they found unmerited, charging that it was little more than the equivalent of the elder or presbyter. Hooker pointed out that the apostles were themselves bishops (as he envisioned the office) as their role had been to spread the gospel, guard, and settle the church. Some had a mandate to travel about, some to care for a particular location, or a particular people (e.g., Paul being sent among the Gentiles). As the number of Christians grew, however, bishops were created among those who had not been apostles themselves—Hooker noted that this was a mechanism designed to combat potential factions and schisms in the growing church. The jurisdiction of bishops over clergy and laity alike sprang from the apostles acting as ordinary judges where Christian churches were established. It was a logical continuation that among the many a few would be instituted as

---

107. Hooker, *Works*, 3:147 (VII, ii, 2); Harrison, "The Church," 315–16.
108. Hooker, *Works*, 3:148–49 (VII, ii, 3).

higher officers if only for the settlement of disputes (finally replacing the apostles altogether as they died out). Thus, the position of the bishop in the church is of long-standing tradition and their authority is both the ordination of lesser offices (pastors, elders and deacons) as well as ecclesiastical governance. Over time, elders took on the role of counsellors and assistants to bishops and as the numbers grew, archbishops were designated superior to bishops and invested with the power to ordain bishops. Hooker found nothing sinister in the growth of the office, simply logical developments over time and place. Cartwright, however, had charged that bishops have no distinctive work or duties derived directly from Scripture, to which Hooker countered with lengthy examinations of the citations 1 Tim 5:19 and Titus 1:5, making a case for a superior authority over pastors and presbyters as "most probable . . . even in all ecclesiastical affairs."[109]

All other arguments aside, the opponents of the settlement and of episcopal authority argued that while bishops and archbishops are ancient offices they did not then have the same extent of authority as they do in the contemporary church. Their claims went further: ordinations were never then made without the consent of the people (that would be tyranny); excommunications are now made on the authority of the bishop himself without reference to congregational discipline or any reference to lay-elders; bishops now imprison the wicked themselves, hold civil office (in direct violation of the strict separation of the two kingdoms), becoming counsellors to kings and princes. Hooker's response incorporated the idea of the church as a politic society which has the necessary power of protecting itself, making laws for its own conduct, changing, or strengthening old laws as conditions present themselves. So, yes, once, ministers were selected with the consent of the community as a whole. As the community grew, however, representative magistrates made the selection of ministers on behalf of the people. Eventually, the ruler made the decisions. "In these things the experience of time may breed both civil and ecclesiastical change from that which hath been before received, neither do latter things always violently exclude former, but the one growing less convenient than it hath been, giveth place to that which is now become more."[110] The magistrate took on the duty as a matter of convenience and to ensure a peaceful turnover of new ministers. This is not unlike how civil society itself developed.

With regard to questions of discipline and judicial decision making, Hooker took the position that justice needs to be served clearly. As for civil affairs, he admitted that there are aspects of temporal matters which it is

---

109. Hooker, *Works*, 3:208–9 (VII, xi, 6).
110. Hooker, *Works*, 3:221 (VII, xiv), 222 (VII, xiv, 3), 226 (VII, xiv, 7).

not appropriate for bishops to interfere in, but this does not include the full range of civil matters. For instance, a community of Christians isolated in hostile territory would naturally look to its spiritual leaders for guidance in a range of activities; a university community and the institutions therein are often overseen by clergy; temporal states themselves are sometimes under the authority of clergy, noble or royal by blood, and therefore obliged to rule (as in some of the imperial elector states). Toward the end of book seven Hooker changed the nature of the discussion from a defence of the office to a brief examination of the benefits episcopal rule brings, noting bishops as a pillar of royal power, order in society, and as the means by which the exercise of true religion is maintained. The unity of the covenanted society comes out clearly in that "amongst the Jews the benefit of civil government grew principally from Moses, he being their principal civil governor; even so the benefit of spiritual regiment grew from Aaron principally, he being in the other kind their principal rector, although even herein subject to the sovereign dominion of Moses . . . The one's authority therefore being so profitable, how should the other's be thought unnecessary?"[111] Book eight rounded the collection off with a defence of the queen's ecclesiastical supremacy against both Catholic and Protestant opponents.

Much evangelic writing agreed that the church and the state were two distinct and separate spheres, and Cartwright absolutely denied the possibility that a man of one sphere could even belong to the other (much less participate in its governance).[112] For Hooker and the Anglican tradition there are indeed two regiments—the church and the commonwealth—each having unique features *but intertwined*. Cartwright had defined the two kingdoms in such a way that members of the temporal sphere could not even participate or perform duties in the spiritual and *vice-versa*, verging upon Anabaptist theory. He termed the members of the temporal sphere as heathens and members of the spiritual sphere as Christians, drawing no practical division between the church visible and invisible. For Hooker and the conforming Anglicans, however, people were of both earthly corporations (the ideal expression of God's will);

> Wherefore to end this point, I conclude: First, that under dominions of infidels, the Church of Christ, and their commonwealth, were two societies independent. Secondly, that in

111. Hooker, *Works*, 3:265 (VII, xviii, 3).
112. Eppley, "Supremacy," 503–4.

those commonwealths where the bishop of Rome beareth sway, one society is both the Church and the commonwealth; but the bishop of Rome doth divide the body into two diverse bodies, and doth not suffer the Church to depend upon the power of any civil prince or potentate. Thirdly, that within this realm of England the case is neither as in the one, nor as in the other of the former two: but from the state of pagans we differ, in that with us one society is both the Church and commonwealth, which with them it was not; as also from the state of those nations which subject themselves to the bishop of Rome, in that our Church hath dependency upon the chief in our commonwealth, which it hath not under him. In a word, our estate is according to the pattern of God's own ancient elect people, which people was not part of them the commonwealth, and part of them the Church of God, but the selfsame people whole and entire were both under one chief Governor, on whose supreme authority they did all depend.[113]

Hooker proceeded to a systematic examination of the civil magistracy's power in ecclesiastical government.

Society, he argued, must be based on the laws of good order—an organizational principle upward from the lowest and weakest to the highest and most powerful. No foreign power had a higher authority in either the civil or spiritual realm than God's lieutenant or agent, thus preserving the covenant state. God's agent is the Christian king exercising spiritual dominion or supreme power in ecclesiastical affairs and causes "within their own precincts and territories" and "even in matters of Christian religion."[114] As did the external arrangement of the church (i.e., the church visible), the organization of the civil magistracy very much also depended on the nature of the people, their history, their geographical location, and any number of other factors (e.g., the traditional nature of their governance). These factors may determine, for instance, whether they are ruled by a monarchy and whether that monarchy is imposed (by conquest), or hereditary, or even elected.

The royal supremacy, the headship of the church, is not an authority based on Scripture *per se* (although Scripture could be understood to support extensive magisterial power). It is instead the expression of an agreement of the community to a certain pattern of rule over external institutions. Hooker was making the laws and traditions of England the true "loci" or foundation of the crown's authority. Presbyterians (and Catholics) often searched Scripture for a statement of royal supremacy or of God's

---

113. Hooker, *Works*, 3:340 (VIII, i, 7).
114. Hooker, *Works*, 3:342 (VIII, ii, 3).

placing of the queen in her position. Hooker dismisses such searches. There are many biblical models of rule, of church governance, but these apply only to the people of the time—ancient Israel—and not to modern day Elizabethan England. He is not denying that royal supremacy can be supported in Scripture, but the Bible shows many formats as equally legitimate. Presbyterians are not taking the weight of historical developments (in which the hand of God can also be discerned) under consideration. Civil authority depends on the needs and agreements of the community, not upon God directly in Christian times, so that the extent of the prince's authority is determined by the customs of the realm. Hooker made the case against a "divine right" argument in order to combat opinions of scripturally justifiable rebellions or regicide. If royal power depended upon God, then God could remove that authority, and person, through a human agent and then pass rule on to someone else. If, however, the crown's authority depended upon heredity, legal right, and long standing traditions and community standards, the possibility of rebellion are dramatically reduced.[115] Rule by communal mandate—crown-in-parliament as the highest expression of royal authority in temporal affairs could be matched by a similar expression of crown-in-convocation for ecclesiastical matters. In any case, as we have seen many times, voiced by many different reformers, the powers of the chief magistrate are to confront and eliminate heresy, make laws for the peace and order of the church, declare and defend sound doctrine (e.g., the articles of religion)—which defines the royal supremacy well—alongside the many temporal duties. There are some things even the prince cannot do, however, like ordinations, administration of the sacraments, "to judge as an ordinary, to bind and loose, to excommunicate";[116] but the bishops' power to do these things is a delegated authority from the prince.

The various Protestant sects in England—conformists, Presbyterians, separatists—had arisen over questions of precisely how the powers of the bishops and prince are understood, connected, and the extent in which the limitations have been acknowledged. Given the relationship between the *two kingdoms* and the division of the church into two aspects there can be little argument that kings, as the principal civil magistrate, are God's primary agents in the outward governance of the church visible, and Hooker examined a number of associated powers—the summoning of councils and synods, the appointment of bishops to their offices (investiture not ordination as bishops), the creation of ecclesiastical laws. The Presbyterians argued that the determination of canons was in the church's own power

---

115. Eppley, "Supremacy," 511–12.
116. Hooker, *Works*, 3:357 (VIII, ii, 16).

but, for Hooker, such a condition was inconsistent with both equity and reason. "A law, be it civil or ecclesiastical, is as a public obligation, wherein seeing that the whole standeth charged, no reason it should pass without his privity and will, whom principally the whole doth depend upon." But, as in other delegated authorities Hooker agreed that the king's power is better expressed in the negative: "principally in the strength of a negative voice"—that is, the veto of laws created by his ecclesiastical subordinate officers if these do not satisfy the king's duty as a guardian of orthodoxy and order.[117] The prince also therefore judges ecclesiastical causes, which the Presbyterians also found questionable. Hooker broke down the issue into three preconditions—the reality of laws, the need for judges and, of course, the necessity of a supreme judge—to explain his point. Ordinaries served as ecclesiastical judges over matters which required that level of authority but other matters could be judged by commissaries who could be laymen appointed to specific duties. In the past, the Bishop of Rome acted as the overriding authority and court of appeal, but this condition had been transferred to the crown over the course of the fifteenth century and, finally, during the reign of Henry VIII.

Finally, the question before Hooker was whether the prince was himself/herself subject to ecclesiastical censure? Recall that some theories held the king or chief magistrate as a member of the church—not as a king but as a brother—and as such equal in status to all other members and equally subject to ecclesiastical censure. Hooker agreed that, where specific spiritual duties were concerned, the prince is indeed as any other member of the covenant—a Christian man (separate from any office). However, "indeed the king is a brother; but such a brother as unto whom all the rest of the brethren are subject," for instance, where judicial matters are concerned. Excommunication is an exception as no power or superior could be brought forward to carry out that sentence on a king or queen. Excommunication, for Hooker, does not remove identification of the excommunicated as a Christian (as a pope might think) or as a member of the political nation, or as a member of the church external. It bars him only from those mystical practices like communion and public worship. We have seen some controversy surrounding this issue in England. Tyndale, for instance, mooted the point in 1532 arguing in his *Exposition* that the king was subject to the spiritual officer as the vessel of God's word: "what he ought to believe, and how to live, and how to rule, as is the poorest beggar in the realm," and this sentiment was echoed by Knox, but Hooker would not have it, seeing it as another potential foundation of an argument for rebellion and regicide.[118] He took the extreme case in order to defend

---

117. Hooker, *Works*, 3:404 (VIII, vi, 8), 411 (VIII, vi, 11).
118. Hooker, *Works*, 3:433 (VIII, viii, 3), 447 (VIII, ix, 3); Tyndale, "Exposition," 67;

the queen against ecclesiastical censures of the old papal variety as well as from Presbyterian charges of scriptural incorrectness. Yes, historically speaking, some popes did excommunicate some emperors, but Hooker could not imagine the heinous crime the queen would have to commit before her own subjects and subordinate magistrates in the church rose up collectively and took such a step. In reality, the possibility existed, but it was so unlikely as to be nearly unimaginable.

Hooker in *Ecclesiastical Polity* defended the royal supremacy and governance of the church as it developed finally and uniquely in Elizabethan England, based on principles which ran the gamut from Scripture, to the laws of nature, to human reason and, consequently, refuted objections from opponents Catholic and Protestant. This being the case, the prerogatives claimed by the crown in England (e.g., headship, governance, supremacy) and by the bishops (e.g., formulation of canons, ecclesiastical discipline, determination of officeholders) are, indeed, expressions of God's sovereign will which can be relied upon by all members of the Christian Commonwealth (including Presbyterians). Book eight, and indeed the entire treatise, called upon all members of the commonwealth to obey the laws of the church—their church—theirs, "in the sense that they themselves collectively as a community of Christians have determined its polity and formulated its laws."[119]

McGiffert, "Covenant, Crown and Commons," 37; Eppley, "Supremacy," 506.

119. Eppley, "Supremacy," 534.

6

Royal Ecclesiastical Authority in Catholic Europe

IN A PREVIOUS BOOK on a related topic the last chapter and conclusion examined the council and canons of Trent, looking at how Catholicism had changed (if at all) as a result of the spread and success of rival theologies and practices, assimilating or condemning them.[1] That cannot be done here; Trent did not deal with the relevant themes of our examination. Neither the relationship between Church and state, nor the extended power of the civil magistrate into ecclesiastical matters were dealt with at the great council. There was some indirect commentary, however, with the new emphasis on, and reform of, episcopal power in the localities (but change was directed from Rome).

The focus here will be on the fact that, as the council met, and then beyond the meetings, the spread of reforming canons in Catholic Europe came to depend not solely on papal approval but on a series of negotiations between the papal office and local magistrates. The temporal rulers, however, would agree to publish nothing in their realms which they found derogatory to, or in denigration of, national interests (and/or temporal/royal authority). What this means is that localism was strongly reinforced by the Catholic Church's attempted centralization. It also means that the published canons approved by the crowns in France or Spain were not *verbatim* that which had been negotiated and passed at Trent specifically, or approved by the popes, and were also often unlike what was published in Venice, Portugal, Austria, Bavaria or in the Spanish satellite states in the Italian peninsula (Sicily, Naples and Milan), except perhaps in generalities. The process of localism, increasing bureaucratic professionalism, and other political realities forced the Tridentine and post-Tridentine popes into a serious of compromises with the Catholic rulers of Europe. These

1. Chibi, *The Wheat and the Tares*.

compromises built upon earlier negotiated agreements, like the *Pragmatic Sanction* for example, and resulted in the chief temporal magistrates of those states exercising a similar authority to their Protestant counterparts without the necessity of schism. The Habsburg rulers of Spain and the Valois rulers of France did not go down the path of the Tudors of England, and they were greatly rewarded for that choice.

In the introduction I noted a few instances prior to the Reformation that bore witness to a shift in power from the church as an institution to the institutions of the state and from the clergy to the magistrates. This was not to say that the church lost all power in relation to the state merely to acknowledge that the relationship had changed over the mediaeval period. Moving into the early modern era the emergence of nation-states had a massive impact on the church *v.* state tension producing cause of the Reformation. In what became Protestant Europe, the tensions were eased by simply throwing off the universal claims of the papacy, dividing the church into visible (i.e., local) and invisible (i.e., universal) forms, and applying new understandings of justification theology to the division. In this way Protestantism allowed the temporal rulers to advance their own powers of jurisdiction, legislation, governance, and control over the visible aspect of the church (while leaving the invisible technically outside the control of any one human altogether). The shift included schism and the establishment of new ecclesiastical institutions and new arrangements with the magistrates who, in many places emerged with new powers of influence and increased treasuries. In Catholic Europe, however, the shift produced new expressions of local Catholic forms and practices under the authority of national rulers but without actual schism, although by the mid-sixteenth-century papal claims to universalism were looking quaint and perhaps amusingly old-fashioned to many. In the late mediaeval period local rulers used the rising tide of complaints against Rome's universalism and, because of the secular needs of the popes for political allies or funding, they gained beneficial compromises or won outright significant powers over their own "national" spiritual structures (giving them a means of moulding the local church to their own criteria). I had made reference to the *Pragmatic Sanction* in France earlier, that is a good place to begin.

— § —

France:
Sanction, Concordat, Royal Power, and Gallicanism

In the 1530s and 1540s Henry VIII repeatedly invited Francis I to join him in anti-papal, reform actions of one sort or another throwing off the yoke of Rome. Francis always politely declined the invitations. The fact of the matter was that the idea held little attraction for him because the kings of France already dominated their church to an extent Henry VIII was only just beginning to imagine was possible. The crown controlled the character of the church through vast powers of appointment and nomination to offices and benefices; the king was recognized as the protector of the French Church against heretical doctrines; the king had the right to summon and preside over ecclesiastical assemblies and to interfere in diocesan matters while still paying respect to the popes as spiritual leaders. Nor was this new thinking; the kings of France were distinctive in Europe with regard to the church in that their coronation oaths recognized them as "both king and priest," holding with some of the benefits of ordination. This dominance also suited the church. From the fourteenth-century it was generally acknowledged that the Church of France was autonomous from papal interference in its affairs as much as the king was autonomous in his political dealings. The Church of France was in a unique position to develop and safeguard its own character and pursuits—sometimes labelled *Gallicanism*. This unique status was supported by Parlement (the chief law court)—which as a final court of appeals for ecclesiastical matters gave it heightened jurisdictional influence—and by the universities, particularly the Sorbonne (the theology school). Consequently, a third of all benefices were reserved for graduates. The determination of orthodoxy in France depended on a wide range of opinion both lay and clerical, academic and political. All three institutions looked to the crown to protect their privileges against the potential ravages of Roman influence, abuse, and greed, and the crown had built up a controlling dominance over the centuries by so doing.[2] The *Gallican* position was further strengthened in the fifteenth-century by the consequences of the Great Schism (discussed earlier in the introduction).

We know that there had been many problems raised for the Roman position due to the Avignon captivity, not the least of which had been the schism at the heart of it (with French popes challenging the authority of their Italian rivals), and with the subsequent contest between the papacy and supporters of the political theory of conciliarism (many of whom were French) which had originated at the Sorbonne. The theory that councils

---

2. Knecht, *Francis I*, 51.

were superior in authority to popes could only ever benefit papal opponents and, in France, royal ordinances were issued advancing the ancient liberties of the church and strengthening its fiscal and jurisdictional autonomies. Such contests came to the foreground in the 1430s at the Council of Basel which, after the pope's attempt to draw it to a premature conclusion, pursued a motion to deprive Pope Eugenius IV of his office (proclaiming his deprivation on 7 July 1439 along with the election of a rival pope).[3] Coincidentally, these incidents strengthened the self-image of the French Church, increasingly looking to the king for protection against the further incursions of Italian power and against papal abuse of its claimed authorities. Charles VII's own political cache was on the rise at this time, in that France was emerging victorious in the so-called Hundred Years' War with England, and he was casting his nets wide to exercise his new found military strength. His attention was drawn to events in Basel and he was not opposed to the council's anti-papal direction. In 1438 the king summoned a synod of the French church to Bourges to settle upon what the French response should be to the Basel propositions, receiving representatives of both papal and council interests. Although *Gallicans* among the French clergy at the synod favoured the actions of the council, Charles remained officially neutral. On 7 July 1438, the resulting *Pragmatic Sanction* was enacted by royal authority and without delay registered by Parlement. This was the start of a distinctive French establishment.

Rival views of ecclesiastical governance and discipline in French Catholicism had been planted. *Gallicanism* looked to the king as a defender of long held ecclesiastical, political, and social privileges, while *Ultramontanism* looked to popes as the source of all power. Over the course of the fourteenth and fifteenth-centuries, however, a new position emerged—a *de facto* royal ecclesiastical supremacy. Concessions had been extracted from the council and pope advantageous to both the *Gallican* position and to royal authority.

In brief, *Sanction* provided a foundation document legitimizing long held French liberties. The document had three parts—an introductory section decrying the many papal abuses current in the church (like nepotism or non-residence), followed by a statement of the twenty-four decrees of Basel (modified to suit French conditions) and, finally, a statement of royal approval and recommendation of the Bourges synod's modifications. The French Church and royal authority emerged stronger as a result of the Basel's

---

3. "Council of Basel," 121–25.

anti-papal stance. Financially, Annates and papal taxes were abolished in France (much to the pleasure of the first estate). Judicially, papal power was severely limited with regard to appeals against ecclesiastical judgements of the higher French clergy, papal interdicts, and excommunications (much to the pleasure of Parlement). Doctrinally, the relationship remained much as it always had been, however. As important as these considerations are, perhaps the most significant change affected nomination and election to high ecclesiastical office in France. Papal election was converted to "canonical" election. This means that the institutions themselves elected their own candidates. Candidates were nominated with a very high degree of royal input and influence—"benign and benevolent recommendations"—which legalized the influence of the king over episcopal or monastic elections, placing nearly the entirety of the visible institution into the royal patronage network.[4]

For perhaps obvious reasons, subsequent popes tried very hard to have these provisions revoked, and the Kings of France used this desire to play *Gallicans* and *ultramonists* off against each other when conditions made this necessary (e.g., in support of royal policy in the Italian peninsula or to punish the pope for political opposition). The French Church, in essence, had a charter of liberties and freedoms from Rome, localism was strengthened, and the king's position *vis-a-vis* the French Church was strengthened. Beyond the advantages inherent in the position as a result of his coronation, the *Sanction* made the king the true master of the Church and gave the Church a heightened sense of liberty from papal influence and interference. As noted, the clauses of the document could be and were subsequently loosened or reinforced as the political relationship between the kings of France and the popes went through the motions of European diplomacy.[5] And it was due to these self-same forces that the *Sanction* was eventually scrapped (much to the annoyance of the upper churchmen, Parlement, and the universities), to be replaced by the far more crown friendly *Concordat of Bologna*.

The level of crown backing for *Sanction* had come to depend, case by case, on the successes or failures of French diplomacy or military action in the Italian peninsula. If French conquests of territory were successful, then *Sanction* decrees were waived in favour of securing continued papal support of French actions. When these efforts or actions failed, or the support of the pope proved negligible, weak, or non-existent, the decrees were adhered to

---

4. "Pragmatic Sanction of Bourges," 112–21.
5. Baumgartner, *France in the Sixteenth Century*, 42: Rady, *France*, 41.

more firmly or reconstituted. The situation changed in the early sixteenth century, when in 1515 the new King of France, Francis I, invaded the peninsula and won a resounding victory over his rivals at the Battle of Marignano. His political cache increased but, as the victory and subsequent dominance raised the spectre of foreign alliances against him it was clear that some new level of accommodation with the pope was necessary. There was really only one thing that Rome wanted and that was the scrapping of *Sanction*.

Against the wishes of *Gallicans* in the church, in Parlement and at the universities, a conference with the pope, Leo X, was convened in Bologna to thrash out a new agreement on both church affairs and for the consolidation of French military gains. In reality Francis risked next to nothing here besides some domestic grumbling by accommodating papal wishes at this time. His effective control of ecclesiastical governance, appointments, and finance was in no way threatened by the revocation of *Sanction* and, indeed, the extended good will and gratitude of the papacy (plus papal recognition of recent gains in Milan) was a useful boon to the crown.[6] The king agreed to revoked royal support for *Sanction* (it became a dead letter except in the hearts and minds of fervent *Gallicans*) and the canonical elections of the previous agreement were modified in favour of both the king and the pope—in that the king would nominate directly his own candidates (as bishops, archbishops, abbots, abbesses and priors) which the pope would then appoint (allowing again for the collection of fees and rising influence in domestic religious affairs). There were a very few extraordinary conditions set on the king's nominations, however, in terms of personal qualifications of the candidates, and the election principle was still maintained at some select elite institutions. As before, if the holders died "*in curia*", the power of nomination passed to the pope. These qualifications were honoured more in the breach as it turned out, however, and never applied to the king's relatives or candidates from the higher social classes. The other decrees of *Sanction*, and those of Basel approved or modified therein were negotiated through, or silently passed over, by the two leaders (so, in effect, the judicial and legislative conditions remained much the same). In essence Francis achieved a *de iure* mastery of the French Church which he had enjoyed previously only *de facto* as the wealth of the Church was now placed into his hands by papal grant. Needless to say, perhaps, *Gallican* sentiments were greatly offended by the king's action in Bologna as power over their own church had been taken out of the hands of the rank and file members, and the pope's authority symbolically returned.

6. Knecht, *Francis I*, 55. For a useful overview see, Richardson, *Renaissance Monarchy*, 134–37.

Political objections aside (and Parlement raised 116 articles against *Concordat*), ecclesiastical concerns were raised over long-standing financial and jurisdiction issues. It was objected, for example, that reverting to a nomination and appointment system left the door open to papal interference elsewhere and would drain the kingdom of money through papal greed. If "major causes" were removed from the ecclesiastical courts of France this also opened the door to papal interference. *Gallicans* feared the loss of French uniqueness. The new arrangements were ideally suited to royal aspirations, however, as church leaders (bishops and abbots) became pliant royal agents. Governance of the Church and ecclesiastical discipline were absorbed into royal patronage networks across the realm.

Historians mark the eventual registration of *Concordat* as that point where *Gallican* independence was broken but where Catholicism was guaranteed as the constituted religion of the state.[7] As such, the French Church was spared many of the disturbances of the early years of the Reformation as a result of the agreement; what need would any French king have in pursuing a break with Rome? There was no contested divorce on Francis's horizon and the crown already dominated ecclesiastical fiscal practices and governance. Protestant doctrines were resisted by the king as unnecessary to his own needs (although Francis appreciated humanist works), and the crown still had the power to block papal bulls being promulgated in France by virtue of his "*droit de vérification.*" Francis I could afford to remain "loyal" to Rome and the unity of the Church survived even the advent of Huguenotism in the second half of the century.[8] In effect, the church in France survived the ravages of the early Reformation by becoming more firmly a tool of crown power, and this is nowhere better illustrated than in the episcopal nominations made by Francis I and his son Henri II.

Marilyn Edelstein used instances of appointments to foreigners to illustrate Francis I's traditionalism in his practice of church patronage. That is, he used his authority to off-set diplomatic and administrative costs and to bolster foreign policy objectives (particularly to strengthen French presence in Milan and Naples). More foreign bishops were appointed in these two reigns than at any other time in the late mediaeval and early modern period, and the cause is obvious—after the reign of Henri II foreign policy took a back seat to the civil wars. A third of Francis's appointments went to foreigners—mostly Italians and mostly to men of the great military families. The obvious conclusion to draw from this is that he wanted to buy the loyalty

---

7. Knecht, *Francis I*, 64.

8. "Concordat of Bologna," 134–44; Rady, *France*, 41–42; Koenigsberger et al., *Europe in the Sixteenth Century*, 277–8; Potter, *A History of France*, 219–25.

and services of the military classes of Italy for support of his intended territorial expansion into the northern and southern parts of the peninsula. That many of his appointments went to men from Florence (providing obvious associations to the de Medici family), or to men from Milan (providing obvious support in his contest against Spanish interests in the duchy). Papal interests were worth courting because Rome dominated the corridor between Milan and Naples where French interests lay.[9] *Gallicans* in the church argued that his appointments were bringing disrepute to the unique character of the French Church and draining money from the treasuries of the kingdom, but the fact is these fears were exaggerated. Plurality was quite rare among the foreign bishops (they were resident), appointments were mainly in the south of France (those sees nearest to Milan), and French clerics dominated the wealthiest sees. In 1525, after his armies were soundly defeated at Pavia, the policy of nominating foreigners declined to the end of the reign. Henri II revised the practice; his foreign policy was anti-Habsburg, he needed Italian support, and his wife was Catherine de Medici. Where Henri can be differentiated from Francis is in the fact that instead of military families he patronized men from the highest, mostly Florentine, social ranks.

Concordat covered the kingdom *as it stood* in 1516. This means that such later additions as Brittany, Provence and other territories were not covered by the agreement. While we might think that this allowed the papacy a loophole to plant Italian bishops and thus subvert *Gallican* aims further in that way, the crown protested and effectively blocked all such potentialities (unless the appointed bishop was somehow pro-France or could further crown political pursuits).[10] The truth of the matter is that any bishops forced on the French Church through papal nominations (of the "*in curia*" or other varieties) were bishops in name only and, if there were genuine problems, revenues could be effectively withheld and bulls never processed in Parlement. For example, relations became strained with Rome as Pope Julius III proved himself more the ally of Charles V by reconvening Trent to Bologna over Henri's objections. The king recalled all French bishops from Rome, cut off Annates and other payments, and summoned a French council as an alternative to the "Imperial" council. When Julius threatened excommunication, Henri replied with a threat of complete separation (a break with Rome or schism) as the King of England had done a decade earlier. A compromise was found at the last minute which greatly favoured Henri. The episode shows that the king was clearly willing to uphold *Gallican* liberties and interests against Rome if and when he thought

---

9. Edelstein, "Foreign Episcopal Appointments," 452.
10. Baumgartner, "Henry II's Italian Bishops," 54.

it necessary. Like the Tudors, the Valois kings used royal ecclesiastical power effectively and maintained their authority through the advancement of their relatives (i.e., princes of the blood) and members of the nobility whose commitment to the king would be sure.[11] The uniqueness of the French Church was not lost through these efforts; the underlying heated doctrinal debates which affected England simply did not have the same heightened impact in France, that is, until the death of Henri ushered in a series of minority kings and factions at the royal court turned to religion as a means of gaining power over their rivals.

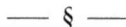

France:
The Wars of Religion and Royal Power post-1559

Patronage and politics aside, the relationship between the Church and state was largely static from 1517 onwards—the Reformation in German and Swiss lands did not generally interest either Francis I or Henri II unless they could somehow use it to their advantage in dealing with the Habsburg empire. Henri was also much more devoted to a doctrinaire Catholicism *per se* than had been Francis, and more conservative generally. In 1547, for instance, he created a new court called the *Chambre Ardente* (the burning chamber) or sometimes the "Second Tournelle" which was exclusively dedicated to hear or appeal heresy cases, blasphemy, and sacrilege (it was in operation for only twenty-three months). Parlementaires objected to its unsanctioned innovative methods, while the ecclesiastical hierarchy objected to their own loss of competence. The power of the crown was so extensive, however, that little real opposition could be put forward until the king actually needed something or changed his mind. Henri died unexpectedly, however, and opened the floodgates to factions at court with rival support networks across the realm.

It is not our purpose to discuss the Reformation in France or the wars of religion which spanned the thirty years following Henri's death. Calvinism had been on the rise in France since the 1520s, however, due to one king's (Francis I's) inability to see heresy as anything more than a lower class vice. Francis failed to acknowledge that it could have serious noble support, while Henri II's concentration on anti-Habsburg foreign policy necessitated a more liberal attitude toward Lutherans and evangelicals

---

11. Holt, *The French Wars of Religion*, 12.

in France (but not to Calvinists who were condemned *sacramentaires*).[12] Indeed, shortly before his death, Henri declared the *Edict of Compiègne* which enforced the death penalty against Calvinists without appeal, for all who preached heresy otherwise in public or private, and for anyone found in commune with Geneva. He even toyed with the idea of establishing a French inquisition on the Spanish model.[13] The next powerful, competent, adult king would not take the throne until the mid-1590s. In the meantime crown authority declined under weak, incompetent, or minority kings left to the mercy of predatory nobles. If not for the skills of their foreign born mother, the crown's ability to mould the visible church (and perhaps crown authority in general) would have been severely compromised or lost entirely. We will examine a few key matters relating to the wars of religion mainly to illustrate that religion was less a key policy worry for the kings (or their regent mother) than was the maintenance of royal power itself. Ultimately, the Calvinists were brought under the royal ecclesiastical supremacy in the same way the Catholics already had been.

The situation in France in 1559 is similar to that of England in 1547. Religion was an issue, but it had been pushed down the list of crown concern below near bankruptcy, harvest failures, famine, rampant inflation, and ongoing dynastic rivalry with the Habsburgs. Like Edward VI, the new king of France, Francis II, was a minor and, as in England, the major families around the royal court exploited the situation to their advantage. As in England, religion formed an aspect of the factionalism which was to plague the court for decades to come. In many ways the kings of this era became political footballs at the mercy of two major noble factions, each of which represented powerful religious interests. Caught in the middle was the queen-mother, and sometimes regent, Catherine de Medici. Initially surprised, the queen's manoeuvring behind the scenes, eventually, saved crown authority despite the unsure abilities of her sons. Francis II was too easily influenced by his Guise mentors, Charles IX could not tame the factional nobles, and Henri III had little real political savvy.

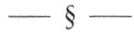

---

12. Baumgartner, *France in the Sixteenth Century*, 144.
13. Roelker, *One King, One Faith*, 231–32.

Immediately after the death of Henri II the court became dominated by the ultra-conservative Guise family who were determined to step into the breach and carry on the policies (political and religious) of the previous king. The Duke of Guise, Francis de Lorraine II, was a wily politician, a prince of the blood, and a war hero—it had been he who had engineered the capture of Calais from the English. Guise could count on the support of the church (it was influenced by his younger brother Charles, Cardinal of Lorraine), and Guise dominated the royal court, having earlier been awarded the honour of a marriage between Henri II's heir and the duke's niece, the young princess of Scotland, Mary Stuart (whose mother was the duke's sister). Guise also established a rapport with the queen-mother and with the head of the rival noble faction at court, Anne de Montmorency—scion of the oldest noble family and Constable of France (i.e., the chief minister and senior military officer).[14] Montmorency was Catholic, but his sons were less devoted, and his nephews, of the powerful Châtillon family—the Admiral of France Gaspard de Coligny, the Colonel-General of the Infantry Dandelot, and the bishop and cardinal Ôdet—were practising Huguenots. The Bourbon family were also Huguenots, princes of the blood, and the rulers of the kingdom of Navarre. This was an autonomous realm on the France-Spain border. While Navarre faced threats from both larger realms, it did give the Bourbons some independence of action. Guise stepped into the breach created by the death of the king and the accession of a boy first, determined to steer the ship of state into safe harbour. This required a consolidation of authority which, it turned out, disadvantaged rival patronage networks. At a political loss, the Châtillon and Bourbon families turned to religion as a rival means of advancement. In the Huguenots they found a ready-made resistance force.

Prior to the death of Henri, French Protestantism consisted largely of small groups, badly organized, meeting only occasionally for prayer and religious discussion, keeping very much in the background. With the king's death, with the accession of a minor, with major noble families casting about for support across the country, and with the Guise determined to make a point, Huguenot fortunes took a dramatic turn for the better. As both the great and lesser magnates embraced Protestantism as a weapon against the duke and the cardinal or as a tool for their own dreams of political power and social authority, the number of congregations boomed as street level Huguenots also benefited. The noble families found a ready-made support network across the realm and the Calvinist sectarians gained political protection. A military structure was easily imposed

---

14. Carroll, *Noble Power during the French Wars of Religion*, 90.

on the ecclesiastical structure of the Huguenot's and, as we might expect, violence rapidly escalated from the public assembly in defiance of heresy laws to rioting, iconoclasm, and armed clashes.[15] Calvinism, we've seen, had by this time developed a theology of resistance to ungodly magistrates and, with Calvin largely silent on the issue, the Huguenots and the nobles supporting them became identified by the Guise faction as both traitors and heretics and, in essence, they therefore had nothing to lose therefore in opposing Guise power or moving from resistance to active rebellion. Catherine's interest remained the defence of crown authority, and the fluid situation of the period forced her into a series of associations and power sharing schemes first with one faction than with the other.

The so-called *Tumult of Amboise*, for example—a failed Bourbon plot to capture the king, kill the Guise leadership, and move one of their own into political dominance—forced the queen-regent into action. Against the raising threat of Guise power (heightened by the foiling of the plot), Catherine urged the duke to defy convention and support the chancellor's efforts to push the *Edict of Romorantin* through Parlement. This would supply a little toleration for the radicals and allow the crown and government to concentrate on France's massive financial problems. The edict met resistance, however, due to the fact that it not only removed the death penalty for heresy but moved competence to judge heresy cases back to the Church. Catherine had become convinced that the safety of her son depended on accommodating powerful Huguenot nobles and princes of the blood against the Guise.[16] The duke approved the edict, and there may have been more negotiated at an on-going great council meeting at Fontainebleau in August 1560, had the king not died on 5 December. The duke had been caught out by this death, but Catherine had made provision and assumed the position of regent to her next son, the ten-year-old king Charles IX.

To safeguard royal power Catherine negotiated a deal with Antoine de Bourbon. In exchange for an agreement to renounce his right to act as regent (as First prince of the blood) he would become "lieutenant-general"—a vague but powerful position with few restrictions.[17] This hinted that Calvinist nobles could expect increased patronage, but the queen's ploy only infuriated the Guise faction as well as the Estates-General (who were demanding solutions to the religious and economic questions). Up to this point the estates had been led by strong kings and expected the same now. While the regent and her ally attempted to ease the religious

---

15. Rady, *France*, 42–44.
16. Reolker, *One King, One Faith*, 241.
17. Rogers, "The French Wars of Religion," 403.

situation (e.g., by freeing religious offenders), Guise made common cause with other leading Catholics (like Montmorency) and in spring of 1561 formed a coalition (or Triumvirate) accepting support offered by the pope, Philip of Spain and the Duke of Savoy.

This was traditional diplomacy, however, putting *Gallican* independence at risk in exchange for heightened political/military support. The relaxation of persecution mixed with the heightened threats occasioned by the coalition spurred on the growth of Calvinism in the countryside, movements which degenerated into violence. Catherine issued a royal edict condemning Protestant assemblies, but later relented and summoned instead an assembly of Catholic and Protestant church leaders to a colloquy at Poissy to settle the church question. Catherine wanted either a *via media* for France (similar to Henry VIII's supremacy which relied on neither Rome nor Geneva) or was sending a signal to the Spanish dominated papacy that Roman Catholic destabilization of the French monarchy would not be tolerated.[18] Sadly, the *sine quo non* for both sides at Poissy was the elimination of the other side's central doctrines. To stem the tide of violence, Catherine issued the *January Edict* or *Edict of Saint Germain* on 17 January 1562.

It was a moderation effort which for the first time gave royal recognition to another religion and ecclesiastical establishment in France. The king would tolerate certain spiritual acts, granting some limited rights of assembly (outside of town walls), tolerate Protestant synods, and equal taxation status, but he would not suffer the continued existence of seditious preaching and divisive literature. Calvinist nobles could host congregations on their estates if they so desired, but the mobilization of arms would be dealt with severely. Catherine had tried to place the king in a position as patron of both churches, but this policy offended the Catholic leadership and violence ensued.[19] It took nearly a year for Catherine to assemble the faction principals at the negotiation table, talks which eventually (19 March 1563) led to the *Peace of Amboise*.

Tying these events into the book's central themes, many Protestant regimes have featured some variation on the basic *two kingdom* motif. Anabaptists, for instance, opted for complete separation of the church from the state. Others preferred some overlapping of temporal and ecclesiastical spheres, while others still opted to subsume governance of the visible church under

---

18. Baumgartner, *France in the Sixteenth Century*, 239.
19. Holt, *The French Wars of Religion*, 47.

temporal authority (as an indifferent or not so indifferent matter). Could the chief magistrate (a king in this case) really place himself at the head of rival interpretations of what the church was and tolerate two visible churches in his kingdom, each with a distinctive doctrinal program specifically opposed to the other? Could the Tudor's title *Defender of the faith* be modified to *Defender of faiths*?

The answer is no. Catherine did manage to bring temporary stability (only by giving both sides the belief that the king was secretly on their side).[20] *Amboise* did normalize France's religious situation for a time, outlawing associations with foreign leagues and powers, and granting nobles a freedom of private worship. For the rank and file Huguenots, however, only one authorized point of public Protestant worship was allowed in each local jurisdiction.[21] Parlement resisted registering the *Peace*, however, as far too generous (unsurprising for a stubbornly *Gallican* institution already disappointed by the failure of French Tridentine representation to achieve any of its objectives). Despite the backdrop of factional struggle at court, spiritual and practical reform in the parishes was slowly building (the returning bishops implemented variations on the Tridentine decrees).[22] Over the course of the mid- to late-1560s, however, the Catholic faction courted the doctrinaire conservative Duke of Anjou (the king's brother and heir), the king matured into his role, and Catholic power in general solidified at the expense of previous Huguenot gains. Fearing the worst, Huguenot leaders had tried to kidnap the king at Meaux in late 1567; the resulting *Edict of Longjumeau* (23 March 1568) stripped the sect of political credibility.

The so-called wars of religion, which were little more than factional struggles using religion as a convenient smokescreen to conflicting noble ambitions, swung back and forth between the principals thereafter. Royal edicts shifted advantage from one faction to the other, extending rights of worship, designating locations of Huguenot influence, and suspending heresy legislation (e.g., the *Peace of St Germain*, 8 August 1570) always short of full-fledged recognition, however, when Protestant nobles were in the ascendency, or planning and executing massacres (e.g., St Bartholomew, 24 August 1572) when Catholic nobles held the upper hand. Political privileges and garrisons aside, it seems clear that what Charles and Catherine were doing was no more than Francis I or Henri II had done—manipulate the visible aspects of the Church to gain the ends of royal policy (e.g., peace, stability and guarantees of crown authority). Over the objections of

---

20. Christin, "Making Peace," 431.
21. For further details, see Greengrass, *Handbook*, 124–25.
22. Baumgartner, *France in the Sixteenth Century*, 240.

the universities and Parlement, the king protected a minority church which came to depend on his patronage just as much as the Catholic majority depended on his protection of *Gallican* principles. Admittedly this was achieved in a sometimes much more threatening way, but the elements of a Tudor-like ecclesiastical supremacy is in evidence. Through royal edicts the king designated areas of worship and suspended discipline when it suited him to do so, and Calvinism's influence in France was marginalized to fringe locations (e.g., La Rochelle) and the south. Calvinism lost its mass appeal under restrictions agreed to or forced upon its noble leaders (who lost the support of Calvin and Beza).[23] This last point brings up an interesting local theological variation (one rejected by Geneva) modifying Calvinist discipline theory and pastor candidate selection processes.

Jean Morély, sire de Villiers became briefly famous in the 1560s as the tutor of a young Henri of Navarre and client of the Châtillon brothers, Ôdet and Gaspard de Coligny. Recall the *Presbyterian* doctrines of Knox and Cartwright (in which discipline and selection were to be handled by elders of the Church) and the Geneva Synod model (where following Company nominations, new pastors were approved by civil magistrates before presentation to the congregation, all under the disciplinary oversight of the Synod). In 1562 Morély published a treatise entitled *Traicté de la discipline & police chrestienne* (or *Treatise on Christian discipline*), decrying both models as unsuited to French conditions and prejudiced against the masses. He favoured a decentralization of discipline and selection away from national and international bodies in favour of the localities where the need was greatest. Like Richard Hooker, Morély argued in favour of popular Church government founded on the principles of law (the Word of God and nature) carefully administered first through the congregation (perhaps by elders for spiritual punishments like the ban), supported by the magistrates (for the application of temporal punishments). Unlike other Calvinists, however, Morély did not see the need to go beyond provincial synods, questioning hierarchical organization altogether (except perhaps in big cities or sparsely populated rural areas). From the starting point of recognizing the need for discipline (in the first part of his book) due to human nature he developed a theory of proper disciplinary methods (in the second part), and from a consideration of biblical writings on clerical office and selection processes (in the third) he moved on to a fully developed organizational and disciplinary method (in the final part) he thought better suited to France. In essence Morély objected to the heavy involvement of civil magistrates in church discipline, arguing that this led to many other

---

23. Rogers, "The French Wars of Religion," 409.

dangerous usurpations, as well as against appointment methods to clerical office which stemmed from other Reformed or magisterial forms (whether invested in bishops or popes or in the clergy as a synod) as against the authority and needs of the local church. Appointment to office and discipline would both be vested in autonomous congregations led by leading local lay figures with little or no outside interference.

For a time French Protestantism was divided between the Morély "Congregationalist" model and the Geneva "centralizing" model of synods and hierarchy.[24] *Two kingdoms doctrine* and *priesthood of all believers'* theology is clear in Morély writing, but there is also an element of late mediaeval conciliarism. Morély advanced a democratic principle based on evidence from the Word of God as found in Scripture and arguments from natural reason in which key functions such as discipline, social control, and the appointments of pastors and elders should be in the hands of the local congregations as the Church or body of Christ. For perhaps obvious reasons (e.g., lack of appropriate pastors) he proposed to make the members of the congregation collectively responsible for ecclesiastical governance and discipline. This was sensible as too radical pastors were periodically exiled. Morély assumed that such a structure would solidify the relationship between the congregation and its noble defenders in genuine fellowship. Morély and his doctrine was eventually condemned by Calvin and the Geneva consistory, a decision upheld by the French national synod under the influence of Beza (who had initiated a huge letter writing campaign, reviewing Morély's scriptural exegesis and natural law conclusions). Bullinger called Morély a crypto-Anabaptist. The Morély reforms were officially condemned at the sixth national synod in La Rochelle (which Beza attended along with many nobles and court notables) in 1571.[25]

The Rise of the Politiques

It was beginning to look as if France was incongruous with both Calvinist and Tridentine dogmas. *Gallican* Catholicism, protected by the king and long tradition, was able to withstand *Ultamontane* pressure and adopt/adapt Tridentine decrees as desired, but *Gallican* Protestantism (Huguenots) could not seem to do the same with Genevan theology. As a result

---

24. Kingdon, "Calvinism and Democracy," 393. Also see, Kingdon, *Geneva*, 43–50 and Baker, *Protestantism, Poetry and Protest*, 197–201.

25. Baumgartner, *France in the Sixteenth Century*, 246–47.

the former thrived in isolation while the latter declined in the second half of the sixteenth century. Queen Catherine, arguably the chief magistrate throughout the period, was concern primarily with safeguarding crown authority and knew the church was a central support. She had the advantage that neither faith could advance without reciprocal crown support (unless they could successfully appeal to foreign backing, unlikely after St Bartholomew's). Antithetical to both the Geneva consistory and Tridentine Catholicism, therefore, Catherine summoned the Estates-General to begin the process of reclaiming order. This would be difficult as the events of St Bartholomew's day had initiated a period of intense emotion throughout the realm. At the extremes, horror and anger on the Protestant side was matched by jubilation among *Gallicans*. Others, recognizing that matters had gone too far, stepped back into deliberately moderate political and religious positions—they were called *Politiques*.

They were an association of like-minded Catholic magistrates and bishops who supported religious toleration (now believing uniformity to be a secondary concern) and a strong monarchy as the only way to solve the problems, both religious and fiscal, facing France. Theirs was a moderate philosophy which appealed to a widespread mix of interests in both the political and non-political classes (including support from like-minded Huguenots who recognized that extremism had not led to increased numbers or the advancement of their cause either). The crown was portrayed as a unifying force for the nation, but one threatened by religious extremists on both sides as well as by foreign interference. It was a practical compromise; the moderates simply recognized that the Huguenot minority was just too big to be easily suppressed but not powerful enough to finally force recognition and equality. The state could, however, implement an outward religious uniformity (for practical reasons of social behaviour) reasoning that trying to enforce a specific confessional piety, where the minority is so large, merely led to civil unrest.[26] The intellectual position of the *Politiques* was codified by Jean Bodin in his 1576 treatise *Six books of the Republic*.

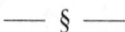

Bodin was an Angers-born civil lawyer and professor at Toulouse who had some humanist training as well as experience of both religions, having spent time as a novice in a Carmelite monastery and later having been a brief convert to Calvinism while living in Geneva (sometime in the 1550s).[27] He

---

26. Remer, "Dialogues of Toleration," 321; Ford, "Dimensions of Toleration," 137.
27. Baldwin, "Jean Bodin and the League," 160.

was politically active as a deputy in the Third Estate in 1576 (the source of many of the themes explored in *Six books*) that which Catherine had summoned. The order the queen desired depended on resolutions to three main problems—the religious peace, the fiscal situation, and the Estates' level of participation in the governing of the realm. These are worth a brief digression as Bodin was intimately involved in all three debates.

With regard to religious peace, the question before the assembly was support for the recent royal *Edict of Beaulieu* which granted the Huguenots concessions to forestall rioting and violence. The Estates-General risked the anger of the Holy League and other powerful Catholic interests should they support *Beaulieu*, but further violence should they oppose it. Bodin influenced many of the deputies to support a program of toleration. He presented his colleagues a stark choice—try to enforce religious uniformity and expect on-going and costly warfare (the cost of which the Third Estate would have to bear) or a simple toleration of the minority, dissenting creed, and peace (which cost nothing and gained much). The deputies in the First and Second Estates wanted to pursue the issue of uniformity at all cost, and the eleven governments that made up the representation in the Third supported the proposal of uniformity *via* warfare *if necessary*.[28] Since that decision was sure to raise taxes (which the first two estates were not all that concerned about) Bodin considered whether a more equitable taxation principle might be found? This became a key theme in his treatise as well, the development of an equitable tax system wherein no-one was exempt—neither clergy nor nobility—and where all would take a proportional responsibility.

Obviously the middle class dominated Third Estate would enthusiastically support such a proposed restructuring but the First and Second would not, having the most to lose thereby. The state of the crown's finances (which the Estates-General was meant partially to solve) forced members of the Third Estate to rethink their previous vote on the religion question and Bodin's toleration plan looked very tempting. The deputies of the First and Second estates approved forced uniformity still, and portrayed members of the Third Estate to the king as somehow unpatriotic, suggesting further alienation of crown properties as a financial solution which, again, would benefit the First and Second estates and disadvantage the Third. It is no doubt on this point that Bodin developed his ideas on inalienable positive law. The king's sovereignty depended on domain (i.e., on revenue producing properties attached to the crown) which he could not, according to the law and customs of the country, alienate. Alienation of domain was equated with the surrender of judicial, administrative, and fiscal power, all

---

28. Ulph, "Jean Bodin and the Estates–General of 1576," 289–90.

of which formed the foundation of royal authority. These discussions led to the third great issue of the day. A proposal was made that the three estates send representatives to the king and council's decision-making sessions over the *cahiers* (reports, grievances and complaints) forwarded to them. Bodin resisted this suggestion as it would give the clergy and nobles some level of sovereignty, and because royal power should not be beholden to the estates (even as a simple review body). He feared that to give the Estates a share in sovereignty would be to open the country up to the special interests of the first two estates (and to aristocratic or oligarchic rule), leaving the Third Estate at the mercy of the special interests of the privileged. He pinned his hopes for the future, instead, on a pseudo-absolutist approach as that one least likely to disfavour the middle classes and that one clearest in God's and natural laws.[29] It was undoubtedly for these same reasons that he was later active in the League and in the entourage of the Duke of Anjou (up to the prince's death in 1584).

Six books argued that the ideal of good social order would be achieved only when the godly prince, ruling in a godly fashion (according to the laws of God and nature), was obeyed by the masses. This was not unlike absolutist theory as seen expressed in Protestant views of the chief magistrate beholden to no authority other than God and natural law. Similar elements are seen in Bodin's claim that the king makes laws for all and can expect to raise taxes or use property as he sees fit (within only two qualifications of French positive law—Salic law and the inalienability of crown property). Although he conceived of the king's power as indivisible, there is nonetheless a clear element of agency within it—that is implementation through delegated power and subordinate magistrates familiar as temporal or ecclesiastical governors. Bodin called these "extraordinary commissioners" as they exercised *ad hoc* authority based on royal commissions (short-term) rather than hereditary or elected office.[30] He recognized the separation of the two kingdoms, however, seeing the visible church and temporal kingdom both under the king as a temporal authority rather than as the "king-priest" of French tradition. He held that the king's power to compel belief, combat zealotry, and protect his people against the wicked were temporal powers in nature rather than spiritual (as others saw it). Indeed, it had been the investment of the king with spiritual powers *per se* that had become the source of so much of the anarchy of the age. The point being that the king's power became invested in one faith and one expression of the visible church and, consequently, all others became naturally inferior and threatening as

29. Ulph, "Jean Bodin and the Estates–General of 1576," 296.
30. Bonney, "Bodin and the Development of the French Monarchy," 48–50.

a result. Toleration of other visible expressions would alleviate much of the tension. If the king's power was based solely on his temporal position, however, religious squabbles should evaporate along with many of the fiscal burdens on the crown treasury and the realm. The king then, as he should, takes up a position as the guarantor of equity and justice for his people rather than the enforcer of spiritual orthodoxy *per se* for only some of his people. In the third book Bodin reasoned that, "it may be, that the consent and agreement of the nobilities and people in a new religion or sect, may be puissant and strong, as that to repress or alter the same, should be a thing impossible, or at leastwise marvelous difficult, without extraeme peril and daunger to the whole estate."[31] Force, in his opinion, would and often did have the opposite result to that one intended. A prince, trying to force a faith in which he has a stake may well push some away from his faith or embolden the stubbornness of those who hold the opposed view. Bodin considered these issues in the fourth book.

Commentators think it ironic that Bodin later joined the Catholic League in 1589 (despite calls for toleration), a partisan of the Catholic Cardinal of Bourbon rather than Bourbon's nephew, the Huguenot Henri of Navarre. Perhaps, but Bodin predicted that Henri would convert and he saw the king's Catholicism was itself an expression of a third positive law in France.[32] Bodin viewed the Catholic and Protestant faiths, in the broadest sense, as civil expressions (in the way Hooker saw the visible church as a type of society) and, thus, conformity to either was dependent on considerations at least partially political in nature. He conformed to Catholicism therefore as the superior civil religion, it having a "better foundation for a just constitution and for good citizenship" in France. Henri III, having had the opposition assassinated, acted contrary to divine and natural law, so the king and those magistrates who supported him gave up the protection of God, who withdrew "the fear of kings." Bodin joined a potent opposition force.

This suggests that he consequently aligned himself with the later generations of Reformed theorists who argued that the subject could be justified in rebellion against the wicked magistrate or the political tyrant. The *Politiques*, who supported and emphasized the authority of the crown, also recognized that order sometimes necessitated resistance to the orders of the king. This is familiar theory in that it echoed earlier Calvinist theology which placed the onus on subordinate magistrates to safeguard the covenant and Christian commonwealth should the prince's decisions conflict

---

31. Ford, "Dimensions of Toleration," 137, quoting Bodin, *Six Bookes*, 382.

32. Ford, "Dimensions of Toleration," 138; Baumgartner, *France in the Sixteenth Century*, 305–7.

with divine or natural laws.[33] Protestantism survived at the grass roots level in France because, in essence, agents of the crown could not agree a solution other than that one offered by the *Politiques*. Moderation may have stabilized the country in the way Bodin envisioned had Charles IX not died on 30 November 1574. The Duke of Anjou succeeded his brother as Henri III. Had he been a strong and decisive king the situation need not have disintegrated (he was neither). Henri was a fickle man, intelligent, but easily swayed under the influence of his favourites (who were young and attractive men with neither political nor diplomatic savvy).

Political issues aside the fact of the matter was that after 1572 there was no chance that France would abandon Catholicism as the duly constituted religion of the state. The question of how much toleration of the Protestant minority would be granted exercised the government and the leading faction figures from that point on; both sides took part in league building exercises none of which were particularly successful in the short term or long lasting and both sides recognized that their success and survival depended on a strong monarch. The late 1570s and 1580s saw a period of relative peace in which the king tried to turn his attentions toward other urgent matters (failing to resolve any of them). After the death of his brother, the Duke of Anjou, in June 1584, the wars of religion (such as they were) turned into a war of succession. The heir to the throne was the Protestant prince Henri of Navarre. The threat of a Huguenot king, however, raised fears in Catholic France to such an extent that the reformed Catholic League—already a treaty with Spain agreed—threw its support behind its own candidate, Henry of Navarre's elder uncle Charles, Cardinal of Bourbon. These events, and secret negotiations, threatened to displace the king as head of the Church. Indeed, the Catholic League seemed to be forcing a wedge between the two institutions. Faced with this reality, and with financial insolvency, Henri III had no option but to agree the *Treaty of Nemours* with the Duke of Guise. All religious and political concessions once made to the Huguenots were withdrawn; they now faced a stark choice—conversion or forced exile.[34] Henri was trying to placate Guise while building up the royal forces behind the League's back but he was not an astute military leader. Consequently, he found himself between two men—Guise and Navarre—who were effective leaders. Henri was

---

33. Baumgartner, *France in the Sixteenth Century*, 414.

34. Baumgartner, *France in the Sixteenth Century*, 418; Holt, *The French Wars of Religion*, 128.

forced to concede power to Guise and the League, and Charles was formally recognized as his lieutenant-general and heir.

Rather than make the best of it, however, Henri arranged for the assassination of the duke (for 23 December 1588) which resulted in the deaths of Guise, his brother Louis, Cardinal of Guise, and other leaguers. Rather than relieve tension, however, these actions exacerbated the already tense situation and brought royal authority to its nadir. Both Catholic and Protestant publicists declared the king a tyrant. The Sorbonne publicized the verdict, excusing his subjects from obedience. Unable to appeal to Catholic forces thereby—having created martyrs of the Guise leadership—the king turned to Navarre for Huguenot military aid in a campaign to re-take Paris. On 1 July 1589, however, before anything was accomplished the king was himself assassinated, followed soon thereafter by the death of the cardinal (through natural causes). To forestall years of dynastic struggle Henri of Navarre resolved all the outstanding issues by simply renouncing Calvinism.

The Leaguers may have doubted the sincerity of the conversion, but Navarre gained support among the episcopal leadership, satisfied to have a strong, adult king on the throne once again. He was crowned Henri IV in July 1593, which prompted the conversion of many other high-ranking Huguenot leaders. The king was next able to reconcile conflicting religious forces first by rallying all loyal Frenchmen to the royal banner against the presence of Spanish forces (old League allies) and, second, by resolving the religious situation with the *Edict of Nantes* (30 April 1598). Nantes offered the Huguenots many familiar privileges and rights (of conscience and practice) within Catholic-dominated France. Henri forced Parlement to register and enforce *Nantes*. Consequently, both the Catholic majority and Protestant minority recognized the king as their protector and head of the church. On the one hand the rights and privileges of the Calvinists' depended entirely on royal goodwill, and through his nominations and appointments to high church office *Gallican* interests were safeguarded against papal incursions. The popes of the late sixteenth century contributed to the weakening of papal and *Ultramontane* power with a refusal to recognize the king's rights (under *Concordat*) prior to 1595. This also would have left no less than a third of the dioceses vacant had Henri IV not acted unilaterally, thus moulding the character of the French Church well into the seventeenth century. Although slow to realize the potentialities he eventually filled offices with *Politique* candidates (opting for moderation) bolstering royal authority and improving the state of the episcopate (his candidates were selected on their merits, maturity and enthusiasm for reform rather than on socio-political considerations). Moreover, Tridentine reform was also tested and royal officers began to attend Huguenot synods and national councils in the same way they monitored Catholic assemblies.[35] Both churches now depended on the king's good will for their existence and Henri IV proved both tolerant and even-handed in his rule, ordering visitations, summoning synods, and imposing discipline, improving the character of the lower and higher clergy alike.

— § —

Spain under the Most Catholic Kings —Regalism and Cooperation

As was the case in France, the kings of Spain were in a position by the 1520s which did not require a Tudor-like statement of royal ecclesiastical supremacy sanctioning their control over the institutions of religion. Unlike the French case, however, this was the result of a series of largely cooperative measures between the kings of the Iberian states and the papacy over the course of the late mediaeval period to their mutual benefit. The Spanish kings sought to gain as firm a temporal sovereignty within their territories as possible, recognizing papal supremacy over spiritual issues and the church, but with themselves or their agents (rather than papal agents) in positions as legates or vicars-general. The papacy maintained both a theoretical supremacy over the Iberian institutions of the church as well as a few firmly held judicial, jurisdictional and doctrinal powers (although many others had been whittled away). The "sanctified" crown (supported by churchmen in key governmental positions) moulded the Spanish institutions to its own needs through vast patronage networks, fiscal controls over secularized properties, a series of economic arrangements with the papacy, as well as through dedicated guardianship of an idealized Catholicism (enforced through a well maintained inquisition and the expulsion of alien influences). The international political and diplomatic needs of the Iberian kings were also quite different to those of France (not to mention often in opposition), but they also strove to protect a uniqueness in their visible church as well as to use it as one of the great foundation stones of increasing royal sovereignty. Whereas the French kings sought to safeguard a distinctive *Gallican* Catholicism (when it suited them to do so) against foreign influences (and looked with suspicion upon most things "papal"), the Spanish kings sought to extend a distinctive Iberian Catholicism outwards in defence of the souls of Christian Europe and beyond (and coming to

---

35. Rogers, "The French Wars of Religion," 420–24; Rady, *France*, 103; Baumgartner, *The French Wars of Religion*, 248.

dominate the papacy and the Universal Church as a result). Part and parcel of this effort was the uniquely Hispanic sense of spiritual mission.

—— § ——

The Iberian Kings and the Papacy
—A Sense of Mission

As noted earlier the relationship between the French kings and the papacy in the fifteenth-century was based primarily on the fluidity of international politics. As a safeguard to their own domination of the local institutions, French scholars had developed an idea in support of localism which proved a serious (and therefore useful) threat to the power of the papacy—conciliarism (i.e., the advancement of the authority of the Ecumenical council over that of the pope). France was a powerful and rich state and its monarchs were willing to manipulate political realities to their own benefit to safeguard *Gallican* practices or, when necessary, recognize *Ultramontane* aspirations (for the short term). They opposed or cooperated with Rome, provided Rome serviced the wants and desires of the French Church and the French king. Mostly, the latter was concerned territorial expansion into the Italian peninsula rather than any particular spiritual issue. What was best for the Universal Church as a whole rarely entered the equation (although what was best for the Church of France occasionally did). Rather than take up this French strategy, the kings of the major Iberian states of Castile and Aragon sided with the papacy against the *Gallican* threat. This was not altruism; the Iberian kings were just as willing as the French to manipulate international politics, but they recognized that their own goals of territorial expansion depended on a strong Roman presence in the Italian peninsula and at the heart of Christendom. A weak papacy suited French and Imperial ambitions which the Iberian states could not yet challenge directly.

Alphonse V, for example, needed papal cooperation and investment if his ambitious expansionist plan was to be realized. A greater crown presence in Sicily, Sardinia, and the Kingdom of Naples was a necessary step toward greater Aragonese/Catalonian presence in the western Mediterranean. Alphonse threatened conciliarism to manoeuvre the pope into recognizing the unification of his diverse realms, extracting privileges of the Aragonese Church in return for his firm support of papal ambitions *vis-à-vis* France and the northern Italian peninsula. John II of Castile (nominally an ally of France) opposed conciliarism as a potential threat to crown authority, fearing Castilian regional Cortés (high courts and parliaments) might apply the principles in the temporal realm.[36] Both kings opposed the French-led, Basel deposition of Pope Eugenius as well as wider conciliar efforts as General Council domination threatened to bring the Universal Church too much under the sway of French or Imperial plans (both of which threatened Aragonese interests in Naples).

When Isabella and Ferdinand married and united the crowns they continued the policy of papal cooperation. Castile adopted the Aragonese cause of Hispanic hegemony in Italy and Aragon repudiated threats of conciliarism, adopting instead the *Hispano-Roman* alliance through which Spain became the papacy's (only) reliable ally. From this point on the Spanish position remained fairly consistent (despite blips during the reign of Carlos I)—in church matters the pope was superior to the General Council (and so to any regional council as well). This sent out a clear political message that, for Spain, the pope governed the Universal Church. It also winked at papal claims of temporal superiority and acknowledged that with regard to new canon laws and doctrinal interpretations popes could not ignore or void at whim the decisions of councils. How the *Hispano-Roman* alliance advanced magisterial authority over the church in Spain is surprisingly straight-forward.

Over the course of the late mediaeval period the Iberian rulers drove out the last vestiges of Islamic power from Christian lands. This purification effort meant little, however, if the Iberian Church was also tainted by the same spiritual immoralities that had surfaced elsewhere—anti-clericalism, abuses in church practice, higher offices dominated by nobles dedicated to familial ambitions rather than episcopal improvement, and so on. Elimination of these offenses became the next "crusade." As the papacy was dependent upon Spanish support, concessions were wrung out over issues of jurisdiction, appointments and finance.[37]

In the first instance crown rights of patronage were recognized *via* papal bulls, over nominations to church posts, the Christianizing of the Muslim populations, the collection of tithes, jurisdiction, and other fiscal controls in lands recovered from the Moors. As more territory was recovered, as more souls were saved, more rewards were granted. Eventually, similar authorities were extracted from the papacy over the *Christian*

---

36. Hermann, "Settlements," 506.

37. Hermann, "Settlements," 507; Mackenney, *Sixteenth Century Europe*, 178; Richardson, *Renaissance Monarchy*, 139.

Iberian realms as well. The more control gained, the more the kings (of Castile especially) were determined to ferret out all foreign interference (not solely of the Islamic variety).

Papal interference was finally targeted through the "ancient custom" of "supplanting." What this means is where once Islamic clerics were supplanted by Christians, now papal (i.e., foreign) nominees were supplanted by equally qualified crown nominees.[38] Ferdinand and Isabella then summoned a Church Council to Seville to settle ecclesiastical policy for Castile (which they expected the papacy to hand-wave), to establish the Inquisition, and to affirm crown oversight of the clergy (to weed out foreigners and the consequent non-residency this entailed). Unlike the cases of France and England the shift of spiritual power to the crown in Spain was more than an issue of sovereignty; the dual-monarchy was implementing genuine reform. That the Spanish crown strategy was successful is finally clear with test cases in the dioceses of Cordoba and Cuenca (1479).[39] The dual-monarchy was aided by the fact that, unlike France and England, the Iberian Peninsula featured a unique spiritual-cultural diversity as the meeting place of Christian, Judaic and Islamic influences. The crown pursued an effort of religious and cultural purity across the peninsula based on the consolidation of Christian supremacy and the channelling of the fanaticism brought on by the success of the *Reconquista*. By the sixteenth century, with Reformation efforts disturbing stability elsewhere, the Spanish sense of spiritual mission was turned toward the purification of Christendom itself.

The *Reconquista* brought increasing numbers of Jews and Muslims into Christian society. Aragon had a large Muslim populace and, as in Castile and the conquered lands of Granada, they were mostly rural farmers who caused little problem for the aristocratic landowners who employed their expertise and labour. The Jewish population of conquered Moorish lands, however, were problematic. They had provided an urban, professional, administrative class for their Moorish overlords which was not so easily assimilated into Christian society (or dismissed from it). Some converted (genuinely or nominally) and these so-called *new Christians* integrated into society as best they could but their efforts were hindered by mistrust in both higher and middling social circles (despite reputations as superior doctors, lawyers and bureaucrats among the social elites and at court).

---

38. Elliott, *Imperial Spain*, 100–102.
39. Elliott, *Imperial Spain*, 100–102; Lea, "The First Castilian Inquisitor," 48.

Many *new Christians* became high ranking professors and churchmen on the basis of their educations and merits, but this was undermined by lingering unconverted Jewish communities and the reconversion of some of their number.[40] Combined with the atmosphere of Spanish spiritual mission, a distinctively Iberian aspect of the tension-producing church *v.* state cause developed. Eventually the Iberian rulers bowed to popular religious pressure and forced the conversion or expulsions of their remaining Jewish populations in 1492. While the masses in general, and the nobility for specific causes may have resented the success of the *new Christians* and complained of the suspected Judaizing tendencies they brought into the church, it is further interesting to note that it was these very tendencies which Protestants, half a century later, would strive so hard to instil in their own churches. Let's pause and consider what this means.

As noted earlier, Protestant theorists were looking for a means to return their national institutions and practices to a more primitive Christian church structure and ideal, and this desire had both doctrinal and institutional consequences. The Iberian churches had already achieved this goal, had built upon it, and were pressing Rome to recognize it as the direction Catholic reform should take across Christendom. "The New Christians suffused Spanish religious culture with a rich spiritual, philosophical, and exegetical tradition . . . ," it was written, characterizing the Protestant Reformation elsewhere as pursuing the restoration of an early Christianity, which "meant also a recovery of the Jewish heritage" that had been a clear part of it and which Spain already experienced.[41] Indeed, all the influences we discussed elsewhere—Erasmian or humanist evangelicalism, spiritualism, anti-clericalism, the clear-cut separation of magisterial and religious authorities—also touched Spain (to a lesser extent but sometimes much earlier). For example, Luther's principle of the *priesthood of all believers* and Erasmus's Scripture-based spiritualism were being explored by a pre-existing and influential mystical tradition which would produce such figures as Ignatius Loyola, Teresa of Avila and John of the Cross and which was deeply influential on Isabella (and to a lesser extent on Ferdinand). In order to safeguard this unique Hispanic Catholicism and its reforming tendencies, however, it was necessary to ensure crown control. Three means were available—the redevelopment of the old inquisition from a church- into a crown-controlled court, the wresting of power over high church nominations away from both a far off pope and self-interested noble magnates, and

---

40. Friedman, "Jewish Conversion," 6–8.
41. Hermann, "Settlements," 495.

the consequent re-moulding of the clerical classes (both regular and secular) into concerned spiritual shepherds.

The establishing of a Castilian inquisition was called for by both *old* and *new* Christians as a means to eliminate Jewish and/or the influence of false *conversos* on the one hand, and as a means of vindicating genuine *new Christians* on the other. The monarchs, however, realized quickly how much more the institution could benefit them as a supra-provincial and interstate body. A papal inquisition had existed in Aragon since the thirteenth century but was largely under-employed. Ferdinand reconstituted the court under the auspices of the crown, independent of both papal and episcopal controls, by manipulating the nomination and appointment of officials who would be in power at the crown's pleasure (owing their positions to crown patronage). Ferdinand and Isabella re-imagined the court as a tool of royal centralization and *regalism*, as a weapon against the independent-minded noble classes in their kingdoms, as a means of bringing the big urban trade centres (often controlled by *new Christians*) under the umbrella of the crown, and as the means of ensuring *new Christian* assimilation. Again, due to the fluidity of international politics this new model was introduced into Castile in 1478 (with the compliance and *de iure* consent of Pope Sixtus IV) to operate *de facto* under the crown's direct control.

In a subsequent letter to the town council of Seville the extensive powers of the new court were sketched out by the crown. The inquisition was an expression of royal power to be used "as we see fit . . . it is our will that these Inquisitors should carry out and practice their work of Inquisition without any impediment. And for this purpose, you will grant them any form and assistance, to uproot from our kingdoms and domains all abominations, apostasy, and heresy." In other words, all local officials were thereby ordered to place their offices, men, and equipment (from jails to stocks) into the hands of the inquisitors if requested to do so, "and you shall adhere to and carry out any sentence, censure, and penalty they give, and you shall denounce the infidel and their supporters and those who help conceal, no matter what their estate, position or status. And you shall do this under penalty of the confiscation of all your property and the loss of your position."[42]

In essence, therefore, the Castilian Inquisition had two key policy concerns, one social and the other religious. The former was the establishment of a court of inquiry with regard to the "blood purity" rules developed in the interest of the established noble class against n*ew Christian* ambitions as landowners with increasingly noble connections. The rules

---

42. Ferdinand and Isabella, "Letter of Commission," 10–11; Friedman, "Jewish Conversion," 12; Lea, "The First Castilian Inquisitor," 46–47.

were to be a means of attesting Catholic orthodoxy on the basis that heretical or unorthodox ancestry somehow equated with tainted blood (which was officially seen as a threat to the established noble class). Rules to distinguish the old faithful from the new (the descendants of converts) were written into the statutes of fraternal associations, religious and military orders, and even some diocesan chapters. In theory (although not strictly in practice) each new postulate had to submit to an extensive background check designed to establish cultural purity and therefore suitability for office. These practices seldom affected professional bodies like universities, however, which had no real interest in discriminating against men of useful talent but could be invaluable to the crown as a means of checking noble ambition. As one of the few institutions with cross-border powers and access to extensive records the Inquisition became the ideal forum for these sociological investigations.[43] These investigations were secondary, however. The primary purpose of the inquisition was to investigate and combat heterodox opinion and practice.

As a tool of the crown the Inquisition extended the monarchy's powers over the church and it extended their spiritual authority over their subjects as a whole (as Ferdinand achieved the introduction of the re-moulded Inquisition into the kingdoms of Aragon in 1483). The crown controlled appointments to the senior offices—the inquisitor-general and the six members of the *Council of the Supreme and General Inquisition* (or the *Suprema*)—of the court, which had both central and regional expressions (in the form of thirteen mainland tribunals as well as bodies established for Sicily, Sardinia and the Canary Islands later)—all of which under the patronage of, and thus answerable to, a crown enforcing papal determinations.[44] By the 1520s the Inquisition was also dealing with issues of censorship, social behaviour, clerical discipline, and economic practice. Clearly there was no need for royal supremacy legislation.[45] Like their French counterparts, the kings of Castile and Aragon had also gained episcopal nomination rights at the expense of the papacy during the schism and conciliar crises of the fifteenth century and these efforts were also carried on into the sixteenth century as part of an overall effort to reform religious institutions across the board.

Although the kings of the late mediaeval period did not exclusively nominate to all higher church offices, through a number of agreements and concessions from the popes they did control a vast majority. In this way they were able to shield the Iberian church from much direct papal interference.

---

43. Pérez, *The Spanish Inquisition*, 55–56.
44. Rawlings, *The Spanish Inquisition*, 56–57.
45. Kilsby, *Spain*, 19–20.

For example, most appeals from the church did not get beyond the borders of the state in which the complaint originated. First John II, and then Isabella (both quite pious individuals with serious reforming tendencies)—less so Enrique IV (1454-74) perhaps—sought to purify the religious institutions of Castile and, later, these efforts influenced the crown of Aragon and were taken up the Habsburg rulers, by the Cortés of the individual realms, and the senior churchmen (bishops, abbots and inquisitors).

Isabella's pious sensibilities, more so than Ferdinand's, were often offended by both secular (church) and regular (monastic) practices which also offended the Spanish spiritual mission which the monarchs had taken control of and wanted to direct towards more positive ends. The conditions which led to anti-clericalism elsewhere in Europe were also present in the states of the peninsula, of course—bishops living in luxury and ignoring their pastoral duties in order to participate in politics and warfare, bishops and higher churchmen holding multiple offices leading to rampant non-residency, bishops ignoring the state of their parish priests (e.g., poor, insufficiently educated), while monasteries, friaries and convents were the sources of rumour, scandal and humorous writings rather than being recognized for their piety, charity and education works. The monarchs (especially Isabella) sought to combat these perceived imperfections. They had a three-prong approach: the expansion of royal authority; the re-channelling of excessive and ill-used church wealth; and, the general reform of monastic institutions. The effort illustrates the extent of temporal power.

The monarchs first removed much of the basis of the bishops' and archbishops' political and military powers by handing their fortresses (which had been gained in warfare against the Moors) over to civil administrators (crown appointments), reducing direct papal power. The years 1478-9 witnessed the crown gaining the power of appointment to senior clerical positions in the recaptured territories of Granada and, subsequently, whenever the papacy needed Spanish support in the Italian peninsula Ferdinand took the opportunities presented to extend royal privileges at home. For example, in 1508 a papal bull handed over patronage of church positions in the new world lands to the crown, which gave the monarchs the right of nomination, dismissal, taxation and exclusion from papal edicts overseas. In 1523, Carlos I secured from Pope Adrian VI the right (i.e., in confirmation of a pre-existing agreement) of episcopal nomination across Spain (examined below).[46]

---

46. Rawlings, "The Secularisation of Castilian Episcopal Office," 55.

Exercising their power the monarchs tended to appoint reform-minded bishops who, in turn, sponsored programs of increased preaching, poor relief, and work programs as part of their duty of pastoral care. These programs blended well with the monarchy's push for general reform. One of the best known reformers, Archbishop Jimenez de Cisneros, was placed in charge of the initiative and he began with the regular institutions (e.g., monasteries and convents). His reform of choice was the establishment of "observant" orders to counteract the more liberal "conventual" orders of the day. He did much the same with the seculars, focussing on sexual incontinence, absenteeism and the other known abuses rampant at the time. Bishops were ordered to reside in their sees and take seriously the role of spiritual shepherd to their lesser clergy and laymen and, through the better supervision of the lives and education of the clergy more directly, through a greater availability of sermons, through the expansion of teaching, and through a more appropriate garb and regulation of their own moral behaviours a much more impressive clergy developed (later, Tridentine decrees tried to achieve the same result across Christendom).[47] In this way the authorities sought to establish as clear a distinction between the laity and the improved secular and regular clergies as possible (entirely opposite the goal of Protestantism) which raised both anti-papal and patriotic principles favourable to the crown going forward.

Alphonse and John, and their children Ferdinand and Isabella, in service to that Spanish sense of spiritual mission sought the removal of so-called reserved benefices (so that natives could be promoted over whatever foreign candidates the popes might appoint), and they sought to restore episcopal authority (through the elimination, for example, of such things as monastic exemption) as well as to bring church courts and physical properties more firmly under crown authority. Not secularized (as in other realms) but subjected to closer scrutiny and oversight. The demands of the Iberian church reform were sometimes resisted in Rome (due to diplomatic fluidities and the realities of political power) but the *Reconquista* made Spanish demands almost irresistible. By the start of the early modern period the dual monarchs of Spain were simply able to impose increased "observant" practices and reform principles as well as to block papal jurisdictional interference (in the form of disallowing appeals, for instance, if they choose to do so). Cisneros was the crown's major agent in the reform process and his merits allowed him to rise quickly through both the clerical and political ranks (a Spanish Thomas Wolsey). Through Cisneros's domination of religious and political offices he showed the kings how to dominate both institutions

---

47. Kilsby, *Spain*, 22.

more firmly themselves. Of course, reform across the board was difficult. So much of Castile was vast rural territory with settlements few and far between linked by ill-constructed road and communications networks, but there were some great successes. Cisneros established the University of Alcalà (1508), for instance, which offered not only an extensive ecclesiastical education but taught in the sciences and the liberal arts as well. Indeed, with the *Reconquista* of Granada, Alcalà featured otherwise hard-to-get Arabic resources which attracted scholars from across Europe. This had the positive knock on effect of increased book printing (particularly of religious themes). As great as these achievements were, however, his greatest achievement was the publication of the *Polyglot Bible* (1522), a boon to scholarship as it featured the Latin text next to the original Greek and Hebrew sources.

While the Spanish Church was not perfect, and the problems inherent in reform did not disappear simply *via* increased crown control of the institutions, finances and discipline, it is the case that Spain was able to avoid those Protestant threats and anticlerical movements other major Catholic powers were just starting to face by the 1520s. Spanish bishops were also in the vanguard, later, of Catholic and Counter-Reformation efforts, taking the battle to the Protestants often on their own chosen grounds of biblical scholarship, treatises, apologia, and effective sermons.[48] The successes of the *Reconquista* and the Inquisition forged a Spanish state, not *via* political cohesion but *via* a common faith, a sense of spiritual mission, and crown control over religious institutions. Every military, spiritual, and political achievement became infused with religious significance and was portrayed as another Spanish victory on behalf of Christendom as a whole—unity was founded on that Holy mission. Unlike in France and England therefore, where increased magisterial control of the spiritual institutions was claimed as the defence of national characteristics, in Spain the crown was placed at the service of the Church Universal and in the service of Christendom itself. The crown became the ultimate servant of the Church by placing itself at the head of a coherent Spanish spiritual mission aimed outward rather than entirely inward. The mission passed to the Habsburg rulers (*via* Ferdinand and Isabella's daughter Joanna and her husband Philip—who reigned briefly as Philip I). Carlos I and his son Philip II maintained and reinforced *"regalism"*—the crown-led church service in which the kings were, in essence, the vicars or legates of the pope—to the point where even papal publications became subject to royal

---

48. Hermann, "Settlements," 501; Richardson, *Renaissance Monarchy*, 138–40.

censure. Through the combination of his Spanish kingdoms with the Holy Roman Empire, Carlos brought the Spanish mission to focus on the state of the church in Europe too (in Germany and the Low Countries, in France and England), trying to mould Christendom in the Spanish model (and defend it from Islamic threats on its south-eastern borders).[49]

— § —

Habsburg Spain—Regalism

With regard to the issues of civil magistrates and ecclesiastical authority, the Spanish crown emerged out of the late mediaeval period acknowledging the spiritual authority of the papacy but otherwise dominating all aspects of the Spanish Church (in the realms of Spain and the New World). The common ideal of the temporal authority as a divinely ordained institution became a source of legitimacy for the Habsburgs on par with the divine providential order of creation. Spanish intellectuals, theoreticians and propagandists acknowledged the importance of spiritual authority in temporal matters, however indirect, whilst reinforcing the crown's hard won prerogatives over the Church as an institution (and sometimes directly over doctrinal issues). So, as in *Gallican* France and *Anglican* England, in Spain, a royal commissioner always presided over church councils and synods, new canons were not published without prior royal approval, church wealth had been (pseudo-)secularized as a resource in the use of the state, church courts had been integrated into the state's judicial systems, papal bulls could not be published and promulgated without the prior examination and approval by the royal council and, in the church hierarchies of the separate realms church offices were reserved for natives (e.g., Castilians for Castilian posts). The crown could, however, naturalize foreigners nominated to posts, as Adrian of Utrecht had been, when it was opportune to do so.[50] Unique to Spain (but subsequently exported) was a re-vamped inquisition which moulded a national character through powers of discipline and investigation (in the exclusive service of the crown).

In the first half of the sixteenth-century, however, Carlos I (who was also Emperor Charles V from 1519) recognized a division in his territories. As the champion of Christendom (the emperor's role was to defend Christian Europe from Ottoman-Turk invasions) he recognized the need for doctrinal, disciplinary, and institutional reform across the board. If the papacy

---

49. Llobera, *The God of Modernity*, 140–41.
50. Hermann, "Settlements," 510.

could be convinced to accept this, take the lead even, his problems with the evangelical reformers of Germany would be eased (as would his diplomatic problems with France). As the Archduke of Austria and as Duke of Burgundy the theories explored by Protestants on the relationship between the magistrates and the church may have been quite useful and interesting, but as King of Spain he recognized that papal supremacy worked to his benefit and to the benefit of the local church and, therefore, he was never fully convinced of the royal supremacy argument, of Luther's *two kingdoms* doctrine, or of Calvin's pseudo-theocracy. Officially, in many ways, the *de iure* Roman primacy and *de facto* autonomy of the Spanish Church was maintained but, practically, the institution was subject to royal domination as much as it was in France or post-supremacy England. This can be illustrated in two ways—*via* the unique taxation arrangements for the church and *via* prosopographical comparisons of episcopal benches.

In Aragon, the clergy were not exempted from normal taxation; in Castile, however, the clergy were exempt (at least to direct taxation). Although not uncommon in pre-Reformation Europe, in Castile clerical tax exemption was supported by the crown as a series of special arrangements with the popes had secured other special financial concessions. Special taxes—like the *cruzada* (clearly intended to support the *Reconquista*)—became permanent over the course of the late mediaeval and early modern periods (making about a third of clerical income subject to crown extraction at any time). Another cooperative effort had been the spread of royal patronage over the church through the assumption of the Grandmasterships of quasi-military religious orders—that is, the crusader orders of Santiago, Calatrava, and Alcántara. By assuming control of the leadership, Ferdinand opened up the land-holdings and treasuries of the orders' to crown administration through a dedicated *Council of the military orders* (created in 1489). Moreover, it was mentioned that from 1523 the crown gained nomination rights to all bishoprics, and the right to collect income from all vacant sees (practices which existed in France and England). This had been granted to Carlos by Adrian VI (somewhat in reflection of the *Concordat of Bologna* agreed with Francis I).

What this means is that, as in France, the right of election and appointment of bishops had finally passed completely from the Cathedral chapters to negotiated cooperation between pope and king, finally to the crown itself. We noted earlier that the crown sought to achieve not only the moral and educational improvement of the bishops (and through them the entire clerical establishment) but also to formalize episcopal power (later reflected in Tridentine decrees). It is the case that long periods of vacancy resulted due to the political realities of a ruler with widespread realms, but the evidence informs us that Carlos still pursued an ideal in Spain (if not in Germany or the Low Countries). The episcopate that slowly emerged under the first Habsburg king can be positively described as a professional body—university educated, experienced bureaucrats and administrators, men of proven ability rather than the family-obsessed noble dilettantes of the past. Carlos was aided in his efforts first by the creation of the *cámara de Castilla* (a court meant to rationalize and normalize the nominations procedure) and by the deaths of so many of the old guard in the first few years of his reign. He also learned quickly what the Spanish spiritual mission meant, as his early appointments—Flemish and Italian courtier types—raised popular discontent and became one of the underlying causes of the *comunero* revolt.

Carlos altered his nomination practices after the revolt was put down and, with the papal bull of 1523 in hand, turned initially to the career-minded cadre of second and third sons of the nobility (family advancement were less an issue for men who were churchmen first). By the 1530s, as the Inquisition was trying to shut out all foreign influences, the nobility came under increasing focus (through the blood purity laws) and the king turned increasingly to the *dons* (i.e., to men representative of the emerging professional, non-noble, middle classes) and such men came to dominate his appointments.[51] It is not exactly the case that local chapters were completely removed from the picture and, indeed, the chapters were still able to maintain a fair degree of autonomy from episcopal control (even in the age of Trent), particularly over the now regular collection of the *"Tres Gracias"*—those contributions to the royal treasury known as the *cruzado*, the *subsidio* and the *excusado*. The king was recognized in all the kingdoms as the defender of the church and of orthodoxy, the crown held the patronage of all royal chapels, monasteries, and convents (reformed to restrict the authority of foreign superiors), collegiate churches, hospitals, and special parishes—but compromise was sometimes still the order of the day.[52]

By mid-sixteenth-century the Spanish took it for granted that (to paraphrase Roger Lockyer) *what was right for Spain was right for Christendom*. There was really no need to doubt that this was the case. Compared to the empire or the Netherlands, his Spanish territories had given Carlos I/Charles V little cause for complaint (spiritually speaking) over

---

51. Rawlings, "The Secularisation of Castilian Episcopal Office," 56, 60–61.
52. Hermann, "Settlements," 511, 517–8; Perrone, *Charles V*, 17, 24.

years in which Germany had been rocked by religious warfare, schism, radical sectarianism, and the threat of Islamic invasion. Indeed, when Philip succeeded his father (16 January 1556) it appeared to be the case that Spain was a perfect Catholic nation (unlike France with its massive heretic population). The Inquisition had been so successful over the years, tireless in their work, that the *conversos* issue had been reduced practically to nothing at all. It had also been so long between infamous heresy cases that the Spanish Church could afford a liberal phase. It may be the case, as Henry Kamen speculated, that success had led the Church, the country, and the emperor into a kind of complacency out of which they needed to be shocked, and the shock came in 1557–8.

It is commonly acknowledged by historians that pre-1560 Protestant heresy *per se* was never really much of an issue in Spain. There was a small assortment of Karlstadtian spiritualists known as *Illuminists*. Never greater than forty in number, these were purists advocating a salvation theory of complete personal surrender to God in the pursuit of mystical union with the Holy Spirit. They emphasized meditation and interior piety at the expense of common external ceremonial practices. It has been said that a number of *new Christians* became interested in *Illuminism* as well, looking perhaps for some deeper spiritual meaning outside the formal structures of their adopted faith. Although these few never aimed at undermining or replacing Catholicism, or papal authority, or even the material church, still they were all but wiped out by the Inquisition in the early 1530s as a precaution. Detailed investigations have not revealed what the supposed threat was, however, but have revealed lose connections to a much more sophisticated religious practice based on Erasmus-inspired humanism, which also had an extensive spiritual element and which also de-emphasized external practices.

While Erasmus and his many books were popular and enjoyed in Spain, in the 1520s a connection was being made by doctrinaire conservatives between he and Luther (particularly in the exposure of the weak theology behind many ceremonies and their criticisms of materialism and the monastic life). Sir John Elliot noted that despite the patronage of the emperor and the inquisitor-general, a writer who brought derision on monastic institutions and the practices of friars would hardly be endearing to an organization dominated by monks and friars. And, frankly, Erasmus was a foreigner, and the Spanish spiritual mission had little truck with foreign influences. Erasmus-inspired humanism became connected to *Illuminism* and

Lutheranism and was therefore targeted (not forcefully, however, at least before Charles V left Spain for Germany in 1529).[53] From that point inquisitors and religious conservatives searched out instances of Lutheranism—by which they understood any and all unorthodox practices. As the Inquisition had oversight of both domestic book production and the importation of foreign books, little beyond the occasional bundle of heretical works seized in a port town evinced a heterodox audience. Indeed, with the release of an *Index of forbidden books* in 1551, inquisitorial practices had been firmed up and normalized considerably. This may explain how at the very start of the new reign, new Lutheran cells were uncovered.

Elliot provides a useful snapshot of the religious climate in Europe at the time of Philip's succession in 1556. The Inquisition was under the leadership of Fernando de Valdés (described as stern) whose standing had been somewhat on the wane since his appointment in 1547. The court was a victim of its own success; it had little to do but Valdés was determined to close the gates against Protestantism as well as raise the Inquisition's standing with the new king. In Europe, a more dogmatic form of Protestantism had grown up around Calvin in Geneva, which all but eliminated the possibility of reconciliation with Rome. In Rome, of course, the pope was nurturing the revitalization of Catholicism's own dogmas with Trent and with the policing force known as the Jesuits. Valdés's vigilance led to the discoveries of small cells of "Lutherans" and their supporters in Seville and Valladolid, and this gave him the means to an end.

The cells have been characterized as remnant *Illuminists* and "humanist" circles, but it was troubling for religious conservatives that they included court figures among their wider contacts, men like the emperor's former confessor and his favourite preacher. A shocked Charles, from his retreat, urged the regent (his daughter Juana) to deal forcefully with them. The Inquisition swept in and arrested all those involved and the regent promulgated a new publications censorship law and a new *Index of forbidden books* was assembled, followed by a series of *autos de fe*. Valdés took this new attention to heart and arrested the Archbishop of Toledo as well, Bartolomé Carranza, the primate of Castile. Carranza had been only a year earlier Philip's personal chaplain and had only recently returned to Spain to take up his new duties as primate. It seems that his personality and closeness with the new king clashed with Valdés's sensibilities and ambitions and, on the pretence of suspicions of heresy hidden in his new *Catechism* (recently published in Antwerp), Carranza was accused and taken into custody.

---

53. Coleman, "Spain," 300–301; Elliot, *Imperial Spain*, 213–15.

Valdés augmented the arrest with unusually spectacular *autos de fe* in Toledo, Seville and Valladolid (breaking with tradition) including a series of sermons, Masses, processions, abjurations, and finally burnings before several thousand spectators. Philip attended some of these as soon as he arrived in the country in an effort to emphasis his power and ultimate authority over ecclesiastical discipline (as if all this was done on his orders). He found in Valdés a willing servant and the inquisitor-general found in the king a man mostly willing to listen to his concerns and charges.[54] Clearly, Philip could not have been unaware of the build-up of more militant religious expressions and their impact. He was kept abreast of events in the England of his wife, Mary Tudor, and of events in the France of Henri II. Philip knew that violence and schism were only avoided with firm repression of unorthodoxy and he upheld the work of the Inquisition thereby. The repression, according to Kamen, was still not all that harsh—even with the index and inquisitional oversights Erasmus was still bought and read and the book trade flourished—even anti-*converso* sentiment was diminishing. Philip tried to navigate a middle course. He refused to step in and protect Carranza from the Inquisition but he also resisted Valdés's calls for an expansion of the court's remit. Philip pinned his hopes on the Tridentine regeneration of Catholicism, which he sought to popularize and re-characterise for Spain *via* tried and true methods.

Castilian and Aragonese rulers acknowledged the pope as the spiritual leader of the universal Catholic community. Philip did likewise but, as the lay protector of the Spanish Church and faith he considered himself free to disregard papal decrees not to his liking within his own realms. Philip, fully in command of the Spanish and territorial churches, acknowledged the pope but focussed on spiritual regeneration, unburdened by any need for compromise. His bishops and cardinals reflected his stance. While French and Imperial cardinals demanded Tridentine accommodation with the Protestants, Philippine spokesmen effectively blocked all attempts to do so. As a result Philip approved the council's doctrinal and disciplinary reforms, implementing them wholesale in his Spain territories.[55] Moreover, he summoned local councils to amend and apply the Tridentine decrees while pursuing a number of anti-heresy initiatives.

---

54. Kamen, *Philip of Spain*, 79–80.
55. Lockyer, *Habsburg and Bourbon Europe*, 281.

According to Patrick Williams the connections between Philip, Spain, and the Council of Trent were many and varied over the course of the council. This tells us quite a lot about the role of temporal authority and the Church in Habsburg Spain. For example, over the course of the council more than 1000 Spanish clerics had been involved in its work (along with diplomats, scholars and observers) and these enthusiastic churchmen returned to Spain determined to implement the canons and reforms (particularly those which more firmly defined doctrine and practices like education reform). The Spanish position had been "parity among bishops" (including the Bishop of Rome) as a necessary first step along the path to regionalisation and localism (a stance ultimately rejected). However, Spanish attendees did encourage the idea that bishops lead national reform movements from the heart of their own dioceses, heading new disciplinary efforts and reforming education practices. The Tridentine canons were published in Spain on the king's authority (July 1564), but with the caveat that implementation depended on the safeguarding of crown privileges—the power of interpreting the decrees had been reserved to the king. It is telling that the canons more or less validated and embodied Spanish qualifications of moral and educational standing, residency, regular preaching, and visitation practices (embodying and thus defusing Protestant positions on the work of the deacon/pastor/elder.[56] Philip recognized the key role played by the bishops in reform and governance of the Church and was determined to direct their efforts himself. He was particularly meticulous with regard to nominations and appointments (at home and in the Spanish empire), and his preference for theologians over canon lawyers gives us insight into his Reformation strategy—the prosopographical evidence referred to earlier.

Over the course of his reign Philip nominated 127 men to 172 episcopal positions in the Castilian church alone, all of them meeting the stated standard of education, judgement, reputation, pure-bloodedness, and morality, most of whom were also "new men" (that is, of the emerging urban professional classes) with career experience of service to the crown or the Inquisition or participation at Trent. Most appointments also came only after a lengthy and detailed consultation process. It was the king's purpose to match the qualities of the candidates to the specific needs of the vacant diocese, regardless of wealth or status. Thus, the generally low-income, peripheral, coastal, or mountainous sees of Castile were seeded with devoted pastoral shepherds while men with legal or theological expertise were posted to larger cosmopolitan sees. Philip began to look at promotions and translations less as an opportunity to reword loyal servants and more

---

56. Rawlings, "The Secularisation of Castilian Episcopal Office," 65.

as an opportunity to enhance the realm's spiritual life. The evidence is that he preferred to promote from outside the established episcopate too, depending on the universities of Alcalà and Salamanca (and a few others) for candidates. In Spain the so-called *colegios mayores*—six universities of Castile and Aragon—collectively played a Paris-like role in the guardianship of religious standards and theological orthodoxy. In any case, not only were Philip's bishops selected from among the best candidates Spain had to offer, they also took up the *regalist* banner (obviously owing their advancements to the king and wishing to keep his patronage). The king also had Carlos I's *cámara* in place through which mandatory annual financial updates from the bishops were available. Regular reports on the merits of the parish clergy gave Philip important intelligence into the who were ideal candidates for promotion.[57]

In turn, Philip's bishops (resident, single office holders) also promoted the decrees of Trent in the way that the king understood them. Local synods were mentioned earlier. These were held at Toledo, Granada, Salamanca, Zaragoza, Valencia and Tarragona, each one summoned by the king for the specific purpose implementing reform. Through these ideal subordinate ecclesiastical magistrates the entirety of Spanish religious life was legislated for, supervised, and controlled by the crown. From the codification of practices to the education of children, and from disciplinary norms to the surveying of church properties, Philip was in charge. The bishops would summon diocesan councils to implement the decrees of the provincial councils as well. Thus, for example, the Tridentine decree to found seminaries in every diocese was actually carried out in Spain with some seriousness, and twenty-one foundations were operational by 1600. This had the knock on effect of creating an influential, disciplined, and effective pastoral service.[58] Otherwise, with the canons being implemented, Philip picked up where his grandparents had left off and mounted the dissolution of failing monasteries (reminiscent of Henry VIII's scheme of the 1530s). By the last years of the century Philip was setting his hand toward making textual changes to the Spanish Mass. The *Hispano-papal* partnership of the fifteenth-century was still going strong at the start of the seventeenth and Philip had established a reform commission which included the inquisitor-general, royal confessors, and papal nuncios at Madrid.[59] By his death in 1598 the King of Spain directly oversaw spiritual reform, episcopal reform, and monastic reform, and practically determined

---

57. "The Secularisation of Castilian Episcopal Office," 56–57.
58. Williams, *Philip II*, 72–75.
59. Hermann, "Settlements," 497–98.

the religious life of every Christian from Madrid to Mexico and from Lisbon to Manilla well into the seventeenth century.

— § —

Concluding Remarks

Back in the introduction to this study I had made reference to a number of key scriptural quotations as illustration of biblical support for magisterial power. Matthew 22:21 says, "Render unto Caesar the things which are Caesar's, and unto God the things that are God's." Romans 13:1 says, "Let every soul be subject unto the higher powers. For there is no power but of God: the powers that be are ordained of God." In 1 Pet 2:13–14 it is written, "Submit yourselves to every ordinance of man for the Lord's sake: whether it be to the king, as supreme; Or unto governors, as unto them that are sent by him for the punishment of evildoers, and for the praise of them that do well." The clearest statement of all is 1 Pet 2:17, which advises to "Honour all men. Love the brotherhood. Fear God. Honour the king." There could be no doubt that the magistrate had a special role to play in the lives of Christians and, therefore, must have some influence over the Church. My purpose in this book was to illustrate what this influence was, and how strong it was featured in the works of both Protestant and Catholic reform programs. This effort was sometimes hampered and sometimes helped by the fact that in the late mediaeval and early modern periods it was extremely difficult to separate what was purely, to borrow from Luther, temporal power from that which was purely spiritual matter. Popes and prince-archbishops claimed temporal rule over vast political bodies while kings and princes and lesser civil magistrates manipulated the local church to their own ends. Over the course of these six chapters I have presented a means to understand why, Protestants in particular, saw the need to advance the power of the magistrate, and how changes evolved over the course of time *via* competing theologies and expectations. The papal-centric doctrine of universal supremacy gave way outside Rome to theories of conciliarism, divine right of kings, two-kingdom doctrine, crypto-theocracy (and outright theocracy), co-terminus cooperation, and royal supremacy as "more accurate" reflections of Scripture and sacred history. All of which forced the papacy into its own reform movement attempting either the re-capture of lost ground or accommodation with new Church/state polities.

It could be said that throughout the dynamic, doctrinal, and dogmatic eras of the Reformation of the sixteenth-century consideration of the influence of the magistrate on the Church and Church/state accommodations were the least spiritually significant of five key themes generally recognized by Reformation scholars (e.g., the sacraments, salvation theology, predestination theology, ecclesiology and the Church/state dynamic). In many ways, however, the last and the subject of this book generated more pure heat in debate and more ink was spilled in polemic dispute than the other categories (save salvation and the Eucharist). This being the case, a longer more detailed study was justified.

Over the course of the book there was also uncovered some very interesting continuities between the ancient, late mediaeval, and early modern thinking about the church and how it was to be overseen by a variety of temporal establishments (from emperors to mayors). As a result of the fluidity of European politics and due to the rise of particularism and nationalism, the temporal authorities came to dominate the external means of religion across the board. While this was theoretically explained, examined, and justified in different ways, it is surprising to note that the general tone of the accounts and rationalizations were very much alike in both developing Protestant and traditionally Catholic lands.

As with salvation and sacramental theology, some division was made between what was internal (and thereby out of man's own hands and sensual awareness) and what was external (and thereby less significant but more obvious to the senses and faculties). The latter was, however, recognized as necessary for the development and protection of the former but, provided the important principles of *sola scriptura* were recognized, it could be safely placed within the sphere of the temporal as that authority best placed to recognize and advance the needs of the particular location (e.g., those historical, cultural and socio-political factors which characterized the population). The result was a variety of justifications and theories which had in common the idea of the temporal authority as the defender of the spiritual and the spiritual as the supporter of the temporal, ranging from Luther's simple *two kingdoms* separation of authorities, to Zwingli's covenantal commonwealth, to Bucer's *co-terminus* view, to the variations on the royal supremacy theme of Tudor England and the Catholic nations of Spain and France. In all cases the spiritual authority was recognized as the means by which genuine salvation, sacramental and ecclesiological theologies were transferred to the people (in control of their interior lives) while the political authority preserved and defended and channelled that spiritual authority in ways relevant to the national characteristics of the people under its control. In rare cases (radical Protestant and modernizing Catholic), the power of the magistrate included the determination of scriptural truth and theological legitimacy. The relationship between the Church and the civil magistrates became so important (and such a dangerous association) that some modern states now maintain a forced separation of the two, an idea which was not available to the thinkers of the Reformation era.

Bibliography

Alexander, Gina. "Bonner and the Marian Persecutions." In *The English Reformation Revised*, edited by Christopher Haigh, 157–75. Cambridge: Cambridge University Press, 1987.

Allen, John W. *A History of Political Thought in the Sixteenth Century*. London: Rowman & Littlefield, 1977.

Almasy, Rudolph. "The Purpose of Richard Hooker's polemic." *JHI* 39 (1978) 251–70.

Ambrose: Select Works and Letters. NPNF2 x. http://www.fordham.edu/halsall/source/ambrose-let21.html.

Arffman, Kaarko. "The Lutheran Reformation of Poor Relief: A Historical and Legal Viewpoint." In *Lutheran Reformation and the Law*, edited by Virpi Mäkinen. Studies in Medieval and Reformation Traditions 112. Leiden: Brill, 2006.

Armstrong, Alastair. *The European Reformation 1500–1610*. Oxford: Heinemann, 2002.

Athanasius: Select Works and Letters. NPNF2, iv].

Augsburg Confession. http://www.reformedited.org/documents/index.html.

Augustijn, Cornelis. *Erasmus: His Life, Works and Influence*. Translated by J. C. Grayson, 43–55. Toronto: University of Toronto Press, 1991.

Augustine. *The Retractions*. Translated by M. Inez Bogan, 226–7. Washington, DC: Catholic University of America Press, 1968, 226–7.

Baird, Henry M. *Theodore Beza: The Counsellor of the French Reformation, 1519–1605*. New York: Putnam, 1899.

Baker, J. Wayne. "Church Discipline or Civil Punishment: On the Origins of the Reformed Schism 1528–1531." *Andrews University Seminary Studies* 23 (1985) 3–18.

———. "Church, State, and Dissent: The Crisis of the Swiss Reformation, 1531–1536." In *The Reformation: Critical Concepts in Historical Studies*, edited by Andrew Pettegree, 312–29. London: Routledge, 2004.

———. "Retrospective: Bullinger, the Covenant, & Reformed Tradition." *SCJ* 39 (1998) 359–76.

Baker, Sue. *Protestantism, Poetry and Protest: The Vernacular Writings of Antoinne de Chandieu c. 1534– 1591*. St. Andrews Studies in Reformation History. Farnham, UK: Ashgate, 2009.

Baldwin, Summerfield. "Jean Bodin and the League." *Catholic Historical Review* 23 (1937) 160–84.

Barnes, Robert. "A Supplicatyon Made by Robert Barnes Doctoure in Diuinite / Vnto the Most Excellent and Redoubted Prince Kinge Henrye the Eyght [1531]." In *A Critical Edition of Robert Barnes's A Supplication Vnto the Most Gracyous Prince Kynge Henry The VIII. 1534*, edited by Douglas H Parker, 486–696. Toronto: University of Toronto Press, 2008.

Baumgartner, Frederick J. *France in the Sixteenth Century*. London: McMillan, 1995.

———. "Henry II's Italian Bishops: A Study in the Use and Abuse of the Concordat of Bologna." *SCJ* 11/2 (1980) 49–58.

Baylor, Michael G. "Thomas Muntzer's First Publication." *SCJ* 17/4 (1986) 451–58.

Bedouelle, Guy. "The Consultation of the Universities and Scholars Concerning the "Great Matter" of Henry VIII." Translated by John L Farthing. In *The Bible in the Sixteenth Century*, edited by David C Steinmetz, 21–36. Durham: Duke University Press, 1990.

Beer, Barrett L. "John Ponet's Shorte Treatise of Politike Power Reassessed." *SCJ* 21 (1990), 373–84.

Bender, Harold S. "The Anabaptist Vision." In *The Recovery of the Anabaptist Vision*, edited by Guy F. Hershberger, 29–56. Waterloo, ON: Herald, 1957.

Bente, Friedrich. *Historical Introductions to the Symbolical Books of the Evangelical Lutheran Church*. Teddington, UK: Echo Library, 2008.

Beza, Theodore. *Confession du foi Chretien*. In *The Christian Faith*. Translated by James Clark, 68–117. Lewes: Focus Christian Ministries Trust, 1992.

———. *De haereticis a civili magistratu puniendis*. Geneva, 1554.

———. *De haereticis a civili magistratu puniendis*. In *Tractationes theologicae*, 1:85–169. 3 vols. Geneva, 1582.

———. "Right of Magistrates." In *Constitutionalism and Resistance in the Sixteenth Century: Three Treatises by Hotman, Beza and Mornay*, edited and translated by Julian H Franklin, 91–135. New York: Pegasus, 1969.

Bickenhotz, Peter G. *Encounters with a Radical Erasmus*. Toronto: University of Toronto Press, 2009.

Birnbaum, Norman. "The Zwinglian Reformation in Zurich." *Past and Present* 15 (1959) 27–47.

BL, Add. MSS., *48012*, fol. 22.

BL, Cott. MSS. Vit. B ii, fol. 22.

BL, Cott. MSS. Vit. B iii, fol. 122v

Bodin, Jean. *The Six Bookes of a Commonweale*. Edited by Kenneth Douglas McRae. Cambridge: Harvard University Press, 1962.

Bonney, Richard. "Bodin and the Development of the French Monarchy." *TRHS*, 5th ser., 40 (1990) 43–61.

Bornkamm, Heinrich. *Luther in Mid-career, 1521–1530*. Edited and with a foreword by Karin Bornkamm. Translated by E. Theodore Bachmann. Philadelphia: Fortress, 1983.

Bouwsma, William J. *John Calvin: A Sixteenth-Century Portrait*. Oxford: Oxford University Press, 1989.

Bradstock, Andrew. *Faith in the Revolution: The Political Theologies of Müntzer and Winstanley*. London: SPCK, 1997.

Brook, B. *Memoir of the Life and Writings of Thomas Cartwright, B.D.* London: Snow, 1845.

Bucer, Martin. "De Regno Christi [On the kingdom of Christ]." In *Melanchthon and Bucer*, edited by Wilhelm Pauck, 155-394. London: SCM, 1969.
Bullinger, Heinrich. "Answers Given to a Certain Scotsman." In *Knox*, 3:217-26.
———. *The Decades of Henry Bullinger*. 5 vols. Translated by H. I. Edited by Thomas Harding. Parker Society Publication 8. Cambridge: Cambridge University Press, 1849.
———. "The One and Eternal Testament or Covenant of God Zurich, 1534." In *Fountainhead of Federalism: Heinrich Bullinger and the Covenantal Tradition*, translated and edited by Charles M. McCoy and J. Wayne Baker, 99-138.. Louisville: Westminster John Knox, 1991.
Butterworth, C. C. *The English Primers, 1529-45*. Philadelphia: University of Pennsylvania Press, 1953.
Calvin, John. "Articles Concerning the Organization of the Church and of Worship at Geneva." In *Treatises*, 47-55.
———. *Institutes of the Christian Religion: The First English Version of the 1541 French Edition*. Translated by Elsie Anne McKee. Grand Rapids: Eerdmans, 2009.
———. "On Civil Government." In *Luther and Calvin on Secular Authority*, edited by Harro Höpfl, 47-86. Cambridge Texts in the History of Political Thought. Cambridge: Cambridge University Press, 1991.
Calvin, John. and William Farel. "The Genevan Confession." In *Treatises*, 25-33.
Cameron, Euan. *The European Reformation*. Oxford: Oxford University Press, 1991.
Carroll, Stuart. *Noble Power during the French Wars of Religion*. Cambridge Studies in Early Modern History. Cambridge: Cambridge University Press, 1998.
Cartwright, Thomas. *A Replye to an Ansvvere Made of M. Doctor Whitgifte against the Admonition to the Parliament*. London: Stroud, 1573.
Chibi, Andrew Allen. "'Had I but served God with half the zeal . . .': The Career Path of the Men Who Became Henry VIII's Bishops." *Reformation* 3 (1998) 75-136.
———. *Henry VIII's Conservative Scholar: Bishop John Stokesley and the Divorce, Royal Supremacy and Doctrinal Reform*. Bern: Lang, 1997.
———. "The Interpretation and Use of Moral and Natural Law in Henry VIII's First Divorce Crisis." *AfR* 85 (1994) 265-86.
———. "State v Church: Implementing Reformation Cromwell, Stokesley and London Diocese." *Journal of Church and State* 41 (1999) 77-98.
———. "*Turpitudinem uxoris fratris tui non revelavit*: John Stokesley and the Divorce Question." *SCJ* 25 (1994) 387-97.
———. *The Wheat and the Tares: Doctrines of the Church in the Reformation, 1500-1590*. Eugene, OR: Pickwick Publications, 2015.
Christin, Olivier. "Making Peace." In *Companion*, 426-39.
Close, Christopher W. *The Negotiated Reformation: Imperial Cities and the Politics of Urban Reform, 1525-1550*. Cambridge: Cambridge University Press, 2009.
Coleman, David. "Spain." In *The Reformation World*, edited by Andrew Pettegree, 296-308. London: Routledge, 2000.
Collinson, Patrick. *The Elizabethan Puritan Movement*. London: Cape, 1967.
"Concordat of Bologna between Pope Leo X and Francis I, King of France, August 18, 1516." In *Church and State through the Centuries*, edited by Sidney Z. Ehler and John B. Morrall, 134-44. New York: Biblo & Tannen, 1988
Confessions and Catechisms of the Reformation, edited by Mark A. Noll. Vancouver, BC: Regent College Publishing, 2004.

Cooper, J. P. D., *Propaganda and the Tudor State: Political Culture in the West Country.* Oxford: Oxford University Press, 2003.

"Council of Basel: Deposition of Pope Eugenius IV, July 7, 1439." In *Church and State through the Centuries*, edited by Sidney Z. Ehler and John B. Morrall, 121–25. New York: Biblo & Tannen, 1988.

Coy, Jason P. *Strangers and Misfits: Banishment, Social Control, and Authority in Early Modern Germany.* Studies in Central European Histories 47. Leiden: Brill, 2008.

Cranmer, Thomas. "An Exhortation concerning Good Order and Obedience to Rulers and Magistrates." http://www.anglicanlibrary.org/homilies/bk1hom10.htm.

———. "An Exhortation Concerning Good Order and Obedience to Rulers and Magistrates." In *Certain Sermons or Homilies Appointed to Be Read in Churches in the Time of the Late Queen Elizabeth*, 95–108. Oxford: Oxford University Press 1844.

Crofts, Richard A. Coleman, David. "Spain." In *The Reformation World*, edited by Andrew Pettegree, 296–308. London: Routledge, 2000.

Danner, Dan G. "Christopher Goodman and the English Protestant Tradition of Civil Disobedience." *SCJ* 8/3 (1977) 60–73.

———. "Resistance and the Ungodly Magistrate in the Sixteenth Century: The Marian Exiles." *Journal of the American Academy of Religion* 49 (1981) 471–81.

Davies, Catherine. *A Religion of the Word: The Defence of the Reformation in the Reign of Edward VI.* Manchester: Manchester University Press, 2002.

Denck, Hans. "Concerning True Love (1527)." In *Outline*, 249–50.

Deppermann, Klaus. *Melchior Hoffman: Social Unrest and Apocalyptic Visions in the Age of the Reformation.* Edinburgh: T. & T. Clark, 1987.

Dickens, A. G., and Whitney R. D. Jones. *Erasmus the Reformer.* London: Methuen, 1994.

The Divorce Tracts of Henry VIII. Edited by Edward Surtz and Virginia Murphy. Angers: Moreana, 1988.

Dixon, C. Scott. "The Politics of Law and Gospel: The Protestant Prince and the Holy Roman Empire." In *The Impact of the European Reformation: Princes, Clergy and People*, edited by Bridget Heal and Ole Peter Grell, 37–62. St. Andrews Studies in Reformation History. Aldershot, UK: Ashgate, 2008.

———. *Protestants: A History from Wittenberg to Pennsylvania, 1517–1740.* Oxford: Wiley-Blackwell, 2010.

Dodds, Gregory D. *Exploiting Erasmus: The Erasmian Legacy and Religious Change in Early Modern Europe.* Toronto: University of Toronto Press, 2009.

Doran, Susan. *Elizabeth I and Religion 1558–1603.* Lancaster Pamphlets. London: Routledge, 1994.

Ebeling, Gerhard. *Luther: An Introduction to His Thought.* Philadelphia: Fortress, 1970.

Edelstein, Marilyn M. "Foreign Episcopal Appointments during the Reign of Francis I." *Church History* 44 (1975) 450–59.

Edward VI. *The Chronicle and Political Papers of Edward VI.* Edited by W. K. Jordan. London: Allen & Unwin, 1966.

———. "Discourse on the Reform of Abuses in Church and State [April? 1551]" In *The Chronicle and Political Papers of Edward VI*, edited by W. K. Jordan, 159–67. London: Allen & Unwin, 1966.

Eells, Hastings. "The contributions of Martin Bucer to the Reformation." *HTR* 24 (1931) 29–42.

Ella, George M. *Henry Bullinger: Shepherd of the Churches*. Eggleston: Go Publications, 2007.
Elliot, J. H. *Imperial Spain, 1469–1716*. Harmondsworth, UK: Penguin, 1963.
———. *Imperial Spain, 1469–1716*. London: Penguin, 1970.
Elton, G. R. *Reform and Renewal: Thomas Cromwell and the Common Weal*. The Wiles Lectures 1972. Cambridge: Cambridge University Press, 1973.
———. "The Reformation in England." In *Elton*, 226–50.
———. *Tudor Constitution*. Cambridge: Cambridge University Press, 1960.
Eno, Adolf. *Subjects or Citizens? The Mennonite Experience in Canada, 1870–1925*. Ottawa: University of Ottawa Press, 1994.
Eppley, Daniel. "Royal Supremacy." In *Companion*, 503–35.
———. *Defending Royal Supremacy and Discerning God's Will in Tudor England*. St. Andrews Studies in Reformation History. Aldershot, UK: Ashgate, 2007.
Erasmus. "Adages III iv 1 to IV ii 100." In *CWE* 35. Translated by Davis L. Drysdale. Edited by John N. Grant. Toronto: University of Toronto Press, 2005.
———. *The "Adages" of Erasmus: A Study with Translations*. Translated by Margaret Mann Phillips. Cambridge: Cambridge University Press, 1964.
———. *The Complaint of Peace*. Boston: Williams, 1813.
———. "Handbook of the Christian Soldier." In *EE*, 24–93.
———. "Julius Excluded from Heaven." In *Life and Letters of Erasmus*, edited by James Anthony Froude, 156–74. London: Longman, Green, 1899.
———. "Julius Excluded from Heaven." In *Praise of Folly and Other Writings*. Translated by Robert M. Adams, 142–73. New York: Norton, 1989. http://triablogue.blogspot.com/2007/01/julius-excluded-from-heaven.html.
———. "Paraphrase on Luke 11–24." In *CWE* xlviii. Translated by Jane E. Phillips. Toronto: University of Toronto Press, 2003.
———. "Paraphrase on Mark." In *CWE* xlix. Translated by Erika Rummel. Toronto: University of Toronto Press, 1998.
———. *Praise of Folly*, edited by John Wilson. Rockville, Maryland: Arc Manor, 2008.
———. *Praise of Folly*. In *EE*, 94–173. http://smith2.sewanee.edu/erasmus/pof.html.
———. *Praise of Folly*. In *Praise of Folly and Letter to Martin Dorp 1515*. Translated by Betty Radice, 55–208. London: Penguin, 1971
Estes, James Martin. *Peace, Order and the Glory of God: Secular Authority and the Church in the Thought of Luther and Melanchthon*. Studies in Medieval and Reformation Traditions 111. Leiden: Brill, 2005.
———. "The Role of Godly Magistrates in the Church: Melanchthon as Luther's Interpreter and Collaborator." *Church History* 67 (1998) 463–83.
Eusebius: Church History, Life of Constantine the Great, & Oration in Praise of Constantine. NPNF2, 1. http://www.fordham.edu/halsall/basis/vita-constantine.html.
Ferdinand and Isabella. "Letter of Commission to Carry out Inquiries into Bad Christians." In *Early Modern Spain: A Documentary History*, edited by Jon Cowans, 10–12. Philadelphia: University of Pennsylvania Press, 2003.
Fields, John, and Thomas Wilcox. "Admonition to the Parliament." In *Puritan Manifestos*, edited by W. H. Frere and C. E. Douglas, 1–40. London: SPCK, 1907.
Fingers, Thomas N. *A Contemporary Anabaptist Theology: Biblical, Historical, Constructive*. Downers Grove, IL: InterVarsity, 2004.
"The First Helvetic confession of 1536." In *Cochrane*, 97–111.

Ford, Franklin L. "Dimensions of Toleration: Castello, Bodin, Montaigne." *Proceedings of the American Philosophical Society* 116/2 (1972) 136–39.
Foster, Herbert Darling. "Calvin's Programme for a Puritan State in Geneva, 1536–41." *HTR* 1 (1908) 391–434.
Friedman, Jerome. "Jewish Conversion, the Spanish Pure Blood Laws and Reformation: A Revisionist View of Racial and Religious Anti-Semitism." *SCJ* 18/1 (1987) 3–30.
Freudenberg, Matthias. "Catechisms." Translated by Judith J Guder. In *The Calvin Handbook*, edited by Herman J Selderhaus. Grand Rapids: Eerdmans, 2008.
Gardiner, Stephen. "The Oration of True Obedience." In *Obedience in Church and State: Three Political Tracts by Stephen Gardiner*, edited and translated by Pierre Janelle, 68–171. Cambridge: Cambridge University Press, 1930.
Glasse of Truthe. London, 1531 [STC 11919]
"Glasse of Truthe." In *Pocock*, ii, 385–421.
"A Godly Primer in English, Newly Corrected and Printed." In *Three Primers Put Forth in the Reign of Henry VIII*, 1–303. Oxford: Oxford University Press, 1834.
Goertz, Hans-Jurgen. "Karlstadt, Muntzer and the Reformation of the Commoners, 1521–1525." In *A Companion to Anabaptism and Spiritualism 1521–1700*, edited by John D. Roth and James N. Stayer, 7–44. Brill's Companion to the Christian Tradition 6. Leiden: Brill, 2007.
———. "Radical Religiosity in the German Reformation." In *Companion*, 70–85.
Goodman, Christopher. *How Superior Powers Ought to Be Obeyed of Their Subjects, and Wherein They May Lawfully Be by God's Word Disobeyed and Resisted*. Geneva: Crispin, 1558.
———. *How Superior Powers Ought to Be Obeyed of Their Subjects, and Wherein They May Lawfully Be by God's Word Disobeyed and Resisted*, edited by Patrick S. Poole. http://www.constitution.org/cmt/goodman/obeyEditedhtm#chap4.
Gordon, Bruce. *The Swiss Reformation*. Manchester: Manchester University Press, 2003.
Graham, Michael F. *The Uses of Reform: "Godly Discipline" and Popular Behaviour in Scotland and Beyond, 1560–1610*. Studies in Medieval and Reformation Thought 58. Leiden: Brill, 1996.
Greaves, Richard L. "Concepts of Political Obedience in Late Tudor England: Conflicting Perspectives." *JBS* 22 (1982) 23–34.
Green, V. H. H. *Renaissance and Reformation: A Survey of European History between 1450 and 1660*. London: Arnold, 1952.
Greengrass, Mark. *The Longman Companion to the European Reformation c.1500–1618*. London: Longman, 1998.
Greschat, Martin. "The Relation between Church and Civil Community in Bucer's Reforming Work." In *Martin Bucer*, 17–31.
Gritsch, Eric W. *A Tragedy of Errors: Thomas Müntzer*. Minneapolis: Fortress, 1989.
Haas, Steven W. "Henry VIII's Glasse of Truthe." *History* 64/212 (1979) 353–62.
———. "Martin Luther's "Divine Right" Kingship and the Royal Supremacy: Two Tracts from the 1531 Parliament and Convocation of the Clergy." *JEH* 31 (1980) 317–25.
Haigh, Christopher. *English Reformations: Religion, Politics, and Society under the Tudors*. Oxford: Oxford University Press, 1993.
Haight, Roger. *Christian Community in History*. 2 vols. London: Continuum, 2005.
Hall, David W. *Genevan Reformation and the American Founding*. Oxford: Lexington Books, 2003.

Harder, Leland, ed. *The Sources of Swiss Anabaptism: The Grebel Letters and Related Documents*. Classics of the Radical Reformation 4. Kitchener, ON: Herald, 1985.

Harrison, William H. "The Church." In *A Companion to Richard Hooker*, edited by Torrance Kirkby, 305–37. Brill's Companion to the Christian Tradition 8. Leiden: Brill, 2008.

Hegenwald, Erhart. "Acts of the Convention Held in the Praiseworthy City of Zurich on the 29th day of January, an account of the Holy Gospel—being a disputation between the dignified and honourable representative from Constance and Huldrych Zwingli, preacher of the Gospel of Christ, together with the common clergy of the whole territory of the aforesaid city of Zurich, held before the assembled council in the year 1523." Edited by Ulrich Zwingli. In *Selected Works of Huldreich Zwingli 1484–1531 The Reformer of German Switzerland*, edited by Samuel M Jackson, 40–117. Philadelphia: University of Pennsylvania Press, 1901.

Hermann, Christian. "Settlements: Spain's National Catholicism." In *Handbook*, ii, 491–522.

Hill, W Speed. "Hooker's 'Polity': The Problem of the "Last Three Books."" *Huntington Library Quarterly* 34 (1971) 317–36.

Hillerbrand, Hans J. "Andreas Bodenstein of Carlstadt, Prodigal Reformer." *Church History* 35 (1966) 379–98.

Holborn, Hajo. *A History of Modern Germany: The Reformation*. London: Eyre & Spottiswoode, 1965.

Holt, Mack P. *The French Wars of Religion, 1562–1629*. New Approaches to European History 36. Cambridge: Cambridge University Press, 2005.

Hooker, Richard. "The Laws of Ecclesiastical Polity." In *The Works of That Learned and Judicious Divine, Mr. Richard Hooker: With an Account of His Life and Death by Isaac Walton*. Vol. 1. Edited by John Keble. 3 vols. Oxford: Clarendon, 1876. http://anglican history.org/hooker/.

———. "The Laws of Ecclesiastical Polity." In *The Works of That Learned and Judicious Divine, Mr. Richard Hooker: With an Account of His Life and Death by Isaac Walton*, edited by John Keble, vol. 1. 3 vols. Oxford: Oxford University Press. 1845.

Hooper, John. "A Declaration of the Ten Holy Commandments of Almighty God [1548]." In *Early Works of John Hooper*, 249–430. Cambridge: Cambridge University Press, 1843.

Höpfl, Harro. *The Christian Polity of John Calvin*. Cambridge Studies in the History and Theory of Politics. Cambridge: Cambridge University Press, 1982.

———, ed. *Luther and Calvin on Secular Authority*. Cambridge Texts in the History of Political Thought. Cambridge: Cambridge University Press, 1991.

Houde, Sigrun. "Anabaptism." In *The Reformation World*, edited by Andrew Pettegree, 237–56. London: Routledge, 2000.

Housley, Norman. *Religious Warfare in Europe, 1400–1536*. Oxford: Oxford University Press, 2002.

Hubmaier, Balthasar. "A Brief Apologia." In *Hubmaier*, 296–313.

———. "An Earnest Christian Appeal to Schaffhausen." In *Hubmaier*, 35–48.

———. "Eighteen Theses Concerning the Christian Life." In *Hubmaier*, 30–4.

———. "Heretics." In *Hubmaier*, 63–4.

———. "On the Sword." In *Hubmaier*, 492–523.

———. "Recantation at Zürich." In *Hubmaier*, 150–9.

———. "Statements at the Second Zurich Disputation." In *Hubmaier*, 21–9.

"The Institution of a Christian man." In *Formularies*, 21–211.

Issak, Helmut. "The Struggle for an Evangelical Town." In *The Dutch Dissenters: A Critical Companion to Their History and Ideas*, edited by Irvin Buckwalter Horst, 66–84. Kerkhistorische Bijdragen 13. Leiden: Brill, 1986.

Jaussen, Johannes. *History of the German People at the Close of the Middle Ages*, edited by A M Christie, 16 vols. London: Kegan, Paul, French, Trubner, 1906.

Jordan, W. K. ed. *The Chronicle and Political Papers of Edward VI*. London: Allen & Unwin, 1966.

Kamen, Henry. *Philip of Spain*. New Haven: Yale University Press, 1997.

———. *The Spanish Inquisition: An Historical Revision*. London: Weidenfeld & Nicolson, 1997.

Karkkainen, Veli–Matti. *An Introduction to Ecclesiology: Ecumenical, Historical & Global Perspectives*. Downers Grove, IL: InterVarsity, 2002.

Karlstadt, Andreas von. "On the Removal of Images and that There Should Be no Beggars among Christians." In *EC*, 100–128.

Keen, Ralph, and Philip Melanchthon. "Political Authority and Ecclesiology in Melanchthon's 'De Ecclesiae Authoritate.'" *Church History* 65 (1996) 1–14.

Korthals, James F. "The Seven Ecumenical Councils." General Pastors' Conference of the Evangelical Lutheran Synod. 1997. http://www.wlsessays.net/authors/K/kindex.html.

Kilsby, Jill. *Spain 1469–1598*. London: Hodder Education Group, 2015.

Kingdon, Robert M. "Calvinism and Democracy: Some Political Implications of Debates on French Reformed Church Government, 1562–1572." *AHR* 69 (1964) 393–401.

———. *Geneva and the Consolidation of the French Protestant Movement, 1564–1572: A Contribution to the History of Congregationalism, Presbyterianism and Calvinist Resistance Theory*. Travaux d'Humanisme et Renaissance 92. Geneva: Droz, 1967.

Klötzer, Rolf. "The Melchoirites and Münster." In *Companion*, 217–56.

Koenigsberger, H. G. et al. *Europe in the Sixteenth Century*. New York: Longman, 1989.

Knecht, R. J. "The Concordat of 1516: A Reassessment." In *Government in Reformation Europe, 1520–1560*, edited by Henry J. Cole, 91–112. London: Macmillan, 1971.

———. *Francis I*. Cambridge: Cambridge University Press, 1982.

Knox, John. "A Faithful Admonition to the Professors of God's Truth in England July 1554." In *Knox*, iii, 251–330.

———. "A Godly Letter of Warning or Admonition to the Faithful in London, Newcastle and Berwick 1554." In *Knox*, 3:157–215.

Knox, John. and Robert M Healey. "Waiting for Deborah: John Knox and Four Ruling Queens." *SCJ* 25 (1994) 371–86.

Kolb, Robert. *Bound Choice, Election, and Wittenberg Theological Method from Martin Luther to the Formula of Concord*. Grand Rapids: Eerdmans, 2005.

Kreider, Robert. "The Anabaptists and the Civil Authorities of Strasbourg, 1525–1555." *Church History* 24 (1955) 99–118.

Kroon, Marijn de. "Martin Bucer and the Problem of Tolerance." *SCJ* 19 (1988) 157–68.

Lane, Jan–Erik. *Constitutions and Political Theory*. Manchester: Manchester University Press. 1996.

Latimer, Hugh. "The First Sermon Preached before King Edward, March 2, 1549." In *Sermons*, 85–103.

———. "The Second Sermon of Master Hugh Latimer." In *Sermons*, 112–28.

———. "The Sixth Sermon Preached before King Edward." In *Sermons*, 194–215.
Lausten, Martin Schwarz. "Lutherus: Luther and the Princes." In *Seven-headed Luther: Essays in Commemoration of a Quincentenary, 1483–1983*, edited by Peter Newman Brooks, 51–76. Oxford: Clarendon, 1984.
Lea, Henry C. "The First Castilian inquisitor." *AHR* 1 (1895) 46–50.
Leroux, Neil R. "'In the Christian City of Wittenberg": Karlstadt's Tract on Images and Begging." *SCJ* 34/1 (2003) 73–105.
Levi, Anthony. *Renaissance and Reformation: The Intellectual Genesis*. New Haven: Yale University Press, 2002.
Lindberg, Carter. *Beyond Charity: Reformation Initiatives for the Poor*. Minneapolis: Augsburg, 1993.
———. *The European Reformation*. Oxford: Blackwell, 1996.
———. "'There Should Be no Beggars among Christians": Karlstadt, Luther and the Origins of Protestant Poor Relief." *Church History* 46 (1977) 313–34.
———. *The Third Reformation: Charismatic Movement and the Lutheran Tradition*. Macon GA: Mercer University Press, 1983.
Literae Cantuarienses. Edited by J B Sheppard, 3 vols. London: Eyre & Spottiswoode, 1889.
Littell, Franklin H. *The Anabaptist View of the Church*. Paris, AR: Baptists Standard Bearer, 2000.
Llobera, Joseph R. *The God of Modernity: The Development of Nationalism in Western Europe*. Oxford: Berg, 1994.
Lockwood, Shelley. "Marsilius of Padua and the Case for the Royal Ecclesiastical Supremacy." *TRHS*, 6th ser., 1 (1991) 89–119.
Lockyer, Roger. *Habsburg and Bourbon Europe 1470–1720*. London: Longman, 1974.
Lohse, Bernhard. *Martin Luther: An Introduction to His Life and Work*. Philadelphia: Fortress Press, 1986.
Luther, Martin. "Admonition to Peace: A Reply to the Twelve Articles of the Peasants in Swabia." Translated by Charles M. Jacobs, 5–43. In *AE* 46.
———. "Against the Robbing and Murdering Hordes of Peasants." In *AE*, 46:45–55.
———. "Babylonian Captivity of the Church." In *AE*, 36:3–126.
———. *Commentary on Romans*. Translated by J Theodore Mueller Kregel, 179–92. Grand Rapids: Kregel, 1976.
———. "The Estate of Marriage." In *AE*, 45:11–49.
———. "Explanation of the ninety-five theses." In *AE*, 31:79–252.
———. "An Exhortation to the Knights of the Teutonic Order That They Lay Aside False Chastity and Assume the True Chastity of wedlock." In *AE*, 45:131–58.
———. "On Marriage Matters." In *AE*, 46:259–320.
———. "An open letter on the harsh book against the peasants." In *AE*, 46:58–85.
———. *The papacy at Rome, an answer to the celebrated Romanist at Leipzig*. In *AE*, 39:55–104.
———. "The Papacy at Rome, An Answer to the Celebrated Romanist at Leipzig." In *Works*, edited by Theodore E. Schmauk, 1:255–301.
———. "Sermon on the Gospel in a Parable." In *The Sermons of Martin Luther*, edited and translated by John Nicholas Lenker, 5:19–20. Albany NY: Books for the Ages, 1997.
———. "Sermons." In *Works*, i/vi, 368–70. [AQ]
———. "Temporal Authority: To What Extent It Should Be Obeyed." In *AE*, 45:81–129.

———. "That Parents Should neither Compel nor Hinder the Marriage of Their Children and That Children Should not Become Engaged without Their Parents' Consent." In *AE*, 45:379–93.

———. "The Persons Related by Consanguinity and Affinity Who Are Forbidden to Marry according to the Scriptures, Leviticus 18." In *AE*, 45:5–9.

———. "To Cardinal Albrecht, October 31, 1517." In *AE*, 48:43–49.

———. "To George Spalatin, August 28, 1518." In *AE*, 48:73–76.

———. "To George Spalatin, May 31, 1520." In *AE*, 48:163–65.

———. "To John Hess, c. June 13, 1528." In *AE*, 49:196–99.

———. "To John Lang, January 26, 1520." In *AE*, 48:148–51.

———. "To John Rühel, May 4, 1525." In *AE*, 49:106–12.

———. "To John von Staupitz, May 30, 1518." In *AE*, 48:64–70.

———. "To the Christian Nobility." In *Three Treatises*. Translated by A. T. W. Steinäuser, 1–112. Philadelphia: Fortress, 1970.

———. "Whether Soldiers, too, Can Be Saved." In *AE*, 46:87–137.

———. "War against the Turk", in *AE*, 46:155–205.

Luther, Martin, and Philip Melanchthon, "To Elector John, May 1 or 2, 1528." In *AE*, 49:189–95.

———. "To Duke John Frederick, May 18, 1528." In *AE*, 49:195–96.

Luther, Martin et al. "To Elector John, September 6, 1525." In *AE*, 49:125–30.

Mabry, Eddie. *Balthasar Hubmaier's Doctrine of the Church*. Lanham, MD: University Press of America, 1994.

Macek, Ellen A. *The Loyal Opposition: Tudor Traditionalist Polemics, 1535–1558*. Studies in Church History 7. New York: Lang, 1996.

Mackenney, Richard. *Sixteenth Century Europe: Expansion and Conflict History of Europe*. London: Palgrave Macmillan, 1993.

Mann, Stephanie A. *Supremacy and Survival: How Catholics Endured the English Reformation*. New York: Scepter, 2007.

Marius, Richard. *Martin Luther: The Christian between God and Death*. Cambridge, MA: Belknap, 1999.

Marpeck, Pilgram. "Confession (1532)." In *Outline*, 251–2.

Marsilio of Padua. *Defensor Pacis*. http://www.fordham.edu/halsall/source/marsiglio4.html.

Mayer, Thomas. "On the Road to 1534: The Occupation of Tournai and Henry VIII's Theory of Sovereignty." In *Tudor Political Culture*, edited by Dale Hoak, 11–30. Cambridge: Cambridge University Press, 1995.

———. *Thomas Starkey and the Commonweal: Humanist Politics and Religion in the Reign of Henry VIII*. Cambridge Studies in Early Modern British History. Cambridge: Cambridge University Press, 1989.

McCoy, Charles S. and J. Wayne Baker. *Fountainhead of Federalism: Heinrich Bullinger and the Covenantal Tradition*. Louisville: Westminster John Knox, 1991.

McGiffert, Michael. "Covenant, Crown and Commons in Elizabethan Puritanism." *JBS* 20 (1980) 32–52.

McGrath, Alistair E. *The Intellectual Origins of the European Reformation*. Oxford: Blackwell, 1987.

———. *Reformation Thought: An Introduction*. Oxford: Blackwell, 1988.

Melanchthon, Philipp. *Didymi Faventini adversus Thomam Placentinum pro Martino Luthero theologo, Oratio*. Wittenberg, 1521.

———. "Letter no. 85." In *AE*, 48:256–63.
———. "Themes for the Sixth Holiday." In *Melanchthon: Selected Writings*. Translated by Charles Leander Hill. Edited by Elmer Ellsworth Flack and Lowell J. Satre, 89–92. Minneapolis: Augsburg, 1962.
Moots, Glenn A. *Politics Reformed: The Anglo-American Legacy of Covenant Theology*. Columbia: University of Missouri Press, 2010.
Morison, Richard. *An Exhortation to Styre All Englvsche Men to the Defence of Theyr Couintrye*. London, 1539.
Mühling, Andreas. *Heinrich Bullingers europäische Kirchenpolitik*. Zürcher Beiträge zur Reformationsgeschichte 19. Bern: Lang, 2001.
Müntzer, Thomas. "Interpretation of the Second Chapter of Daniel." In *CWTM*, 230–52.
———. "Interrogation and 'Recantation' of Müntzer." In *CWTM*, 433–40.
———. "Letter no. 13." In *CWTM*, 18–22.
———. "Letter no. 19". In *CWTM*, 27–28.
———. "Letter no. 31." In *CWTM*, 43–46.
———. "Letter no. 35." In *CWTM*, 50–51.
———. "Letter no. 37." In *CWTM*, 52–53.
———. "Letter nos. 41A.B." In *CWTM*, 60–64.
———. "Letter no. 44." In *CWTM*, 66–67.
———. "Letter no. 45." In *CWTM*, 67–70.
———. "Letter no. 50." In *CWTM*, 79–81.
———. "Letter no. 52." In *CWTM*, 82–83.
———. "Letter no. 53." In *CWTM*, 83–85.
———. "Letter no. 54." In *CWTM*, 85–86.
———. "Letter no. 55." In *CWTM*, 86–91.
———. "Letter no. 56." In *CWTM*, 91–92.
———. "Letter nos. 57–8." In *CWTM*, 95–98.
———. "Letter no. 59." In *CWTM*, 100–101.
———. "Letter no. 70." In *CWTM*, 132–34.
———. "A Manifest Exposé of True Faith." In *CWTM*, 253–323.
———. "The Prague Manifesto (German version)." In *CWTM*, 357–61.
———. *Revelation and Revolution: Basic Writings of Thomas Müntzer*. Translated and edited by Michael G. Baylor. London: Associated University Press, 1993.
———. "The Testimony of the First Chapter of Luke." In *CWTM*, 253–323.
———. "Vindication and Refutation." In *CWTM*, 327–50.
Müntzer, Thomas, and Heinrich Pfeiffer, "The Mühlhausen Articles." In *CWTM*, 455–59.
Murphy, Virginia. "The Literature and Propaganda of Henry VIII's First Divorce." In *The Reign of Henry VIII*, edited by Diarmaid MacCulloch, 135–58. London: Macmillan, 1995.
Neff, Christian, and Werner O. Packull. "Melchior Hoffman." In *GAMEO*. http://www.gameo.org/encyclopedia/contents/H646.html.
Neff, Christian et al. "Rothmann, Bernhard ca. 1495–ca. 1535." In *GAMEO*. http://www.gameo.org/encyclopedia/contents/R6852.html.
Nelson-Burnett, Amy. "'Kilchen ist uff dem Radthus'? Conflicting Views of Magistrate and Ministry in Early Reformation Basel." In *Debatten über die Legitimation von Herrochaft: Politische Sprachen in der Frühlen Neuzeit*, 44–66, edited by Luise Schorn-Schütte and Sven Tode. Berlin: Akademie, 2006.

Noll, Mark A. *Turning Points: Decisive Moments in the History of Christianity*. Grand Rapids: Baker Academic, 1997.
Oakley, Francis. "Almain and Major: Conciliar Theory on the Eve of the Reformation." *AHR* 70 (1965) 673–90.
Ogle, A. *The Tragedy of the Lollard's Tower*. Oxford: Pen-in-Hand, 1949.
Oyer, John S. *Lutheran Reformers against Anabaptists: Luther, Melanchthon and Menius and the Anabaptists of Central Germany*. The Hague: Nijhoff, 1964.
———. "The Reformers Oppose the Anabaptist Theology." In *The Recovery of the Anabaptist Vision*, edited by Guy F Hershberger, 202–18. Waterloo, ON: Herald, 2001.
Pabel, Hilmar M. "The Peaceful People of Christ: The Irenic Ecclesiology of Erasmus of Rotterdam." In *Erasmus' Vision of the Church*, edited by Hilmar M. Pabel, 57–94. Kirksville, MO: Sixteenth Century Journal, 1995.
"Panegyric for Archduke Philip of Austria." 1504. In *CWE*, edited by A. H. T. Levi, 27:54–56. Toronto: University of Toronto Press, 1986.
Pater, C. A. *Karlstadt as the Father of the Baptist Movements: The Emergence of Lay Protestantism*. Lewiston, NY: Mellen, 1994.
Peardon, Barbara. "The Politics of Polemic: John Ponet's Short Treatise of Politic Power and Contemporary Circumstances, 1553–1556." *JBS* 22 (1982) 35–49.
Pérez, Joseph. *The Spanish Inquisition: A History*. New Haven, Conn: Yale University Press, 2006.
Perrone, Sean T. *Charles V and the Castilian Assembly of the Clergy: Negotiations for the Ecclesiastical Subsidy*. Studies in the History of Christian Traditions 141. Leiden: Brill, 2008.
Ponet, John. *A Short Treatise of Politike Power, and of the Obedience which Subjects Owe to Kynges and Other Civile Governours, with an Exhortation to All True Naturall Englishmen*. Strasbourg: Köpfel, 1556.
Potter, David. *A History of France, 1460–1560: The Emergence of a Nation State*. London: MacMillan, 1995.
Potter, G. R. "Church and State, 1528: A Letter from Zwingli to Ambrosuis Blarer 4 May 1528." In *Occasional Papers of the American Society for Reformation Research* 1 (December 1977) 108–27.
———. *Huldrych Zwingli: Documents of Modern History*. London: Arnold, 1978.
Poythress, Diane Marie. "Johannes Oecolampadius' Exposition of Isaiah, Chapter 36–37." Ph.D. thesis, Westminster Theological Seminary, 1992.
———. *Reformer of Basel: The Life, Thought and Influence of Johannes Oecolampadius*. Grand Rapids: Reformation Heritage Books, 2011.
Pragmatic Sanction of Bologna. http://www.fordham.edu/halsall/source/1438pragmatic.html.
"Pragmatic Sanction of Bourges Enacted by Charles VII, King of France, July 7, 1438." In *Church and State through the Centuries*, edited by Sidney Z. Ehler and John B. Morrall, 112–21. New York: Biblo & Tannen, 1988.
Preus, James S. *Carlstadt's Ordinaciones and Luther's Liberty: A Study of the Wittenberg Movement 1521-22*. London: Oxford University Press, 1974.
PRO, SP 1/13, fol. 127v
Raath, Andries. "Covenant and the Christian Community: Bullinger and the Relationship between Church and Magistracy in Early Cape Settlement 1652–1708." *SCJ* 33 (2002) 999–1019.

Raby, Martyn. *France: Renaissance, Religion, and Recovery, 1494–1610*. London: Hodder & Stoughton, 1992.
Rawlings, Helen. *The Spanish Inquisition*. Oxford: Blackwell, 2006.
———. "The Secularisation of Castilian Episcopal Office under the Habsburgs, c. 1516–1700." *JEH* 38 (1987) 53–79.
Reardon, B. M. G. *Religious Thought in the Teformation*. London: Longman, 1981.
Reid, W. Stanford. "John Knox's Theology of Political Government." *SCJ* 19 (1988) 529–40.
Remer, Gary. "Dialogues of Toleration: Erasmus and Bodin." In *The Review of Politics* 56 (1994) 305–36.
Rex, Richard. "The Crisis of Obedience: God's Word and Henry's Reformation." *HJ* 39 (1996) 863–94.
Richardson, Glenn. *Renaissance Monarchy: The Reigns of Henry VIII, Francis I and Charles V*. London: Arnold, 2002.
Roberts, Adrian. "Ferdinand and Isabella." In *Years of Renewal: European History 1470–1600*, edited by John Lotherington, 28–60. London: Hodder & Stoughton, 1999.
Roelker, Nancy Lynan. *One King, One Faith: The Parlement of Paris and the Religious Reformations of the Sixteenth Century*. Berkeley: University of California Press, 1996.
Rogers, Caroline. "The French Wars of Religion." In *Years of Renewal: European History 1470–1600*, edited by John Lotherington, 395–424. London: Hodder & Stoughton, 1999.
Rothbard, Murray N. "Karl Marx—Communist as Religious Eschatologist." *Review of Austrian Economics* 4 (1990) 123–79.
Rothmann, Bernhard. "Restitution." In *Outline*, 253–4.
Rott, Jean. "The Strasbourg Kirchenpfleger and Parish Discipline: Theory and Practice." In *Bucer*, 122–28.
Rück, Stefanie. "Patriotic Tendencies in Pamphleteering during the Reigns of Henry VIII and Edward VI." In *Writing the Early Modern English Nation*, edited by Herbert Grabes, 1–46. Amsterdam: Rodopi, 2001.
Rupp, E. Gordon. *Patterns of Reformation*. London: Epworth, 1969.
———. "The Reformation in Zurich, Strassburg and Geneva." In *Elton*, 96–118.
Scarisbrick, J J. *Henry VIII*. Berkeley: University of California Press, 1968.
Schaff, Harold H. "The Anabaptists, the Reformers, and the Civil Government." *Church History* 1 (1932) 27–46.
Schoeck, R. J. *Erasmus of Europe, the Prince of Humanists 1501–1536*. Edinburgh: Edinburgh University Press, 1993.
"The Schwabach Articles." In *Sources and Contexts of the Book of Concord*, edited by Robert Kolb and James A Nestingen, 83–87. Minneapolis: Fortress, 2001.
Schwerin, Philip J. "How the Bishop of Rome Assumed the Title of "Vicar of Christ." South Central District Pastoral Conference: 1998. http://www.wlsessays.net/authors/S/sindex .html.
Scott, Tom. "Hubmaier, Schappeler and Hergot on Social Revolution." In *The Impact of the European Reformation: Princes, Clergy and People*, edited by Bridget Heal and Ole Peter Grell, 15–36. St. Andrews Studies in Reformation History. Aldershot, UK: Ashgate, 2008.
"The Second Helvetic Confession of 1566." In *Cochrane*, 220–302.

Secor, Philip Bruce. *Richard Hooker: Prophet of Anglicanism*. Tunbridge Wells, UK: Burns & Oates, 1999.

Selderhuis, H. J. *Marriage and Divorce in the Thought of Martin Bucer*. Translated by John Vriend and Lyle D Bierma. Kirksville MO: Truman State University Press, 2009.

Sider, Ronald J., ed. *Karlstadt's Battle with Luther: Documents in a Liberal-Radical Debate*. 1978. Reprint, Eugene OR: Wipf & Stock, 2001.

Simons, Menno. *A Foundation and Plain Instruction of the Saving Doctrine of Our Lord Jesus Christ*. http://www.mennosimons.net/fulltext.html.

———. "A Foundation and Plain Instruction of the Saving Doctrine of Our Lord Jesus Christ." In *The Complete Works of Menno Simons, edited* and Translated by John F. Funk. Elkhart IN: Funk, 1871.

Skinner, Quentin. *The Foundations of Modern Political Thought*. 2 vols. Cambridge: Cambridge University Press, 1978.

Spijker, W. van't. *Calvin*. Translated by Lyle D Bierma. Louisville: Westminster John Knox, 2009.

———. *The Ecclesiastical Offices in the Thought of Martin Bucer*. Translated by John Vriend and Lyle D Bierma. Studies in Medieval and Reformation Thought 57. Leiden: Brill, 1996.

Spooner, F. C. "The Reformation in Difficulties [3] France, 1519–59." In *Elton*, 210–25.

Stayer, James M. "The Anabaptist Revolt and Political and Religious Power." In *Power, Authority, and the Anabaptist Tradition*, edited by Benjamin W. Redekop and Calvin W. Redekop, 50–72. Baltimore: John Hopkins University Press, 2001.

———. "The Anabaptists and the Sects." In *The Reformation, 1520–1559*, edited by G. R. Elton, 118–43. New Cambridge Modern History 2. Cambridge: Cambridge University Press, 1990.

———. "Anabaptists and the Sword Revisited: The Trend from Radicalism to Apoliticalism." In *The Pacifist Impulse in Historical Perspective*, edited by Harvey L. Dyck, 111–24. Toronto: University of Toronto Press, 1996.

———. "Swiss–South German Anabaptism, 1526–1540." In *A Companion to Anabaptism and Spiritualism, 1521–1700*, edited by John D. Roth and James M. Stayer, 83–118. Brill's Companion to the Christian Tradition 6. Leiden: Brill, 2007.

Stephens, W. Peter. *The Theology of Huldrych Zwingli*. Oxford: Clarendon, 1986.

Stokesley, John et al. *The Determinations of the Moste Famous and Mooste Excellent Vniuersities of Italy and Fraunce*. Translated by Thomas Cranmer. London: Berthelet, 1531 [STC 14287]

———. *Gravissimae atque exactissime illustrissimarum totius Italie et Galliae academiarum censurae*. London: Berthelet, 1530 [STC 14286].

Sunshine, Glenn S. *Reforming French Protestantism: The Development of Huguenot Ecclesiastical Institutions, 1557–1572*. Kirksville, MO: Truman State University Press, 2003.

Swinnerton, Thomas. *A Litel Treatise against the Mutterynge of Some Papistis in Corners*. London, 1534 [STC19177].

———. "A Litel Treatise against the Mutterynge of Some Papistis in Corners." In *Pocock*, 2:539–52.

Thompson, Glen L. "Trouble in the Kingdom: Church and State in the Fourth Century." History-Social Science Division Symposium, Martin Luther College, 1999. http://www.wlsessays.net/authors/T/tindex.html.

Tyndale, William. "An Exposition on the Fifth, Sixth and Seventh Chapters of Matthew." In *Writings of Tindale, Frith and Barnes*. 2:128–246. 2 vols. London, 1831.

———. *The Obedience of a Christian Man and How Christian Rulers Ought to Govern*. http://www.godrules.net/library/tyndale/19tyndale7.htm.

———. "The Obedience of a Christian Man and How Christian Rulers Ought to Govern." In *Tyndale*, 1:163–379.

Ulph, Owen. "Jean Bodin and the Estates-General of 1576." *JMH* 19 (1947) 289–96.

Urry, James. *Mennonites, Politics, and Peoplehood: Europe–Russia–Canada, 1525 to 1980*. Winnipeg: University of Manitoba Press, 2006.

VanDrunen, David. *Natural Law and the Two Kingdoms: A Study in the Development of Reformed Social Thought*. Grand Rapid: Eerdmeans, 2010.

Wabuda, Susan. "Bishops and the Provision of Homilies, 1520 to 1547." *SCJ* 25 (1994) 551–66.

Werrell, Ralph S. *The Theology of William Tyndale*. Cambridge: James Clarke, 2006.

Whitgift, John. "The Defence of the Answer." In *The Works of John Whitgift, D.D., Archbishop of Canterbury*, edited by John Ayre, 3:298–300. 3 vols. Cambridge: Cambridge University Press, 1851–1853.

Wilkins, David. *Concilia Magnae Britanniae et Hiberniae*. 4 vols. London: Gosling, 1737.

Williams, Patrick. *Philip II*. New York: Palgrave, 2001.

Wollman, David H. "The Biblical Justification for Resistance to Authority in Ponet's and Goodman's Polemics." *SCJ* 13/4 (1982) 29–41.

Wriedt, Marcus. "'Founding a New Church...' The Early Ecclesiology of Martin Luther in the Light of the Debate about Confessionalization." In *Confessionalization in Europe, 1555–1700: Essays in Honor and Memory of Bodo Nischan*, edited by Bodo Nischan, et al., 51–66. Aldershot, UK: Ashgate, 2004.

———. "Luther on Call and Ordination: A Look at Luther and the Ministry." *Concordia Journal* 28 (2002) 254–69.

Wylie, James A. *The History of Protestantism*, 4 vols. Rapidan, VA: Heartland, 2002.

Zagorin, Perez. *How the Idea of Religious Toleration Came to the West*. Princeton: Princeton University Press, 2005.

———. *Rebels and Rulers, 1500–1660*. 2 vols. Cambridge: Cambridge University Press, 1984.

Zeeveld, W Gordon. "Thomas Starkey and the Cromwellian Polity." *JMH* 15 (1943) 177–91.

Zwingli, Ulrich. "Commentary on True and False Religion (1525)." Translated by Henry Preble, 43–343. In *Commentary on True and False Religion*, edited by Samuel M. Jackson and Clarence N. Heller. Durham: Labyrinth, 1981.

———. "Divine and Human Righteousness." In *Huldrych Zwingli Writings*, edited by H. Wayne Pipkin, 2:1–43. 2 vols. Allison Park, PA: Pickwick Publications, 1984.

———. "The Exposition of the Sixty-Seven Articles." In *Huldrych Zwingli Writings: Volume One: The Defence of the Reformed Faith*. Translated by E. J. Furcha. Allison Park, PA: Pickwick Publications, 1984.

———. "Letter of Huldreich Zwingli to Erasmus Fabricius about the proceedings, on the 7th, 8th, and 9th of April, 1522, of the delegates sent to Zürich by the bishop of Constance." In *Writings*, 113–29.

———. *The Sixty-Seven Articles*. In "The Acts of the First Zurich Disputation, January 1523." In *Selected Works of Huldreich Zwingli 1484–1531: The Reformer of German Switzerland*, edited by Samuel M. Jackson, 111–17. Philadelphia: University of Pennsylvania Press, 1901.

———. "A Solemn Warning by Huldriech Zwingli, a Simple Preacher of the Gospel of Jesus Christ, Addressed to the Honourable, Wise, Steadfast, Senior Confederates at Schwyz, that They Should Beware of, and Free Themselves from, the Control of Foreign Lords." In *Writings*, 130–49.

———. "Subsidiary Essay on the Eucharist." In *Huldrych Zwingli Writings*, edited by H. Wayne Pipkin, 2:187–231. 2 vols. Allison Park, PA: Pickwick Publications, 1984.

Subject Index

A Brief Apologia, 111
A Brief Exhortation, 190
A Godly Letter, 188
A faithful admonition to the professors of God's truth in England, 189
A foundation and plain instruction of the saving doctrine of our Lord Jesus Christ, 127–28
A Litel Treatise ageynste the mutterynge of some papistis in corners, 202–3
A Manifest Exposé of True Faith, 95–96, 97
A profitable and necessarye doctrine, 223
A supplicatyon made by Robert Barnes doctoure in diuinite / vnto the most excellent and redoubted prince kinge henrye the eyght, 201
Aarau, 144–45
Aaron, 33, 75, 253
Abbess of Naundorf, 91
abbots, 264, 287
absenteeism, 288
absolution, 74
Absolutism, 276
ad fontes, 21–22, 24, 58
Adages, 25
Adam, 91, 175
Address to the Christian nobility, 132–34
adiaphora, 204, 234, 239, 243, 247, 271
Admonition of Peace, 40, 41–42, 43, 44
Admonition to Parliament, 235, 236–42
adult baptism, 105, 110
adultery, 51
Africa, 7–8, 10, 162
Against the Robbing and Murdering Hoards of Peasants, 43–44
Ahab, 70
Albrecht of Mansfeld (count), 43
Alcalà, University of, 289, 297
alienation of domain, 275–76
Allstedt, 88–90, 95, 96, 97
  Brotherhood of, 90–91
  St John's in the New Town, 88
Alveld, Augustine von, 32–33
altruism, 80
Amaria, 241
Amsdorf, Nicolaus von, 76, 78
Amsterdam, 122
An Exhortation to the People instructing them to Unity and Obedience, 203
An Exhortation concerning good order and obedience to rulers and magistrates, 213
An exposition of the Faith, 69
An exposition on the fifth, sixth and seventh chapters of Matthew, 199
An open letter on the harsh book against the peasants, 44, 97
Anabaptist (-ism), 55, 72, 98–101, 110, 115–18, 126–27, 140, 144, 147, 149–51, 153, 163, 165, 218, 227, 229, 239–40, 247, 270
  cryto-, 273
  on marriage, 127
  Stäbler (staff bearers), 100, 105, 116

Anabaptist (-ism) *(continued)*
    Schwertler (sword bearers), 100
anarchy, 183–84
Angers, 274
Anglican (-s, -ism), 191, 233, 243, 248, 253, 290
annates, 262, 275
Anselm (saint), 10
Antichrist, 88
anticlericalism, 14, 17, 39, 86–87, 120, 145, 158, 195, 282, 284, 287, 289
antimaterialism, 24, 26
antinomian (-s, -ism), 35, 106, 207, 212, 227
antipapalism, 14, 17, 195, 221, 288
anti-Trinitarian, 218
Answere to a certain libel, 239–40
Antwerp, 294
apocalypse, 116, 118, 120
apolitical (-ism), 115, 128
Apology, 55, 137–38
Apostles, 64, 248–51
    as office, 249
Apostles' Creed, 208
apostolic age, 117
apostolic messengers, 119–20
apostolic renovation, 86
Aquinas, Thomas (saint), 5
Arabia, 289
Aragon, 186, 281–82, 285, 286–87, 291, 295, 297
    Catherine of, 50, 221
        divorce of, 194, 198, 200–201
    Church of, 281
    Inquisition of, 20, 286
    Kings of,
        Alphonse V, 281, 288
        Ferdinand II, 20, 282–89, 291
Archangel Gabriel, 76
archbishop, as office, 11, 14
Archbishop(-s)
    of Canterbury, 13, 212, 222, 233, 235
        Thomas Cranmer, 191, 212–14, 218–19, 222–23, 232, 234
        John de Grey, 13
        Edmund Grindal, 191
        Matthew Parker, 235, 236
        William Warham, 193
        John Whitgift, 233–36, 239–42, 247
    of Mainz, 84
aristocracy, 70
Aristotle, 2
Arius, 8
Army sermon against the Turks, 49
Articles of Schwabach, 54
Augsburg, 32, 157, 161, 163
    Confession, 52, 54–55, 131, 137–38
    Diet of, 54, 137–38
Augustine (saint), 10, 38, 161, 162, 180
    mandate, 23, 27, 55, 64
Austria, 72, 107–8, 115, 258
    Archduke of, 291
    Ferdinand of, 52, 108, 115
authority,
    ecclesiastical, 2, 5–6, 11
    secular, 1, 3, 9, 19–20
    spiritual, 20, 23, 27–28
    temporal, 1, 3, 8, 30, 34–45
auto de fe, 294–95
Ave Maria, 208
Avignon, 14–17, 21, 260

Babylonian captivity, 14, 17
Babylonian captivity of the church, 50
Baden, colloquy of, 141
ban, 105–6, 109, 114
Baker, J. Wayne, 143
Baptism (see Sacraments)
    believer's baptism, 72, 105, 127
Barnes, Robert, 201, 206
barons, 193
Basel, 57, 140–41, 145, 147, 154, 157, 175–76, 179
    Council of, 140–41
    edict, 141–42, 145
    Mayor of, 147
    morality court, 147, 152
    ordinance, 141–42, 148
Bavaria, 161, 258
Baylor, Michael, 87
Becket, Thomas, 193
begging, 79–80
benefice, 18, 184
Bern(e), 63, 147, 157, 177
    Colloquy, 141, 152–53
    guilds, 141–2, 160

SUBJECT INDEX

Beza, Theodore, 130, 146, 180–88, 190–92, 220, 233, 239, 272–73
Biberach, 161
Bible (see Scripture)
   vernacular, 204, 212, 222
biblical exegesis, 58, 61, 182
biblicist (-s, -ism), 73, 86, 98–99, 117
bilateralism, 156
binding and loosing, 34, 255
bishop (-s), 7, 9–10, 14, 25, 27, 58, 60, 219, 232, 235, 239, 241–42, 250, 252–53, 255, 267, 271, 273–74, 277, 287–88, 291–92, 296–97
   abuses, 31
   as apostles, 249
   as civil officers, 264, 287, 290, 292
   characteristics, 264–65
   duties of, 34, 50, 60, 64, 71, 251–52, 256–57
   of England, 201, 206, 210
   Roman, 114, 118
Bishop of Rome, 9, 10, 254, 256, 296
Bishops' Book (a.k.a., *The Institution of a Christian man*), 208–9, 211
Black Death, 3
Blansch, Martin, 59
Blarer, Ambrosius, 68, 158–59, 161
blasphemy, 139, 153–54, 162, 181, 266
Blessed Virgin Mary, 60, 91
blood purity, 285–86, 292, 296
Bockelson, Jan (*alias* John of Leiden, King John, Jan van Leiden, King Jan), 119, 123–26
   marriages of, 126
Bodin, Jean, 274–78
body analogy, 60
Bohemia (-n, ns), 87
Bologna, 19, 263, 265
   University of, 194
Bonifacius (Count Boniface, General Boniface), 162
Bonner, Edmund (bishop), 220, 222–23
Book of Homilies, 212, 214, 222
Borgia (family), 20–21
   Cesare, 21
   Lucrecia, 21
Bourbon (family), 268–69
   Antoine de, 269

Charles (cardinal), 268, 276, 278
Bourges, 18, 261 (synod)
Bradstock, Andrew, 85, 88
Breslau, 85
Brittany, 265
Bucer, Martin, 117–18, 121–22, 130, 137, 144, 146, 156–69, 170–71, 174–79, 184, 191, 198, 204, 299, 305
   sanctification doctrine of, 158, 162, 167
Bullinger, Heinrich, 57, 69, 72, 130, 140, 143, 146, 146–56, 157, 171, 187, 189, 191, 214, 220, 223, 233, 273
Burgundy, 181
   Duke of, 291

Caesar, 105
Caesaro-papist (-ism), 196
cahiers, 276
Cajetan, Thomas (cardinal), 32
Calais, 268
Calvin, John, 26, 56, 71, 106, 130, 146, 170–80, 182, 184, 187, 189–91, 220, 226, 233, 239, 269, 272–73, 291, 294
   exile, 177
Calvinist, 189, 220, 233, 266–70, 272–74, 277, 279
Cámara de Castilla, 292, 297
Cambridge University, 235
Canary Islands, 286
canonical election, 262, 265
Canterbury,
   Archdiocese, 193
   province of, 193
capitaines, 178
Capito, Wolfgang, 117–18, 121, 144, 158, 165, 177
Cardinal (-s), 11, 27
   College of, 15–16
Carranza, Bartolomé, 294, 295
Cartwright, Thomas, 233–36, 239–43, 246–47, 249, 252–53, 272
Castello, Sebastian, 182
Castile, 281, 283, 285–87, 289–91, 294–97
   Cortes of, 281

Castile *(continued)*
  Inquisition of, 20, 285
  Kings of,
    Enrique IV, 287
    John II, 281, 287–88
    Philip I, 289
  Queens of,
    Isabella I, 20, 282–85, 287–89
    Joanna, 289
Catalonia, 281
catechism, 138, 161, 174–75, 222, 294
Catholic (–s, –ism), 29, 45, 55, 63, 65, 144, 158, 184–85, 191, 207, 219, 221, 226–27, 231, 250, 253–54, 256, 258–59, 264, 266–68, 270–71, 275, 279–80, 286, 293, 295, 298–99
  as *papists*, 67, 201
  clergy, 220
  hierarchy, 132
  League, 277–79
  princes (*mad-dogs*), 95
  reform, 284, 289
  theology, 223
  Tridentine, 222
censors, office of, 144, 146
censorship, 286
ceremonies, 129, 132, 175
Chamber Ardente, 266
charity, 63, 80, 225
Charlemagne, 11
Châtillon, 268, 272
Christ, 2, 8, 17, 22, 24, 25, 30, 32–34, 60, 64, 82, 92, 102, 107, 113, 127–28, 144, 175, 198–99, 207–9, 238
  authority of, 199
  body of, 22, 24, 145, 158, 171–72, 240–41, 251, 273
  kingdom of, 170
  risen, 247
  second coming, 105, 117, 120, 125
  vicar of, 8, 13, 16, 22
  yoke of, 170
Christ Church (monastery), 13
Christendom, 3, 6, 11–12, 14–15, 25–26, 32, 37, 49, 51, 87–88, 93, 193, 229, 281, 283, 284, 288–90, 292
  socio-political hierarchy, 30, 33
  Western, 9

Christian (–s), 7, 22–23, 31, 41–42, 72, 76, 79–80, 84, 87–88, 92, 104, 134, 137–38, 144, 152, 154, 160, 165, 174, 176, 184–85, 197, 199, 204–5, 229–30, 237, 247, 250, 252–53, 256, 282–83, 285
  and tyrants, 66, 70
  duty of, 54–55, 62–66, 68–70, 81, 85, 100, 134, 203
  duty to the state, 112–20, 124, 128, 154
  magistracy, 103
  new, 283–85, 293
  prince, 38–39
    Commonwealth, 81, 212–13, 215–16, 277
Christian Civic League, 144
Christian doctrines, ceremonies, and life; composed by the preachers, along with the advice of my appointed Lords, 159
Christian Union (Brotherhood), 40
Christianity, 152, 162
Christianity for Dummies, 23
Christianization, 165, 167, 169
Christocracy, 169
Church, as an institution, 1–3, 6, 14, 21–23, 26, 57, 60, 86–87, 248, 250, 259, 266, 269, 285, 289, 290
  authority of, 29, 36–38, 48, 62, 64, 67
  believers' 104, 110, 122, 166
  Catholic, 7, 82, 86, 258, 270
  definition of, 22
  discipline, 139, 142–48, 153
  external, 182
  eternal, 73, 80
  fellowship, 160, 163–64, 166, 179
  history, 117
  in England, 235–37, 243–44, 246, 250
  invisible, 31–34, 37, 45, 59–61, 69, 166, 171, 241, 245, 248–49, 255, 259
  hierarchy, 61, 68
  mandate, 113, 117
  militant, 209
  ministers of, 160
  mixed nature of, 140, 145, 151, 153

SUBJECT INDEX 321

offices,
   antistes, 148, 147, 148
   deacon, 168, 296
   penitentiary, 142
   prophet, 150
ordinances, 173–74, 175
primitive, 78, 86, 87, 89, 94, 104, 133, 153, 237, 238, 240, 244, 249, 250, 251, 284
Roman (of Rome), 1–2, 6, 8, 17, 20, 29, 34, 74, 78, 93, 98, 137, 238–39, 248, 250
Separatist, 103, 105, 116, 118, 122, 126
state, 4, 8
true, 33
true marks of, 177, 184
Universal, 2, 5, 8, 17, 59–61
visible, 31, 32–34, 37, 45, 59–61, 69, 149–50, 152, 166, 170–71, 175–77, 240–42, 245, 248–50, 254–56, 259, 267, 270–71, 276, 280
church and state relationship, 3–4, 6, 17, 27, 30, 43, 45, 47, 51, 55, 59, 93, 98, 129–33, 135–36, 138, 140, 142–43, 146, 148, 151–52, 163, 166–68, 170, 181, 185, 187, 189–90, 193–94, 198–99, 209, 224, 233, 238–39, 241, 253, 258–59, 266, 270, 276, 284, 290, 298–99
   separation of, 105, 108–9, 112, 113, 116, 117, 121, 128
Church of England, 221, 222, 248, 250
circumcision, 151
Cisneros, Jimenez de (archbishop), 288–89
civil authority, 101–3, 104, 107–9, 113–14, 129, 134, 175, 179–80
civil disobedience, 56, 82, 168
civil government, 71
   sword as, 105–6, 108, 110–11, 114, 119, 123–24, 127, 152, 154, 162, 168, 183
civil obedience, 94, 130, 132, 135, 138, 185, 186
class hierarchy, 84

clergy, 3, 24, 27, 61–62, 173
   as civil office, 172, 174, 178, 193, 198, 209–10, 252, 253
   benefit of, 14, 170
   duty of, 65, 68
   immunity from taxes, 13–14
clerical abuses, 108, 140, 157
clerical authority, 83, 86, 111, 171
clerical autonomy, 181, 173, 175, 177–78, 180
clerical duty, 188, 216
clerical celibacy, 50
clerical hierarchy, 75, 78, 83, 86, 89, 96
clerical incontinence, 11
clerical marriage, 11, 60, 204
clerical offices, 130, 235–36, 238, 244, 249
clerical taxation, 15, 287, 291
clerical tyranny, 78, 142, 143–44, 170–71, 178
clerical vows, 61
colegios mayors, 297
Coligny (family),
   Dandelot, 268
   Gaspard de, 185, 268, 272
   Ôdet, 268, 272
Collectanea satis copiosa, 195, 201
Collinson, Patrick, 235
Colloquy,
   Poissy, 270
Cologne, University of, 60
Commentaries on the Epistle of St Paul to the Romans, 138
Commentary on true and false Religion, 68
commonwealth, 30, 144, 146, 149–50, 153, 155, 201, 203, 217, 220, 224–26, 229–30, 234, 239, 241, 245, 253–54, 257
commune, 57, 64, 130, 188
communion, 141
communism (proto-), 84
community, 58, 60–61, 64, 67–68, 71, 75, 78, 81, 83, 106–7, 117, 121, 129, 132, 133–34, 139, 142–43, 147, 149–50, 153, 157, 160, 163
Complaint of Peace (*Querela pacis*), 25

Comunero revolt, 292
Concerning True Love, 116
conciliarism, 14, 17, 27, 186–87, 205, 224, 260–61, 281–82, 286, 298
Concordat of Bologna, 19–20, 260, 262, 264–65, 279, 291
confession, 74, 137, 142, 158, 172
Confession (Marpeck), 54, 116
Confession (Hooper), 215
Confession de foi du Chrétien, 181, 183–84
conformist, 255
congregation, 144, 152, 159, 162, 183, 189
    duty of, 236–38, 240, 244
    of the faithful, 104, 107
Congregationalism, 87, 273
Considerations, 164–65
Consistory, 184, 192
Constantinople, 7, 9, 10
constitutional, 224
conversion, 284
converso, 285, 293, 295
convocation, 6, 192–93, 195, 202, 206, 221, 231, 236
    southern, 193
Constance, bishop of, 58, 59
constituted religion, 221
cooperative grace, 207, 209
Cordoba (diocese), 283
cortes, 287
Co-terminus doctrine, 156–69, 174, 177, 178, 180, 187, 198, 204, 208, 298, 299
Council (–s), 8, 12, 204
    Basel, 261–63, 282
    Carthage, 162
    Constance, 17
    Constantinople (third council of), 10
    Florence, 49
    Lateran, 13
    Nicaea, 8
    of the elect, 104, 107, 125
    Pisa, 17
    Trent, 165, 258, 265, 292, 284, 296
Court of Inquiry, 285
Council of the military orders, 291
Council of the Supreme and General Inquisition (*Suprema*), 286
Counter-Reformation, 289, 295
covenant, 57, 84, 140, 143–44, 146, 149–50, 153, 156–57, 165, 168, 171, 173–76, 187–88, 192, 198, 207, 212–17, 219–20, 224–27, 230–33, 249, 253–54, 256, 277
    Abrahamic, 150
    as political theory, 188–90
    carnal, 175
    spiritual, 175
creation, 197–98, 207, 290
Cromwell, Thomas, 196, 201, 203, 205
crown (office of), 235
crown-in-parliament, 231, 255
Cuenca (diocese), 283
crusade (–s), 12–13, 47–48, 52
crusader orders,
    Alcántara, 291
    Calatrava, 291
    Santiago, 291
cruzada, 291–92
cunctos populo, 8
curia, 18, 263, 265
customs duties, 64
Czech, 86, 87

Dark Ages, 10–13
David, 70, 75, 123–26, 128
    Kingdom of, 124
De Haereticis, 181, 184
De officio principum, 139
De Regno Christi, 167
De testament seu foedera Dei unico et aeterno, 149–50
De vera obedientia, 207, 222
dean (office), 206
Decades, 150, 155
Decalogue, 66, 135–36, 139, 176, 197, 204, 207–9, 214, 249
    two tables, 185, 214–15
Decretals of Isidore, 10
Defender of faiths, 271
Defender of the faith, 232, 271
Defense of the answere, 239, 241
Defensor Pacis, 14, 205, 206
democracy, 70

confessional, 119
democratic localism, 87
Denck, Hans, 100, 116–18, 122
Devil (Satan), 49, 51, 91, 229
Dialogues or Discussion, 162
Dictatus papae, 12
Difference between the Old and New Testaments, 151
Deliberations, 164–65
deposition, 187, 190
discipline, 3, 4–5, 11, 20, 105–6, 117, 154, 157–58, 163–65, 170, 174, 176–77, 179, 181, 184, 200, 205, 210, 219, 221–22, 234–35, 237, 239, 242, 252, 272–73, 286, 290, 296
  authority, 101
  civic board of, 160
  compulsion, 68–69
Discourse on the reform of abuses in church and state, 218–19
disobedience, 190
Divine and Human righteousness, 63
divine right, 196, 197, 206, 219, 255, 298
divorce, 50, 51
Donation of Constantine, 11
Donatist (–s, –ism), 7, 162
dons, 292, 296
Doubting Thomas, 147
droit de vérification, 264
duality, 37, 65, 68, 70, 173, 199–200
Duke of Anjou, 271, 276, 278

Ebeling, Gerhard, 29
ecclesiastical government, 193, 201, 204, 206, 231, 234, 235, 237, 240, 242–43, 248, 251, 254–56
ecclesiastical jurisdiction, 183–84
ecclesiastical (spiritual) magistrates, 135, 212
Ecclesiastical Ordinances, 178, 180
Ecclesiology, 31, 299
  Lutheran, 34
Eck, Johann, 74, 221
economics, 286
Edelstein, Marilyn, 264
Education of a Christian Prince, 26
ego (egocentricity), 74, 91

Egypt, 214
Eighteen Theses concerning the Christian Life, 107–8
elders, 163, 169, 174, 176–77, 179, 183–84, 200, 219, 221, 272, 273, 296
  as bishop, 169
  council of, 125–26, 144–46, 152, 158, 159
  duties, 238, 250, 252
elect, the, 2, 84, 88, 97, 105, 112, 115, 119, 124, 125
  community of, 97–98, 99
  congregation of, 95
  true believers, 171, 176
Elector Palatine, 131
Eleven Mülhausen Articles, 98
Elijah, 70, 117–18, 122, 125
Elliot, Sir John, 293–94
Emden, 118, 122
England, 4, 6, 13, 14, 18–19, 166, 186, 188, 189–259, 261, 266–67, 283, 289, 290–91, 295
  break with Rome, 202
  Bucer in, 166–69
  Church of, 18
  Church in, 195, 206, 208
  Kings of,
    Edward VI, 167, 188, 191–92, 212–20, 222–23, 228, 230–31, 233–34, 237, 240, 267
    Henry VIII, 4, 18, 43, 50, 191–94, 200, 203, 206, 208, 212, 220–21, 228, 231, 233, 237, 240, 256, 260, 265, 270, 297
      divorce of, 194, 198, 200–201, 221
    John, 13, 18
  Queens of,
    Elizabeth I, 191–92, 228, 231, 231–57
    Mary I, 188–92, 218–31, 231–32, 237, 295
      as punishment, 230
      illegitimacy of, 228
Enoch, 117, 122, 125
episcopal hierarchy, 235–36, 240
episcopal jurisdiction, 251–52, 253, 258, 287–88

episcopal parity, 296
Erasmus, Desiderius, 21–27, 29, 30–31,
    34–36, 130, 131, 133, 137–38,
    140, 142, 147, 149, 221–22, 249,
    284, 293, 295
Ernst of Mansfeld (Count), 84, 89–90
Estates (General), 186, 269, 274–75, 276
    First, 262, 275
    Second, 275
    Third, 275
Estes, James, 131, 135
Eucharist (the Sacrament), 33–34
    crisis, 138
Eusebius, 7
evangelicals, 86, 197, 205, 250, 266, 284, 291
    radical, 196
Evangelical princes, 96
evangelist (office), 220
excommunication, 119, 142–45, 147,
    152–53, 158, 160–61, 166, 168,
    173–74, 176, 179, 181, 183–84,
    220, 226, 239, 252, 255–56, 262,
    265; also see, ban
    committee, 145
excusado, 292
Explanation of the Ninety-five theses,
    31, 47
Exposition, 256
Exposition of Romans 13, 215
Exposition of the Sixty–seven articles,
    62–65

Faber (Fabri), John, 59–60, 62
faction, 266–67, 269, 271, 278
Fall, the, 114, 197–98
false teachings of the Anabaptists, 151
Farel, William, 173, 177
federal, 146
Fellows of the congregation, 107, 119, 124
Fellowship of the Lord's Supper, 157, 226
feudal dues, 95
feudalism, 11, 12, 13, 39, 108, 111, 225
Fidei ratio, 121
Fields, John, 234–35, 237–39
filioque controversy, 11
First Book of Common Prayer, 219, 235–36

First Helvetic Confession, 69, 154
Fisher, John (bishop), 197
Flemish, 292
Florence, 265
Fontainebleau, 269
food restrictions, 58, 60
Forty-two Articles, 232
*Four Books to warn the faithful from the
    shameless disturbances, offensive
    confusion and false teachings of
    the Anabaptists*, 151
Fox(e), Richard (bishop), 193
France, 4, 10, 13–14, 17–19, 60, 69–70,
    172, 184–86, 193, 210, 226,
    258–81, 283, 186, 289–91, 293,
    295, 299
    Admiral of, 268
    Constable of, 268
    Edicts,
        Beaulieu, 275
        Compiègne, 267
        January, 270
        Longjumaeu, 271
        Nantes, 279
        Romorantin, 269
        Saint Germain, 270
    Kings of,
        Charles IX, 267, 269, 270, 271, 278
        Charles VII, 261
        Charles VIII, 18
        Francis I, 19, 45, 52, 69, 70, 170,
            260, 263–64, 266, 271, 291
        Francis II, 267
        Henri II, 264–68, 271, 295
        Henri III, 267, 276, 178
        Henri IV, 279, 280
    national synod, 273
Frankenhausen, battle of, 44
Frankfurt, 189, 223
fraternities, 79, 81, 286
Free Republic of Christ, 75
French church, 260–62, 264–66, 279, 281
friars, 293
functional (-ality, -ism), 25, 28, 30, 34,
    35, 43, 56, 62, 71, 74, 75, 79, 80,

89, 114, 120, 130, 132, 155, 157, 168, 198

Gallican (-ism), 260, 261, 262, 263, 264, 265, 270, 272–74, 279, 280–81, 290
Gardiner, Stephan (bishop), 207, 208, 219, 222–23
General Announcement, 161
Geneva, 57, 71, 172, 174, 176–78, 180–81, 189, 191, 220, 223, 234–37, 250, 267, 270, 272–74, 294
   Consistory of, 178, 179, 273, 274
   magistrates of, 172–73, 177, 180
   matrimonial court, 175, 177
   Small Council of, 178
   syndics of, 175, 175(n85), 177, 179
   synod, 272
Geneva Confession, 172–63
Gentiles, 151
geo-political conflict, 49
German, 86, 87
German Theology, 73, 85
Germany, 11, 35, 56, 72, 102, 115, 117, 147, 223, 266, 290, 291, 292, 293, 294
Glauchau, 88
Glasse of Truth, 201–2
Gloucester (Bishop of), 214, 218
God, 2, 4, 18, 29–30, 39, 41–42, 44, 48, 50–51, 55, 56, 58, 61, 63, 66, 71–72, 75, 80–81, 88–89, 91–92, 94–95, 99–100, 106, 109, 111–12, 123–24, 129, 131, 133, 135, 138–39, 149–50, 152–54, 167–68, 174, 182, 184, 186, 188, 193, 197, 204, 207, 212, 216, 226–27, 232, 238–39, 241–47, 249, 254, 257, 272, 293
   glory of, 170–71, 176, 178, 183
   law of, 75, 176–77, 184–85, 213, 276–78
   kingdom of, 76, 198
   messenger of, 79
   people of, 76, 78, 149–50, 157, 214, 227
   servant of, 152
   sovereignty, 197
   will of, 244–46
   wrath of, 154, 162
god-parents, 250
Godly Primer, 205
Goertz, Hans-Jurgen, 85
good works, 35, 48, 63, 79, 175, 197, 205, 207
Goodman, Christopher, 220, 222–23, 226–31, 233, 240
gospel (the Word, Bible, Scripture), 3, 21, 25, 34, 36–40, 43–44, 57, 60, 62–63, 66, 70, 102, 107, 109, 112–13, 125, 129–30, 132–34, 137, 141–43, 148–50, 155–57, 162, 168, 170–74, 183–85, 187–89, 192, 201–2, 204, 206, 209, 212–13, 218, 222, 224, 227, 230–31, 233, 235, 238–44, 246–49, 251, 254, 257, 272–73, 298
   preaching of, 78, 82
gospel (spiritual) regiment, 199, 205
grace, 251
Granada, 283, 287, 289, 297
Gravissimae atque exactissimae, illusstrissimarum totius Italiae, et Gallicae academiarum censurae, 195
Great Schism, 260, 286
Grebel, Conrad (Konrad), 72–73, 98, 100–105, 107, 112–14, 122, 125–26, 151–52
   on magistrates, 100
   on separation of church and state, 113
greed, 98
Greek, 21, 62, 251, 289
Green, Vivian Hubert Howard, 12
Grey, Jane, 220
Gritsch, Eric W., 87
guilds, 79, 81
Guise (family), 184, 267–70
   Francis de Lorraine II (duke), 268–69, 278–79
   Louis (cardinal), 279
   Mary of, 190

Haarlem, 122
habitant, 177

SUBJECT INDEX

Habsburg (family), 120, 259, 265–67, 287, 289–90, 292
    Juana of, 294
Halle, 88
Handbook of the Christian Soldier (*Enchiridion militis christiani*), 23
Hanseatic League, 120
Harpsfield, Nicholas, 223
heathens, 144
heaven, 188
Hebrew, 21, 62, 289
Heidelberg, 31
Hell, 91
hereditary rule, 205
heresy, 9, 16, 106, 109, 151, 153–54, 204, 231, 266–67, 269, 285–86, 293–95
heretics, 162, 181–84
Herod, 70
Hess(e), Landgraviate of, 45, 69, 157
    Philip of, 53–54, 122–23
Hispanic-Iberian Catholicism, 280, 284, 286, 288, 293
Hispano-Roman, 282, 297
Hoffman, Melchior, 72, 85, 116–20
    as theocrat, 125
    church hierarchy, 119
Hohenlandenberg, Hugo von, 59
Holland, 122
Holy League, 275–76
Holy Spirit (Ghost), 17, 33, 36–37, 60–61, 102, 106, 119, 128, 162, 167, 209, 244, 293
Holy Roman Emperor (–s), 47, 162, 164, 224–25, 227
    Charles V, 43, 45, 48–49, 52, 54–55, 90, 118, 138, 265, 290, 292, 294
    Henry III, 11
    Henry IV, 12–13
Holy Roman Empire, 11, 40, 52, 53, 55, 93, 95, 165, 253, 290, 292
homilies, 212, 219, 222, 238
Homilies sette forth by Eddmune byshop of London, 223
Höngg, 102
Hooker, Richard, 191, 234, 242–57, 272, 276

Hooper, John, 191, 214–15, 217–19, 234
House of Commons, 236
House of Lords, 210
housefathers, 79
How superior powers ought to be obeyed, 223, 229
Hubmaier, Balthasar, 72–73, 85, 100, 101, 107–15, 116–17, 119–20, 127
    arrest warrant, 108
    cooperation with magistrates, 116
    on secular government, 112–15
    rebaptism of, 107
Huguenot (–s), 184–85, 226, 264, 268–69, 271, 273–75, 278–79
human reason, 243–47, 256–57
humanism (–ist, –ists), 21, 130, 138, 215, 221, 264, 284, 293–94
Hundred Years' War, 261
Hus, John, 86
Hussite (–s), 17
Hut, Hans, 100, 110, 112, 116–17, 120
    on violence, 116
Hutton, Ulrich von, 35

Iberian peninsula, 282–83, 287
idolatry, 91, 133, 139, 162, 188–89, 227
Illuminists, 293–94
images, 23, 57–58, 67–68, 72, 75, 81, 102, 107, 142, 161, 201
imitatio Christi, 58
immutability, 249
Imperial edicts, 38, 50
Imperial Knights, 35
Imperial mandate, 78
impotence, 51
Index of Forbidden books, 294–95
Indulgence (–s), 3, 21, 23, 31
industrialization, 125
infant baptism, 66, 105, 118, 147, 151, 156, 245
infidel, 285
injunction (–s), 222, 238
Inquisition,
    French, 267
    Papal, 285
    Spanish, 267, 283–86, 289, 292–95
Inquisitor (office), 287, 290, 296

Institutes of the Christian Religion
(1539), 175–76, 187; (1543), 180
Institutions of the Christian Religion
(1536), 171, 173, 175
Interdict, 262
Interim, 166
interior illumination, 76
Interpretation of the second chapter of Daniel, 91
Investiture contest, 12–13
irenicism, 157
Islam, 282–83, 290
isolationism, 113, 127, 137
Israel, 153, 214, 219, 255
Italy (–ian), 2, 10–11, 17, 60, 219, 258, 260, 262, 265, 281–82, 287

Jehoshaphat, 241
Jerome (saint), 10
Jesus, 5
Jew (–s, –ish), 3, 33, 51, 144, 247, 249, 253, 283, 288–89, 291
Joan of Kent, 218
John, 70
John of the Cross, 284
Jonah, 119
Jonas, 76, 78
Jordon, W. K., 218
Jost, Lienhard, 188
Jost, Ursula, 118
Jud, Leo, 152
Judaism, 6, 283
    legalism of, 151
Judaizing, 284
Judah, 241
Judea, 188
Julius banned from Heaven (*Julius exclusus e coelis*), 26
justice,
    human, 65
    natural, 62
Justification, theology, 2, 130, 140, 207, 208, 259

Kamen, Henry, 293, 295
Kappel, 147
    second war of, 69

Karlstadt, Andreas Rudolph Bodenstein von, 41, 72–73, 84–85, 87–88, 95, 99, 104, 129
    as *Brother Andrew*, 80
    mysticism of, 82
    one kingdom doctrine, 73–83
    salvation theology of, 79, 81, 83
Karlstadtian, 293
Keller, Michael, 161
keys, power of the, 9, 61, 145, 177, 182, 184, 201–2, 209
Kidderminster, Richard, 194
king,
    as office, 198, 200–204, 211, 217, 224–25, 255–56
    as papal legate, 289
    as person, 198, 205, 211, 256
    -in-parliament, 220
king-priest, 276
King's Bench (court), 195
King's Book (or *A Necessary Doctrine and Erudition for any Christen Man*), 211
kirchenrat, 146, 223
Klötzer, Rolf, 120, 125
Knaut, Ziliax, 91
Konrad, Sam, 159
Konstanz, 158, 165
Knox, John, 71, 187–91, 218, 223, 226, 230, 233, 256
    as royal chaplain, 188

La Rochelle, 272–73
laity, duties of, 74, 79, 92
Lamentation, 205
Langton, Stephan, 13
Laski, Jan, 130, 191
Later Middle Ages, 13–21
Latimer, Hugh, 215, 217, 219
Latin, 21, 86–87, 289
Lausanne, 181
law (–s)
    canon, 33, 36, 49–50, 61, 210, 282, 290
    ceremonial, 249
    civil, 49–50, 149–50

law (-s) *(continued)*
　divine, 5, 34, 44, 62–64, 66–67, 135, 155, 157, 194, 200–202, 204, 206, 211, 215, 225–26, 228–30, 244, 246
　eternal, 5
　human positive, 5, 33, 64, 100, 134–35, 201–2, 223, 227, 230, 232, 242, 245, 249, 275–76
　Judaic, 176
　judicial, 176, 249
　moral, 150, 155, 176, 249
　natural, 5, 40, 42, 44, 47, 65–66, 99, 135, 155, 176, 190, 204, 211, 218, 220, 225, 227, 230, 232, 234, 242–46, 257, 272–73, 276–78
　pontifical, 135
　Salic, 276
　spiritual, 5
　sumptuary, 61, 165
　temporal, 5, 231
League of Cognac, 52
legalism, 33, 181
Leipzig, 32
Lenten sermons, 216, 217–18
Levites, 241
liberty, 109
　Christian, 177
Liechtenstein, Leonard von, 115
Life of Constantine, 7
Lindau, 165
Lindberg, Carter, 16, 81
Lisbon, 298
liturgy, 57, 141, 234
Loci Communes, 121, 134–36, 138, 203
Lockyer, Roger, 292
Lollard (-s, -y), 17, 191
London (Bishop of), 220
Lords of the congregation, 190
Low Countries, 117, 122, 127, 290, 292
Louvain, university of, 60
Loyola, Ignatius, 284
Luther, Martin, 21, 26–27, 29–59, 61, 63, 69, 71–75, 77, 83, 86, 88–91, 94–95, 97–99, 106, 112, 115, 117, 120–22, 129–34, 145–46, 170–71, 173–74, 182, 191–92, 198, 201–4, 206–7, 210, 224–25, 230, 244, 284, 291, 293, 298–99
　anti-war, 53–54
　heresy of, 34
　Invocavit sermons, 75
　Justification theology of, 30, 35, 207
　on civil authority, 31–39, 134, 136, 137, 139
　on imperial politics, 52–55
　on marriage, 49–52
　on the Peasants' Revolt, 39, 41, 42–43
　on war, 45–49
　salvation theology of, 77
　theology of the cross, 74, 75, 170, 173, 180
　two kingdoms doctrine, 29–56, 71, 75, 80, 83, 87, 93, 99, 100, 106, 108–9, 116–17, 119, 121, 132, 136–38, 145–46, 151, 157, 244, 252, 255, 270, 273
Lutheran (-ism), 55, 63, 121, 123, 130, 132, 135–36, 141, 146–47, 151, 158, 201, 212, 250, 266, 294

Mabray, Eddie, 113
Machiavelli, Niccolò, 21
Madrid, 297, 298
magisterial authority, 3–5, 7–9, 11, 14, 25–27, 29, 35, 37, 54–55, 71–77, 79, 84–89, 92–94, 98–100, 231–32, 234, 238–42, 244, 250, 252, 255, 298
　and the church, 103–4, 118, 127, 140, 150–51, 153, 155–56, 161, 166, 181, 184–86, 189, 194–95, 197, 199, 202, 204, 210–11, 220, 258, 260, 271, 296, 298–300
　cura religionis, 131, 138–39, 147, 171, 173, 176–78
magistrate (-s), 140–41, 147–49, 151, 162, 164, 170–73, 175–77, 179, 213, 221, 230, 258, 271–72, 290
　as churchmen, 163
　as father, 163
　as Old Testament king, 152, 153
　as *presbyteroi*, 68
　as shepherd, 96–97

as godly, 212, 215–16, 227, 229, 290
duties of, 212, 217, 227
sacerdotal function, 195
subordinate, 133–34, 136, 139,
    186–87, 189–90, 192, 197–98,
    200–202, 205–6, 212–13, 215,
    217, 219, 221, 223–24, 230–31,
    240, 243, 249, 257, 268, 276–77
character of, 106, 113, 116
duty of, 80, 81, 84, 85, 87, 89–90,
    92–93, 95, 96–97, 98, 100,
    130, 132, 133, 135–37, 139–
    40, 142–57, 159, 161–62, 165,
    167–68, 171, 173, 176, 182,
    184, 186–90, 197–98, 202–4,
    208, 210, 213, 215, 223, 226
office of, 2, 3, 5, 38, 41, 43–45, 52,
    57, 62–70, 77, 89, 184, 186
Magna Charta, 13, 193
Maigret, Lambert, 69
Mair, John, 187
Mallerbach, 89
    incident, 90–91
Manila, 298
Mansfeld, 89
    miners of, 89
Marignano, battle of, 263
Marian exiles, 220, 224–25, 241
Marius, Richard, 41
marriage (as civil issue), 49–52, 133, 165
    court, 142, 147, 159, 163
    legalities, 195
Marsilio (Marsiglio) of Padua, 14, 25,
    27, 205, 209
material world, 84
materialism, 293
Matheson, Peter, 86
Marpeck (Marbeck), Pilgram, 100, 118
Marshal, William, 205–7
Martinian, 84, 86
Marxist, 84
Mass (ceremony), 3, 23, 67–68, 72, 77–
    78, 101–2, 141–42, 174, 189, 221
    evangelical, 78
    private, 76
    Spanish, 297
materialism, 15
Mathijs, Jan, 119, 122–23, 125
    death of, 125

Mayer, Thomas, 4
McGrath, Alistair, 22, 72, 178
Meaux, 271
Medici (family), 265
    Catherine de, 185, 265, 267, 269–71,
        274–75
Mediterranean, 281
Melanchthon, Philip, 53–55, 76–78, 82,
    87–88, 121, 130–39, 146, 149,
    176, 182, 203–4
Melchiorites, 118–20, 122, 123
Memmingen, 161, 165
Mexico, 298
Middle Ages, 9–10
Milan, 19, 258, 264
military orders, 286
    Grandmaster of, 291
Millenarian (–ism), 49, 105, 110, 116,
    123
Missal, 143
modes of assurance, 246
Mohammad, 76
monarchy, 70
Monastic orders, 286–87, 293
    Augustinians, 31, 73, 76, 85
    Carmelite, 274
    Cistercians, 11
    Conventual, 288
    Dominicans, 11
    Franciscans, 11, 32, 85
        provincial of, 85
    Jesuits, 294
        observant, 288
        reformation of, 288
monastic dissolution, 297
monastic vows, 50, 76, 81
Montmorency, Anne de, 268, 270
Moors, 282, 287
morality, 170
Moravia, 110, 115–16
More, Thomas, 197, 201
    as Lord Chancellor, 201
Morély, Jean, 272–73
Morrison, Richard, 205–6
Moses, 75, 112, 249, 253
Mülhausen, 97–99
    class division in, 97
    eternal council, 99

Münster, 104, 116–17, 119, 120–28, 151, 153, 165, 176
  Aristocratic council of, 120
  as New Jerusalem, 119
  blockade of, 126
  church order, 123
  St Lambert's, 121, 123
  St Mauritz, 121
Müntzer, Thomas, 40–41, 72–73, 75–76, 83, 101, 104–5, 110–12, 116–17
  as theocrat, 87
  on secular authority, 83
  salvation theology of, 86, 91, 94, 95, 97
  sword of God, 83–99
Musculus, Wolfgang, 161
Muslims, 283
Myconius, Frederick, 146
mysticism, 3, 36, 72–73, 85, 99, 117, 151; also see spiritualism
  apocalyptic, 85, 88, 99
  experiential, 85

Naples, 19, 258, 264
  King of, 281–82
Nathan, 70
nationalism, 1, 6, 17, 203, 288, 299
natural order, 89, 97
natural reason, 32, 273
Navarre, 268
  Henri of, 272, 276, 278–79
Nebuchadnezzar, 94
neck verse, 14
Neff, Christian, 118
Netherlands, 292
Neustadt, 86
New Testament, 22, 27, 33–34, 37, 61, 82, 127, 143, 150, 153, 235
New world, 287, 290
Nikolsburg, 110–11
Ninety-five Theses, 31–32
nobles, 285–86
nomination, 282–84, 286–87, 291, 296
non-conformity, 164–65, 236, 243, 247–48
non-cooperation, 72, 137, 151
non-salvific, 24
non-separatist, 100
non-residence, 283, 287

non-resistance, 72, 191
non-Trinitarian, 181
Nordhausen, 88
Northumberland (duke of), 220
Nuremberg, 99

oath (–s), 63, 72, 106, 138, 154, 168, 190, 229
obedience theology, 196, 197, 200–214, 216, 222, 224–27, 233
Oecolampadius, Johannes, 56, 130, 139–46, 152, 157–59, 161, 163, 170–71, 174–79
Of the Laws of Ecclesiastic Polity, 243–57
officers of the crown, 186
officers of the king, 186
Old Testament, 27, 33, 34, 61, 73, 75, 81–82, 92, 126, 140, 143, 150–53, 163, 207, 219, 226, 230, 247, 249
oligarchy, 70
On Earthly power, 124
On heretics and those who burn them, 109
On marriage matters, 51
On Romans, 118
On Secular Authority, 132
On the church's defects and failings, 166
On the office of the Prince, 139
On the pure fear of God, 119
On the removal of Images, 79–81
On the Sword (Hoffman), 117
On the Sword (Hubmaier), 111–13, 115
On the war against the Turks, 48
On Vengeance, 124, 126
Open Letter to the Brothers at Stolberg, 88
Oration concerning the fact that excommunication ought to be reinstated, 143
Oratio de reducenda excommunication, 143
Oratio pro Martino Luthero theologo, 133–34
original sin, 11
Orlamünde, 82–83, 85
Ottoman-Turks, 290

SUBJECT INDEX

pacifist (-s, -ism), 104, 115, 117, 127–28
Packnull, Werner, 118
Padua, 14
parliament, 6, 14, 186, 192–93, 195–96, 202, 205, 210, 218, 221, 224–26
Pater Noster, 208
patronage, 12, 184
Panegyric for Archduke Philip of Austria, 25
papacy, 140, 145, 170, 174, 204, 280–81, 286–88, 290–91
  falsity of, 162
  tyranny of, 152, 167
papal abuses of power, 47–48, 51–52, 58, 70, 133, 139, 201–3, 213, 237, 240, 250, 256, 261, 282
papal appointment, 263–64
papal authority, 29, 32–33, 193–96, 198, 200, 202, 204–6. 217, 221–22
papal bulls, 290, 292
papal claims, 61, 64–65
papal decretals, 33, 61
papal dispensation, 224
papal election, 18, 262
papal infallibility, 10
papal obedience, 192, 202
papal penitential system, 169
papal reform, 298
Papal States, 19–20
papal supremacy, 5–6, 10, 12–14, 18, 20, 27, 187, 203–4, 207, 211, 219, 221, 223, 231, 280, 291–92
papal taxation, 202
papal tyranny, 174, 180
papal usurpation, 197
parable of the vineyard, 76
parable of the wheat and the tares, 182
paradise, 65
Paraphrases on Luke, 25
Paraphrases on Mark, 25
Paris, 279, 297
  University of, 60, 194
parish warden, 159, 163, 166
Parlement, 260–66, 269, 271–72, 279
parliament, 231–32, 234–36, 250

particularism (localism), 1–3, 11, 17, 18–19, 32, 55, 87, 184, 189, 195–96, 203–4, 208–10, 224, 234, 244, 248, 250, 251, 254, 258–59, 262–63, 272, 281, 291, 296, 299
patronage, 39, 193, 225, 262, 264, 266, 268–69, 280, 282, 285–86, 291–93
pastoral authority, 172, 174, 180
pastoral function, 143, 145, 148–49, 168, 222, 288
patriotism, 224, 228
Paul (saint), 36, 38, 82, 135, 138, 159, 176, 226, 229 241, 251
  letters, 201
  mandate, 55, 64
Pavia, 265
pax Europa, 21, 27
Peace of Amboise, 270–71
peasants, duties of, 44–45, 48–49
Peasants' Revolt, 30, 38–40, 45–46, 49, 52, 72, 74, 83, 85, 90, 95, 98, 101–2, 104–5, 108, 121, 126, 138
persons,
  general, 46
  individual, 46
Peter (saint), 5, 9–10, 26, 33, 229
  as rock, 61, 225
  and the sword, 113
  letters, 201
Pfeiffer, Heinrich, 97–99
Pharisees, 97
physical life, 214, 224
physical sphere, 24, 26
piety, 1, 45, 117, 142, 145, 150, 164
  lay piety, 21
pilgrimage (-s), 3, 23, 222
Plato, 2, 30, 85
pluralism, 265
Pole, Reginald, 222
Politiques, 273–80
polygamy, 126
Polyglot Bible, 289
Ponet, John, 220, 222–28, 230–31, 233, 240, 260, 263, 270, 272
  problematic, 219–20
pontifex maximus, 8

pope (–s), 2, 34, 192–95, 203, 219, 221, 224–25, 227, 282, 284, 286, 288, 295, 298
  Adrian VI, 287, 290–91
  Alexander V, 17
  Alexander VI, 20–21
  as an office, 23
  authorities of, 18, 27
  Boniface VIII, 14
  Clement V, 14
  Clement VII (anti–pope), 16–17
  Gregory VII, 10, 12
  Eugenius IV, 261, 282
  Innocent III, 13
  Julius II, 20, 26
  Julius III, 265
  Leo I, 9–10
  Leo III, 11
  Leo X, 11, 263
  Martin V, 17, 20
  Sixtus IV, 285
  Urban VI, 16–17
popery, 214
Portugal, 258
Pragmatic Sanction, 18, 259–63
Prague, 86, 87
Prague Manifesto, 86–87
Praise of Folly (or *Encomium Moriae*), 27
Peace of Saint Germain, 271
predestination, 2, 33, 299
Presbyterian (–s), 234–36, 239, 242, 244, 246–48, 250–51, 254–55, 257, 272
presbyters (*presbyteroi*), 144
Preus, James, 76, 78
priesthood, pastorship (as office), 14, 27, 34, 52–53, 71, 73, 75, 82, 149, 157, 200
priesthood of all believers, 30, 34, 35, 39, 41–43, 71, 74–75, 80, 83, 87, 90, 92, 97–99, 101, 114, 119, 121, 125, 129–30, 132–33, 160, 170, 178, 225, 238, 273, 284, 296
prince as steward of the church, 131–39
prince-bishop, 41, 135, 298
prince(s) of the blood, 266, 268–69
prophet (–s), 70

as office, 76, 92, 124, 126, 188, 220
false, 184
proportional taxation, 275
Provence, 265
providence, 60, 140, 290
Protestant, 192, 200–201, 204, 206, 212, 216, 218–19, 221, 231, 233, 253, 257, 259, 264, 268, 270–71, 273–76, 278–79, 284, 288
purgatory, doctrine of, 208
Puritan (–s, –ism), 73, 191, 223, 234, 236, 242, 246–48, 250

Reardon, Bernard Morris Garvin, 24
rebellion, 223
Recantation, 110
Reconquista, 283, 288, 289, 291
Reformation, 2, 4, 6, 20, 39, 55, 58, 71, 76, 83–85, 88, 97–98, 102, 112, 117, 124, 129, 140, 158, 164, 170–72, 188, 190–91, 235, 259, 264, 266, 283, 291, 296, 298–300
  causes, 2
  Edwardian, 221
  magisterial, 42, 273
  Protestant, 284, 289, 291, 293–96, 298–99
  socio-political, 40
Reformation Parliament, 195, 202, 231
Reformed Church, 145, 171, 181, 250
Reformed religion, 130, 191, 226, 273, 277
Reformed theology, 232
reformers, 22, 27
  magisterial, 72, 84, 99, 100–101, 112, 120, 122, 129, 152, 158
regalism, 280, 285, 289–98
Regarding the abolishment of church vices, 165
Regency council, 53, 213
regicide, 255, 256
relics, 3, 222
repentance, 230
Replye, 239
Renaissance, 205
reserved benefices, 288
residency, 288

resistance, 184–87, 189, 213, 220, 223, 228
resistance theology, 191, 201, 205, 211, 219–20, 230–31, 269, 277
Restitution, 123
Reublin, Wilhelm, 118
Reuchlin, Johann, 107
revelation, 3, 78
revolt, 153, 184
Rhineland, 122
Ridley, Nicholas, 215
Right of Magistrates, 181, 185
righteousness, 113, 128, 152, 168
  divine, 63–65, 67, 69, 73–74
  human, 63–67, 69, 73–74, 79, 201 (worldly)
Rochester (Bishop of), 223
Roman Emperor (–s),
  Constantine, 6–7, 8, 14
  Constantius, 7
  Gratian, 8
Roman Empire, 72, 162
Roman society, 104
Rome, 7, 16, 31–32, 58–59, 61–62, 124, 129, 132, 172, 193–94, 203, 208, 212, 216, 219, 222, 229, 258, 260, 262–65, 270, 281, 284, 288, 294, 298
  clergy of, 189
  as New Jerusalem, 33
Rothmann, Bernard, 120–29
  as pastor, 121
  church order of, 122
royal authority, 276, 279
royal nomination, 263–64
royal supremacy, 191–97, 203, 206–11, 213, 218, 220–22, 231–38, 261–62, 264, 266–67, 270, 272, 276, 280, 284, 286–87, 289, 295–99
Rückert, Nicholas, 88, 91, 95
Rule of Christ, 109, 114, 144, 158, 160, 167, 169, 174, 239
Rupp, Gordon, 84, 146

St Andrew's University, 187
St Bartholomew's Day massacre, 184–85, 187, 271, 273
St Paul's mandate, 23, 27

St Peter's Basilica, 21
saints, 60
Sacraments, 30, 35, 45, 168, 176, 208, 212, 255, 299
  Baptism, 9, 24, 33, 66–67, 137, 141
  Eucharist (Lord's Supper, the sacrament), 58, 66, 77, 105, 122, 137, 145, 165, 173–74, 177, 201, 209, 299
  transubstantian, 223
  Marriage, 49, 50
  rites, 141
  Ordination, 34, 208–9, 255, 260
  Penance, 32, 142, 168, 250
sacramentarian, 212, 267
sacred history, 77–78, 182, 185, 212, 298
saints, 222
Salamanca, 297
  University of, 297
Salvation theology, 2, 3, 11, 16, 27, 30, 33, 57, 59, 60, 63–64, 71–72, 79, 105, 113, 129, 133, 139, 170, 175, 197, 203, 207–8, 248, 250, 293, 299
salvific, 24
Samuel, 70
sanctification process, 204
Sangerhausen, 94
Sardinia, 281, 286
Sattler, Michael, 100, 105–7, 111–14, 116, 118–19, 122, 127
  and isolationism, 113, 116
Saul, 70
Savoy, duke of, 172, 270
Saxony, ducal, 31
  Duke George, 37, 45, 53, 84, 95
Saxony, electoral, 53–54, 72, 77, 192
  Duke John Frederick, 88
  elector of, 76, 81–82, 90–91, 93–95, 97
  Elector Frederick, 77, 78, 133
  Elector John, 53–54, 85, 88, 91, 137
Scandinavia, 117
Schaff, Harold, 101
Schaffhausen, 108, 147
schism, 166
schismatics, 162

Schleithiem Articles, 72, 100, 105–7, 112, 114–16, 119
Schmalkaldic League, 123, 138, 158, 161
scholasticism, 32
Schwenckfeld, Caspar von, 151–52
Scotland, 10, 71, 187–88, 190, 213, 268
Second Admonition, 235, 239
Second Helvetic Confession, 148, 154–55
Second Replie, 239, 242
Second Tournelle, 266
sectarian (–s, –ism), 30, 37–38, 45, 57–58, 63, 67, 69, 71–128, 132, 136–38, 146, 151, 154, 158, 164–66, 170, 176, 182, 239, 247, 250, 268, 293
seculars, 287–88
secular government, 56, 58, 106, 110–11
　duty of, 108–9, 113–15, 117, 119, 121, 123, 128
secular history, 65, 247, 254, 267
secularization (church property), 32, 79, 139, 142, 288
seminaries, 297
Sentences, 22
separatism, (–ist, ists), 3, 101, 103, 105, 108, 110, 112, 151, 234, 255
sermon on the mount, 63
Servetus, Michael, 181–82
Seville, 283, 285, 294, 295
Seymour, Edward, 213, 215
Short treatise of politike power, 223–24
Sicily, 258, 281, 286
Sickingen, Franz von, 35
Simons, Menno, 100, 115, 127
simony, 11
Sir Christian, 48
Six books of the Republic, 274–77
Sixty-seven Articles, 59–62, 65–66, 107
social control, 273, 286, 290
social order, 214–15, 221, 235, 239, 245, 254, 276
Socialism, 80
sociology, 4
socio-economics, 15–16
socio-political, 46–47, 55
sola fide (–ism), 35, 101, 197, 201, 207, 212

sola scriptura, 22, 32, 59, 60, 68, 73, 77, 79, 90, 92, 101, 121, 129, 132, 134, 137, 162, 172, 235, 237, 240, 242–43, 245–48, 299
soldiers, 45, 47
Solomon, 119, 124–25
Sorbonne, 260, 279
Spalatin, George, 31
Spain, 52, 60, 225, 227, 258, 259, 268, 270, 278, 280–98, 299
　Church of, 290
　Kings of
　　Carlos I, 282, 287, 289–91, 292, 297
　　Philip II, 190, 270, 289, 293–97
Speyer,
　First Diet of, 53
　Second Diet of, 54
sphere,
　external (spiritual), 173, 175, 298–99
　internal (temporal), 173, 298–99
spiritual authority, 129, 134, 144, 148, 166, 169
spiritual life, 214
spiritual mission, 281, 283–84, 287–89, 292–93
spiritual (ecclesiastical) sphere, 24, 26, 219, 224, 270, 284, 288
spiritual sword, 216, 229
Spiritualism, 3, 36, 72–73, 284, 293
Stadion, Christoph von (bishop), 161
Standish, Henry, 194
Starkey, Thomas, 203–6
Statutes,
　Praemunire, 18, 193, 193n3, 195, 202, 222
　Provisors, 18, 193n3, 222
　Supremacy, 196
　Uniformity, 232
Stayer, James M, 102, 115, 127
Stolberg, 88
Stork, Nicolas, 75–76, 85
Strangers' Church, 172, 218
Strasbourg, 54, 117–18, 121–23, 125, 157, 159, 161, 163, 165, 177, 179, 192, 223

as New Jerusalem, 118
church order, 164
council of, 118–19, 158, 163
mandates, 166
toleration policy, 118
wardens, 163
Stuart, Mary, 190, 268
Stumpf, Simon, 101–2, 104, 107, 151–52
subsidio, 292
Suleiman II (sultan), 53
supplanting, 283
supreme governor, 221
supreme headship, 202, 221–22, 232
Swinnerton, Thomas, 202–3, 206
Swiss Brethren, 72, 98–99, 101–5, 107, 112, 114, 140
Swiss cantons, 182
Swiss Confederacy, 140, 141, 143, 144, 146, 147
civil war of, 147
Switzerland, 56, 72, 102, 108, 115, 231, 266
syndics, 186
synod (–s), 8, 12, 142–43, 146–48, 152–53, 155, 159, 164, 204, 208, 290, 297

Tarragona, 297
Temporal Authority, 37
temporal government as necessary, 198, 209–10
temporal kingdom, 199
temporal regiment, 199, 202, 205
temporal sphere, 57, 62–63, 64, 65, 66, 67, 70, 218, 219, 241, 270, 276, 284, 288, 290
temporal sword, 99, 129, 134, 197, 201, 203, 209, 216, 222
temporalities, 5, 12
Ten Commandments (see: *Decalogue*)
fourth as fifth, 200, 204, 208, 211
Teresa of Avila, 284
testamentary jurisdiction, 193–94
Tetrapolitan Confession, 165
Teutonic Knights, 51
That parents should neither compel nor hinder the marriage of their children and that children should not become engaged without their parents' consent, 51
The determinations of the moste famous and mooste excellent vniuersities of Italy and Fraunce, that it is so vnlefull for a man to marie his brothers wyfe, that the pope hath no power to dispence therewith, 195, 201
The estate of marriage, 50
The First Blast of the Trumpet Against the Monstruous Regiment of Women, 190
Themata ad Sextam feriam discutienda, 135–36
The Christian Faith, 181, 183–84
The Obedience of a Christian man, 196–98
The one and eternal testament or covenant of God, 149–50
The papacy at Rome, an answer to the celebrated Romanist at Leipzig, 32
The Prince, 21
The rest of the second replie, 239
The Second Blast of the Trumpet Against the Monstruous Regiment of Women, 190
The Testimony of the First Chapter of Luke, 95
theocracy, 94, 120, 291, 298
crypto-, 298
Theses for the Friday Disputation, 136
Thirty-nine Articles, 232, 235
Thuringia, 42, 137
tithe, 42, 63, 108, 111, 229, 282
dispute, 101–2
To the Christian nobility, 29, 31
Toledo, 295, 297
Archbishop of, 294
Torgau, 54
toleration, 109, 138, 153, 163–64, 182, 190, 269, 274–76, 278
Toulouse, 274
Tournai, 4, 193
trade guilds, 120–21, 123
Traicté de la discipline & police chrestienne, 272

SUBJECT INDEX

transparency, 98
Treatise on Christian discipline, 272
Treaty of Nemours, 275
Tres Gracias, 292
Tridentine, 271, 273, 279
  decrees, 288, 291, 295–97
Triumvirate, 270
tribute, 197
Tübingen, 59
Tudor (family), 259, 266, 271–72, 280
Tudor England, 191–258, 299
Tumult of Ambroise, 269
Turks (as invading force), 45, 47–49, 52, 54, 115
  as cleansing force, 117
twelve tribes of Israel, 125
two kingdoms doctrine, 198, 201, 204, 206, 208, 219, 223–24, 229, 291
two swords, doctrine, 5, 6, 11, 23, 25, 29, 41, 43–45, 56, 216, 229
Tyndale, William, 191, 196–203, 205, 207, 226, 256
tyrannicide, 220, 226, 229, 230, 233
tyranny, 115, 146, 168, 183, 184–87, 189, 190, 252
tyrant (–s), 197–98, 201, 205, 211, 225–26, 228–30, 277, 279
  fate of, 94–97

Ulm, 54, 157–60, 163
  Bucer in, 161
  church ordinance of, 162–64
  council of, 161, 163
  morality court of, 159, 161
  wardens' court, 159–60
Ultramontanism, 261, 262, 273, 279, 281
Unam Sanctum, 5, 14
uniformity, 274–75
United States, 4
  Constitution of, 4
universal monarchy, 32
universal supremacy, 298
universalism, 204, 208, 246, 259, 281–82, 289

Valdés, Fernando de, 294–95
Valencia, 297
Valladolid, 294–95
Valois (family), 259, 265
Venerable Company of Pastors, 179, 181, 272
Venice, 69, 258
Verba Dei, 74
Vermigli, Peter Martyr, 130, 191, 218
Vestiarian controversy, 234, 236
via media, 212, 222, 250, 270
Vienne, 181
Vindication and Refutation, 97
visitations, 136–38, 159, 222
Von dem unverschampten fräefel ergerlichem verwyrren und unwarhafftem leeren der selbsgesandten Widertoeuffern viergespraech Buecher, 151

Waldshut, 111
  disputation of, 107
wardens, 175, 177, 179
Wars of Religion, 264, 266–73
War of Succession, 278
Wartburg, the, 134
Weimar, 91
  alliance of, 53
Wellenberg, 110
Western Schism, 16
Westphalia, 122
What the duty of the magistrate is in the church of Christ, who lawfully defends it against the seditions of heretics and the attacks of tyrants, 153
Whether it is the duty of the honorable magistracy to punish in honor, body or goods men who lead astray or have been led astray from the faith, 153
Whether soldiers, too, can be saved, 45
Wilcox, Thomas, 234–35, 237–39
Williams, Patrick, 296
Winchester (diocese), 193, 207
  Bishop of, 223

Wittenberg, 31, 74–77, 82–83, 90, 95, 121
  city council, 77, 78, 81
  Collegiate Church of, 77
  disturbances, 73, 76, 81–82
  Ordinance, 78–79, 81
  reform commission, 77, 78
  Six Articles of, 78
Wollman, David, 223
Wolsey, Thomas (cardinal), 195, 288
Worcester (Bishop of), 214–15
Wyatt, Thomas, 226
Wyatt's Rebellion, 223, 225

York (archdiocese), 195

Zabadiah, 241
Zaragoza, 297
Zeiss, Hans, 88, 91, 94–96
Zöfingen, 153
Zürich, 57, 59–60, 63, 66, 69, 78, 98, 142–43, 145–47, 150, 179, 189, 191–92, 212, 220
  Church of, 63, 68, 148
  Council of two-hundred, 68, 110
  First disputation of, 58, 102
  Great council of, 57, 66–68
  Grossmünster, 101
  magistrates of, 142, 147, 153
  Marriage court of, 101
  Reformation of, 66, 147
  Second disputation of, 67, 101–2, 107, 110, 122
  Senate of, 59
  Small council of, 57, 102, 110
  synod, 101
  understanding of the covenant, 151–55, 157Zwickau, 85, 86
  prophets, 75–76, 78
  St Mary's Church, 85
Zwingli, Ulrich, 26, 55, 56–70, 71, 75, 77, 84, 99, 101–2, 104, 106–10, 112–13, 117, 120, 122, 125, 139, 140, 143–47, 149–52, 171, 176, 188, 299
  civil authority theory of, 56–70
  covenant theology of, 146, 299
  death of, 69
  ecclesiology of, 59
  justification theology of, 64
  on tithes, 102
  predestination theology of, 146
  theocrat, 57, 58
Zwinglian (–s, –ism), 121–22, 141, 146, 148, 152, 158–59, 161–62, 165

Scripture Index

Genesis
3:16	227
17:1–14	150

Leviticus
18	50

Deuteronomy
17:4	215, 217
32	197

1 Samuel
	235
14:43–45	230

1 Kings
8	97

2 Chronicles
19:8, 11	245

Psalms
51:1	14
101	215

Isaiah
56:10	85

Ezekiel
14:19	81

Daniel
2	94
7	90
7:27	97

Matthew
	114, 169
5:32	127
5:39	106
5:40	111
6:22–23	44
7:12	65
10:34	94
11:12	76
16:18–19	9
17:24–27	65
18	144
19:4	127
22:21	3, 64, 298
23:9	61
26:52–54	113

Luke

3:14	134
9:54–56	113
12:13	113
20:9–18	76, 97, 115
22:25	114
22:38	5

John

6:40	60
8	97
18:36	113
20:25–29	247

Acts (of the Apostles)

	235
5	135
5:29	135, 229
15	67, 68
20:28	251

Romans

	123, 138, 229, 241
13	84, 89–90, 92, 97, 135, 197, 202, 211, 226
13:1	3, 95, 115, 134, 184, 203, 298
13:1–3	128, 134, 135
13:4	44
13:7	114
14	241
14:6, 7	248
14:23	241

1 Corinthians

	183
1:2	61
6:12	247
10:31	248
10:32	248
12:28	176
14:26	248
14:34–35	227
14:40	248

2 Corinthians

10:4	114

Galatians

5:21	127–28

Ephesians

	168
1:22–23	114
4:11–12	158

Colossians

1:18	114

1 Timothy

2:1–2	134
2:11–12	227
5:19	252

2 Timothy

2:14	87

Titus

1:5	252

James

5:16	142

1 Peter

	229
2	211, 226
2:9–19	3
2:13–14	3, 134, 298
2:13–17	65
2:14	44
2:17	3

2 Peter

2	202
17	298

Revelation

6:14	97
11	125

www.ingramcontent.com/pod-product-compliance
Lightning Source LLC
Chambersburg PA
CBHW071151300426
44113CB00009B/1168